OP   250

POETS'
HANDBOOK

TO

GLORIA GODDARD

POETS' HANDBOOK

By

CLEMENT WOOD

GARDEN CITY PUBLISHING CO., INC.

GARDEN CITY, NEW YORK

1942

GARDEN CITY PUBLISHING CO., INC.

CL

PRINTED IN THE UNITED STATES OF AMERICA

FOREWORD

The impulse to write poetry and verse is as common and wide-spread as the impulse to speak and write prose. It may be suppressed, but always harmfully to the personality that thus throttles the more concentrated, impressive and enduring half of its expression. It is an arrogant impulse, and often assumes from the start that the impulse is enough: that "poets are born," and, since they have been born, perfection is already attained. Too late such writers discover the cost of not having familiarized themselves with the materials of which poetry is compounded: life, its desires, and the devices already invented to express these.

But there are enough who are not so arrogant, and who see the need of mastering the technique of verse-writing for strangely diverse purposes: these including professional, potential, and amateur poets, verse-writers, and lyric-writers; all students of versification in university, college, and even secondary schools; all prose-writers, who need the discipline of versification, with its major emphasis on choosing the right word, to improve their prose styles; all composers of songs, who must comprehend the problems confronting their lyricists; all persons who ever feel the urge to write a poem, light verse, song-lyric, greeting-card, verse drama for stage, radio, or television, advertising writers who occasionally use verse, clear down to those who merely wish to know how to add the right line to a limerick. And, of course, librarians and teachers, who are called upon to aid the embryonic versifiers. The list includes almost the whole human race. And all these need a book giving, simply and clearly, accurate information about all the devices open to the versifier or poet.

This book started out to be precisely that: an omnibus of verse technique. It grew into more. In order to make it indispensable to the professional, as well as to the apprentice and the amateur, it had to present every verse device, with the emphasis on how best it could be used in writing; but, deeper than that, it had to dig deep into the beginnings of each verse device, so that any prior stage of the form's development, or any stage yet unreached but inevitable in the development so far, could be utilized by the verse-writer at any time. This was more of a challenge to the author, and more of an adventure in the doing.

Some of the results of these excavations are startling. In every instance, it seemed wisest to progress throughout from the simplest to the most difficult: an obvious course that should have been discovered long ago. Thus the rhythms of prose, free verse, and accent verse are considered before the artificial alien importation, metric verse, which came in to alter significantly the stream of natural English verse and poetry. Sound repetitions progress in the order in which they originated: mere repetitions of complete words and groups of words coming first, and then alliteration, assonance, and consonance, before the "crowning ornament," rhyme, is given the floor. Stanza forms commence with one-line stanzas and poems, and progress to the most intricate stanzas known. Poem forms begin with the most familiar and homegrown, the sonnet—nine or more types are included—and the limerick; before mounting through the intricacies of French and other alien forms, from forms so simple that they are used in ignorance that they are fixed forms, to the resplendent chant royal and the rhymed sestina. The basic convention of Anglo-Saxon and English verse, the four-accent line, is traced back to its dawn lair: and its development thereafter, down to today, is given with thoroughness. Ballad meter, its major offspring, is for the first time fully explained. Classic quantity meters, natural in music but unnatural without music from the start, and their gradual development into alien accent meter, now familiar, and yet forever threatened by the native accent verse, are made clear. The essential opposition between natural scansion and pattern scansion, and methods of effecting an armistice, are not neglected. The inevitability of the form of the Shakespearean sonnet is made manifest. And, throughout, the book ranks the light verse writer on a parity with the poet, and deals with Tin Pan Alley lyrics on an equal footing with Dorothy Parker and Shakespeare.

The book is functional throughout. The museum pieces in versification—poetic license, classic meters, assonance, odes—are all included. But the living forms are stressed most: simple lyrics, songs, popular song-lyrics, ballads and poems telling a story, sonnets, accent verse, free verse, poetic dramas, chants, limericks, novels and stories using devices found in versification—all the forms for which there is an actual demand and a market. The problems of marketing are surveyed fairly. The valuable by-products of versification, including all reproduction rights, are treated fully.

There are inevitable omissions. All readers of the book are invited to cooperate in making later editions as complete as possible.

My thanks are due to more than I can mention, for assistance in making this book comprehensive. Outstanding among these are Etta Josephean Murfey, Ralph Cheyney, Lucia Trent, Margarette Ball Dickson, Aimee Jackson Short, Arthur Guiterman, Louis Untermeyer, James Oppenheim, Arthur Davison Ficke, and most of all Gloria Goddard, whose healthy scepticism and loyal cooperation throughout aided in shaping the whole.

CLEMENT WOOD

Bozenkill
Delanson, N. Y.

CONTENTS

Contents

Contents

Contents

Contents

Contents

[xiv]

Contents

Contents

I

POETRY, VERSE AND PROSE

POETRY DEFINED

POETRY is classified as one of the fine arts, along with painting, sculpture, architecture, music, drama and dancing. From the inclusive standpoint of the cultural history of the human race, it may be defined: *Poetry is verse which produces a deep emotional response.* This calls for a definition of verse, of which poetry constitutes a subclass: *Verse is words arranged according to some conventionalized repetition.*

It is this conventionalized repetition which distinguishes verse from prose. It may apply to some element in speech with whose repetition we are familiar: as, the repetition of rhythm, either accent or durational; or the repetition of complete words or parts of words, as shown in refrains, alliteration, assonance, consonance, and rhyme. It may be a repetition less familiar to us: as, the repetition of meaning, in the parallelism of ancient Hebrew poetry; or that requirement, found alike in certain French and Oriental poetry, of so many syllables to each line. A repetition conventionally required of verse in one culture may be labeled prose in another; but it is, in essence, verse, in any culture.

From the standpoint of our English and American culture—a standpoint shared by many Western nations—we may narrow the definition of verse: *Verse, in our culture, is words arranged with repetition in their accent rhythm, which tends toward uniformity or regularity, rather than toward variety.* The other repetitions referred to may be present; but they are regarded as ornaments merely. The essence of our verse and poetry is repetition of accent rhythm.

[3]

DISCUSSION OF THIS DEFINITION

The latest unabridged *Webster's New International Dictionary* defines poetry as "the art or work of poets; the embodiment in appropriate language of beautiful or high thought, imagination or emotion, the language being rhythmical, usually metrical, and characterized by harmonic and emotional qualities which appeal to and arouse the feelings and imagination." It lists also the extended meaning of "something poetical; poetical quality; as, the poetry of nature," or of motion, or of Rodin or Chopin, or of orchid-raising. Such a treatment reminds us anew that a dictionary is valuable for description, but cannot be relied upon for scientific definition. Phrases such as "appropriate language" and "beautiful or high thoughts" are either too vague to be helpful, or are not sufficiently inclusive. Moreover, the definition, by limiting the technique merely to "rhythmical language," fails to exclude prose; and, as we shall find out in the treatment of rhythm, all language, used either in prose or in poetry, is rhythmical.

The definition of poetry in the latest *Encyclopedia Britannica* is: "Absolute poetry is the concrete and artistic expression of the human mind in emotional and rhythmical language." This is no improvement. "Artistic" is vague, unspecific, and evasive; and, as above, "rhythmical" includes all prose, as well as all verse and poetry.

If we consult the authorities in the field of poetics, most of them furnish small aid. Among the best of the definitions or descriptions are "the breath of beauty" (Leigh Hunt), "the eloquence of verse" (Bryant), "invention . . . which surprises and delights" (Samuel Johnson), "words producing illusion on the imagination" (Macaulay). The looseness of these needs no comment. Shelley's dictum, "the record of the best and happiest moments of the best and happiest minds" is a masterpiece of slack misdefinition. Few would care to sustain the opinion that poets are of necessity the best minds, or the happiest minds: since their emotional natures are far more important than their cold logical acumen. Nor need "the record of the best and happiest moments" of poets constitute poetry; it may, instead, be merely a receipted bill, or a cryptic notation in a diary. Coleridge makes a differentiation without value or accuracy, when he writes, "prose—words in the best order; poetry, the best words in the best order." This limits prose with glaring inaccuracy; and the treatment of poetry, here made a subhead of prose, is no improvement. Nor is Wordsworth accurate or properly inclusive, in his famous definition, "emotion recollected in tranquillity"; poetry can flame out of a hot heart, as well as out of one cold as old lava. Matthew Arnold errs as fully in writing, "Poetry is simply the most beautiful, impressive and widely effective mode of saying things." This can apply as well to the most effective prose. Ruskin comes closest of all, when he defines poetry as the expression, in musical words, of thoughts which appeal to the higher and nobler emotions, or their opposites. But "musical words" include all words, the crisp *Connecticut* no less than the lingering *amanita;* and the best prose comes within his definition.

We have encountered no definitions as accurate or serviceable as the two first given. Let us add to them a third: *Prose, in our culture, is words whose rhythm tends toward variety, rather than toward uniformity or regularity.* As commonly used, poetry, verse and prose call for the expression of thoughts, usually grammatically. Exceptions to this occur, varying all the way from nonsense jingles and magical runes to certain modernistic writing.

Versification is the art or practice of writing verse, which, of course, includes its subclassification, poetry.

The twofold nature of poetry, its technique (verse) and its content (producing a deep emotional response), calls for our accurate use of at least three words: poetry, verse, and prose. From the standpoint of technique—our conventional test being whether there is repetition in the accent rhythm, tending toward uniformity or regularity, or the lack of such repetition, causing the accent rhythm to tend toward the variety of prose—*verse* (including its subclass, *poetry*) is to be distinguished from *prose*. From the standpoint of content—the test being whether or not the product produces deep emotional response—*poetry* is to be distinguished from mere *verse,* used as a subhead of the more inclusive *verse.*

VERSE DISTINGUISHED FROM PROSE

Starting with the understanding that our convention places that repetition in the accent rhythm which tends toward uniformity or regularity as verse, and an accent rhythm tending toward variety as prose, what is to be our precise dividing line between these nearly related methods of expression? Where does verse end, and where does prose begin? Who is to determine where the dividing line is to be placed, and what is to be the precise standard of differentiation?

"Tending toward" is as vague as an explanation by Hitler. Yet anything more precise would be dogmatically erroneous, and would bog us in the quagmire of futile logic.

Let us approach the solution of these questions by appraising specific examples. Clearly most people would regard the following as poetry—that is, as in the higher bracket of verse:

> Music, when soft voices die,
> Vibrates in the memory—
> Odours, when sweet violets sicken,
> Live within the sense they quicken.
>
> Rose leaves, when the rose is dead,
> Are heaped for the beloved's bed;
> And so thy thoughts, when thou art gone,
> Love itself shall slumber on.
> —PERCY BYSSHE SHELLEY

It is not the artificial typography—brief lines, with capitals commencing them, which makes poetry of this; it would be as surely poetry, if set up in the natural format commonly used with prose:

Music, when soft voices die, vibrates in the memory. Odours, when sweet violets sicken, live within the sense they quicken. Rose leaves, when the rose is dead, are heaped for the beloved's bed.

And so thy thoughts, when thou art gone, love itself shall slumber on.

No matter what the typography, nevertheless the repetition in the accent rhythm, the tendency toward regularity, makes this definitely verse, and not prose; while its emotional appeal, to most people, makes it poetry as well. Set up the opening of the first chapter of this book in the same line division:

[6]

Poetry is classified as one
Of the fine arts, along with
Painting, sculpture, architecture,
Music, drama and dancing. From the

Inclusive standpoint of the cultural
History of the human race, it may
Be defined: Poetry is verse which
Produces a deep emotional response.

This is prose. No magic worked by the line division can bring it any closer to poetry. Only the presence of repetition in the accent rhythm could make it acceptable verse; this, plus the proper emotional appeal, alone could make it poetry.

Remember, if the number of syllables per line in this had been uniform, and had fitted an accepted convention, this would be verse, in cultures—such as French and Japanese—where this is the accepted convention. We are dealing here with our own culture, where repetition in accent rhythm is the test. Except where otherwise noted, the whole discussion will be limited to poetry, verse and prose in our own culture.

The two examples given just above have been respectively definitely verse and definitely prose. Suppose we have something nearer to the borderline, as this passage from Walt Whitman's *One's Self I Sing:*

One's self I sing, a simple separate person,
Yet utter the word Democratic, the word En-Masse.

Of physiology from top to toe I sing,
Not physiognomy alone nor brain alone is worthy for the use,
I say the Form complete is worthier far,
The Female equally with the Male I sing.

Of Life immense in passion, pulse, and power,
Cheerful, for freest action form'd under the laws divine,
The Modern Man I sing.

In which category, verse or prose, shall we place this? We are dealing with it as verse, now, and not as poetry. Sidney Lanier did go so far as to describe Whitman's product as "huge raw collops slashed from the rump of poetry"; but many of Whitman's contemporaries emphatically screeched that all of *Leaves of Grass* was merely chopped-up prose.

Certain lines are definitely verse, "Of Life immense in passion, pulse, and power," an accurate five-foot iambic line, being our clearest example. A few changes, illustrated in parentheses, would alter this into accurate iambic blank verse—that is, un-rhymed verse:

> One's self I sing, a simple separate person,
> Yet (speak) the (phrase The Crowd,) the word En-Masse.

> Of physiology from top to toe I sing,
> Not physiognomy alone nor brain alone
> Is worthy for the use,
> I say the Form complete is worthier far,
> The Female (equal to) the Male I sing.

> Of Life immense in passion, pulse, and power,
> Cheerful, for freest action formed under the laws divine,
> The Modern Man I sing.

We have made only three changes, in order to alter the original into acceptable iambics. Did these three changes turn loose verse into iambic verse, or prose into iambic verse? The repetition in the accent rhythm, the tendency toward uniformity or regularity, was there all the time: at least, to me, as one reader. This clearly comes within the more liberal technique of free verse, which now has wide acceptance. Analysis reveals that this selection from Whitman is clearly verse, as distinguished from prose.

Or so it seems to me. At the same time, you may hold to the opposite conclusion, with absolute correctness and a full right to your own opinion. For, even after the lines are scanned, by the method we will reach under Rhythm, the problem remains: Does the whole tend toward uniformity and regularity, or toward variety? The final arbiter is the individual judgment of each reader. For yourself, you may come to your own independent conclusion, if you prefer; or you may give weight to or even swallow uncritically the consensus of opinion of the authorities. Yet never forget that each of these has had to arrive at his opinion after first fixing his own dividing line between verse and prose.

PROSE AND VERSE: THE TWILIGHT ZONE

It is important to remember that there is, between unquestioned verse and unquestioned prose, as between all things in nature, a twilight zone in which the two blend. Man makes sharp, straight boundaries; nature does not. Night dawns into day, day softens into night, and there is in each case a time when each observer may say that it is still day, or already night, or a blend of both; or neither, but the period separating them. The fact is the meeting and blending, a trait shared by everything in nature, at some point in their contact. So it is with prose and verse. Certain lines are definitely verse; certain ones are definitely prose; and, between these, come those which partake of the nature of both, and are one, or the other, or both, or neither, as your judgment dictates.

Once you have analyzed the rhythm by scansion, the final test, then, between prose and verse—the location of the dividing line you establish between rhythms tending toward variety, and those using a repetition which tends toward uniformity or regularity—is a subjective one. Seventy years ago, the Whitman selection would have been classified as prose, by the majority of the authorities. Critical standards today are almost united in calling it definitely verse. You must let your own inner sense of music determine the boundary you set up; and at the same time allow to others the right to place their dividing lines where they please.

ALIEN CONVENTIONS OF VERSE

So far, we have considered only English and American verse, with repetition in accent rhythm as the basis of its differentiation from prose. In what category would you place this selection from Psalm VIII?

When I consider Thy heavens, the work of Thy fingers, the moon and the stars, which thou hast ordained;

What is man, that thou art mindful of him? And the son of man, that thou visitest him?

For Thou hast made him a little lower than the angels, and hast crowned him with glory and honor.

The ear hears a definite repetition rhythm in this. Scansion reveals a faint preponderance of the foot called anapest over the iambs: both being feet mounting from unaccent to accent, and hence parts of an obvious accent rhythm scheme. Shall we, then, place this without hesitation in the category called verse?

This is accurate, so far as verse in English is concerned. But recall that this was originally Hebrew poetry, and that its technical convention is essentially parallelism—that is, repetition of the idea or meaning of the first half of the line in the second half. Thus the first half of each of these three *verses*, in the Biblical sense, is repeated with slight variation in the second half; and the use of this convention makes it verse, to those familiar with Hebrew poetry. No matter what our verdict on it as English verse, its ranking as Hebrew verse is certain.

What would you make of this?

When washing and rinsing were done, they brought the linen down on to the seashore, and set it all out thereupon in rows, where the pebbles thrown up by the waves most thickly abounded.

To my ear, this is extremely varied, and prosy: and the knowledge that it is William J. Stone's translation of the *Odyssey, vi, 92-94,* in classic durational verse in English, does not alter my opinion that it is not verse in English, but adequate prose. From the standpoint of the alien convention of meter based upon quantity or duration, it is adequate verse.

Here is another example:

More fleeting than the flash of withered windblown leaf, this thing men call life.

From the standpoint of English scansion, this is obviously lovely and emotion-rousing prose; but not verse. Yet set it up—

> More fleeting than the
> Flash of withered windblown leaf,
> This thing men call life,

and measure it by the Japanese yardstick for verse—the *hokku* requiring technically three lines, of respectively five, seven, and five syllables—and it becomes accurate verse, from the Japanese standpoint. This lacks the essential English convention for verse, repetition of the accent rhythm. It has the ornamental convention of alliteration: *f*leeting, *f*lash; *w*ithered, *w*indblown; *l*eaf, *l*ife; and traces of a less familiar ornament, the repetition of unaccented identical or related consonants. From the standpoint of rhythm, it is prose to us.

Note that the Japanese requirement is purely objective, depending merely on the counting of syllables. So is the classical convention, the length of syllables, judged by purely arbitrary rules. Even the Hebrew parallelism, or repetition of ideas, is objective. The test for verse in English, a tendency toward regularity in the accent rhythm, is more natural, as well as somewhat more subjective; for here the precise dividing line must be placed according to the subjective preference of each reader.

VERSE AND ITS SUBCLASS, POETRY

The distinction here is: Do the verses produce a deep emotional response, or not? If not, they remain mere verse; if they do, they are properly labeled poetry. The qualifying "deep" leaves each reader to decide for himself how much of an emotional response he requires, to allocate or promote verse into the charmed inner circle of poetry. Clearly the only person who can decide whether or not any given group of verses is poetry—to *you,* that is—is yourself. This test is more subjective even than the test for technique.

To most readers, this glorious old song of Thomas Campion's is definitely poetry:

> There is a garden in her face,
>   Where roses and white lilies blow;
> A heavenly paradise is that place,
>   Wherein all pleasant fruits do grow;
>   There cherries grow that none may buy,
>   Till Cherry-Ripe themselves do cry.

Yet, in any particular reader, this may fail to awaken deep emotional response, and will therefore be classed by him as mere verse. Similarly, the last stanza of Milton's *Ode on the Morning of Christ's Nativity,*

> But see! the Virgin blest
> Hath laid the Babe to rest;
> Time is, our tedious song should here have ending:
> Heaven's youngest-teemèd star
> Hath fixed her polish'd car,
> Her sleeping Lord with hand-maid lamp attending:
> And all about the courtly stable
> Bright-harness'd Angels sit in order serviceable,

to me is mere verse, and not good verse either. To any other reader, it may be impressive poetry of high ranking. Each of us

is right; for the test is individual and subjective. When we come
to a witty classic like:

> Willie and two other brats
> Licked up all the Rough-on-Rats.
> Father said, when mother cried,
> "Never mind—they'll die outside,"

most of us would definitely place this as verse, and not poetry.
But the minority have the right to classify it as poetry, saying
that they see nothing whatever in the deep stuff.

There are far more definite borderline instances that could
be cited. Indeed, the average book proffered as poetry seems, to
the qualified critic, entirely verse; while, to its author and to
those who prefer cottage cheese to Camembert in poetry, it is
pure poetry. The popular sentimental classics, *The End of a
Perfect Day, My Rosary,* come in this group. To the author, no
doubt, and to those who love the songs, they are high poetry;
to the sophisticates, they range from fair verse to moronic bilge.
The thing to remember is that the test is entirely subjective; and
that you, and no one else, are the final arbiter, the Supreme Court
with no appeal beyond, as to whether any verses are poetry or
not, to you. With, of course, full power to take the dicta of
recognized authorities, as far as you will, recalling always that
the dictum of each had to be originally subjective, whether original or shopworn.

And there is always the twilight zone, in which the opinion
may oscillate. The standard of judgment tends to rigidify as you
grow more learned in poetry, and weakens complacently as second childhood approaches. But it always remains subjective.

What expressions in words are to be classified as prose, and
what as mere verse? Is a given example of verse mere verse, or
does it mount into poetry? The final answer is always left to you.

POET AND VERSIFIER

The underlying purpose of your versification will determine
your method of preparation, and the slant of your attack toward
achieving whatever goal you aim for. The simplest of all objec-
tives is merely a desire to become an adept in versification. This
can be for any of a number of reasons:

Because you want the social grace of being able to play your part in games requiring versification, as well as the ability to write acceptable verses on such special occasions as a birthday, an anniversary, a holiday, or the like.

Because you want to round out your all-important powers of self-expression, and do not want this half of oral and written speech to be denied you. Because you want the valuable by-products in improvement of your prose style, by mastering the kindred art, versification.

Because you want to increase your prestige, by being known as a versifier or poet.

Because you want to add to your income by the use of versification, whether from winning last-line limerick contests, writing and selling greeting-card mottoes, or light and humorous verse, or sentimental verses suitable for especial magazine markets, or song lyrics ranging from such Tin-Pan Alley products as *Don't Look Now* or *Over the Rainbow* to the *Indian Love Lyrics* of Lawrence Hope, or poems with a wide enough appeal to have sales value.

Because you wish to be a poet, with your song as perfected as possible.

Where the object is merely technical skill in versification, the chief requirements are to master the details of the poet's craft, and to understand the needs of your market, and write to satisfy them. As to the first of these, a recent article of mine in *The Writer's Digest* stated:

Learn the rules of versification! Follow them, until you know enough to know how to break them. Don't dream of submitting amateur work to editors, and expect to be paid for your clumsy foot-faults.

These rules are far simpler than the rules and procedure for playing contract or solving crossword puzzles. They are incredibly easier than mathematics or any science. It is infinitely simpler to be a master in versification, than to learn to be a qualified mechanic, lawyer, doctor, pharmacist, trained nurse, stenographer, or cook. The rules for writing verse are as simple as the rules for writing prose. Writing good verse is as easy as writing good prose.

Once technical mastery is yours, the understanding of market requirements, and meeting "the trial by market everything must come to," is precisely parallel to the problem of the farmer with eggs or potatoes to sell, the merchant with wares to vend, the professional man with services to exchange for coin of the realm or something of value in barter. This will be taken up later in detail.

The mood of your application to versification will differ as the objective of your verse-writing differs. Where your aim is to achieve the highest of all distinctions in the field, that of an authentic poet, and to produce satisfying and enduring poetry, the practice of the masters indicates certain additional essentials. The major one is a deep sincerity of soul. Elsewhere I have described poetry as the concentrated expression of desire, the attar of dreams and longings. You will never be satisfied to your depths by the concentrated expression of sham and artificial desires; they will always seem to you the shoddy that they are. For a time they may fool others, whose desires they do express, and be hailed as the authentic expression of genuine desire; but sooner or later they will pale in comparison with more genuine poems phrasing the same desire, and your repute will wilt from that of poet to that of mere versifier, however deft, graceful and tuneful your lines may be.

This sincerity calls for an unending display of originality. Why? Because you are original, unique, a total synthesis of impressions and materials that has never been precisely paralleled in the whole history of the race, and will never again be produced after you. The mere matter of difference in timing will mark you off from any earlier or later almost-identity. Recall that no two animals or birds are precisely identical; no two leaves in the forest; no two grains of sand on the shore; possibly no two molecules or atoms or ions or lesser constituents of matter or energy throughout the universe. Likeness and classification are man-made attributes and conveniences; each thing is itself, individual, unique. Your genealogical background is different from that of every other human being who ever lived, except your own blood brothers and sisters; and think how different you are from each of these! Again, the matter of timing differentiates you from all except that rare person called your identical twin; and slightly, even in this case. You have taken in different impressions, with different degrees of receptivity, every second of your existence. The sum total is you, and there is no duplicate. How, then, can your product, your poetry, the expression of your deepest personality, be identical with that of any other person?

We will deal with this more fully under the treatment of the proper poetic vocabulary. It is enough to note in advance that you see everything differently from any other person that ever lived. To be faithful to this unique vision, and your individual conclusions drawn from it, your words must possess the same subtle uniqueness.

And, always, technical mastery is required, to let your product reach its maximum of effectiveness. Some distinguished poets lacked a large equipment of self-criticism. Vachel Lindsay thought his lines to Mary Pickford much better than *The Congo* or *Simon Legree*. To the extreme contrary were such self-perfectionists as E. A. Housman and Edwin Arlington Robinson, who might possess faults of stature or outlook on life, but whose lines always more than satisfy technically. Much poetry and verse sags into doughiness forever because of ignorance or heedlessness of the basic fundamentals of good verse-writing. It is not such that constitutes bread for the soul of the race.

The final advice is, always secure as wide publication as possible. When you read your poem aloud to the first listener, or give it to the first other person to read to himself, publication begins. It never ends. Unless you wish to live a life as poet more crypted and sealed than a bottle gentian or a clam, you will gain by every reaction from outside, even if you disagree thoroughly with its evaluation. A constant pertinent fact about your poems is, How will others regard them? Go for the best markets; but, if they turn aloofly from you, find some home that will give the fledgeling soul-child a chance. Wean it by publication, the wider the better; that you may the better produce its more effective brothers and sisters.

GREATNESS IN POETRY

The bottle gentian or clam of a poet, providing that he or she expresses his own desires in verse to his own complete satisfaction, thereby becomes a poet of major ranking to himself or herself. In proportion as others recognize and hail the result as the expression of their own desires, the versifier becomes a poet to them. This identification of desire is usually unconscious; yet it is the final determinant of poetic ranking. Amy Lowell, in her poems definitely tending toward the love that Sappho sang, made herself the spokesman and laureate of that group; but the public at large heard no word of its soul in such verses, and these remained unimpressive verse to the world at large. Walt Whitman was regarded as "a lecherous old man" by the hypocritical Victorian moralists of his day; younger generations have been fired by his frankness about the body, mating, democracy, and liberty, until he is hailed today as the major poetic voice of America. All because he better expresses the desire of America than any other poet, even if his product was comparatively un-self-critical, and ranked technically below such adepts of versification as Longfellow, Swinburne and Housman. Thus crude lumbering Dreiser is properly hailed as a greater novelist than a flawless patterned pigmy in novel-writing.

The major test, to the poet himself, is whether or not he has fully expressed his own desire, to the best of his technical ability. Thereafter, the weaned poem must be foster-parented by others; and only when the desire it expresses relatively coincides with the desires of others do they hail the result as poetry, and great. Your own experience in the widening reactions of others, tending toward your being hailed as a poet, and great, will in the end drive home to you the accuracy of this analysis.

Murder will out, truth crushed to earth will do a handspring again, and in the end a composite picture of you will emerge from your poems. Make them all masquerades for your real desires, yet still the desires will force themselves into them, in unguessed devious ways: as desires suppressed by the conscious mind seethe and fester inside, until they burst forth into dreams or slips of speech or jokes or some other activity of the unconscious, that will bare them in the end. George Arliss by turns sank himself, as fully as he could, in such roles as Disraeli, Paganini, Zakkuri, Shylock, Rothschild, even the devil; but he remained George Arliss throughout, the sheer domino slipping soon enough in each instance. Each poem reflects, frankly or with such concealment as you dress it in, some facet of your personality. The sum total of these facets will build a clarifying picture of what you are and do and want and dream. The composite picture your poems present will be the etching of you on the soul of the race: not

for praise or blame primarily, but for recognition and disciple-
ship, if you speak the word waiting in the hearts of others for
utterance.

VERSE AND POETRY IN HUMAN AFFAIRS

Verse was remembered before prose, because of its mnemonic
advantages. "Thirty days hath September," "First William the
Norman, then William his son," "Now I lay me down to sleep"
—these jingled their way into our memories before a prose calen-
dar or tabulation of rulers or the Lord's Prayer could be absorbed
and retained. It was so in the childhood of the race. Lacking
writing, primitive men remembered the concentrated more than
the unconcentrated, the formalized more than the unformalized,
the ornamented more than the unornamented. Prose to be remembered was at first concentrated and formalized into verse,
which became the all of the first literary expression. Lyric out-
bursts, folk wisdom, tales and myths of tribal heroes, demigods
and gods, individual or collective jubilation or sorrowing, religious teachings, philosophies, budding sciences, chronicles, developed first in the form of verse or its more concentrated offspring, poetry.

And now came the inevitable breaking of the first artistic wave
on the shore of reality—a parallel to the process in each of the
arts. The form of the verse or poetry became formalized, wor-
shiped for its form rather than for the content which had found
its most suitable and natural form. Lesser imitators came, not
creatively wedding meaning to natural form, but pouring newer
and often lesser meaning into forms ever growing more rigid and
petrified. It was easier to remember a hexameter or a line of
marching iambics than a line of prose; but the prose might be
the more natural form of expression, and the rigid metric line
unnatural. Poets created the natural forms, but varied them as
the poem demanded. It remained for the formalizing grammarians
to give a name and set bounds and limits to meters and poetic
devices, and to ukase that thereafter all verse and poetry must
come within the tiny fenced yard, or be branded as mere prose.
When writing came in, this process quickened. As a result, the
more humble things, and then the greater ones, began to be
written down in prose. Natural prose encroached more and more

upon the domains of unnatural verse, until today most of the fields once pre-empted by poetry have been reclaimed by the more natural prose.

The art itself suddenly witnessed the first of many upheavals: the revolt of the authentic poets, who refused to have their lines corseted and straightjacketed by the desiccated grammarians. New and more liberal poetic forms were created. In turn, as the creative fury waned, the rigidifying process set in, and dearth and death came to real poetry. So it has been with all the arts, from the beginning; so it may be forever with all the arts. Yet at the core the description of poetry as the most concentrated expression of desire remains true; and this may, even now, be calling for a redefinition of the conventions of poetry itself. A new generation may alter the position of the boundaries entirely, and definitely label as poetry effective novels and other books now called prose, which utilize aspects of repetition more native to poetry than to its more diffuse sister, prose.

And the process may be unending, the core definition of poetry always remaining.

In the main, few domains have still been left to poetry and verse. The song, often set to music; the pastime of light verse, humorous, witty, in dialect; the lyric outburst; and, recently resurrected, the poetic drama—poetry still lords it over these. Yet, for all this loss in territory, it is still true of poetry that the more diffuse and unconcentrated prose is comparatively temporary, as a living expression of desire. The great novel of today will lose its immediacy perhaps a decade or a score of years from the time of its birth. The adult prose classics of yesterday are relegated to the schools today, to the kindergarten tomorrow. The message of prose has to be resaid for each generation, in most instances. Poetry lives longer. We need no reshaping of the lyrics of Keats, Shelley, and Burns, of the poetry of Shakespeare, of the Psalms or the bright dawn song of Sappho.

The poet was once also the man of affairs, the ruler, the prophet or spiritual leader, the military conqueror. Today he has become more specialized, and in general smaller. A d'Annunzio took Fiume for Italy, a Paderewski steered his country through the bloody young aftermath of the World War near the beginning of the century. But we do not look to a Maxwell Bodenheim or a W. H. Auden to be such a king as the psalmist David was, or to Father Divine to sing forever to the human heart as Isaiah did. Nor do we expect from Hitler, Stalin, Mussolini, Chamberlain, Reynaud, or Franklin Roosevelt trills of song as they steer mankind toward whatever tomorrow man will next encounter.

It is urged that this concentrated peak of human utterance be generalized and freshened, until more men of human glittering share in it, and until it becomes again the speech, not of weaklings and incomplete men and women, but of the completer ones; and that the poets themselves become such men and women as once strode the singing earth.

THE METHOD OF POETIC CREATION

The essential thing is that poetry is created first by the poet, as the concentrated expression of his desire; and only thereafter is it sharpened and formalized and perfected by the critical part of his personality.

It does no harm, but infinite good, for the poet to be saturated in the lore of technique; so that, when the sonnet mood, for instance, comes, the desire seething within for expression will automatically shape itself into the bounds of a sonnet. The same is true of free verse and all the other methods of poetic expression. But, when the impulse to write becomes too great to be resisted, the time for critical control of the flow has ceased. Let the poem come out in its natural form; and always preserve this for comparison, and perhaps for a far later return toward the original vision and its utterance.

With some poets, a mood is the inception, and thereafter the pencil writes almost automatically what the unconscious dictates. With others, a first line may come first, and set the tempo for all the rest; the beginning may even be a last line, to which the whole will be unconsciously and consciously built up. Also, the poet may do all of this without writing a line down, shaping and perfecting the whole before the first word of it is put to paper. All of these methods are right, depending on the poet's preference and tendency.

Since, however, often a poetic flash comes at a time when there is no opportunity for full creation, or when the brain stubbornly refuses to do more, it is highly wise to write down poetic notes or outlines as they come, and preserve them. Some may later develop into poems. Some may be used, as were Sidney Lanier's exquisite *Poem Outlines*, to make a book, even if issued only posthumously. And this is as true of ideas for light and other mere verse.

Sooner or later the poet, and the light versifier as well, will discover the importance of keeping a pencil or pen and a sheet of paper always handy. Each poet will in the end build up amazing memories of the strange deliveries of some of his brain-children.

THE THEMES OF POETRY

Since poetry is the most concentrated expression of your desires, cosmic or trivial, and since your desires may deal with anything in the universe, from a beloved man or girl you desire to win, to a dead horse you desire to see removed; from love for a mother or daughter to a thrilled exultation at thought of an ion, a widening universe, or a world at peace—there is no limit whatever to the themes of poetry.

However, always remember that the use of an unpopular theme may to that extent limit your audience. If you are deliberately writing for a market which wants verses of a sentimental slant, avoid themes and treatments not appropriate to the market demands—at least, for those verses offered to the market. With this one limitation, write on any theme you choose. Louis Untermeyer once wrote a sonnet on a dead horse. Other versifiers have dealt autobiographically with material no less odorous. Choose the theme you prefer; and then let your verses phrase your desire to your own complete satisfaction, and trust that you have been keyed to a wide desire, whose voice you thereupon become.

USING A LIVING VOCABULARY

We have defined verse as "words arranged according to some conventionalized repetition." Before turning to the detailed technique of the conventions of versification, a major problem emerges: what words should be chosen, and how are they to be used? For if the wrong poetic vocabulary is used from the start, the whole product will have to be rewritten with the proper word usage; hence it is wise to learn what words are appropriate to poetry and verse, before starting to write these.

At first glance, the question sounds superfluous. One who knew nothing of versification would answer, "Why, *any* good words—any words that would be right in prose." And this is the right answer. But most beginners in versification come with a different answer mistaught them in advance; and it is this toxic teaching that must be corrected, at the very beginning.

The answer is simple: *The words that the poet or versifier uses in his best actual conversational speech.*
The vocabulary used by the poet or versifier who knows his trade, is the contemporary living vocabulary.

Prose of all kinds invariably uses this, or else it becomes stilted, affected, and repelling, instead of persuasive. If a public speaker commenced his tribute to the Fourth of July,

O thou holiday sacred beyond what any man conceiveth, thou wast conceived of yore by our forebears, while tyranny lowered athwart the perturb-ed welkin; and, for more years than man computeth—

all his hearers would wonder hazily whether he was quoting from some interred worthy who should have known better, or whether he was merely temporarily unbalanced. Suppose a short story or novel began,

Since Eos hath woken the bedrowsing vale of Bilgewater Flats, a forlorn wight meandered featsomely up a bosky dell, eftsoons carolling matins to the God of Day.

Unless we read on, imagining this to be humor or, at best, parody, we should know right away that the author was not speaking our language; and we would leave him to wither unread in the solitude he so richly deserved. If a friend or a man with something to sell greeted us,

I give thee gentil greeting betimes, fair sir,

we would take his outburst as clowning and forgive him, or else we should know that something was shockingly out of kilter. The use of a dead language is not forgiven, in prose. The same reasoning applies to verse and poetry: a dead language has no place in either.

Let us consider this genetically, from the beginning, as the language of poetry developed. It is clear that the earliest poets and versifiers had to use the living language—there was no museum of dead word-usages to draw from. Since verse expressed nothing that prose could not express and nothing that prose ultimately did not say, how could it require a different and more corpse-like language to express matter common to itself and prose, which invariably used a living language? Since poetry was primarily a concentrate of man's desires, which are always real far beyond mere thought, how could this need to be spoken in an unreal language, least of all in a dead language?

At no stage was there any reason why any other language should have been adopted. Except a reason unflattering to the users, and damaging to their product, namely: a slavish imitation of poets of the past, mistaking their word-usages, which in the meantime had become archaisms, as somehow essential to the poetic equipment and products, whereas these, in the first place, had been used only because they were part of the current living speech.

In the concluding verses in *Anonyma,* in *The Glory Road,* this point is touched on when the modernistic poet proposes to his lady, "And his raw yawp beat like a hammer hitting tin:"

> Twili
> g
> ht pushed down his
> GRAY DERBY theda is SOME jaz
> z quee
> N
> another flapper with her be
> side has no
>   GASoline
> Love (O!ITS!EATING!ME!) love
> ME be
> fore i sUIcide if you don't
>   SMACK
> me and of me be the
> wif!   !!   !!!

The lady replies, "in a murmur soft as a hammer hitting mush:"

> O prithee, my coz, my minion,
> Athwart the cerulean span
> I lift on a daedal pinion,
> An ye at the barbican.

> Like asphodel all awither
> I waste, with dejected poll.
> Buss me, string to thy zither,
> Earth to Sol!

Neither, naturally, can understand the other's language:

> And Love spread wide his fleecy
> Wings, and fled soon, I trow;
> Since she dwelt somewhere in B. C.;
> He, in now!

The insistent defense for this use of a dead or moribund vocabulary is that it was what the masters used. "But it's the poetic vocabulary; you wouldn't want us to write like *prose,* would you?" It is obvious that the bulk of the world's great poets and light versifiers wrote in the living language of their own time and land: Homer, Sappho, the great Greek tragic and comic dramatists; Virgil, Catullus, Horace, Lucretius, Dante, Petrarch, Camoëns, the epic and saga writers; Chaucer, Shakespeare and all his resplendent company; Burns, Shelley, Byron, Browning, Housman, Kipling, Chesterton; Poe, Whitman, Lanier, Emily Dickinson, Frost and the other leading moderns. There have been exceptions. Spenser tended to echo words alive in Chaucer's day, but alive no more. Milton, far more rarely, listened backward, instead of around him, for his words to use. Keats's ears were turned back to Spenser, himself too much an echo. Tennyson at times cocked his ear too tensely toward the past. There are countless minor exceptions. Again Whitman comes to reassure us:

> Poems distill'd from poems pass away,
> The swarms of reflectors and the polite pass, and leave ashes,
> Admirers, importers, obedient persons, make but the soil of literature.

When we come to the matter of craftsmanship in the masters, we will find this established beyond argument.

Again, the using of a living vocabulary is definitely an affirmative requirement. Only incidentally does it prohibit voting the cemeteries in word-usage. Before we come to its more positive aspects, there is value in digging deeper into the word-usage that it calls for.

THE NEED FOR ORIGINALITY IN YOUR VERSE AND POETRY

Anyone can spend all his energies in verse in echoing the verse and poetry already said by others; in being a rubber-stamp to forms and phrases already popular, and merely dressing them up slightly and offering them with a new turn of phrase or locale, as original verse. This often sells, in Tin Pan Alley song-lyrics. This was the essence of the two centuries of Provençal verse. It is all emphatically dead today; it constitutes no part whatever of the treasure-house of French poetry, in which the poems of Villon, from almost the same age, are so important. But no one looks to an echo for anything but an astonishing acoustic phenomenon; and one may turn to the one who makes the echo, to heed. A rubber-stamp is a mere convenience, never looked to as having personality or originality of its own. If being an echo, or a rubber-stamp, is the versifier's objective, it is not difficult to achieve; and this book will be of material assistance to him. But it is written primarily for those whose aim is far different: those who desire their verse and poetry to express their own words, their own desires, and not merely to mimic the words and the wishes of others.

We start with desires, each one of us. Man has developed words to express these desires. Poetry is the concentrated use of words, to express them. It is possible to use these vital tools— words—for amusement, in embroidering little toys with which to titillate ourselves and others. There is no harm in this. But it is play—it is *not* putting those instruments to the use for which they were shaped. The genuine poet or versifier will in the end use his tools as such, to cohere his desires and dreams into reality.

These desires and dreams can never precisely coincide with the dreams and desires of any other individual of the past, the present, or still to be. Any more than any one of us is a mere replica of any other person; as no animal repeats precisely the pattern of another; or no flower or leaf; or no grain of sand; or, if science reports correctly, no molecule, no atom, no ion or lesser constituent of energy-matter-time. Resemblances are human generalizations, not innate qualities of things: they are our mental pigeon-holes, for convenience and efficiency, and always faintly blur reality. No other person has ever precisely shared with you the same heritage of the past, which you received at the moment of birth, and added to thereafter: even an identical twin has a faint difference of timing. The phenomena that have altered into preceptions within you since birth, and your intermittent reception of them, dulled by inattention and almost blanked by sleep, differ from those experienced by any other individual. The emotions, thoughts and generalizations you have drawn from these of necessity differ from those of any other individual. Get this clearly: a specific tree, a sunrise, any definite human relationship, to you, differs from what it is to any other individual. Your report of it must differ correspondingly, if you are to be a faithful reporter and chronicler of it. Your every emotion and desire must differ similarly; and so must your report of it. If you seek to report merely the lowest common denominator of your desires, combined with those of others, this may pass for an authentic statement of desire for a time; but in the end it will fade of its very tepidity, to be replaced by more authentic reporting. Even where you are writing a *Marseillaise* to focus and heat to a white-hot point the collective desires of you and others, you cannot hobble yourself merely to echoing the desires of others; they must be the collective desires, passed through your soul as a conduit, and altered of necessity by the unique nature of that conduit.

You cannot write like anyone else, and still be yourself, and be true to yourself. You cannot write poems like Keats or Dorothy Parker, and still be yourself, true to yourself. An imitation is always inferior to the original: the latter had the merit of originality, for one thing. A restatement with improvements, whittling the original to a statement true to yourself, is a different matter. It was so that Shakespeare took the crude matrix of his plots, and touched them with his own inner divine fire, and so refined and annealed them to the metal the world uses still for its blade. If he had echoed these as they were, his name would be meaningless to us today.

And yet, your words must be intelligible; or they will speak only to yourself. What language can you use, in which to clothe your thoughts and desires? Obviously, the only language you employ in *all* your speech: the living vocabulary of your time, as altered in subtle and unique ways and nuances by your own speech. It should be colloquial, conversational in the highest sense, unwarped, uninverted, natural, in every line of poetry and verse you write. This is the goal to strive for; this is the goal the masters tend to reach.

There are exceptions, of course; or, rather, specialized cases. If you are writing dated period verse, imitating the speech of a bygone person or time, either in parody, or drama, or for any other purpose, naturally you must be faithful to this speech of another, as far as you can. It is always sure to reflect your own desire in some way; indeed, your use of this idiom of another is to incorporate and embody your own desire in it, for reasons of your own. Another exception is when you are writing for a specific market, which requires that you write to a pattern laid down and prescribed for you by the editor. All you can do then is write in the stipulated pattern. The result tends to be verse, rather than poetry.

AVOIDING A DEAD VOCABULARY

We find the wrong usage of words, at times, in poetry which otherwise has high merit, and which meets with great critical acclaim. Of this type was William Ellery Leonard's *Two Lives,* which had stretches of great beauty and effectiveness in it. But when we reach, in this sonnet sequence, a line like,

For that she died not ere she won her quest,

we realize that some mistaken inner compulsion has driven this writer far from the use of his living speech-vocabulary—unless he speaks a speech none of us has ever heard from living man or woman. Clearly, in actual speech, this would have been something like, "Because she did not die before she won what she sought," or "her objective," or "what she was after." *For that, she died not, ere, quest,* are all out of the current of living speech. They are not actually uttered, to convey desires and thoughts, even in the most literate and cultured circles; except in clowning. The sequence is full of similar lines:

Ye that *do hear* my story, *wroth* with me. . . .

Hands *'gainst* my temples *as to* crunch the brain. . . .

[26]

When I *bethink me 'tis* a husband's pen. . . .

> *Ye*
> Who *reft* your sister thus, in *reaving* me. . . .

Not one of the italicized expressions has any part in living speech. Most unforgivable of all, not one is rhyme-induced: living synonyms can be substituted in each instance, without jeopardizing the rhyme-pattern. Of course, if one did jeopardize the rhyme-pattern, this would merely place the stern mandate on the versifier of altering the rhyme-pattern, until the result was natural speech. The most that can be said in extenuation is that the words chosen here fitted the rhythm scheme. But, in turn, it suffers from monotony; it would be the gainer, by the addition of such rhythmic variations as the masters use. Take a line whose meaning is as colloquial as:

> I sat *in sweater* with the college boys.

Here it is the idiom that is at fault. The remedy is so simple,

> I sat, sweatered, among the college boys,

or

> I sat, in my sweater, among the college boys,

and we would have living speech at last.

John Livingston Lowes, in *Convention and Revolt in Poetry*, phrased words of gold for poets to remember:

> The very greatest effects of poetry are often produced without the use of a single word which might not be employed in ordinary speech.

To the extreme contrary was what Thomas Gray wrote, in one of his letters:

> The language of the age is never the language of poetry. . . . Our poetry . . . has a language peculiar to itself.

While this language can explain the use, by Leonard and so many others, of dead words and phrases, it cannot resurrect them from the graves dug by their following of it. Wordsworth was moved by this, when he preluded *The Force of Prayer* with the double archaism:

> What is good for a bootless bene?

Mary Lamb, when her brother Charles read this to her, wittily flashed back, "A shoeless pea," and punned this absurd line into immortality. Similar is this line of Rossetti's, in his rendition of the most famous of the Villon ballades,

> From Love he won such dule and teen!

Walt Whitman boasted, in a memorandum dealing with his writing of *Leaves of Grass*,

> I had great trouble in leaving out the stock "poetical" touches, but succeeded at last.

Yet even this great plain-speaking master slipped back, as he aged, into such stale stock poeticisms as:

> 'mid, unrecked, know I, yield we, ye valleys grand, laws divine.

It might aid to enumerate some of the things that should be avoided.

Classical Tags and Illusions.—Walt Whitman wrote, in *Song of the Exposition:*

> Come Muse migrate from Greece and Ionia,
> Cross out please those immensely overpaid accounts,
> That matter of Troy and Achilles' wrath, and Aeneas',
>   Odysseus' wanderings,
> Placard "Removed" and "To Let" on the rocks of your
>   snowy Parnassus.

If you live a life dominated by Greek and Latin deities, and think and speak commonly in classical tags and illusions, it would be natural for your poetry to move in the same enmummied aura. But you would limit your audience to the few today who suffer from the same adulation of entombed antiquity. There is no gain in comparing the automobile or the subway to Phaeton's chariot, or the airplane to the wings of Daedalus or Icarus: the modern things are reality, and have small kinship to the bright dawn dreams of the ancient Hellenes. There is small compliment in likening Napoleon, Pershing or Goering to Mars, for Mars had no strategy to meet modern artillery, tanks, and mustard gas. If your theme is a modern embroidery of the myths, or a psychoanalytic treatment of them, as Freud did with the misadventures of Jocasta's young, you will of course use the old stories, but in a living way. When you are describing the Empire State or San Francisco's Treasure Island, you gain nothing by dislocating chronology, and seeing minor Greek deities on major modern structures.

Clichés and Hackneyed Phrases.—All the phrases classified today as clichés, banal and hackneyed from overuse, shopworn and tarnished, were once fresh creations, and then of course deserved use. But, without individual repolishing by yourself and other later users, they must always be rigorously excluded. *Red as a rose, white as snow, black as night, the boundless blue, the dewy earth, teeth like pearls, eyes like stars* or *violets* or *woodland pools, cheeks like roses* or *sun-encarmined peaches, a throat like the swan*—suspect all these, and eliminate them sternly. Make your own similes, fresh and original—or alter the old ones until they are so new that they have become your own.

The same thing applies to repeating stock saws and axioms, "Honesty is the best policy," "The early bird catches the worm," and all the rest. Never use them, without freshening them until they are your own; or without making such a novel application of them that the application establishes them as your own.

Plagiarism.—Plagiarism, or adopting the idioms and phrases of other poets, or their whole lines, stanzas, or even poems, is of course to be avoided like the plague or housemaid's knee. At times phrases or lines come to you which you hail as original, and which become embedded in your own work. These may be lines once encountered in some other poet's work, and then forgotten, only to emerge unfathered in the unconscious process of poem creation. As soon as you or any one identifies the phrase or line as borrowed, purge the poem of it, or make clear your indebtedness. A poetry pupil submitted his volume to me recently, with the refrain "Spirit of Night" lifted bodily from Shelley; with a reference to "forest primeval," poached from Longfellow's preserve; whose love was like "a red, red rose"—page Burns; and who altogether had concocted a jambalaya of echoes, instead of speaking his own words. After this was called rather forcibly to his attention, he discontinued the practice. Once, while this dedicatory poem of mine was in page proofs,

> What if I coasted near the shore
> Of ultimate utter sleep?
> You were the tide that swung me back
> Into the living deep.
>
> I did not heed what all the world
> Held in its proud embrace.
> But it was life to hear you speak,
> And heaven, to see your face.

a friend pointed out to me that the ending came, almost word for word, from Ralph Hodgson's *The Mystery*. For all that his was a religious poem, the kinship was too close. A note, "With apologies to—" Hodgson and the particular poem, placed after my title, cured the matter. These things can happen. But be on guard against them, and remove them, or give credit, as soon as you learn of the borrowing.

Archaisms and Obsolescent Expressions.—All archaisms and obsolescent expressions—anything not in the living vocabulary —must be deleted sternly, as soon as you notice them. Perhaps you treasure them, and hate to see them go. Did not Keats use them, and Tennyson? True; but the vitality, the enduringness, of these poets was when they surmounted being echoes, and spoke authentically as themselves.

> Knowledge enormous makes a god of me.

The inversion is regrettable. But the breadth of the vista suddenly spread before us makes this one of Keats's starred lines.

> Not so much wind as on a summer's day
> Robs not one light seed from the feathered grass,
> But where the dead leaf fell, there did it rest. . . .

> Twilight and evening star,
> And one clear call for me.

There is a common and ruinous misconception that verse only becomes poetry, insofar as it uses a "poetic vocabulary," different from the living prose vocabulary. Gray and others contributed to this poisonous teaching. The poetic vocabulary is merely the speech vocabulary; and so is the prose vocabulary. All else must go out. Even in worship, where old customs linger longest. When *thou, thee, thy, thine* were part of the living vocabulary, to be used, among other usages, toward the deity, such usage was appropriate. It is so no longer. *You* and *your* are the pronouns to use in the second person, even in a direct invocation to Jehovah. The Quakers crystallized an allied usage, to show humility; but they have forgotten the grammar that went with it, and use *thee* for a nominative, instead of *thou,* which alone has grammatical standing. As harmful is any perpetuation of the archaic, even in the so-called "solemn style."

Among other archaic forms that must automatically and rigorously be deleted from the vocabulary of the living poet or versifier, except where he is writing verse definitely dated as of some archaic period, are:

Ye, mineself.

Art (as a verb form), *wast, wert, dost, wilt* (as a verb form), *wouldst, shouldst, shalt,* and all verb forms ending in *-est, -st, -eth,* and the like.

Intensive verb forms, such as *do go, did turn*—except where used as part of the living vocabulary.

'Tis, 'gainst, 'gin, 'tween, 'neath, e'er, ne'er, e'en, wa'in (for wagon), *ta'en* (for taken), and all other contractions not in the living vocabulary. *It's* and other contractions still used are permissible, where they do not too greatly lower the dignity of the speech.

Wroth, bethink, reft, reaving, athwart, welkin, rathe, in sooth, fardel, burthen, murther, nave, chaps, gins, Norweyan, proof (for armor), *composition* (for terms of peace), *ronyon,* and all other archaic, obsolete or obsolescent words.

Begirt, beplumed, bedecked, beribboned, and so on, except where part of the living speech. Many of these are. *Enwreathed, emplumed, empined,* and the like, with the same limitation. *A-Maying, a-hunting, a-swimming,* with the same large exception.

Except for *unless, memorize* for *make memorable, an* for *if,* and other outworn word-usages. All unnatural and elliptical expressions, improper to living speech; such *as to* for "as if to," *bethink me* for "recall," *for to that* for "for to that end," and so on.

All inversions and strained expressions improper in living speech, such as *the soldier brave, have I seen, I battles fought,* and the like. These are definite blemishes, when rhyme-induced. They are no less harmful when mere pointless echoes.

Poetic License.—The outworn plea of poetic license is used to excuse deviations from the normal word-usage and word-order; including especially inversions, ellipses (omissions of necessary words), mutilations of words for rhyming purposes, and so on. Obviously, since the speech used must be the living conversational vocabulary, none of these instances of poetic license must be used. Of course, any word-order or word-treatment permissible in good spoken prose is at home in good verse or poetry.

THE CHOICE OF WORDS

It must never be forgotten that poetry appeals primarily to the emotions, rather than to the intellect. Didactic poetry gains most when it has the same appeal. As a mnemonic device, it may direct itself toward the intellect primarily; but examples of this are rare today. Even witty verse appeals to the emotions also; for all forms of wit and humor release suppressed emotions, and gain their appeal thus. Thus, we do not "see a joke" where it is directed against us or against a cause we hold sacred. One of *The Eagle Sonnets* drives this whole point home:

> We cling to life, because we are a veil
> Of thought, over a vast unthinkingness.
> For its few seconds, thinking lifts its frail
> And timid form. And then all the bottomless
> Urges of being, blinder than the mole,
> Blind as the battered rock that sleeps forever,
> Speak the authentic mandate of the soul,
> Ruling the brain, so impotently clever.
> If the bedevilled brain, driven and breaking,
> Ask of the self: "Should I not rather die,
> Than stretch forever on a rack of aching?"
> Gloating stupidly, whip lifted on high,
>   The will beneath, as rank as swampland fennel,
>   Lashes dog reason back into his kennel.

When all other things are equal, out of the many words that the language affords, those must be chosen which appeal to the emotions most strongly. This means primarily the short sharp native words, rather than the overlong alien ones; the Anglo-Saxon, rather than the Greek and Latin stems. When Shakespeare wrote the first line below, in *Macbeth,* he at once glossed it with the Anglo-Saxon equivalent: and the whole power speaks in the second line:

> The multitudinous sea incarnadine,
> Making the green one red.

The impressions received during the formative years of childhood are the ones that etch themselves most deeply on the soul, and tend to rouse deeper emotions than words learned later. These words are primarily the short native words, rather than the ponderous exotic polysyllables. Where the vocabulary offers words of both types, in general the effective word for poetry, in proportion to the depth of its appeal, is the briefer and more native one.

This applies even more strongly to those words which, by long association, are heart-warming, automatically releasing our emotions, even against our will. *Home . . . mother . . . god . . . heaven . . . father . . . the flag . . . right . . .* these and many more, and many of their opposites as well: *wrong . . . enemy . . . traitor . . . Satan . . .* the glow-words have an automatic power that their synonyms can never have. Here we trespass on the subject to be taken up in dealing with translations. Note that, in these instances, it is not the thing, the idea, that is preferable: *mother* has all the appeal that its precise synonym, *maternal ancestor,* lacks; *home* has the tug and pull that *domicile* does not share at all. In cases where *maternal ancestor* had been used throughout instead of *mother,* from childhood on, clearly it would be the phrase to use. The proper word is the word with the ancient emotional overtones. My *More Power to Your Words!* develops this so fully that it need merely be mentioned here.

The vocabulary must be living; and slang is a part of the living vocabulary of most of us. But not the same slang. Some words are temporary neologisms—notice how the emotional reaction is drained out, by the use of the polysyllables!—and die as soon as they are born. Clearly they make your verse dated, and swiftly lose all appeal. Other slang words expand into wider and wider use, and in the end become an authentic part of the accepted language. The latter group are naturally to be preferred to the former. The only danger in the use of slang is that it limits your audience to those who are familiar with and accept the particular slang in question.

Here we have a stanza which clearly is in a modern idiom:

> I sit in one of the dives
> On Fifty-second Street
> Uncertain and afraid
> As the clever hopes expire

> Of a low dishonest decade;
> Waves of anger and fear
> Circulate over the bright
> And darkened lands of the earth
> Obsessing our private lives;
> The unmentionable odor of death
> Offends the September night.
> *September: 1939*, W. H. AUDEN

If it fails to affect us, the blame must rather be put on the erratic pattern of rhyme, consonance, and more remote sound-repetitions, often spaced so far apart that the ear fails to hear them. Here is an example, where the language is as living, but the emotional effect as definite as it was diffuse in the example from Auden:

> No puppet master pulls the strings on high,
> Portioning our parts, the tinsel and the paint;
> A twisted nerve, a ganglion gone awry,
> Predestinate the sinner and the saint.
>
> Each, held more firmly than by hempen band,
> Slave of his entrails, struts across the scene;
> The malnutrition of some obscure gland
> Makes him a Ripper or the Nazarene.
> *Slaves*, GEORGE SYLVESTER VIERECK

The final comment on word-usage may also sound superfluous: Be sure that, grammatically, your poetry or verse is as good as prose. This is obviously sound; if it isn't at least as well written as prose, why write it at all? But this calls for a survey of your poem or verses as a whole, from the standpoint of sentence-structure and the whole field of composition and rhetoric. For instance, it is a common practice of sonnet-writers to write either the whole sonnet as one fourteen-line sentence; or to write an opening sentence of eight lines, followed by one of six lines. Would either of these be good sentence-structure, if written in prose? Obviously not. Then never let the hypnotic effect of the devices of versification, rhyme-scheme, stanza pattern and the rest, blind you to the need for following the same rules of grammar, composition and rhetoric that good prose must follow.

II

THE KINDS OF POETRY

THE field covered by verse and poetry is so vast that it early became necessary for man to classify it, in order to make the study of versification more easily comprehensible. From the standpoint of content or subject-matter, the basis of classification was primarily the poet's method of expressing his desire: whether he worded it directly as a desire, embodied it in a description, implied it in a story, or had various persons speak it in a drama.

Lyric Poetry.—The first and most spontaneous device occurring to the poet is to express his desire directly. Thus an anonymous early English lyric implored:

> Blow, northern wind,
> Send thou me my sweeting.

Geoffrey Chaucer, hailed as the father of English song, in *The Complaint to His Empty Purse,* worded his plea directly:

> For which unto your mercy thus I cry:
> Be heavy again, or elles might I die!

The same personal utterance appears in Shakespeare's sonnets:

> When, in disgrace with fortune and men's eyes,
> I all alone beweep my outcast state. . . .
> Haply I think on thee. . . .
> For thy sweet love remember'd such wealth brings,
> That then I scorn to change my state with kings.
> *xxiv.*

Such poetry is called *lyric,* because the early Greeks sang poems of this type to the lyre; although it could be accompanied as appropriately by the harp, or the piano, or the jungle drum, or by any

[35]

or no musical instrument. Lyric poetry expresses primarily the poet's feelings directly, rather than emphasizing outward incidents and events. It is the most direct and subjective of all the types of poetry.

Descriptive Poetry.—The poet's desire might be centered in a sense of satisfaction or dissatisfaction with outward things, and the poem might consist merely of a description of these, as in this famous old anonymous English song:

> Summer is i-comen in,
> Loud sing cuckoo.
> Groweth seed and bloweth mead,
> And springeth the wood new.
> Sing cuckoo!

The same outward observation of nature can mount at times into such a magnificent apostrophe as Shelley's *Ode to the West Wind:*

> O wild West Wind, thou breath of Autumn's being,
> Thou, from whose unseen presence the leaves dead
> Are driven, like ghosts from an enchanter fleeing,
> Yellow, and black, and pale, and hectic red,
> Pestilence-stricken multitudes.

The end of the great ode alters into a direct personal lyric. But this is not necessary; the mood of description may continue to the very last word. The subject described might range from the Taj Mahal seen by moonlight to a fern lifting its spore-spears; from Mount Blanc to a poverty-blasted tenement; but the emphasis has been shifted, from the poet's direct expression of his desire, to his desire as embodied in outward things. This is called *descriptive* poetry. It is often included, purely for convenience, under lyric poetry. But the direct wish has become more remote, and may remain merely implied, as an unexpressed desire for the continuance or discontinuance of the thing described. Prose has increasingly replaced verse in description.

Narrative Poetry.—The poet's handling of his material may consist in the telling of a story of outward incidents and events, which have somehow aroused his interest, and which involve, directly or remotely, his desire:

> Come listen to me, you gallants so free,
> And all that love mirth for to hear,

> And I will tell you of a bold outlaw
> That lived in Nottinghamshire.
>
> As Robin Hood in the forest stood,
> All under the greenwood tree,
> He was aware of a grave young man,
> As fine as fine might be.
> *Robin Hood and Alan-a-Dale,* ANONYMOUS

This is called *narrative* verse or poetry, since it narrates or tells a tale. It may range from the most trivial description of a trivial happening, to an epic like the *Iliad* or the *Niebelungenlied:*

> Of man's first disobedience, and the fruit
> Of that forbidden tree, whose mortal taste
> Brought death into the world, and all our woe,
> With loss of Eden, till one greater man
> Restore us, and regain the blissful seat,
> Sing, heavenly Muse.
> *Paradise Lost,* JOHN MILTON

A narrative poem is usually told by the poet in the third person. In the great majority of cases, it involves what happens to others, with the poet merely an omniscient but imaginary spectator, our enterprising reporter, giving the latest flashes from the Trojan War or the Garden of Eden. It always has its elements of desire: the direct desire to tell the tale, plus some more concealed desire that the reader share the poet's admiration or detestation of the actions of the participating characters.

It may, however, be told in the first person, providing the emphasis is on telling the incidents, rather than on individually characteristic words used in the telling, or on the thoughts of the narrator. If the emphasis is shifted in either of these directions, the poem tends to alter from true narrative poetry to dramatic, which we reach next.

The field of narrative poetry has been largely usurped by the less artificial, more natural prose—as exemplified in the short story, of varying degrees of shortness, clear up to *Gone with the Wind;* as well as the expanding universe of prose fact stories, histories, biographies and so on. Masefield and others indicate that there is still a place for poetry in narration, if it compensates for its artificiality by added appeal.

Dramatic Poetry.—A fourth method of expressing the poet's desires is to place on a real or an imaginary stage the person or persons whose words or actions will express this desire, and let him or them tell the tale or express their feelings and thoughts in their own words. This may be merely one person speaking, in an autobiographical narrative emphasizing the personality of the speaker, as seen for instance in Browning's dramatic monologs, such as *My Last Duchess:*

> That's my last Duchess painted on the wall,
> Looking as if she were alive. I call
> That piece a wonder, now: Fra Pandolf's hands
> Worked busily a day, and there she stands:
> Wilt please you sit and look at her? I said
> "Fra Pandolf" by design, for never read
> Strangers like you that pictured countenance,
> The depth and passion of its earnest glance,
> But to myself they turned (since none puts by
> The curtain I have drawn for you, but I)
> And seemed as they would ask me, if they durst,
> How such a glance came there; so, not the first
> Are you to turn and ask thus.

And then the whole tragedy, of the volatile woman soul shrivelled in the not causeless jealousy of her lord and owner, comes forth. It may consist of a dialog between two persons, as in the gripping old ballad, *Edward, Edward:*

> "Why does your brand so drop with blood,
>   Edward, Edward?
> Why does your brand so drop with blood,
>   And why so sad go you, O?"
> "O, I have killed my hawk so good,
>   Mother, mother;
> O, I have killed my hawk so good,
>   And I had no more but he, O."

It may rise to a complete play, as in Shakespeare's *Othello;* or to a trilogy or longer, as among the great Athenian dramatists. Always the poet has the characters speak their own words; and, until we come to Shaw, the descriptive portions—the stage directions—are minimized. This is another field in which the naturalness of prose has largely replaced the artificiality of verse, with shining recent exceptions.

Didactic Poetry.—Verse may be used to teach a lesson, or to express an exhortation to conduct, or indeed a philosophy of life:

> Thirty days hath September,
> April, June, and November.
> ANONYMOUS FOLKRHYME

> Life is real, life is earnest,
>   And the grave is not its goal.
> Dust thou art, to dust returnest,
>   Was not written of the soul.
> *A Psalm of Life*, HENRY WADSWORTH LONGFELLOW

Such verse is called *didactic* (that is, teaching) poetry or verse. Where its appeal is primarily to the intellect, to that extent it strains its effectiveness as poetry; since poetry's primary appeal is to the emotions. The wish is often a moralistic desire to influence the conduct of others. Prose has made tremendous inroads upon this field. But, as verse, it has a definite mnemonic advantage, and is still popular.

Occasional Verse.—Verse may be used to signalize some especial occasion—an anniversary, a dedication, a holiday, a birthday. The annual odes expected of the laureate of England are of this nature; and so are the memorial verses still printed on the deaths of some relatives, friends, or celebrities. Occasional verse can at times rise to impressive poetry, as in Chesterton's dedicatory verses to *The Napoleon of Notting Hill,* and other similar verses.

Light Verse.—Verse may be used to amuse, in the form of dialect verse, witty verse, humorous verse, vers de société, sarcastic verse, parody, and the many variations employed by the funmakers and wits who turn to verse to impart their inner laughter. Since the psychologists have indicated how jokes of all kinds are used to release dislikes, the existence of the desire here is not to be doubted. This is called collectively *light verse.*

A WARNING CONCERNING THE CLASSIFICATION OF POETRY

It must always be remembered that poems were created, before they could be classified; that the poems are facts, and the classifications merely mental conveniences, to enable us to comprehend poetry and verse better. Any single poem may partake of the nature of any two of these various groups of verses or poetry, or of more, or even of all.

A narrative poem may include description, dramatic speech

of its characters, lyric interludes, and comic relief. Shakespeare's starkest tragedies usually insert descriptive portions, narration, and the inevitable clowning, to relax the otherwise overbearing tension. The same is true of much poetry. It is written by poets, to no mold but their own; and it does not gracefully fit into convenient pigeonholes.

A. E. Housman, whose *A Shropshire Lad* has been the most popular model for minor versifiers since the turn of the century, is properly called a lyric poet; and his verses are predominantly lyrical. But the rousing opening chorus ends didactically:

> Oh, God will save her, fear you not;
> Be you the men you've been,
> Get you the sons your fathers got,
> And God will save the Queen.

Again and again a sophisticated adolescent didacticism creeps in:

> Clay lies still, but blood's a rover;
> Breath's a ware that will not keep.
> Up, lad: when the journey's over
> There'll be time enough to sleep.

The very next poem, the popular—

> "O see how thick the goldcup flowers
> Are lying in field and lane. . . .
> 'Twill do no harm to take my arm."
> "You may, young man, you may,"

is a dialog between the wooer and the wooed, and hence uses the device of drama to express its lyric mood; while at the same time it is delicious light verse. "Farewell to barn and stack and tree" is only one of the brief bitter dramatic monologs. It, if course, tells a story as it proceeds, and is to that extent narrative as well; but the device of having the character tell the story, in his restrained understatement, makes it drama. *Bredon Hill* and "Is my team plowing?" use understatement and subtlety still further, to bring out their moving stories. The famous "Terence, this is stupid stuff," lxii, is first of all a dialog between the friend and the poet—and hence drama; and its essence is bitter didacticism. In addition to this, many of the verses partake of the nature of descriptive poetry, in whole or in part, and also frequently of light verse. Thus there is no classification entirely omitted; and there are complete specimens of each type of verse, except the pure narrative.

This is a typical collection of poems, one of the most popular of the present half century. For all that the academic mind desires to classify it as a collection of lyrics, closer scrutiny discovers traces of every other type of poetry, and full-grown examples of many of these. If this is so, what are we to do with our classifications? Have they any value, any utility? And how may they be best understood to be of use, since any one poem can partake of the nature of all of them?

We recall the discussion of the twilight zone contiguous to the two areas involved in any two touching definitions: Man makes sharp straight boundaries; nature does not. These classifications will be most valuable to us if we define them *from the center,* and not from the boundaries. Thus we can locate a poem that is definitely a lyric: as xxxv, "On the idle hill of summer," ending:

> Far the calling bugles hollo,
> High the screaming fife replies,
> Gay the files of scarlet follow:
> Woman bore me, I will rise.

Just as surely xlv, "If it chance your eye offend you," is wholly didactic. And xxvii, "Is my team plowing," is, in device, dialog, that is, drama—for all that it has elements of narration and description.

The spirit of our definitions, to make them of most use, will then follow somewhat this pattern: "It expresses *primarily* the poet's feelings directly." The poet and versifier will always remember that he will encounter many poems primarily lyrical, yet with elements of one or more or all of the other classifications in them; and these he will still, as matter of convenience, classify as lyrics. He will remember, when he comes to write his own lyrics, that he is given the same latitude in using the other devices; the sole ultimate criterion being what will most effectively express his desire.

When we come to a poem or verses exactly balancing two or more of the classifications, the subjective decision must be that it is one, or the other, or both, or neither. The poem is the fact;

never let the mere mental convenience, the classification, assume too great importance.

Fix firmly in the mind the core of the definition, and a few poems which precisely fit it, as cases in point. Recognize that most poems do not fit the straight-jacket classifications with any grace; and that this is their merit, not their fault. Always feel free to write with any combination of devices that will best express your desire. With the one exception of a contest restricting you to one classification: in which case, the closer you shave to the core of the definition, the better.

1. LYRIC POETRY

History of the Lyric

The birds developed architecture, in their most elaborate nest-building; the formal dance; and the formal song without words. Certain mammals also made some progress in all three of these. It is possible that architecture, dancing and music may well have been the first of the three fine arts to spring up among primitive men. We know that painting and sculpture came in at least as early as 25,000 B.C., as the Altamira murals and the Brassempuoy Venus indicate. The arts of design—architecture, painting, and sculpture—by virtue of using more enduring materials, have left surviving vestiges antedating and exceeding in amount those of the arts of music, poetry, and the dance. From the standpoint of function, the early need for a dwelling stimulated the early development of architecture, which may well have come as the first of the arts of design, before the more ornamental arts of painting and sculpture. Of the three non-design fine arts, music, poetry, and the dance, there is little definite evidence of priority of origin. From a functional standpoint, since, unlike the songs of birds, man's words were primarily for communication to others, poetry may have come first.

After written records commenced, there is ample evidence of the antiquity of all three of the non-design arts; and relatively nothing as to their respective priority. Among the early Hebrews, according to Genesis iv, the sixth generation from Cain produced Jubal, "the father of all such as handle the harp and organ";

while his father, Lamech, is credited with uttering this early Hebrew verse,

I have slain a man to my wounding, and a young man to my hurt.

The victory song of Moses, in Exodus xv, is even more famous; and, at its end, Miriam the prophetess, sister of Aaron, "took a timbrel in her hand; and all the women went out after her with timbrels and with dances," as she sang her song.

Among the Greeks, the great Homeric epics refer to pre-existing hymns, harvest-songs, warsongs, dirges and the like. After Homer, who may be dated 950 B.C., and his immediate Ionian followers, came Hesiod and the Boeotian school; and the development of the lighter elegiac and iambic poetry, the former sung to the oboe. Now came the brief personal poems sung to the lyre, or lyrics proper; the outstanding poet among them being Sappho of Lesbos, in the seventh century B.C. The lyric, and no doubt earlier poems also, coexisted with music and the dance; but again we are entirely in the dark as to which came first.

For decades, there was a plausible theory that the arts developed practically simultaneously, as a social product rather than as the result of the creation of individual artists. This theory has fallen into disrepute, especially when faced with Louise Pound's poser: "Did primitive man sing, dance and compose in a throng, while he was yet unable to do so as an individual?" It is of course possible that it required collective emotion to release the individual artist; but even then artistic creation could not have come simultaneously to a group. The most that could have happened was group-inflamed individual creation, with immediate group acceptance, and further improvisation, extension or improvement. No matter how fully we conjecture alterations in original musical or literary creations, from hundreds of later collaborators, extending over long periods, the original creation must have been individual. Thus what are called folk music and folk literature are in essence anonymous creations with anonymous alterations, rather than group-created.

We are on slightly firmer ground when we come to the question of which came first, lyric, descriptive, narrative or dramatic poetry. There is a comparative equality in the antiquity of the earliest preserved fragments. In biology, such a dilemma would be solved by embryology—utilizing the fact that the development of each form of life before birth recapitulates the past history of that branch of the animate world. We shall see whether we can discover any comparable evidence as to the classifications of poetry, as to their respective priority.

Let us start with a homely modern example, to see which of these devices of expression of desire would automatically come first. Let us take a situation of individual desire: a man wants a certain girl. Would he first, assuming that his emotion required the concentrated outlet of verse, say that he wanted her; or describe her or himself; or tell a story dealing with his want; or compose it as a drama? The answer is self-evident. He would first phrase his desire directly—the lyric method.

A more complicated group example would be that of a group of workers who felt the pinch of their working conditions, and, by strike or otherwise, took action against it. Would their first versified expression of their desire for improved working conditions be: A direct demand, "We want more wages, more food, better working conditions?" A description (by its nature less concentratedly emotional) of the harassing conditions, or the desired improvement? A narrative of how one or many had suffered, or a parallel narrative of similar past sufferings, with the resultant improvement—or the reverse? Or, lastly, a play or pageant dealing with their condition?

No doubt, if the contest lasted long enough, all these would be created. But the first to be created would, in the common run of cases, be the direct lyric cry for improvement and an end of the harassments.

The lyric apparently came first.

From a standpoint of the embryology of poetry, the inquiry is clouded by the fact that these five dominant types of verse are as specialized and distinct, in perfect specimens, as, for instance, the squid family, the insects, the spiders, the birds and the mammals. Yet, when we study the inception of each type of verse— the actual creation by you or any other versifier—one is simpler, by a step, than any of the others; and this step the others must include. Hence the others apparently stem out of this one. In four of these, the intermediate step occurs as a rule before the first word is written down, and hence it will be enclosed in parentheses in the outline given below. This, of course, is merely parallel to development before birth, in biologic embryology. But this missing step is always present, at least in the unconscious, and has itself dictated the form of the creation. Let us skeletonize the coming of verses in these varied classifications:

Lyric. I want something. I write out that want.

Descriptive. (I want something. I connect it with a liked or disliked locality or thing.) I describe this thing.

Narrative. (I want something. Some series of happenings expresses my desire.) I write out the happenings.

Dramatic. (I want something. Some series of happenings or expressions of opinion express my desire.) I write it out.

Didactic. (I want someone else to do or believe something.) I write out the thing to be done or believed.

The common element is the desire. This is expressed simply and directly only in the lyric. It is reshaped into a description, a story, a drama, or a teaching or command, in the other cases. The un-reshaped clearly precedes the reshaped. Poetic embryology corroborates that the lyric must have come first.

THE SIMPLE LYRIC

In the dawn of our culture, Sappho wrote *To Gongyla:*

Tonight, Gongyla, my rosebud,
I urge you, come to me,
bringing your Lydian harp.

O, how my hunger
flutters forever
around the lamp of your beauty.

For the sight of your dress
makes me tremble,
and I shiver with rapture.

There was a time when I found fault
with Cyprus-born Aphrodite.
That hour is past.
I pray for no more
than she has given me,
to fold you again in my arms, my adored one.

This and the other translations from Sappho are from my own *The Song of Sappho,* which presents her poetry directly to our hearts, without the intervention of the alien Sapphic stanzas, a form of quantity verse conditioned by her accompaniment on the lyre and with dancing.

This first direct expression of wish is broadened in another poem into description of bodily anguish which Longinus and Plutarch hail as the sublimest expression in verse of physical passion:

> One with the Gods he seems to me,
> that man who sits before you,
> and close beside you
> listens to your sweet voice
> and your trilled laughter—
> this, this indeed
> causes the heart in my breast to shiver.
>
> For if I see you only a tiny moment
> my voice fails me,
> my tongue is broken,
> and at once beneath my flesh
> untouchable fire runs.
> My eyes are blinded,
> there is a roaring in my ears,
> sweat runs down my limbs,
> I tremble all over,
> I am paler than winter grass,
> and death seems so near I can touch it.
>
> But now, since I must lack you,
> I must bear all this.

Here we have the direct lyric as achieved by a master, whose greatness in poetic stature has not yet been equaled by any other woman. The modern lyric does not differ in impulse from these. The lyric is almost the most important of all forms of poetry to the modern poet, because of the great demand for .it, and its resultant wide modern use. It is frequently conditioned by the requirements of the periodical and book markets, which demand excessive brevity, and prefer an epigrammatic quality: the sort of O. Henry ending that Housman excelled in. Yet the more leisurely lyric still lives in men's hearts, as is evidenced by this opening of the bird's carol from Walt Whitman's *Out of the Cradle Endlessly Rocking:*

> Shine! shine! shine!
> Pour down your warmth, great sun!
> While we bask, we two together.

Two together!
Winds blow south, or winds blow north,
Day come white, or night come black,
Home, or rivers and mountains from home,
Singing all time, minding no time,
While we two keep together. . . .

Blow! blow! blow!
Blow up sea-winds along Paumanok's shore;
I wait and I wait till you blow my mate to me.

The modern tendency often prefers rhyming, as in Robert
Browning's *Home-Thoughts from Abroad:* I:

Oh, to be in England
Now that April's there,
And whoever wakes in England
Sees, some morning, unaware,
That the lowest boughs and the brushwood sheaf
Round the elm-tree bole are in tiny leaf,
While the chaffinch sings on the orchard bough
In England—now!

It prefers even the more formal stanza, as in Vivian Swerig's
Bring With You:

Bring with you but the touch of your slim fingers,
And with the quietness which bending skies
Have learned from leaning down to hold the still earth,
Lay them upon my hair, upon my eyes.

Bring with you but the softness of your small breasts;
There my lips will dwell in blind delight,
And sun and moon and stars may dim, nor stir me
Who know your beauty singing through the night.

The core of the definition of the simple lyric is that it sings
the poet's feelings directly. These feelings may be far subtler
than the simple "I want," and may tend in the direction of
description until they merge with pure description, the definite
desire being implicit and unspoken. The lyric wealth of the
language is so great, that it is impossible to do more than give
a few typical lyrics, to indicate how widely the aim and pattern
may vary. Here is one of Emily Dickinson's triumphant lyric
cries:

I taste a liquor never brewed
From tankards scooped in pearl;
Not all the vats upon the Rhine
Yield such an alcohol!

[47]

Inebriate of air am I,
And debauchee of dew,
Reeling, through endless summer days,
From inns of molten blue.

When landlords turn the drunken bee
Out of the foxglove's door,
When butterflies renounce their drams,
I shall but drink the more!

Till seraphs swing their snowy hats,
And saints to windows run
To see the little tippler
Leaning against the sun.

The lyric exultation is here seen at its height. Elinor Wylie's passionate longing for death is expressed with infinite art in *Escape:*

When foxes eat the last gold grape,
    And the last white antelope is killed,
I shall stop fighting and escape
    Into a little house I'll build.

But first I'll shrink to fairy size,
    With a whisper no one understands,
Making blind moons of all your eyes,
    And muddy roads of all your hands.

And you may grope for me in vain
    In hollows under the mangrove root,
Or where, in apple-scented rain,
    The silver wasp-nests hang like fruit.

The quality of frantic imagination, far beyond the bounds usually attributed to sanity, is seen here, and may result in the quality hailed as magic. It must never be forgotten that the essence of poetry is desire; and that desire far precedes thought and logic and sanity, and is more anciently rooted and sounder than man's fumbling logic.

Rose O'Neill, in *Apollo Senex* and so many more, speaks with a jewelled tongue reminiscent of Campion and the lordly Elizabethans:

Give me an old poet,
    Not these young,
Crying, crying, with a hurt in the tongue
This *much* of pretty words—
    Books are more than birds.

Give me an old poet,
Thick with scars,
Quit with babbling of the stars
And of disasters more or less,
Who chirps with bitter pleasantness;
Full of quaint wisdom, but inclined
To let alone the neighbor's mind,
Abstemious of fury, yet
Adept of all regret. . . .
Wine-colored as a stricken leaf,
And Sybarite of grief.
The soundless laugh in the Alas,
The old last cricket in the grass.

John V. A. Weaver's *To Youth* speaks directly to us:

This I say to you,
Be arrogant! Be true!
True to April lust that sings
Through your veins. These sharp springs
Matter most. . . . Afteryears
Will be time enough for sleep. . . .
Carefulness . . . and tears. . . .

Now, while life is raw and new,
Drink it clear, drink it deep!
Let the moonlight's lunacy
Tear away your cautions. Be
Proud, and mad, and young, and free!
Grasp a comet! Kick at stars
Laughingly! Fight! Dare!
Arms are soft, breasts are white,
Magic's in the April night. . . .

Never fear. Age will catch you,
Slow you down, ere it dispatch you
To your long and solemn quiet. . . .
What will matter then the riot
Of the lilacs in the wind?
What will mean—then—the crush
Of lips at hours when birds hush?

Purple, green and flame will end
In a calm, gray blend.
Only . . . graven in your soul
After all the rest are gone
There will be the ecstasies. . . .
These alone.

Notice how the lyric passion strides over the rhyming scheme,
leaving the lines ending "stars," "dare," "wind," "soul," "ecsta-

sies," unmated. This is no blemish, when authentic poetry speaks. The advice here is, Live! There is no mention of the kindred command,—And write! But the poet knows that the living, for all its rainbow solace as the sun swells and flattens and vanishes, will be as forgotten as Susa or Ecbatana, unless it be graven at its moment in enduring words. Rose O'Neill, in one of her most graphic pictures, has represented the compulsion to write as a mighty hand driven, with its imperative index finger outreached in command, sheer through the shrinking body of the poet. The poet is impaled upon the great finger-commanding hand. So it must be, when poetry is about to be born. And so to this poem I would add the two additional words, before passing out of the triple circle of man's most concentrated utterance, to its contiguous territories.

THE SONG

The song, especially when set to music, shares with the simple lyric major functional importance in poetry today; and it is often far more remunerative. Whether the simple lyric originated with its tune or not, or originated independently, and soon thereafter became coalesced with a tune and an accompaniment upon some musical instrument, there were long centuries when the lyric involved not only verse but a tune to which it was to be sung, usually with some instrumental accompaniment. During this period, definitions and classifications were thoroughly blurred; the lyric might include elements from descriptive, narrative, dramatic or didactic poetry, or might consist entirely of one of these, or of a combination of two or more. Among recent favorites among songs, *In Old Madrid* tells a story with a lyric refrain; *The Two Grenadiers* tells a story with dramatic dialog and a lyric outburst at the end; while *Anchored* prefaces each use of the refrain with a story emphasizing descriptive passages. The use in *Othello* of one stanza of *Take Thine Old Cloak About Thee* shows that this dramatic-didactic favorite was sung; while a majority or all of the old English ballads, many of them mainly or wholly narrative, were sung. Even during this period, however, the closet lyric—the lyric for reading only—had become well known. While the interspersed songs in the Elizabethan dramas, the lyrics of Campion, and the like, all had tunes, increasingly the lyric for reading only wandered off—although any such lyric might at any time be set to music; while the main trend of lyrics used as songs, which we shall hereafter simply call songs, became more and more formalized to meet the market demands of music. It is worthy of mention that, in popular usage, a lyric for reading is more often referred to as a poem; while the verses to be sung, even to *Hold Tight, Mamma* or *Flatfoot Flugie,* are called by the trade the *lyric,* and their author is the lyricist.

We have pointed out that the periodical and book market for lyrics tends to shorten the production of custom-built lyrics into packed concentrated epigrammatic verses. The same tendency is seen in song-writing. The sprawl and spread of *Casey Jones, Frankie and Johnny,* and most of the ballads and Negro spirituals, have been replaced by a demand for a stanza of limited range, and a chorus of one of several general patterns; while the number of stanzas is greatly limited since, for instance, the recent hour of the appearance of *The Man on the Flying Trapeze.* The stanza-forms preferred for modern lyrics to be set to music will be considered in the treatment of stanza-forms.

The remunerative aspect of lyric-writing, in the sense of writing verses to be set to music, comes from royalties from sales of sheet-music, mechanical reproduction rights, movie, radio, and television use, and many other rights. What will be said later on the subject of the versifier's vocabulary applies with immense force to the writing of song-lyrics, with certain important additions. The words chosen to be sung should, by preference, be words with the more singable sounds. While a patter-song, as in a Gilbert and Sullivan opera or Noel Coward's *Mad Dogs and Englishmen,* might exult in such rhyming combinations as *scratched, embarked, latched, remarked,* these are all difficult to sing; while vowels like long *o, u,* and *i,* and broad *a,* especially when followed by *r, l, n, m,* or followed by no consonant, are correspondingly easy. If the versifier aims especially at song-lyrics, he should specialize in the use, not only in line-terminals but throughout, of sounds not too difficult to sing. Granting that poetry should be suitable to be read aloud, such a combination as Browning's—

> Irks care the crop-fed bird? Frets doubt the
> maw-crammed beast?

is at best doubtful in poetry, except in a line intentionally caco-
phonic; while its use in a concert song or a popular one would be
definitely lethal.

At any time any particular type of song-poem may strike a
responsive popular chord, and become popular. In all but one
case out of a thousand, the chances of publication and popularity
depend upon some adaptation to the current pattern. Accordingly,
the prospective song-lyricist must familiarize himself with the
general type of lyrics used in the type of songs he aims to write
for, and must follow these, rather than waste his energy trying to
convert a tightly organized industry into an acceptance of his
unspecialized efforts.

A study of the lyrics that have survived in popularity, or
become instantaneous favorites, will be of aid. Hardly a budding
baritone emerges from the goslings without trying his talent on
Ben Jonson's famous *To Celia,* as fresh now as it was three hundred years ago:

> Drink to me only with thine eyes,
>   And I will pledge with mine;
> Or leave a kiss but in the cup
>   And I'll not look for wine.
> The thirst that from the soul doth rise
>   Doth ask a drink divine;
> Yet might I of Jove's nectar sip,
>   I would not change for thine.
>
> I sent thee late a rosy wreath,
>   Not so much honoring thee
> As giving it a hope that there
>   It could not wither'd be.
> But thou thereon didst only breathe
>   And send'st it back to me;
> Since when it grows, and smells, I swear,
>   Not of itself but thee!

The magical welding of words to tune have made this outlast
many a more moving lyric, many a finer tune. Clinton Scollard's
Sylvia seems destined to impressive longevity, and rightfully,
in its perfect musical setting. There are recent lyrics, even in
the popular class, as well-wrought and comely—for instance,
Lazybones:

Long as there is chicken-gravy on your rice,
  Everything seems nice;
Long as there's a water-melon on the vine,
  Everything seems fine.
Ain't got no time to work, ain't got no time to play,
Busy doin' nothin' all the livelong day;
He don't seem to care, no matter what you say,
  He's just built that way.

Chorus: Lazybones, sittin' in de sun,
How you 'spec' to git yo' day's work done,
  How you git yo' day's work done,
  Sittin' in de noonday sun?
Lazybones, sittin' in de shade,
How you 'spec' to git yo' cawn-meal made?
  Never git yo' cawn-meal made,
  Sittin' in de noonday shade.
When 'taters need sprayin', I know you keep prayin'
  De bugs fall off o' de vine;
An' when he goes fishin', I know he keeps wishin'
  De fish won't bite on his line;
Oh, Lazybones, sleepin' all de day,
How you 'spec' to make a dime dat way?
  Never make a dime dat way—
    Well, looky here!
  He never heard a word I say!

If memory has tricked me on some of the pronouns, full apologies are hereby tendered. The lyric is splendid, and splendidly fitted to the tune. It will earn and receive many revivals.

The same cannot be said for the lyrics to such appealing tunes as *Smoke Gets in Your Eyes, Sunrise Serenade,* and so many more. Lyrics which violate the technique of good verse-writing sag of their own doughiness, and unaccountably fail of the continuing popularity the music entitled them to. Such off-rhymes as *Norfolk, war talk,* in George M. Cohan's *I Was Born in Virginia,* and *childhood, wildwood* in *Childhood* and so many more, are blemishes that add their share toward the speedy demise of a song. Excellence in the technique of versification pays dividends in lyric-writing, and its absence exacts in time its price.

THE ELEGY

An elegy is a formal expression of the poet's grief at death, whether of an individual or in the abstract.

Why should the poet's reaction toward death be singled out

to form a complete class of lyrics, when the same is not done with his desire for love, beauty, food, travel, a palace to live in, money, and countless other things? Do not lullabies, drinking songs, hunting songs, warsongs, and so many more, deserve equal isolation? Undoubtedly; yet it is a fact that we have here a class illogically separated, and we must accept this as a fact. One possible explanation lies in the fact, pointed out in Freud's *Beyond the Pleasure-Pain Principle,* that the primary instinct of life is to return to lifelessness (or death) in its own time in its own way. The fact that this instinct is so universal, and treatments of it so immensely popular, may have been partially responsible for its elevation to this separate category, the elegy.

Among the Greeks, a special form, the elegiac couplet, was invented about the seventh century B.C. It will be analyzed under Classic Meters. But it was invented merely as a lighter form than the ponderous hexameters, and at first was used for poems of war, love, and conviviality, and probably at first not to express grief at death at all. Since the beginning of the sixteenth century, *elegy* has been restricted in English to the meaning first given. A morbid Christian preoccupation with death and a world beyond has undoubtedly contributed to this.

The elegy may be a mere reflection upon death in general, as in Gray's celebrated *Elegy Written in a Country Churchyard.* More usually it is dedicated to the death of a single person, as in Milton's *Lycidas,* Shelley's *Adonais,* Tennyson's *In Memoriam,* Whitman's *When Lilacs Last in the Dooryard Bloomed,* and many shorter elegies. The absence of personal feeling in most of the longer elegies in English is noteworthy; the death is rather used as a peg upon which to hang the poet's particular views, than to express personal grief. The *Encyclopaedia Britannica* seeks to differentiate between an extremely short elegy, which it calls a dirge; an elegy; and a long elegy like *In Memoriam,* which it calls a collection of elegies. There is no gain from such academic finickiness. It is best to treat as elegies all poems and verses expressing the poet's desire regarding death, no matter what that desire is, remembering that this is the English usage of the word, and not the Greek.

The custom of inserting rhymed obituaries in newspapers perhaps reached its culmination in the heyday of the verses of Mrs.

Julia A. Moore, whom the nation remembers as "The Sweet Singer of Michigan." Among her famous obituary elegies, this one, *Hattie House,* is to be sung to the tune of *Lily Dale:*

Come all kind friends, wherever you may be,
    Come listen to what I say.
It's of a little girl that was pleasant to see,
    And she died while out doors at play.

Chorus.

Oh! Hattie, dear Hattie,
    Sweet little Hattie House—
May the flowers ever bloom o'er the little tomb
    Of our loved one, Hattie House.

She had blue eyes and light flaxen hair,
    Her heart was light and gay,
She said to her mother, that morning fair,
    "Mother, can I go out and play?"

Her mother tied her bonnet on,
    Not thinking it would be the last
She would ever see her dear little one
    In this world, little Hattie House. . . .

Those little girls will not forget
    The day little Hattie died,
For she was with them when she fell in a fit,
    While playing by their side. . . .

One fine morning, the fifth of July,
    The summer flowers were in bloom,
Eighteen seventy-one, little Hattie died,
    And is sleeping in her tomb.

Nor can we possibly omit one key stanza from *Little Libbie:*

While eating dinner, this dear little child
    Was choked on a piece of beef.
Doctors came, tried their skill awhile,
    But none could give relief.

We observe at once that these verses amuse, rather than move us with deeper emotions. Yet the happenings must have moved the author and others in a way deserving of a far different emotional response from us. We will learn later that this comes from the poet's ignoring all the requirements of acceptable verse. These elegies refer, after all, to actual deaths, that brought shocking grief to parents, friends, and at least a morbid interest to the singer. If she had known her technique, she might have produced poems that survive for their power, rather than for their faults. The subject deserved better treatment.

To the opposite extreme is the art displayed by Edna St. Vincent Millay in her elegies, including the poignant *Memorial to D. C.*, with this exquisite sextet:

> Heap not on this mound
>   Roses that she loved so well;
> Why bewilder her with roses
>   That she cannot see or smell?
> She is happy where she lies
> With the dust upon her eyes.

It must never be forgotten that the public taste prefers the simpler and more concentrated poem to the longer, more erudite one. Thus of Whitman's poems on the death of Lincoln, *O Captain, My Captain* is far more of a popular favorite than *When Lilacs Last in the Dooryard Bloomed*. There is still a market for obituary verses in many periodicals; and surely there would be a general gain in improving the technique of those that appear. Occasions arise in which any poet, deeply stirred at the coming of death to some loved or admired one, wishes to phrase this in enduring form; and then the elegy is at hand. Beyond this, the classification is of minor importance. But it may always include verses as lovely as those which Mark Twain had engraved on the tomb of his wife, "Warm summer sun, Shine kindly here"; or that exquisite elegiac lyric by Stevenson, *Requiem:*

> Under the wide and starry sky,
> Dig the grave, and let me lie;
> Glad did I live, and gladly die,
>   And I lay me down with a will.
>
> These be the words you grave for me:
> "Here he lies, where he longed to be;
> Home is the sailor, home from sea,
>   And the hunter home from the hill."

THE PASTORAL

A pastoral is a poem dealing with the lives of shepherds; or one in which the characters are pictured as ideal shepherds; or, by extension, one dealing with outdoor and country life.

Why should there be a separate classification for poems of shepherd life, when there is none for those of hunter or farmer, lawyer, dentist or laundryworker, and so on? Or for poems of country life, when there is no corresponding category for poems of city life, or life in a jungle, or on a glacier? There is no logic in this classification, but it does spring from a development of literary history. It came out of man's nostalgic desire to return, during an agricultural and urban culture, to the imagined ease of the shepherd's life, as he idly watched his flock browse contentedly, while playing some pensive air upon his pipe, and awaiting the arrival of some complaisant shepherdess. The court dilettantes of Greece, Rome, Bourbon France, Cavalier England, and other provincial spots, adopted the convention of the pastoral as a graceful masquerade. The names given to the characters were fanciful and light: Corydon, Thyrsis, Strephon, Phyllis, Amaryllis, Chloe, Sylvia, Celia, Lucasta, Althea; the verses were often as light. Even such elegies as *Lycidas* and *Adonais* take their titles from the pastoral mood, and move under its influence:

> Alas! what boots it with uncessant care
> To tend the homely, slighted, shepherd's trade,
> And strictly meditate the thankless Muse?
> Were it not better done, as others use,
> To sport with Amaryllis in the shade,
> Or with the tangles of Neaera's hair? . . .
> At last he rose, and twiched his mantle blue:
> Tomorrow to fresh woods, and pastures new.
>
> *Lycidas,* JOHN MILTON

This presumably referred to Milton's own grief at the death of his college friend, Edward King; and here, of course, the shepherd's trade symbolizes the pursuit of poetry. The unfortunate use of the pastoral setting lends an air of unreality to the grief. It was a similar convention which caused John Erskine, when writing a poignant happening in the World War just after the turn of this century, in which a soldier bayonetting one of the enemy sudenly discovered that it was a woman in man's attire that he was killing, to tell this as if it had happened in the Peloponnesian war between Athens and Sparta. Artificial conventions are a late blemish to poetry, and soon enough there is always a return to direct speech, without tinsel make-believe.

Milton's *L'Allegro* and *Il Penseroso* are charming reflective poems of the pastoral class; and Whittier's *Snowbound* is frequently classed as a humbler cousin. But this should bring us up with a start. Here we have no conventional shepherds and shepherdesses out of an impossible Arcady, but a well-knit picture of American country life snowed in for a hard winter. Call it pastoral if you insist; it is primarily descriptive verse dealing with country life, and needs no artificial category.

A similar craze for academic classification has caused the splendid poems of Robert Frost to be described occasionally as pastorals. This is as erroneous. His poems reflect faithfully a certain section of New England gone to seed, in lyrics, descriptive poems, and narratives, with tense drama appearing in some of them. If we use the term pastoral at all, let it be limited to artificial verses dealing with conventionalized shepherd life. These are remote from the concerns of life today, except as an unreal ivory tower to cell oneself within, or for the spice of light verse.

THE ODE

The dictionary definition of *ode* is a poem suitable to be set to music and sung or chanted, originally by a chorus moving rhythmically. It is academically divided into (1) the regular or Pindaric ode, each section containing a strophe and an antistrophe of identical stanzaic form, followed by a contrasting epode; (2) the irregular or pseudo-Pindaric ode, with no correspondence between its parts; and (3) the Lesbian or Horatian ode, a simpler form, with uniform stanzas.

According to this, Gray's *The Bard* and *The Progress of Poesy* would come under the first classification; Wordsworth's elaborately titled *Ode on the Intimations of Immortality*, under the second; and Shelley's *Ode to the West Wind* and, in general, the odes of Keats, under the third.

We may throw out of the window, as far as modern odes are concerned, the requirement that an ode is to be set to music or sung or chanted, either by a chorus or an individual. An ode is simply the longest and most dignified form of lyric verse. The elaborate machinery invented by Pindar is similar to the canzos and sirventes of the medieval Provençal troubadours, and has met with a similar forgetfulness. Attempts of the French Pleiad and of Victor Hugo and his confrères in France, like those of Gray and a few more in England, failed to receive wide following.

The great odes in the English language use either the irregular line and stanza form employed by Wordsworth in the ode mentioned:

> Our birth is but a sleep and a forgetting;
> The Soul that rises in us, our Life's star,
>   Hath elsewhere its setting
>   And cometh from afar.
> Not in entire forgetfulness
> And not in utter nakedness,
> But trailing clouds of glory do we come
>   From God, who is our home:
> Heaven lies about us in our infancy!

Shelley's *Ode to the West Wind,* one of the highwater marks of descriptive-lyrical writing in English, is in terza rima, fourteen lines to the stanza, and tightly rhymed. The great odes of Keats tend to have a uniform stanza, such as:

> Thou wast not born for death, immortal Bird!
>   No hungry generations tread thee down;
> The voice I heard this passing night was heard
>   In ancient days by emperor and clown:
> Perhaps the self-same song that found a path
>   Through the sad heart of Ruth, when, sick for home,
>   She stood in tears amid the alien corn;
>   The same that oft-times hath
> Charmed magic casements, opening on the foam
> Of perilous seas, in faery lands forlorn.
>
> *To a Nightingale*

At that, *On a Grecian Urn, To Melancholy* and *To Autumn* repeatedly vary their precise stanza forms, a prerogative a poet or versifier may always take, to improve his presentation.

THE CHANT

A chant is a poem to be chanted, rather than spoken or sung: that is, to be recited musically, with liberal use of monotone, occasionally broken by more definitely tuneful parts. The chant is a recent revival of an old art form, apparently related to its use in public religious worship. The growth of this poetic form within our memory is typical of the erratic way in which poetic forms develop.

In 1911, G. K. Chesterton's *Lepanto* appeared, a rousing narrative, surcharged with lyric feeling. He called several similar poems ballads. As far as is known, it was written to be read aloud, with such moving music as:

Dim drums throbbing, in the hills half heard,
Where only on a nameless throne a crownless prince has stirred,
Where, risen from a doubtful seat and half attainted stall,
The last knight of Europe takes weapons from the wall,
The last and lingering troubadour to whom the bird has sung,
That once went singing southward when all the world was young.
In that enormous silence, tiny and unafraid,
Comes up along a winding road the noise of the Crusade.
Strong gongs groaning as the guns boom far,
Don John of Austria is going to the war,
Stiff flags straining in the night-blasts cold,
In the gloom black-purple, in the glint old-gold,
Torchlight crimson on the copper kettle-drums,
Then the tuckets, then the trumpets, then the cannon, and he comes,
Don John laughing in the brave beard curled,
Spurning of his stirrups like the thrones of all the world,
Holding his head up for a flag of all the free.
Love-light of Spain—hurrah!
Death-light of Africa!
Don John of Austria
Is riding to the sea.

This poem deservedly swept itself into swift popularity. Gloria Goddard wrote a biography of Don John of Austria, *The Last Knight of Europe,* expanding the rhythm and repetition devices found here into a book offered as prose, one of the books which may cause the definition of poetry to be broadened. Chesterton's lyrico-dramatic outburst is apparently based on the seven-foot movement of the early ballads, a norm line being:

Comes úp / alóng / a wínd- / ing róad / the noíse / of the / Crusáde,

It was recited or chanted by Floyd Dell to Vachel Lindsay, the American poet, on the shore of Lake Michigan. Dell's rendition was based on the theory of William Butler Yeats that poems should be chanted, and not spoken; which no doubt stems out of an ancient Irish custom. Chesterton had probably intended his verse to be divided, with (P) to indicate pauses,

Dim (P) / drums (P) / throbbing / in the / hills (P) / half (P)
heard (P)

But Lindsay heard this as four-foot time:

Dim′ drums / throb′bing in the / hills′ half / heard′,

and utilized it in three of his first chants as four-foot or 4-accent time:

Booth′ led / bold′ly with his / big′ bass / drum′
General William Booth Enters Into Heaven

Fat′ black / bucks′ in a / wine′-barrel / room′
The Congo

I′ am the / Kal′ lyope, / Kal′ lyope, / Kal′ lyope,
Tooting hope, / tooting hope, / tooting hope, / tooting hope,
Wil′ ly willy / wil′ ly rah / HOO′!
The Kallyope Yell

The same 4-accent line dominated *The Chinese Nightingale; The Ghost of the Buffaloes; Bryan, Bryan, Bryan, Bryan; The Drunkard's Funeral; The Santa Fé Trail; Daniel;* and *Simon Legree,* among his earlier chants; though he later ventured into 5-accent and other rhythms.

The opening of *The Congo* gives one phase of his handling of the chant:

1. THE BASIC SAVAGERY OF THE NEGRO

Fat black bucks in a wine-barrel room,
Barrel-house kings with feet unstable,
Sagged and reeled and pounded on the table,   *A deep rolling bass*
Pounded on the table,
Beat an empty barrel with the handle of a broom,
Hard as they were able,
Boom, boom, BOOM,
With a silk umbrella and the handle of a broom,
Boomlay, boomlay, boomlay, BOOM.
THEN I had religion, THEN I had a vision,
I could not turn from their revel in derision.
THEN I SAW THE CONGO, CREEPING THROUGH THE
    BLACK,   *More deliberate*
CUTTING THROUGH THE FOREST WITH A GOLDEN
    TRACK.

Then along that riverbank
A thousand miles   *Solemnly chanted*
Tattooed cannibals danced in files;
Then I heard the boom of the blood-lust song
And a thigh-bone beating on a tin-pan gong.
And "BLOOD" screamed the whistles and the fifes of the warriors,
"BLOOD" screamed the skull-faced, lean witch-doctors,
"Whirl ye the deadly voo-doo rattle,   *A rapidly piling climax*
Harry the uplands,   *of speed and racket*
Steal all the cattle,
Rattle-rattle, rattle-rattle,
Bing.
Boomlay, boomlay, boomlay, BOOM."
A roaring, epic, ragtime tune
From the mouth of the Congo
To the Mountains of the Moon. . . .
"Be careful what you do,   *All the "o" sounds very*
Or Mumbo-Jumbo, God of the Congo,   *golden. Heavy accents very*
And all of the other   *heavy. Light accents very*
Gods of the Congo,   *light. Last line whispered.*
Mumbo-Jumbo will hoo-doo you,
Mumbo-Jumbo will hoo-doo you,
Mumbo-Jumbo will hoo-doo you."

Such chants, especially as given by Lindsay in his best mid-Western Methodist revivalist manner, were very effective. As he used them, the form was primarily lyric or descriptive, or a combination of both; although *Simon Legree* tended to the narrative. The form was a distinct contribution to the technique of poetry; and, by bringing the poet, and not his book, directly to his audience, it helped bring poetry out of the cloistered study into the currents of life again.

2. DESCRIPTIVE POETRY

Purely descriptive poetry is one step more complicated than the simplicity of the pure lyric. For, in the lyric, the poet utters his desire directly; in descriptive poetry, he describes something outside of himself, followed by the expression of his desire regarding it, or quite as often leaving the desire unexpressed and implicit.

Many of the poems treated under "The Lyric," above, might with more accuracy be dealt with here. Whittier's *Snowbound* is a good example. Take, for instance, this lyric by Orrick Johns:

They are unholy who are born
To love wild plum at night,
Who once have passed it on a road
Glimmering and white.

It is as though the darkness had
Speech of silver words,
Or as though a cloud of stars
Perched like ghostly birds.

They are unpitied from their birth
And homeless in men's sight,
Who love better than the earth
Wild plum at night.

The emphasis here is on the evocative description of the wild plum blossoms, with an opening and closing faintly didactic, and no direct lyric expression whatsoever. The tendency recently has been to make the word *lyric* a catch-all for anything that is not definitely a narrative or a drama; and there is no gain in this.

The desire may be fairly close to the surface, as in Gloria Goddard's *A Sycamore in Spring:*

Naked and unabashed, you wait on the hilltop,
Flaunting your uxorious want
Against the dull dismay of a gray farmhouse.
Your bare limbs,
Ivoried by winter's feasting,
Yearn toward an aching sky;
In fingers tenuous with longing,
You clutch a raucous crow.
Still as figures scrawled on paper
You wait for the spring wind
Creeping stealthily over the hill,
To quicken you with its throbbing kiss,
To tumble you
To ripe leaf and riper fruit.

This clearly comes under the category of descriptive poetry; as do Robert Frost's *An Old Man's Winter Night, The Cow in Apple Time,* Keat's *To Autumn,* Tennyson's *The Splendor Falls on Castle Walls,* Poe's *The Bells,* and many more. Yet even in the most objective descriptive poem, the wish is still there. It may be that, in the end, *lyric* will be applied loosely to cover descriptive verse, similar to its loose usage in song-writing. It always remains that descriptive verse differs from the pure lyric in that it gives merely the data on which the desire is based, with the final expression of the wish left for the reader's heart to speak.

3. NARRATIVE POETRY

The Ballad and Its Origin

The ballad in English is of especial interest to us. This is less because of its importance and popularity as an art form, than because a search into its origins will take us to the beginning of native English poetry, with its essential convention, the four-accent line.

Verses telling a story must have been of almost as great antiquity as lyric verses expressing the versifier's desire directly. The impulse to tell a story—whether that story deal with one's own experiences, or whether it mount in importance until it deals with the adventures of a king or a god—must have come early to man. It is hard not to predicate it of the hunters' camp-fires of men of the primitive Stone Ages. Verse came to be used, with whatever conventions slowly came into vogue, because this was easier to remember than prose. But the initial impulse of the lyric, a direct expression of desire so concentrated it could no longer remain silent, itself produced repetition conventions naturally; while the story tended naturally to mount to such repetition conventions only at its climax. Hence verse is less natural to the story as a whole than to a desire expressed directly. An ultimate result of this is that the pure lyric still persists as the major method of expressing concentrated desire; while the narrative poem has been largely replaced by the short story, the novel, the history, and other prose works. The application of verse to the whole of a narrative was hence artificial from the start; while it was natural to lyric utterance.

But, in the absence of writing, with verse and its conventions developed from the lyric, and with memory as the sole perpetuator of man's earliest literary creations, the mésalliance had to be made, and the complete narrative in verse resulted. In spite of this, we have few early brief narratives perpetuated, compared to the number of the more formal longer narratives, epics and the like. References in Homer establish that the Homeric Greek possessed prior hymns, harvest-songs, warsongs, and dirges; but only by implication are heroic narrative ballads also included.

When we turn to such a collection as Mother Goose, however, the preponderance of verses with some narrative element is remarkable. For one direct lyric.

> If I'd as much money as I could tell,
> I never would cry old clothes to sell,

and two dialogs primarily dramatic, "Who killed Cock Robin?" and "Where are you going, my pretty maid?", there are more than a score with story elements: "The Queen of Hearts she made some tarts," "Old King Cole," "When Good King Arthur ruled the land," "Little Miss Muffet," "Little Jack Horner," "Simple Simon," "There was a little man and he had a little gun," "There was a man in our town," the versions of "There was an Old Woman," and so on. All this in addition to lullabies, definite dance songs, didactic descriptions ("What are little boys made out of?"), riddles, alphabet and letter songs, and the like. Here we have a vestigial collection of anonymous verse accepted as folkverse, with the narrative element predominating; which indicates that it was no late development.

To return to our Stone Age campfire and the verses chanted around it, it is clear that the story element would predominate. Narration must have come first and most naturally in prose; but it came memorably only in verse. Lyrics, except in such times of collective strain as general hunger, an attack by a hostile power, or collective oppression by a conqueror, were largely secrets to be told man to man. A man did not shout aloud his love desire to the group, until it had failed, or been definitely postponed, or perhaps had succeeded. Yet consider how large a part love lyrics play in the history of lyric poetry! In those days before the knight-wanderings of chivalry had evolved romantic love, love lyrics were largely spells for capture, or announcements of capture; they had not yet become the intimate advertisements of failure that of late have become so popular, among a race where achieved mating is diminishing, with individuals becoming collectively so bee-like.

If the development of the Greek ballad is obscure, and that Roman ballads down to the tarnished silver age of Augustus more so, at least the direct ancestry and development of our own ballads, the English ballads, is becoming increasingly clear. Louise Pound is one of many who have clearly established that the original authorship of the ballad was individual, and not collective; that the task of others in the group was merely to join in the chorus and make further improvisations, and to preserve the whole in memory, with constant alterations and corruptions.

Clear thinking upon the *ballad* can come only from clarifying the altered meanings of the word. We have seen *lyric* alter from any song to be sung to the lyre, to the specialized meaning of a direct expression of the poet's desire; and then wandering off in two directions, as any words to be sung, and as a catch-all for all poetry not narrative or dramatic. *Ballad* has wandered in meaning quite as much. It came from the Latin *ballare*, and meant primarily a dance-song. Like *Oats, Pease Beans and Barley Grow,* or *Jeepers-Creepers*. It developed independently into meaning a simple song, primarily sentimental. None of these meanings is of primary concern, when dealing with narrative poetry. Narrative ballads did not spring from these; the word *ballad* was borrowed later to apply to narrative verses. Quite independently, the word began to be applied, late in the eighteenth century, to popular short narrative poems, simple in structure and often utilizing the favorite narrative verse stanza. It was Ritson, in 1813, who first restricted *ballad* to "mere narrative pieces." Formerly these had been called *songs;* and the use of ballad for dance-song was then so definite that Burton, in his *Anatomy of Melancholy,* refers to an old English translation of *The Song of Songs* as *The Ballad of Ballads.*

English drama originated in the miracle and morality plays produced by the church, to teach religion and ethics in the vernacular. Similarly the ballad, in the sense of story-to-be-sung, originated in ecclesiastical ballads for the same purpose. Such early ballads as the 13th century *Judas* and *A Ballad of the Twelfth Day,* and the fifteenth century *Inter diabolus et Virgo, St. Stephen* and *Herod* preceded the earliest of the secular ballads. Religious tags were long added to the early secular ballads, further establishing the ecclesiastical influence. From the clerics the ballads passed into the hands of the medieval minstrels—at first largely connected with noble houses, and only later being forced, by the constant breaking-up of the noble houses from continual warfare, to look to the loose populace for patronage.

DEVELOPMENT OF THE FOUR-ACCENT LINE

According to Merriam-Webster and many earlier authorities, there is in English a definite ballad meter or stanza: the meter being "the seven-accent verse, or pair of verses"—the rhythm being, of course, 4,3 when divided into a pair of lines. The misconception here will be clarified on closer analysis of the rhythm of the ballads themselves, and what these rhythms stemmed from.

Since the earliest ballads were written in the vernacular, the rhythm of the first ballads had to be the rhythm of the English vernacular. This was neither 7-accent verse nor 4,3 verse. It was the conventional line found in *Beowulf* and other early English poems, which was popular as late as William Langland's *Piers Plowman,* a poem appearing about the time Chaucer was importing alien meters and stanzas from France and Italy to replace native English verse. The *Britannica* follows other authorities in describing the norm of this verse as "the alliterative long line, the lax rhythm of which shows that it was intended, not to be sung to regular melodies, but to be recited." The illogical conclusion aids as little as the loose use of "long line," which is as unspecific, without further analysis, as if the Greek hexameter or the English iambic pentameter were merely described as a "long line."

Old English verse had three conventions: four accents to the line; two (or three, or four) alliterations to the line; and each line bisected by a cesura, or pause. The number and position of the unaccented syllables was regarded as unimportant. Just as alliteration and cesura are unimportant to modern English verse. Here are typical opening lines, the cesura marked by (/):

> *W*idsith made utterance, / his *w*ord-hoard unlocked,
> He who *m*ost of *m*en / a*m*ong *m*einies on the earth
> And *f*olks had wandered; / oft on the *f*loor he took
> *Widsith, c. 600* A. D.

> "It is never the *h*orns / of the *h*ouse are burning?"
> *B*rake then into speech / the *b*attle-young king:
> "This nor *d*awneth from the east, / nor here any *d*ragon flieth,
> Nor *h*ere on this *h*all / are the *h*orns burning."
> *Finnsburgh*

Weland among the Wurmas / wandered in exile,
A single-minded earl / he suffered hardship,
He had for his comrades / care and longing,
Winter-cold wretchedness; /woe he often found.

Deor

Charles Scott Moncrieff insists that these were composed for the harpist, and were not merely to be recited. He points out, "The line consists of two metrically equivalent halves, . . . In each half there are normally two accented syllables. . . . At least one accented syllable in the first half-line is alliterated with one in the second." The original opening of *Beowulf* is:

Hwaet! we Gar-Dena / in gear-dagum
theod-cyninga / thrym gefrunon,
hu tha aethelingas / ellen fremedon.
Oft Scyld Scefing / sceathena threatum,
monegum maegthum / meodo-setla ofteah.

Note the alternate alliteration in line 1 (g, d, g, d); the secondary *fr* alliteration in lines 2 and 3; and the subordinate alliteration or phonetic syzygy in line 4 (th, th): so intricately could the device be used. Moncrieff's translation of this misses some of the subleties of alliteration in the original:

What! We of Spear-Danes / in spent days
Of the Folk-Kings' / force have heard,
How the Athelings / excelled in fight,
Oft Shield of the Sheaf / from scathing hordes,
From many meinies / their mead-stools tore.

Approximately seven hundred years after *Widsith,* the same rhythmic line is used in *Piers Plowman;* always with four accents to the line:

In a summer season, / when soft was the sun,
In rough cloth I robed me, / as I a shepherd were,
In habit like a hermit / in his works unholy,
And through the wide world / I went, wonders to hear.

The original, in line 2 for instance, follows the convention far better than the translation.

Two elements of this convention—the formalized alliteration, and the compulsory cesura—were regarded as too artificial to be retained, when the alien element of rhyme had been added to it.

But the four-accent rhythm was adopted wholly by the priests, when they originated the ballad as we know it. Chaucer had brought in the rhymed couplet from France—using 16,000 lines of five-foot metric couplets and 3,500 lines of four-foot metric couplets, as well as 14,000 lines of five-foot iambics rhymed in Rhyme Royal. Couplet and stanza were alike unknown to West Germanic verse, out of which English verse stemmed; it was always stichic—marked by no periods save those of the individual lines—not stanzaic. Of the earliest ballads, says Louis Pound, "The ecclesiastical pieces are in the couplet form usually recognized by scholars as the older for ballads." We shall find, added to rhyme in couplets, all three of the old English conventions, at first: four accents to the line, some formal alliteration, and the cesura. Thus the lovely 14th century *Song of the Incantation* commences:

> I sing of a *m*ayden / that is *m*akeless;
> *k*yng of alle *k*ynges / to here sone she ches.
>
> he *c*am also stylle / ther his moder was,
> as dew in aprylle / that fallyt on the grass.
>
> he cam also stylle / to his moderes bowr
> as dew in aprille / that *f*allyt on the *f*lour.

We note alliteration departing, and word and phrase and clause repetition coming in. Here is another opening, from about the same period:

> Adam lay y-boundyn, / *b*oundyn in a *b*ond
> fowr thousand wynter / thowt he not to long.

Here is one from *Lully Lulley,* written down first during the reign of Henry VIII:

> He *b*are him up, / he *b*are him down,
> He *b*are him into / an orchard *b*rown. *Lully,* etc.
>
> In that orchard / there was an hall,
> Which was hanged / with *p*urple and *p*all. *Lully,* etc.

The famous *Judas* opens:

> Hit wes upon a Scerethorsday / that vre louerd aros;
> Ful milde *w*ere the *w*ordes / he spec to Iudas.
>
> "*I*udas, thou *m*ost to *I*urselem, / oure *m*ete for to bugge,
> Thritti platen of seluer / thou bere up othi rugge. . . ."

So it was that the English ballad started: with the 4-accent line preserved, and the cesura; with rhyme added; with formal alliteration slowly departing. R. Brimley Johnson's collection *A Book of British Ballads* contains eight following this precise original pattern, with a varying use of refrain. In addition to these examples of the earliest form of the ballad, there is *Cospatrick*, in couplet-rhymed 4-accent quatrains. Eleven more have 4-accent quatrains, with alternate rhyming; and one, *Fair Helen*, has three 4-accent lines rhymed together and followed by a refrain. As against this twenty in predominantly 4-accent pattern, there are only thirty-four in the later and more usual pattern of 4,3 accents.

The lesson to ballad-writers is important. The 4,4 accent pattern is more venerable and at least as valuable as the later 4.3 accent pattern.

DEVELOPMENT OF THE 4,3 COUPLET

Where did the 4,3 couplet, often misdescribed as the 7-accent line, come from? Here for the first time we are on speculative ground. But, where there is a problem, the answer will be found sooner or later. The priests used the 4-accent line, because it was the familiar and popular line of old English alliterative verse. They tended toward couplet rhyming, because this was the simplest form of rhyming known, and the one that came in first from France. Even at that, they experimented with the stanza of three 4-accent lines, followed by a refrain:

> Owt of the est a sterre shon bright
> For to shew thre kingis light,
> Which had ferre traveled day & nyght
> *To seke that lord that all hath sent.*

> MS. *Balliol 354, Richard Hill's Commonplace Book*

> Lystyn, lordyngis both gret & small,
> I will tell you a wonder tale,
> Howe holy chirch was browght in bale
> Cum magna inuria.
> A, a, a, al
> Nunc gaudet ecclesia.

> *The Murder of Thomas a Beket, Balliol MS. 354*

We will omit marking the cesura hereafter, since it shrank in importance, and ultimately disappeared as a formal requirement. The same stanza form is still sung in an equally ancient Yule carol, *The Boar's Head:*

> The *b*oar's head in hand *b*ear I,
> Bedecked with yew and rosemary.
> And I pray you, my gentles, be merry,
> Quod estis in convivio.
> (*Chorus*) Caput apri defero,
> Reddens laudes Domino.

This triply rhymed stanza, which appears in the CHESTER *Noah's Flood* and other miracle plays, appears in one famous ballad, if not more:

> I wish I were where Helen lies,
> Night and day on me she cries;
> O that I were where Helen lies,
> On fair Kirconnel Lee!
> *Fair Helen,* ANONYMOUS

Miss Pound suggests that this was abandoned, because the excessive rhyming interfered with the ballad flow of the story. After all, rhyme was still regarded as an alien interloper, unknown to the great heroic old English poems. No doubt for the same reason, the 4-accent couplet rhyming, seen in *Cospatrick,* gave way to the 4-accent quatrain, not alternately rhymed, but containing only one pair of rhymes, 1,2,3,2, separated by eight syllables instead of four. It should be noted that the refrain chorus of *The Boar's Head,* and the refrain line of *Fair Helen,* at last show three accents to the line, instead of four: and this is the element we are looking for, to complete the 4,3-accent couplet.

We must dig a little deeper for the precise origin of this 4,3,4,3 stanza. There are seven 4-accent couplet-rhymed ballads in Johnson' collection, with refrains. The famous *Widdicombe Fair* brings in a 3-accent refrain, the stanza having this intricate pattern: 4, R4, 4, (R2, 2, 2, 3, 3), the repeated tag of the refrain,

> Old Uncle Tom Cobleigh and all,

showing only three accents. *The Brave Earl Bran* emerges into a definite 3-accent refrain:

[71]

> O did you ever hear o' brave Earl Bran?
> *Ay lally, O lilly lally!*
> He courted the king's daughter of fair England,
> *All i' the night sae early.*

The same is true of *Lady Isabel and the Elf-Knight:*

> Fair Lady Isabel sits in her bower sewing,
> *Aye as the gowans grow gay;*
> There she heard an elf-knight blowing his horn,
> *The first morning in May.*

It is not surprising to find alliteration reappearing in both of the refrain lines: old customs die hard. The norm in this ballad is couplet rhyming for the 4-accent lines which carry on the story; and the *gay-May* rhyme for the 3-accent refrain. The dropped foot in the refrain gave a chance for breath for the singer, as well as for a flourish on the musical instrument. It became popular, with the added advantage that it postponed the rhyme from a 4-internal to a 7-internal somewhat as alternately rhymed 4-accent quatrains had done.

Thus the regular ballad meter (more properly, ballad rhythm) came in as 4,3 verse (the 3-accent lines being at first a refrain), and not as 7-accent verse. Kipling was on the wrong track when he united these into the unwieldy lines of:

O East is East, and West is West, and never the twain shall meet
Till two strong men stand face to face at God's great judgment seat.

But he was not original in this. Certain comic scenes in Shakespeare's early *Comedy of Errors* are in this couplet form:

> *Dro.* Your cake here is warm within; you stand here in the cold;
> It would make a man mad as a buck, to be so bought and sold.
> *Ant. E.* Go, fetch me something (Pause), I'll break ope the gate.
> *Dro.* Break any breaking here, and I'll break your knave's pate.
> *III, i.*

It is even possible that the original version of the play, from which Shakespeare borrowed or which he rewrote, was entirely in this loose seven-foot accent verse. Ralph's famous song from *The Knight of the Burning Pestle,* by Beaumont and Fletcher, is in the same contagious popular line:

> And now the birchen-tree doth bud, that makes the schoolboy cry;
> The morris rings, while hobby-horse doth foot it feateously;

The lords and ladies now abroad, for their disport and play,
Do kiss sometimes upon the grass, and sometimes in the hay.

We even have alliteration as an overtone here, as in the famous
line:

Fly Venus and phlebotomy, for they are nothing good.

So it was that the 4,3-accent couplet, or the 7-accent line, developed in English poetry out of the original 4-accent line.

FURTHER DEVELOPMENTS OF THE BALLAD

A typical ballad, in the early 4-accent couplet rhyming, with
a 4-accent couplet-rhymed refrain interrupting it, is *Fine Flowers in the Valley:*

She sat down below a thorn,
Fine flowers in the valley,
And there she has her sweet baby born,
And the green leaves they grow rarely.

"Smile na sae sweet, my bonny babe,"
Fine flowers, etc.,
"And ye smile sae sweet, ye'll smile me dead,"
And the green leaves, etc.

She's ta'en out her little penknife,
And twinn'd * the sweet babe o' its life.

She's howket ** a grave by the light o' the moon,
And there she's buried her sweet babe in.

As she was going to the church,
She saw a sweet babe in the porch.

"O sweet babe, an thou were mine,
I wad clead *** thee in the silk so fine."

"O mother dear, when I was thine,"
Fine flowers in the valley,
"Ye did na prove to me saw kind,"
And the green leaves they grow rarely.

In studying this, we note that the rhythm is based on four
accents to the line, rather than on any metric foot. Yet an extra
accented syllable is permitted, and no doubt slurred over, as in

* Twinn'd—parted, severed, sundered.
** Howket—digged.
*** Clead—clothe. cf. clad.

"sweet babe." The repetition device we have called rhyming is far laxer, and admits related repetition devices: two assonances (*valley-rarely* and *thine-kind*), two consonances (*moon-in, church-porch*), and one couplet with no real repetition link, *babe-dead;* these to only three rhymes, *thorn-born, mine-fine,* and one formed by a misplaced accent, *life-penknife.* Stock phrases are used, as in "sweet babe"; akin to the "wine-dark sea" type of phrase in Homer. This is an instance of complete phrase repetition. The action is swift, the subject matter strong meat. There is a tendency toward dialog, the essence of drama—this development Miss Pound regarding as fairly late in the early ballad. All of these are typically in the ballad mood and technique. In many ballads, these are still further emphasized. Modern ballads with a planned archaic touch may use any or all of these devices.

When the poem becomes pure dialog, it shifts to the classification of drama. Yet it is still in the ballad mood and technique otherwise,—a story to be sung, cast in dialog form. Note the added element of direct word, phrase and clause repetition, in the original form of the famous Scottish ballad-drama, *Edward, Edward:*

> "Quhy dois zour brand sae drop wi' bluid,
> Edward, Edward?
> Quhy dois zour brand sae drop wi' bluid,
> And quhy sae sad gang zee, O?"
> "O, I hae killed my hauke sae guid,
> Mither, mither:
> O, I hae killed my hauke sae guid:
> And I had nae mair bot hee, O."

Barring the invocations and the repetitions in lines 2, 3, 6 and 7, this leaves lines 1, 4, 5 and 8 as a quatrain in the 4,-3,-4,-3-accent pattern. When his mother challenges that his hawk's blood was not so red, the son evades that he has killed his red-roan steed.

> "Zour steid was auld, and ze hae gat mair,
> Edward, Edward:
> Zour steid was auld, and ze hae gat mair,
> Sum other dule ze drie, O."
> "O, I hae killed my fadir deir,
> Mither, mither:

> O, I hae killed my fadir deir,
> Alas! and wae is mee, O! . . ."

> "And quhat wul ze leive to zour ain mither deir,
> Edward, Edward?
> And quhat wul ze leive to zour ain mither deir?
> My deir son, now tell me, O."
> "The curse of hell frae me sall ze beir,
> Mither, mither:
> The curse of hell frae me sall ze beir,
> Sic counseils ze gave to me, O."

The ballad may open with an invocation:

> All gentlemen and yeomen good,
> I wish you to draw near.
> *Robin Hood and the Shepherd*

> I will sing, if you will hearken,
> If you will hearken unto me.
> *The Laird o' Logie*

In the vast majority of cases, it snaps right into the story:

> The king sits in Dumferline toune,
> Drinking the blude-reid wine.
> "O quhar will I get guid sailor,
> To sail this schip of mine?"
> *Sir Patrick Spence*

or even opens with dialog:

> "O where have you been, my long, long love,
> This long seven years and more?"—
> "O I'm come to seek my former vows
> Ye granted me before."
> *The Daemon Lover*

The stripped simplicity and speed of development of the typical ballads, as Miss Pound points out, are evidences of high art in story-telling, not of amateurish improvisation. There are often many literary tags encountered, *dolour, travail, paynim;* as well as accent-shifting evidently derived from the French, which was the court language. Gummere points out the constant use of incremental repetition: that is, repetition used, not as a refrain, but, by successive changes of a word, phrase, or line, to reveal a situation or aid in the development of the story. Thus, in *The*

Hangman's Tree, the groups of three stanzas develop with these
openings:

> "Feyther, feyther, ha ya brot me goold?" . . .
>
> "Meyther, meyther, ha ya brot me goold?" . . .
>
> "Sister, sister, ha ya brot me goold?"

Finally the sweetheart is asked the same question; and, unlike
the negatives of the others, she answers,

> "O I ha brot yo goold,
> And I ha paid yo fee,
> And I ha coom to take yo from
> Beneath the hangman's tree."

This device, and many others found in the ballads, appears in
many of the Negro spirituals, shoutsongs and seculars, where
the individual members of the family, the deacon, the preacher,
and others, successively play their parts; or where a succession
of Biblical characters do the same thing.

The general social attitude is that of the upper classes; which
might have been expected from the clerical and minstrel origins.
The persons are primarily upper-class, on the whole. Where both
classes are represented, the action develops usually as the lower-
class would wish to hear, as in the Cinderella story—kitchen-
maid to princess; or in King Cophetua and the Beggar Maid.
Thus Thomas Potts, a serving man, weds a lady of noble birth,
and is ennobled; the Kitchie Boy weds a lady of noble birth;
Richie Story, an aristocrat, marries a footman; the blacksmith in
The Twa Magicians successfully seduces the lady; Little Mus-
grave becomes the lover of Lady Barnard; and, as the essence
of such romance, in *Hind Horn* the king's daughter, on the day
she is a bride, yields to her humble lover, who has come to her
disguised as a beggar. The themes are typically bloody and sen-
sational: Lord Barnard cuts off his wife's nipples in punish-
ment; the jealous eldest of *The Twa Sisters* drowns her sister,
fair Ellen; Lord Thomas' nut-brown bride at the wedding stabs
Fair Annet to death, and is in turn killed by her husband; the
Jew's daughter murders little Sir Hugh "like a swine," as an
early example of the ritual-murder myth; The Brave Earl Bran
dies, after killing the King of England and sixteen of his fol-

lowers, as an incident in his abducting the king's daughter; the wife of Robin of Portingale plans on the wedding night to have twenty-four knights murder her husband, but instead he kills them all, and punishes his wife by depriving her of her ears and other bodily accessories. The whole is a cheerful mixture of mayhem and murder, and has endured as a vicarious satisfaction of deep-rooted desires in all of us.

LATER BALLADS

The academic mind soon fell into the error of misunderstanding the original accent basis of the rhythm, and insisting upon accurate iambics, a foreign importation into English:

> O waly, waly up the bank,
> And waly, waly down the braw,
> And waly, waly yon burn side,
> Where I and my love wont to gae.
> *Waly, Waly, but Love Be Bonny*

Bishop Percy, in his famous *Reliques,* tends to this emasculation of the lively naturalness of the original rhythm; compare his opening stanza of *The Child of Elle*. The spirit of the ballad is best expressed in accent verse, which alone is native to English speech; and the later machine-made iambics may usually with profit be eliminated, in favor of the more natural rhythm.

The original ballad stanza we have found to be the 4,4 rhymed couplet in accent rhythm, usually with a refrain of greater or less complication, tending toward the 3-accent refrain. An early variation was three 4-accent lines rhymed together, followed by a 3-accent refrain. This never became popular. The 4,4 stanza developed into a 4,4,4,4 stanza, first with couplet rhyming; then rhymed only on the second and fourth lines, or 1,2,3,2. The final development was into accent-rhythm of 4,3,4,3 accents, rhymed 1,2,3,2, with the rhyming sounds seven feet apart.

Modern ballad writers may use any of these or may vary them where there is profit in the variation. Thus Keats, in his *La Belle Dame Sans Merci,* written in soul-agony at his failure with Fannie Brawne, adopted as his stanza form:

[77]

> O what can ail thee, knight-at-arms,
> Alone and palely loitering?
> The sedge has wither'd from the lake,
> And no birds sing.

Here the iambic metric pattern is 4,4,4,2, with the rhyming the familiar 1,2,3,2.

Coleridge's *The Rime of the Ancient Mariner* has for its norm the typical stanza of 4,3,4,3 accent lines, rhymed 1,2,3,2. Among his many variation stanzas—the old ballads especially permitting a 4,3,4,3,4,3 stanza—are:

> 4,4,4,3,4,3 rhymed 1,1,1,2,3,2
> 4,3,4,3,4,3 rhymed 1,2,3,2,4,2
> 4,3,4,4,3 rhymed 1,2,3,3,2

clear up to a nine-line stanza,

> 4,4,3,4,4,3,4,4,3 rhymed 1,1,2,3,3,2,4,4,2

the device called tail-rhyme.

Thomas Babington Macaulay's rousing *Lays of Ancient Rome* make their own use of the ballad technique based upon his understanding of the Roman Saturnian meter, which preceded in Italy the incursion of the alien Greek quantity meters. In *Horatius*, he prefers an eight line stanza norm of 3,3,3,3,3,3,3,3, normally iambics, with an added unaccented syllable wherever desired; and with a 4-accent line, often internally rhymed, inserted in any odd-numbered line:

> Then out spake brave Horatius,
> The Captain of the Gate,
> "To every man upon this earth   (4 accents)
> Death cometh soon or late.
> And how can man die better
> Than facing fearful odds
> For the ashes of his fathers,
> And the temples of his Gods?"

His variations are self-evident. *Ivry* returns to the more usual 4,3 meter, in lines of seven iambic feet each, terminally rhymed in couplets.

G. K. Chesterton's superb *The Ballad of the White Horse* uses its own development of the 4,3 accent rhythm, primarily iambic, the norm being 4,3,4n,3—where 4n means any number of rhymed 4-accent lines. Typical stanzas are:

> Yet Alfred is no fairy tale;
>   His days as our days ran,
> He also looked forth for an hour
> On peopled plains and skies that lower,
> From those few windows in the tower
>   That is the head of a man.
>
> But who shall look from Alfred's hood
>   Or breathe his breath alive?
> His century like a small dark cloud
> Drifts far; it is an eyeless crowd
> Where the tortured trumpets scream aloud
>   And the dense arrows drive. . . .
>
> "I tell you naught for your comfort,
>   Yea, naught for your desire,
> Save that the sky grows darker yet,
>   And the sea rises higher.
>
> "Night shall be thrice night over you,
>   And heaven an iron cope.
> Do you have joy without a cause,
>   Yea, faith without a hope?"

Among outstanding modern ballads, authored where the original ones were anonymous, are Oscar Wilde's didactic *The Ballad of Reading Gaol,* Tennyson's stirring *The Revenge,* Browning's *Herve Riel,* Lanier's *The Revenge of Hamish* (made more bookish by its anapestic movement and the long intervals between the rhyme sounds, four and fifteen anapestic feet respectively, or 11-12 and 42-45 syllables, yet gripping throughout), and the ballads of Stephen Vincent Benet and other moderns. My *Jehovah,* framing unrhymed ballads in various meters within a framework of heroic blank verse, is the chief example of the unrhymed ballad in modern verse.

THE METRICAL ROMANCE

It is plausibly held by Miss Pound and others that the ballads themselves stemmed out of the metrical romances which preceded them in England and throughout Europe—a simplification, needed alike by nobles and commons, in an age depressed into crudeness by interminable warfare. Similarly in the religious field, the ancient biblical stories had to be brought alive in the vernacular by more popular poems and the vivid gaudy miracle plays.

In any case, the narrative poetry of medieval Western Europe appeared chiefly in the form called the metrical romance. Romance meant originally a composition in one of the languages into which the Roman speech altered: Italian, Spanish, Portugese, French, etc. It came to embody a narrative centered around some quest, usually dealing with war, love, or religion, or a combination of these; and full of adventures, marvels, type characters and the chivalric ideal. For all that Goethe later said, "Classicism is health; Romanticism is disease," by the end of the 11th century Europe was full of this romantic verse. The oldest manifestation was miraculous lives of the saints. Out of these stemmed Norse sagas, the French *chanson de geste,* and the widespread cycles of stories based on Charlemagne, Alexander, King Arthur and his Table Round, as well as Oriental and a few more themes. A few centuries later, these versified romances were re-expressed in prose, and the noon of the metrical romance had ended.

Among the more famous of these romances were the successive treatments of the story of Troilus, the uncle Pandarus (whose name added a verb to the language), and the fair but fickle Cressida; the Song of Roland; and the various developments of the Arthur story, especially those involving Merlin, Parsifal and the Grail, Tristan and Ysolte, and the Lancelot-Guinevere-Mordred entanglements. While the main current of the romance soon flowed into prose, it continued a vestigial existence in verse. In this direct line come the *Orlando Furioso* of Ariosto, *The Faerie Queene* of Spenser, and ultimately the *Idylls of the King* of Tennyson. *The Knight's Tale,* the story of Palamon and Arcite, in Chaucer's *Canterbury Tales,* is clearly akin to these. Shakespeare's *Venus and Adonis* and *The Rape of Lucrece* are allied in spirit, although they have begun to emerge into a more direct and lyric drive, closer akin to the classical than the romantic.

Modern examples include Edwin Arlington Robinson's *Merlin, Lancelot* and *Tristram.* These have dropped the emphasis upon adventure, and lean toward the psychological; the same sort of treatment that Shakespeare gave to the melodramatic matrix of Hamlet. But Shakespeare breathed life as well into his figures, and the more bookish American poet failed in this regard. The metrical romance, in spite of the popularity of *The Idylls of the King,* is at best vestigial today.

STORIES IN VERSE

The conte or tale in verse preceded the use of prose in this field, and still holds a vestigial popularity. Shakespeare's two story poems, already referred to, properly belong here. So do Keats's *Isabella, The Eve of St. Agnes* and *Lamia;* Coleridge's torso of *Christabel,* important for its rediscovery of verse based on accent rather than meter; Longfellow's *Tales of a Wayside Inn;* Lowell's *Vision of Sir Launfal,* and many another story in verse. Burns's *Tam-o'-Shanter* is a rollicking member of the goodly company, with *The Glory Road* in the same bracket. Chaucer's *Canterbury Tales* furnish examples, to go beside Browning's *The Jackdaw of Rheims, The Pied Piper of Hamelin,* and others of his story poems.

Prose, however, holds the inner citadels and the town walls of the short story, although verse survives and intermittently revives its conquest of some salient. The present age has witnessed an overturning of the academic definitions of the short story, in the direction of infinitely greater inclusiveness and variety. The same applies to the shorter stories in verse. The same prerogative is given to verse that has been taken by prose: the story can be as short as is desired, or as long as the subject matter warrants. In spite of the naturalness of prose, the more concentrated medium of verse and poetry has its legitimate place in narration, especially in proportion to the naturalness of the telling. It only requires a mastery of the technique to develop a vein of stories that will again meet the popular demand and acclaim. With always the reminder that the definition of verse may at any time be broadened by the artist in the field.

NOVELS IN VERSE

Here we come again to a field for which there is a modern market and popularity, for all of the advantage now with prose. The whole transition from verse to prose in adventure novels is seen in the work of Sir Walter Scott. He commenced by writing his spirited stories in verse: *Marmion, The Lady of the Lake, The Lay of the Last Minstrel, Vision of Don Roderick,* and *Rokeby,* 1808 to 1813. But, in March, 1812, Byron's *Childe Harold* was published, and went into five editions before the end of the year. *The Giaour* and *The Bride of Abydos* appeared the next year, and *The Corsair,* appearing in the ensuing February, sold 10,000 copies on the day of publication. Scott, sensing the presence of a master, turned to prose romance. He resurrected his 1806 prose beginning of *Waverley,* and it was completed and published in July, 1814, commencing a career which ranks him among the major masters of romantic adventure fiction.

The book-length story in verse was revived with great success by John Masefield, in his *Dauber, The Everlasting Mercy, The Widow in the Bye Street, Right Royal, Reynard the Fox,* and several others. Robinson wrote a number of modern stories in verse, of the general type of *Roman Barthalow,* but they found no wide response. Stephen Vincent Benet's *John Brown* may be mentioned along with these, for all of its deliberate use of prose passages. There is usually an annual crop of book-length poems, which meet as a rule with minor success. Some of the more effective of these have been in some form of free verse.

The objection to the use of verse to tell a book-length story is that prose is more natural, and most readers resent a second veiling of artificiality thrown between them and the story; the first being the fact that it is merely words written upon paper. The reaction is somewhat similar to that of the audience when Caruso, in Puccini's opera, *The Girl of the Golden West,* lyrically warbled out "Give me a glass of whiskey." No doubt the character he represented would have said it, and in a rare moment of clowning or exuberance he might have sung it; but he would not have sung it in the most elaborate Italian vocalization, with subtle orchestral accompaniment. The obligation of the writer, if he determines to write a book-length story in verse, is to face this difficulty squarely. He may seek to make up for the artificial medium by the magical beauty of his telling; or he may seek to avoid it by a use of verse as natural as possible: colloquial in the highest sense, in the choice of words, phrases, and rhythms, so that it rings true. The task is not easy. Yet Shakespeare at will switched to prose for specific purposes, as in *Macbeth, Hamlet,* and *Julius Caesar;* and this might suggest something to the modern tale-teller in verse. The task will be essayed again and again, no doubt, and at times successfully.

All of this has regarded the book-length story in verse as vestigial: not a dominant living art form, but a mere diminished survival, like tiny salamanders faintly echoing the former greatness of the great crawling amphibians. But is this inevitable? Is it not possible to write a book-length story, with a use of words that adopts some convention different enough from prose to entitle it to be called verse? Some combination of stream-of-consciousness writing, perhaps, with a natural free or accent verse for more concentrated passages.

Summer Time Ends, by John Hargrave, appeared in 1935. A few quotations from it cannot communicate the reason for the deep enthusiasm it inspired in many quarters. Yet here are a few fragments from one section:

"I'm going to run out in the car—I'm going to play truant, just for today—" . . . .

away at last
swifter than the moonè's sphere
changing gear
dither, speedometer-needle, dither
30   35   40   45
damn that silly cyclist!   35   40   45
hatless   50   48   50
hair blown back in the speedwindstream
village—pub—vicarage—church—oh
it's lovely it's
50   50   49   40
by-pass—tarring—   45   30
farmcart—pram—crossroads—   20
A. A.—   30   35   40

Here is another passage:

"er—Harris?"
"yes, my lord"
"I thought I gave you notice some time ago—weeks and weeks ago?"
"yes, my lord"
"but—but you're still here?"
"yes, my lord"

"but—but why *are* you still here?"
no answer. . . .
"you understand, Harris?"
"yes, my lord"
"not that I want you to go?"
"no, my lord"
"but you will have to go?"
"yes, my lord"
"matter of fact, I shall be very sorry when you do have to go"
"yes, my lord"
"but there's no way out of it"
"yes, my lord"

Here is yet another:

when she (and everyone else) was thunderstruck to see Ismay stand up
and fling his arms about
"did you *ever* hear such filthy hogwash!" he shouted "hogwash, I
tell you!—pigswill, slush, undiluted slops—foul slobber—slime, sew-
age, bilge! don't believe a word he says, any of you! he's a sowbug and
nothing but a sowbug!"
moments of aphonic astonishment
"I'll tell you what next!" shouted Ismay "this sowbug brother of
mine will be Prime Minister next, if you're not careful! that'll be ten
times worse than any Baldwins or Macdonalds. Solway isn't just a
mug—I know him only too well!—he's a bug—a special kind of political aphis—a plant-louse—an ant-cow—and how you could sit there,
all of you, and listen to the tripe—the loathsome, sickening, nauseat-
ing, unadulterated tripe—and then actually applaud (some off you)—
God! you make me want to spew my heart up!"
puka-pu! puka-pu!

I see no gain in the omission of punctuation here; any more
than in the impressive conclusion of James Joyce's *Ulysses,* the
scene in which Miriam Bloom fingers so thoroughly her mental
dirty linen. After all, punctuation is an important human invention, whose sole purpose is to clarify meaning. Its omission
is as needless as omitting that other early invention, of separating
words by spaces: nogaininrunningwordstogetherlikethis. *Ulysses,*
of course, had a coast-to-coast hookup of clacque applause, while
the other book tapered off into forgetfulness. Yet it is possible
that the more promising trend was in *Summer Time Ends.*
    We have found the essential device of verse to be repetition.
Gloria Goddard, in *Pull, Dobbin, Pull,* written in intended
prose, brought in a word usage and a return to such ancient
customs of verse as the echo and the repetend—a wider gesture

of repetition, in a way indicative of possible future trends in narrative verse, book-length or shorter. A few quotations can at least suggest her use of these devices. The story opens in Schenectady in 1690:

> It was warm and noisy in the tavern, and the wide low room was filled with a greater crowd than even a Saturday night brought out, and this in spite of the bitter cold and the sober morning hour. The chill morning sunlight trickled through the narrow bottle-glass windows and spread a feeble pallor over the room. The dark broad beams, handhewn from trees from the Woestyne beyond the stockade, were lost above a thick swaying ceiling of dun smoke, which seemed to be supported on thin spiral columns rising from long-stemmed Dutch pipes. The tanged damp odor of ale, mingled with the raw leaf scent of tobacco, was a wall within the room's walls that helped to shut out the cold and the snow. Ponderous Dutch voices rose against this ceiling and this wall, and fell back in a muted blur of sound. De Vries himself was making a slow passage among his guests, bekers of ale in each hand, and this was more strange than the undue crowd at this sober hour.

The repetition here is continued every time a similar scene is introduced. Every time Wouter Groot appears, or one of his descendants inheriting his face and his nature, we have the same description of the baby-pink face, the hair sand-hued or gray:

> His pale Delft-blue eyes held the calm innocence of a child. And though he stood still, there was no doubting the strength in those huge shoulders, and that big body. . . . His voice was bland and innocent, as if no worry ever troubled his quiet thoughts. . . . "There is always power," Wouter said quietly. "It makes no difference how you name it." . . .
> "He has sworn to break the power of the Privileged Dutch West India Company." The young voice lashed in furious scorn over the last words. "He will give us freedom to live as we choose."
> "Freedom. . . ." The old man laughed. "It is a swamplight, my son. Always ahead of you, and gone when you near it."

Scene after scene, situation after situation, echoes itself repeatedly in the two hundred and fifty years of the story. The echo device is even applied to the unchanging face of the stream, no matter whether it witness the launching of the first batteau, the coming of the sailboats, the coming of the canal, or the opening of the railroad:

[85]

All the village was clotted along the bank of the Binne Kil. The August sun lay like a copper lid over the motionless water, the motionless trees, and the parched fields. But the villagers, streamered along the bank, gave no heed to the sun.

This device becomes incremental repetition in many places, and indicates how fully the devices of the ballad-makers and other versifiers have been taken over successfully into what is intended as prose. There are many modern novels written in what is superficially called poetic prose, and what, on analysis, turns out frequently to be a definite tendency toward a rhythmic uniformity that is, properly speaking, verse. Others use some other convention, not hitherto included in our definitions of verse, but suitable for such inclusion.

The use of tight formal verse in a book-length story may again command a substantial following; but it is more probable that some unexpected development, in the direction of naturalness, will evolve an art-form of the book-length story in verse. Only then will the academic bookworms crawl up with their vermiform surveying instruments, and announce new metes and bounds.

Any novel can be written in verse, with or without a widened definition. The market for publication is harder to find than for the novel in prose. So it has always been with the innovators in verse. The effort may well be worth the while.

THE EPIC

The epic is a long narrative poem, dealing with heroic events, usually with supernatural guidance and participation in the action. The earliest epics are anonymous, or are attributed to authors possibly wholly or partly mythical. Each one was primarily the creation of some one author or combiner; but, in pre-writing days, countless later persons altered, improved or deteriorated the product.

In Greece, the earliest bulk of literature is in the epic form. There are three chief divisions of the surviving Greek epics. The first deals with war and personal adventures, outstanding among these being the *Iliad* and the *Odyssey* of the semi-mythical Homer. Homer, his date ranging from 1159 B.C. to a date as recent as 685 B.C., had, after his death, seven cities disputing his birthplace—Smyrna, Chios, Colophon, Salamis, Rhodos, Argos, and Athens. Other lists include Ithaca, Kyme, Ios, Pylos, and even remote Sparta, Egypt and Babylon. He is supposed to have wandered, old, blind, poor, spurned, from city to city chanting his verses. This is a more accurate picture of the frequent fate of the great artist, than of the specific author of these poems. By the time of Peisistratus, he was "the poet," whose poems were the only ones that could be recited at the solemn Pan-Athenean festival.

The theme of the *Iliad* deals with the war between the Greeks and the Trojans, a Greek effort to avenge the elopement of Helen, wife of Menelaus of Sparta, and Paris of Troy. The core of the poem is the peevish anger of the Grecian warrior Achilles, deprived by the Greek leader Agamemnon of a girl he has captured. With Achilles sulking in his tent, the Greeks begin to lose. Hector, the Trojan champion, kills Patroclus, best friend of Achilles, mistaking him for the sulking hero, because he is wearing the armor of Achilles. Whereupon Achilles re-enters the fray, slays Hector, foully misuses his body, repents, and permits him a noble funeral. With this, the poem ends. The incident of the Wooden Horse and the return of the chastened Helen with her husband to Sparta are not included.

The story of the *Odyssey* is the wanderings of the Grecian hero Odysseus (Ulysses) from Troy to his native Ithaca, where his faithful wife Penelope fences off her suitors, and awaits her husband's return. There are adventures with the giant Cyclops Polyphemus, with the seductive nymph Calypso, with Nausicaa, princess of Phaeacia, with the enchantress Circe who turned men into animals, and also a descent into Hades, the Greek world after death.

What was the importance of all this to the Greeks, and what is its importance to us today? It is largely fiction, for all that it is no doubt based upon some actual warfare between Greeks and the energetic Hittites of the Troad. But it crystallized national traditions, and embodied national religion, when there was no other way of attaining these objects. It taught them and us the customs, attire, morals, of early Greeks, when there was no other record extant. It gave a tremendous impetus to the fixing of the literate Greek language (for all of its meter-induced mangling of Greek speech away from any actual spoken tongue); as Chaucer did to English, Dante to Italian, and Luther to German. Its verse medium, the Greek dactylic hexameter or six-foot line, became the classical norm in Greek, only broken by the lyricists.

There are Grecian poems almost as ancient celebrating the mysteries of religion, as those attributed to the mythical Orpheus; and of a definite didactic or teaching nature, such as the *Works and Days* and the *Theogony* of Hesiod. But these never gained the place in world acclaim that the epics of Homer have held for so long.

Allied primitive epics are the Sanskrit *Mahabharata* and *Ramayana*, the Persian *Shah-nameh*, the Middle German *Niebelungenlied*, the Anglo-Saxon *Beowulf* and briefer fragments, the Icelandic *Elder Edda*, the Spanish *Poem of the Cid*, the Finnish *Kalevala*, and perhaps the medieval French *Song of Roland* and other national epics. All of these had national heroes for their major figures, with elaborate supernatural participation in the action, or indeed centering it.

The epics, then, came naturally when verse was the only form of literate expression, to embody national or racial ideals, religion, traditions, and the memory of early customs, places and living. What place has the epic in a more literate age? By the vestigial process, epics came to be written imitatively long after the need for them had vanished. Thus we have the *Annales* of the Roman Ennius and the *Aeneid* of Vergil, the latter a labored attempt to recapture Homer's spirit, and base Rome's ancestry on Trojan royalty; as later the British sought to trace British ancestry (and the name of the land and its people) to the noble Brutus. Among later authored epics are the *Jerusalem Delivered* of the Italian Tasso, the spite-ridden *Commedia* of Dante, the Portugese *Lusiad* of Camoens, the French *Henriade* of Voltaire, the English *Paradise Lost* and *Paradise Regained* of the intransigent Puritan, John Milton. Increasingly these failed to isolate the national traditions, religion, customs, morals and living. They became mere imitation of an outworn form, motivated too often by special pleading for some narrow-minded religious or political bias. They enjoyed a long and high repute, which has slowly dimmed as the years pass; while at the same time the effulgence of the primitive epics glows the brighter, for all that they are no longer read primarily for pure emotional delight. Epics are as out of place today as a living dinosaur at large in Atlantic City. Just as there can be no new Bible written, that synthesis of the traditional history, re- ligion, and songs of a whole race, so there can be no new epics written; at least, not unless human culture become again illiterate.

A late effort was Longfellow's *Hiawatha,* which enjoyed at first a brief popularity. But it embodied neither the Indian atti- tude, which it purported to convey; or the Christian attitude, tagged on at the end; and the use of a Finnish meter did not add to its authenticity.

We are most interested in the two epics of Milton, for they at least speak for one aspect of our culture. The form adopted, the unrhymed iambic five-foot line (heroic blank verse), first entered English verse at about the time of Chaucer, as the rhymed iambic five-foot couplet; and this thereafter fell out of popularity for a century and a half, as not native to English speech. It was inde- pendently brought in from France and Italy by Wyatt and Surrey, as the meter for the sonnet, which promptly became anglicized in stanza pattern, as we shall see; and in blank or unrhymed verse, where drama first adopted it. This was apparently because the classic hexameter could not be adapted successfully into English; and because the popular four-foot accent verse was not regarded as dignified enough for the speech of kings and princes, who thun- dered loudest upon the Elizabethan stage. From the first, it tended toward adaptation into five-foot accent verse, Shakespeare being an outstanding example of this tendency. Milton for the first time used it for long narrative poems of the epic nature. Its use by Shakespeare and Milton superimposed it upon our culture as the dominant English meter. But always, beneath it, the tendency toward a return to the original accent verse persisted, and modern poetry shows an increasing tendency in this direction.

4. DRAMATIC POETRY

Origin and Peak of Dramatic Poetry

Dramatic poetry originated among most or all peoples as part of religious worship. Drama is a composition, which may be in verse, for acting, usually with the aid of dialog. Among the Greeks, in Athens, it arose out of the worship of Dionysus. In the sixth century, tradition ascribes to Thespis its development into a series of narrative odes concerning the history of this god, broken by episodes in which one actor represented some adventure by means of narrative, or of dialog with the chorus. A second actor was strictly forbidden. Aeschylus (524-456 B.C.) permitted a second actor, which allowed the dialog to take place without the chorus; and the choral songs became subordinated to the dialog and action. Sophocles, born thirty years later, added a third actor. Although his *Oedipus at Colonus* allowed a fourth, this was rare in Greek drama. These two and Euripides represented the height of Greek tragedy, as the later Aristophanes did of Grecian comedy. The distinction between the two was primarily that tragedy must end in the death of the principal character or characters, and that comedy did not. But all sorts of clowning and burlesquing were added to Grecian comedy, to liven it for popular consumption.

There were strange conventions in Grecian drama. There were first of all, the unities of place, time, and action: the scene must not shift, nor the action consume more than one day, and irrelevant incidents were prohibited. The tragic actors wore masks of dreadful mournfulness; the comic actors, masks writhed in a perpetual grin. The former wore the high-heeled buskin, to add to their tragic impressiveness; the latter the heelless sock. Action within sight of the audience was practically forbidden, and took place offstage, being related by a messenger.

English drama came into existence during the latter half of the sixteenth century, developing from the crude Mysteries (or Miracle plays) and the Moralities (or plays with moral teachings), both being at first under religious auspices, with religious actors. The purpose was to convey the teachings of religion to the populace in palatable doses. Such plays were common throughout Europe toward the end of the Middle Ages, and were chiefly performed on holidays or holy-days. The Passion Plays of Oberammergau and Jersey City are survivals of these.

English drama soon became secularized, at first in the form of Interludes to lighten the more serious miracle and morality plays. Under Shakespeare and his glittering associates, drama reached a height so far unreached among other races. We will trace elsewhere the growth of Shakespeare's metric liberality, as his maturity came and deepened. He wrote in three moods: tragedies, comedies and historical plays or chronicles.

Elizabethan drama was primarily in verse, with prose permitted when desired. Shakespeare used it for some low comedy, such as a prosy speech like that of Brutus in *Julius Caesar;* he used it also as being appropriate to a prosy character, as in the case of certain speeches of Casca in the same play; for such a mental disorder as sleep-walking; and so on. By the time of Goldsmith and Sheridan, drama had taken the second great step, from verse to prose. Since men and women do not, as a rule, talk verse, this transition was in the direction of naturalness. Prose has dominated most drama since that time. But drama in verse has persisted, as a vestigial aftermath, and at times as more. Thus there are many plays in verse (often more suited to be closet dramas, for reading only, than for acting) by Shelley, Byron, Browning, Tennyson, and others. In our own time, Ibsen started with dramas in verse, and soon matured to prose dramas. Drama in verse has been revived with much effect by Maxwell Anderson and a few more.

The purpose of drama in verse is to express somehow the author's desire; and this, of course, is also the purpose of prose drama. This may be by emphasis on character study or on action, or on some other aspect of the characters. As a rule, drama is best received in proportion to its naturalness. Yet natural includes "such stuff as dreams are made of": for dreams are natural, too. Thus romantic and so-called poetic themes, if presented as naturally as they come to the author, have the same chance of success, or more, than realistic dramas. The trouble comes when the dramatist inserts artificial conventions between himself and his play, on the one hand, and his audience on the other. He may still succeed, if the conventions are pleasing. Usually most of them are not.

Dramatists using verse or prose should master the achievements of their forerunners in the field, even if this requires a special course in drama-writing. A direct familiarity with the stage and its demands and permissible illusions is highly valuable— such a familiarity as the Elizabethan dramatists all had. The whole play, as a rule, should build up to one tremendous climax. Shakespeare's usual formula was build-up, climax, descent to the conclusion or dénouement. This last is often omitted today, since we possess curtains and other mechanical devices unknown to the Elizabethans. Each act, each scene, should similarly build up to a climax, and to a "curtain" or last word or action which is breath-taking, and which holds over the interest until the curtain's rise again. Any of these suggestions may be violated, where there is advantage to be gained. The staging may be done realistically, or merely suggestively, as the Elizabethans and the Chinese drama, for instance, prefer. And the commercial rewards for a Broadway success are great.

Drama, it should be noticed, emerged from its thralldom to a musical accompaniment earlier than the lyric or the narrative. Yet music still persists in grand opera, that by-blow of music and literature in which all the speeches are usually sung or chanted; as well as in light opera, opera bouffe, musical comedy, and so on. The poet and versifier are in demand in all these fields. There is also a more limited market for closet drama—drama primarily to be read. Much of this is written, however, with acting in view, and only fails through unawareness of the actual conditions of stage presentation.

The metric norm for Elizabethan drama was the five-foot iambic line, unrhymed, so familiar in Shakespeare:

> Our revels now are ended; these our actors,
> As I foretold you, were all spirits, and
> Are melted into air, into thin air:
> And, like the baseless fabric of this vision,
> The cloud-capp'd towers, the gorgeous palaces,
> The solemn temples, the great globe itself,
> Yea, all which it inherit, shall dissolve,
> And, like this insubstantial pageant faded,
> Leave not a rack behind. We are such stuff
> As dreams are made of, and our little life
> Is rounded with a sleep.
>
> *The Tempest,* WILLIAM SHAKESPEARE, *iv, i.*

The modern dramatist in verse can use this form, with such interspersed lyrics as he pleases, as was the custom of the Elizabethans; or he may use such other poetic conventions, as to rhythm, rhyme, and stanza form, as he prefers.

SHORTER DRAMATIC VERSE

It should be remembered that the essence of drama is that it represents the characters in the story or discussion as actually speaking their own lines; in dialog, in fact. Certain of the poems long classed as ballads are really little dramas. *Edward, Edward* is of this type, as are *The Nut Brown Maid* and that jolly connubial spat, *Take Thine Old Cloak About Thee,* including the stanza Shakespeare has Iago sing in *Othello:*

> King Stephen was and a worthy peer.
> His breeches cost him but a pound.
> He held them sixpence all too dear,
> With that he called the tailor lown.
> He was a wight of high renown,
> And thou art but of low degree.
> 'Tis pride that pulls the country down;
> Then take thine auld cloak about thee.

This has an intricate rhyming scheme, 1, 2, 1, 2, 2, 3, 2, 3, worthy of wider use. Altogether there are fourteen such complete dialog poems in Percy's *Reliques;* while, of course, many of the ballads emphasize dialog greatly; making them a transition form, as it were, between ballad and drama, or at least poems partaking of the essence of each. It must never be forgotten that the core of drama is a method of presentation—the dialog plus acting method—and not a matter of theme or purpose. Even Mother Goose, with "Where are you going, my pretty maid?" "Who Killed Cock Robin?" and many more, includes minim dramas.

The revival of interest in one-act plays, so evident among the little theatre groups in Ireland, the United States, and elsewhere, gives a wider opportunity for one-act dramas in verse than has ever existed before. Any program of such plays can include, for variety, if for no other reason, at least one example of drama in verse. The radio has discovered the drama in verse, one act and even longer; and television promises to broaden this market. All that has been said of poetry and drama in verse applies to these, with the added warning that the appeal of sight is absent in the radio, and the words themselves must do all the picturing, instead of having the picture presented to the eyes as well. A drama to be heard by a blind man must differ from one presented to an audience with eyes, to be most effective; and this difference should mark dramas done for radio. One other field that might be mentioned is the pageant, often designed to commemorate some historical or legendary happening, or some common cause. Here drama in verse finds an admirable and increasing outlet.

THE DRAMATIC MONOLOG OR DRAMATIC LYRIC

Out of one of the artificial conventions of the older drama, the soliloquy, the genius of one poet carved a verse form which still holds its popularity. The soliloquy was the convention by which the dramatist sought to convey to the audience the thoughts and motives of an actor: the expression of thoughts otherwise as a rule unspoken. Eugene O'Neill, by the use of masks in *The Great God Brown,* and other playwrights by the introduction of characters representing the real selves speaking on the stage with the selves that spoke to others, have sought to convey the same thing.

Robert Browning was the poet who first popularized the dramatic monolog, which he called the dramatic lyric. In it one person speaks, and reveals much of his soul in what he says. Such little master dramas, with only one character speaking, as *My Last Duchess, Fra Lippo Lippi, Caliban Upon Setebos, Andrea del Sarto, Mr. Sludge "The Medium,"* and many more, etch endurably the personalities, dreams and aspirations, as well as the stories, of the persons speaking, as in this conclusion of *Andrea del Sarto:*

> I am grown peaceful as old age tonight.
> I regret little, I would change still less.
> Since there my past life lies, why alter it? . . .
> No doubt, there's something strikes a balance. Yes,
> You loved me quite enough, it seems tonight.
> This must suffice me here. What would one have?
> In heaven, perhaps, new chances, one more chance—
> Four great walls in the New Jerusalem,
> Meted on each side by the angel's reed,
> For Leonard, Rafeal, Agnolo and me
> To cover—the first three without a wife,
> While I have mine! So—still they overcome
> Because there's still Lucrezia,—as I choose.
> Again the Cousin's whistle! Go, my Love.

Even Browning's largest work, *The Ring and the Book,* frames ten immense dramatic monologs, giving the same story, told over and over, as it appears to ten differing personalities—a crude old melodrama in essence, sublimated as Shakespeare did to the bald crude skeletons of plots he used to work on. In most of these dramatic monologs of Browning the dominant rhythm is iambic, usually five feet to the line, unrhymed or rhymed as he chose.

Edgar Lee Masters made the dramatic monolog a temporary best seller in his *Spoon River Anthology,* which rediscovered the American village and its suppressed scandals, to the titillation of the avid public. Here is *Daisy Fraser,* the village prostitute, speaking (like all the rest) at the moment of death, without greater illumination than life had afforded her, and this time in a bitter vein:

> Did you ever hear of the Circuit Judge
> Helping anyone except the "Q" railroad,
> Or the bankers? Or did Rev. Peet or Rev. Sibley
> Give any part of their salary, earned by keeping still,
> Or speaking out as the leaders wished them to,
> To the building of the water works?
> But I, Daisy Fraser, who always passed
> Along the streets through rows of nods and smiles
> And coughs and words such as "there she goes,"
> Never was taken before Judge Arnett
> Without contributing ten dollars and costs
> To the school fund of Spoon River!

This is presumably in free verse; but the iambic five-foot pattern obtrudes crudely in such lines as:

> Or speak- / ing out / as the lea- / ders wished / them to . . .
> Along / the streets / through rows / of nods / and smiles,

and this is a defect in free verse. In general, the technique is too suffused with irregularly used iambics to be masterly; but it reached the public, and that is something which poetry once had a habit of doing far more than recently. The poet with something to say can still find his audience. If he says it with superb technique, his audience is always increased and perpetuated.

The dramatic monolog offers wide possibilities for any versifier today.

5. DIDACTIC POETRY

Didactic is defined as "conveying instruction; teaching some moral lesson." Moral, which originally meant merely "customary," has grown to involve the distinction between what is right and what is wrong. This again is a subjective distinction, and each person develops his or her own code, developed by the interaction of his teachings and his own desires. Thus the moral which constitutes the poem or verses, or which is emphasized in them, will be what the poet wants the hearer or reader to learn and believe and follow; just as the teaching will be what the poet wants the hearer or reader to learn.

Neither of these puts its major emphasis upon emotion. To teach a person the names of the Presidents of the United States, for instance, may be as emotionless a procedure as a woodchuck's hibernating. To write, in verse, such conventional morality as, Always pay your debts; Honesty is the best policy; Early to bed and early to rise Makes a man healthy, wealthy and wise—this is apparently as unexciting as licking a postage stamp. It is this consideration which has made many authorities deny that didactic poetry is poetry at all; these holding that it is merely verse applied to a wrong function.

And yet, the teaching of fact or morals may involve tremendous emotion. Longfellow, as he lessoned his contemporaries in the platitudes of *A Psalm of Life,* no doubt felt a glow of righteous exultation:

> Tell me not, in mournful numbers,
>   "Life is but an empty dream!"
> For the soul is dead that slumbers,
>   And things are not what they seem.
>
> Life is real! Life is earnest!
>   And the grave is not its goal;
> "Dust thou art, to dust returnest,"
>   Was not spoken of the soul. . . .
>
> In the world's broad field of battle,
>   In the bivouac of Life,
> Be not like dumb, driven cattle!
>   Be a hero in the strife! . . .
>
> Lives of great men all remind us
>   We can make our lives sublime,
> And, departing, leave behind us
>   Footprints on the sands of time;

> Footprints, that perhaps another,
>   Sailing o'er life's solemn main,
> A forlorn and shipwrecked brother,
>   Seeing, shall take heart again.

What is wrong with this is not that it is didactic, or moralizing; but that it is banal verse, as full of clichés as a gravid shad of roe. Analyze it, and it becomes absurd. It is doubtful whether a forlorn and shipwrecked human ever took much heart from locating the footprints on the sand left by a departed predecessor. Of course, too, wave and weather have their own way with footprints—and life is anything but a "solemn main," except perhaps to Puritans. But, banal or not, this poem was taken to the people's heart, and that was what Longfellow wanted. The words used are heart-warming, a matter we have taken up under "The Poetic Vocabulary"; and they automatically awake some emotions in all of us. The adjurations to heroism and leaving footprints are of the glowword type, embedded deep in us since childhood; and they tend to make us want to stand up and cheer. No matured person, with his intellect functioning, would be moved by an analysis of this. But he would be, if he, as so often, killed the motor of his intellect and let his emotions freewheel down into this slough of clichés. It is a sort of rallying cry for the mass of human beings. To them, it is definitely poetry of high rank. And they are the judges of what is poetry to them. All that we need to do is to label it as banal verse; with the proviso that it might have been good verse, might have said the same thing, and nevertheless have mounted to higher poetic ranking.

A similar fire of moral indignation suffused James Byron Elmore, when he wrote:

> Alcohol is like a snake:
>   It can't be kept in bounds;
> It makes of one a perfect wreck,
>   A wondering vagrant hound.
>
> It steals away an active brain,
>   And fills one with remorse,
> And causes people to go insane,
>   Their soul is all morose.
>
> In dread of those, we stand in awe,
>   Who tipple at the wine.
> They all disgrace the moral laws,—
>   Their manners are unkind.

The same reformistic fervor glows to incandescent heat in Mary
Ann O'Byrne's book-length philippic against the exhibition of a
painting of the Magdalene by her pastor, entitled *On Fine Art:*

> And them little baby angels
> A covering should wear,
> For no mother that will love her child
> Will exhibit it when it's bare.
>
> And as the angels are pure spirits
> Without a body of their own,
> I am sure that for a naked one
> They would not ask the loan.
>
> For when they appear among us
> They are modestly robed in white,
> Or otherwise to our friendship
> They would not have no right.
>
> Therefore their heavenly message
> They could carry back with them,
> For if they appeared in a nude condition
> We would something at them fling.

Even if one is in sympathy with these blasts against alcohol and
nudism, it is clear that the verse technique fails by every test.
There can be no excuse for such illiterate rhyming mésalliances
as *snake—wreck, bounds—hound, remorse—morose, awe—laws,
wine—unkind,* in the first verses; or the *them-fling* in the second; the vulgarisms, "them little baby angels," and "ask the
loan"; the double negative "not have no right"; the inversion
"would something at them fling"; or, finally, the incredible
mangling of the rhythm throughout the same verses. The thing
that is wrong is not that this is didactic, but that it is faulty
versification.

Turn to Walt Whitman, and we hear a different type of song:

> I do not snivel the world over,
> That months are vacuums and the ground but wallow and filth.
>
> Whimpering and truckling, fold with powders for invalids, conformity
> goes to the fourth-remov'd.
> I wear my hat as I please indoors or out.
>
> Why should I pray? why should I venerate and be ceremonious?
>
> Having pried through the strata, analyzed to a hair, counsell'd with
> doctors and calculated close,
> I find no sweeter fat than sticks to my own bones.

This is definitely didactic, and is regarded as inspiring poetry by many, although not by the hoi polloi he aimed at. It may reasonably be the reverse of poetry to you. But Whitman's own emotional simoom here is undisputed, and awakens a like response rather widely.

Take something that fewer will dispute about, as poetry:

> If it chance your eye offend you,
>   Pluck it out, lad, and be sound:
> 'Twill hurt, but here are salves to friend you,
>   And many a balsam grows on ground.
>
> And if your hand or foot offend you,
>   Cut it off, lad, and be whole;
> But play the man, stand up and end you,
>   When your sickness is your soul.
>   *A Shropshire Lad, xlv,* A. E. HOUSMAN

This is all didacticism. It is not even logical. The underlying meaning of the New Testament reference is not understood by this poet. Barring surgical operations removing an eye, hand or foot to save the rest of the body, there is no recorded instance of anyone's plucking out an eye, or lopping off a hand or foot. The final advice is: Commit suicide, if you are soul-sick. Like much of Housman, this is the attitude of a sophisticated adolescent, which a maturing mind tends to label as poison. Yet it is rousing and emotion-wringing, and is popular as didactic poetry, even among some sophisticates.

Much of the *Shropshire Lad* is didactic: that is, it definitely teaches:

> "Empty vessel, garment cast,
> We that wore you long shall last.
> —Another night, another day,"
> So my bones within me say.
>
> Therefore they shall do my will
> Today while I am master still,
> And flesh and soul, now both are strong,
> Shall hale the sullen slaves along,
>
> Before this fire of sense decay,
> This smoke of thought blow clean away,
> And leave with ancient night alone
> The steadfast and enduring bone.
>   *The Immortal Part, xliii,* A. E. HOUSMAN

> Oh many a peer of England brews
> Livelier liquor than the Muse,
> And malt does more than Milton can
> To justify God's ways to man. . . .
>
> Therefore, since the world has still
> Much good, but much less good than ill,
> And while the sun and moon endure
> Luck's a chance, but trouble's sure,
> I'd face it as a wise man would,
> And train for ill and not for good.
> *A Shropshire Lad, lxii,* A. E. HOUSMAN

Throughout both volumes by Housman, the technique tends to be superb; and this played its enormous part in the continuing popularity of this poetry. It has all the heart-glow appeal of a return to the melodramatic poses of adolescence. Few dispute its ranking as minor poetry of a high flight.

Many of our favorite poems, which we imagine we like as lyrics or for some quality other than the lyrical, are in essence didactic, teachy-preachy. Kipling's *L'Envoi* and *The Sons of Martha,* Swinburne's stirring *The Garden of Proserpine* and *Hymn to Proserpine,* much of Browning, Tennyson, and many more, are definitely didactic or suffused with didacticism. There is no gain in merely allocating these to lyric, narrative or dramatic poetry, overlooking the fact that to the personal desire is added the immense impulse to impress a teaching on others.

The classifications of poetry, accepted so long, include an inherent lack of logic. *Lyric* means both an attitude of utterance, the poet's direct expression of his desire, and, differently, a singing quality derived from instrumental accompaniment; and these are based upon entirely different bases of classification. *Narrative* and *dramatic* both refer to the method of presentation; while *didactic* refers to the object, or objective, of presentation: to instruct. Since a lyric, a narrative, or a drama may be intended to instruct, as well as embody a wish, these then become, respectively, a didactic lyric, a didactic narrative, a didactic drama. The academic tendency has been to call poems of these three types—to which that academic tendency subscribes—lyrics, narratives, and dramas; and to dismiss as didactic all verse to which it does not subscribe. There is no justification for this. The antiquity and continuing popularity of didactic verse entitles it to its inclusion, however illogical that may be. No doubt ultimately a poetic Linnaeus will restore order to the domain of poetry. Until that time, didactic verse and poetry hold their inner salient against all comers.

DIDACTIC VERSE DOWN THE AGES

Before prose assumed importance in literature, epigrams, proverbs, early gobbets of information, the first flights toward science, were expressed in verse, to pass them down from generation to generation; this because of the mnemonic value of verse. In Greece, the half-mythical Hesiod was held to be the founder of didactic verse. A supposed Boeotian tiller of the soil, he wrote *Works and Days,* which still exists and which is a versified thesis on agriculture. Works attributed to him, but no longer existing, include studies of astronomy, of the auguries from birds, and one on the character of the physical world.

Soon the Greek teachings dealing with religion, harmonized from the worships of various localities (the way most pantheons are constructed), were expressed in didactic verse. The greatest of all the classic didactic poets was the Roman philosopher Titus Lucretius Carus, of the 1st century B.C. His *De Rerum Natura* ("On the Nature of Things") shouted aloud, in glowing lines, the unalterable conflict between the old superstitions and the laws of nature. He preached a vast universe in evolution, controlled by the original qualities inherent in the atoms that constituted matter. And then Rome decayed, and Christianity spread, and the world entered upon the Dark Ages.

There has been an uninterrupted flood of didactic verse since, but much of it has been too earthbound to soar to continued popularity. We smile at Thomas Tusser's quaint *Hundreth Pointes of Good Husbandrie,* a versified treatise on agriculture appearing in 1557. A new peak of didactic verse came in during the ages of Dryden and Pope, phrased as a rule in polished couplets, too gemlike to do more than glitter. Yet for scores of years the more soaring poetry of Shakespeare and the Elizabethans was ignored for such faceted couplets as:

> A little learning is a dangerous thing;
> Drink deep, or taste not the Pierian spring.
> There shallow draughts intoxicate the brain,
> And drinking largely sobers us again. . . .

> All seems infected that the infected spy,
> As all looks yellow to the jaundiced eye.
> *Essay on Criticism,* ALEXANDER POPE

> Vice is a monster of so frightful mien,
> As, to be hated, needs but to be seen;
> Yet, seen too oft, familiar with her face,
> We first endure, then pity, then embrace.
> *An Essay on Man,* POPE

That he can mount to tremendous passion is shown by the conclusion of *The Dunciad,* telling of the final conquest achieved by Dullness:

> She comes! she comes! the sable throne behold
> Of night primeval and of chaos old!
> Before her, fancy's gilded clouds decay,
> And all its varying rainbows die away.
> Wit shoots in vain its momentary fires,
> The meteor drops, and in a flash expires.
> As one by one, at dread Medea's strain,
> The sickening stars fade off the ethereal plain;
> As Argus' eyes by Hermes' wand opprest,
> Closed one by one to everlasting rest;
> Thus at her felt approach, and secret might,
> Art after art goes out, and all is night.
> See skulking truth to her old cavern fled,
> Mountains of casuistry heap'd o'er her head!
> Philosophy, that leaned on heaven before,
> Shrinks to her second cause, and is no more.
> Physic of metaphysic begs defense,
> And metaphysic calls for aid on sense!
> See mystery to mathematics fly!
> In vain! they gaze, turn giddy, rave, and die.
> Religion blushing veils her sacred fires,
> And unawares morality expires.
> Nor public flame, nor private, dares to shine;
> Nor human spark is left, nor glimpse divine!
> Lo! thy dread empire, chaos! is restored;
> Light dies before thy uncreating word;
> Thy hand, great anarch! lets the curtain fall,
> And universal darkness buries all.

Pope was one of the impressive technicians of the language. Yet the wit and wisdom of his lines, made too artificial by his over-accurate versification, intrigue the mind briefly and the emotions hardly at all; and the bright product dulls of its own too mental glitter.

In America, the *Bay Psalm Book* (*The Psalms in Metre, Faithfully Translated for the Use, Edification, and Comfort of the Saints, in Public and Private, especially in New England*) published in 1640, had a definite didactic aim and treatment. Many of the heart-warming favorites of the people are didactic. Religious poems and hymns tend in this direction, and so do many patriotic and revolutionary verses. The market is wide for this type of verse or poetry; and its income increases in proportion as the ideas expressed meet with wide acceptance. And, always, technical ability will increase the chances of publication and enduring popularity.

6. LIGHT, HUMOROUS, AND OCCASIONAL VERSE

Light verse may fit under any of the categories already studied, or may be merely to amuse. Its various subdivisions will be treated in dealing with the poem as a whole.

III

RHYTHM AND ACCENT REPETITION

RHYTHM DEFINED

WE have defined verse, as opposed to prose, as: *words arranged with repetition in their accent rhythm, which tends toward uniformity or regularity, rather than toward variety.*

Rhythm means movement marked by recurrence of, or alternation in, features, elements, or phenomena used as the means of perceiving the rhythm. Thus we have cosmic rhythm, as in the successive creation and dissolution of solar universes; geologic rhythm, as in the alternation of glacial and interglacial periods, or as in the alternation of night and day, or the recurrence of the seasons; vital rhythm, as in waking and sleeping, inhalation and exhalation, the heartbeats, and so on.

In written or spoken speech, there could be a rhythm based on any detail of speech. Thus we could base our rhythm upon alternate initial *b*'s and *d*'s:

> bobcat, degradation, bite, doping, barracuda, dog.

This could be described as alternating alliterative rhythm. The rhythm could be based on any convention of succession in vowel sounds; on the number of syllables in words—as, words of one, two, three, one, two, three, etc., syllables, irrespective of quantity, accent or any other consideration:

The revered ancestor of Grecian potentates was always regarded as wholly heavenly.

Or it could be based on some conventionalized sequence of Greek, Latin, and Anglo-Saxon words; or on some even stranger convention. The two most important conventions used to mark the rhythm of oral and written speech have been: (a) the quantity of syllables (regarded as long or short) in classic literature; and (b) accent, in English and most modern Western languages. Since we are concerned primarily with verse and poetry in English, we give the following definition: *Rhythm, in English speech, means the movement of words marked by the recurrence of, or alternation in, accented and unaccented syllables and pauses.*

DISCUSSION OF THIS DEFINITION

Merriam-Webster defines rhythm in prosody as "the successive and, in the main, regular rise and fall of sounds (whether in pitch, stress, or speed) in verse when read with attention to quantities of syllables or to syllabic and speech accents, and to pauses, especially as these coincide with cadences determined by a definite metrical pattern; the recurrent alternation of thesis and arsis in verse."

This overlooks the fact that prose has as definite a rhythm as verse. Pitch in music means something definite: the property of a musical tone determined by the frequency of vibration of the sound waves which strike the ear. Pitch could certainly be a determinant in rhythm. I have never heard it so used in English, although some Oriental languages, notably Chinese, are said to employ it. The same is true of speed of utterance; although theoretically classic prosody depended upon quantity, based on speed of utterance. Stress means emphasis or weight given to accented or long syllables in verse; which brings us back to quantity and accent, appearing later. This definition leans decidedly toward a definite metrical pattern; neither prose nor poetry requires one. *Thesis* means the heavier or stressed part of a foot; and also, illogically enough, the unaccented syllable or syllables in a foot, this coming from a misunderstanding of the Greek. *Arsis* means the lighter or unaccented part of a foot; and also, as illogically, the accented part. This part of the definition also excludes prose, which has its own rhythm; and eliminates certain complicated feet, which have two or more accented portions, and/or two or more unaccented portions.

The simpler definition given above—that movement of words marked by the recurrence of, or alternation in, accented and unaccented syllables and pauses—is in every way preferable.

[105]

THE RHYTHM OF PROSE

The opening of the Introduction of my *The Outline of Man's Knowledge* is:

> Men and women have been grouped enduringly into the quick and the dead. The dead know nothing; or what knowledge they have is stagnant. The quick know somewhat, and seek to learn more. In the accelerated tempo of modern living, the quick literally hunger and thirst after knowledge.

Prose or verse is scanned by marking the accented (/) and the unaccented (˘) syllables; and then dividing them into feet. Where these divisions coincide with the natural divisions used by the voice in natural speech, this is *natural scansion*. We will come later to that warping of natural scansion to fit a prearranged rhythmic or metric pattern, called *pattern scansion*. In prose, natural scansion is always used: that is, the division into feet follows the normal division that the voice uses in speaking the words. In some poetry and verse, scanning is done both by natural scansion and pattern scansion. The scansion of the first three sentences above is:

Men / and women / have been grouped / enduringly /

into the quick / and the dead. / The dead / know / nothing; /

or what knowledge / they have / is stagnant. / The quick /

know / somewhat, / and seek / to learn / more.

Here we have four feet of one accented syllable only (/), no doubt followed by a natural pause; two trochees (/˘); five iambs (˘/); two anapests (˘˘/); two amphibrachs (˘/˘); three four-foot syllables (˘/˘˘, ˘˘˘/, and ˘//˘). If you prefer to break *or what knowledge* into two feet (˘/ /˘), this gives three trochees and six iambs; but the tendency toward irregularity is still marked. This in spite of the fact that the author is a versifier, tending in impressive places to slip into a rhythm of verse. This is a typical prose rhythm.

It is necessary to learn to use natural scansion like a master. It is extremely easy. The determinants are naturalness of utterance, and the proper location of the accented and unaccented syllables, followed by the normal division into feet that the voice unconsciously makes in natural speech. It is wise to practice scanning prose and verse, until it becomes a habit with you. Later we will see how irregular off-accents may be fitted into a regular metric pattern: that is, pattern scansion.

All prose has rhythm, and can be scanned. You may at times encounter apparent prose with the regularity usually found in verse. It then becomes verse, and a failure, if prose rhythm is desired. Much of the highly poetic prose of Cabell's Poictesme stories is intentionally written in verse feet, and the reader reads it with no knowledge that it is that modernly disliked and distrusted form, verse; yet receiving from it the emotional thrill of verse. Thus Cabell achieved his purpose—concealing his verse under the mask of prose. This is a device any writer can use, when he finds it suits his purpose. It is not without significance, as an antidote to the earned distrust of verse.

THE RHYTHM OF FREE VERSE

Suppose you wished to write your sincerest desire toward something, as, for instance, toward a girl you felt you were in love with, and wanted. Assume that you did not care to label it in advance verse or prose, but merely wanted to write out your full heart's longing. The result might be something like:

> O beauty that has come into my life,
> Soft brown eyes and ineffable melting smile,
> Body shaped for a god's caresses,
> Yield to that hurricane of love
> That turns me into a tempest of longing!

When we scan this, the result is:

> Ŏ beaŭty / thăt hăs cóme / ĭntŏ mў lífe,
> Sóft / brŏwn eўes / ănd inéffăblĕ / méltĭng / smíle,
> Bŏdў / shápĕd / fŏr ă gŏd's / căréssĕs,
> Yíeld / tŏ thăt húrrĭcănĕ / ŏf lóve
> Thăt túrns mĕ / íntŏ ă témpĕst / ŏf lóngĭng!

This gives us four feet of one accented syllable only; two trochees; one iamb; two anapests; four amphibrachs; one spondee, or two accented syllables ($\prime\prime$); one foot of four syllables ($\smile\smile\smile\prime$); and three of five, two of one pattern ($\smile\smile\prime\smile\smile$) and one of another ($\smile\smile\ \smile\prime\smile$). This sounds superficially as varied as the prose selection. And yet, to my ear, it is indisputably verse: polyrhythmic verse (many rhythmic feet to the line) or free verse, to be sure; but beyond question verse. What is this tendency toward regularity that the inner ear hears here, and that was missing in the quotation from *The Outline?*

Our natural scansion will not suit the exponent of metric scansion at all; for he does not recognize feet of four, five, and more syllables. In general, the only feet that he allows in his patterns are six in number: three two-syllabled feet, iamb ($\smile\prime$), trochee ($\prime\smile$), and spondee ($\prime\prime$); and three three-syllabled feet, anapest ($\smile\smile\prime$), dactyl ($\prime\smile\smile$), and amphibrach ($\smile\prime\smile$). To test whether this fits logically into a metric pattern or not, let us break up the natural scansion far enough to limit our feet to the six that are used in metric scansion. What we are really doing is giving more recognition to secondary accents, as in *into* and *hurricane*. This semi-natural semi-pattern scansion would give us:

Ŏ béaŭty̆ / thăt hăs cóme / íntŏ / my̆ lífe,
Sóft / brówn eýes / ănd ĭnĕf- / făblĕ mélt- / ĭng smíle,
Bódy̆ / shápĕd / fŏr ă gód's / căréssĕs,
Yíeld / tŏ thăt húr- / rĭcáne / ŏf lóve
Thăt túrns mĕ / íntŏ / ă témpĕst / ŏf lóngĭng!

This time, we find three feet of one accented syllable only; four iambs; three trochees; one spondee; five anapests; and five amphibrachs. This shows the regularity expected of verse far more clearly than the first or natural scansion.

The exponent of metric scansion, confronted with this, would explain it one of two ways. He would point out that iambs and anapests move from unaccent toward accent, and hence may both be used in the same line: and, of course, that an anapest may omit the first unaccented syllable, or even both of them. He might cite this game rhyme from *Mother Goose:*

Chic- / ory chic- / ory cra- / ny crow,

I went / to the well / to wash / my toe,

where anapests, perfect or defective, and iambs are used interchangeably. Of course, too, he might add that dactyls and trochees,
moving from accent toward unaccent, similarly may both be used
in the same line. And then he would fall back to the other line
of defense, and explain that, after all, iambs and trochees are interchangeable, in an iambic or a trochaic line; and so are anapests
and dactyls, as well as an amphibrach, too, if you insist on including it. And a spondee can pinch-hit for any of these. And
that defective foot, consisting of only one syllable, with only an
accent in it: you could regard it as an iamb or a trochee, with a
pause replacing the unaccented syllable.

But what kind of verse *is* it, you insist?

Well, he retorts, why not try it to the pattern of heroic blank
verse—unrhymed iambic pentameter? Most verse in English that
doesn't fit into anything else can be made to fit into that. And
now we come to pattern scansion: fitting this verse into an artificial pattern of five iambics to the line. The first line, we find,
fits fairly well. The rest strain the pattern. But, if we put a P
for pause, to replace a missing unaccented syllable; and recall
that an anapest may be crowded into the iambic pattern, as if a
grace-note were added; and that an amphibrach (⌣ ╱ ⌣) ending an
iambic line is accepted as merely an iamb with an extra unaccented syllable, we do get some sort of tolerable iambics out of it:

O beau- / ty that / has come / into / my life,

Soft / brown eyes / and inef- / fable melt- / ing smile,

Bod- / y shaped / for / a god's / caresses,

Yield / to that / hur- / ricane / of love

That turns / me / into / a tem- / pest of longing.

Here we have seventeen iambs, including those with pauses and
one with an added unaccent; four trochees, including those with
pauses; three anapests, including one with an added unaccent;
and one spondee. Are we to call this, then, iambic verse, extremely

[109]

irregular, since it permits pauses, substituted trochees, spondees, and anapests, and two extra unaccented syllables terminating two lines?

This would probably be the academic decision. And may I point out that *all* of these scansions are correct, depending on the amount of artificial patterning introduced?

Yet there are two simpler answers, equally correct. This may be regarded as irregular accent verse: the convention being five accents to each line, let the unaccents fall where they will. This calls for pattern scansion too. The first line fits; the second calls for only one major accent on the spondee, on *eyes;* and the last three lines qualifying by accenting the *that* in the fourth, and the pauses in the third and fifth.

But let us revert to the original natural scansion, and classify this as free verse or polyrhythmic poetry, with 3, 5, 4, 3, 3, feet to the lines, either with an upward cadence (iamb-anapest type) or an amphibrachic cadence (unaccent, accent, unaccent, with liberty to have as many unaccents as desired either side of the accent), or a combination of both. To me it is indisputably verse; and, technically, excellent free verse.

Incidentally, this work in scansion has not been wasted. The last example especially is the way the verses would have been scanned and divided into feet by a composer who was setting them to music. He is used to the need for pauses; and can fill out any desired pattern by means of them.

One final question. If these lines could be treated so, and established as verse, could not the prose selection from the *Outline* be similarly regarded? First of all, it consists of only three sentences—and each one constitutes a natural line in itself. This would then give the number of accents as 7, 5, 5. The place of the boundary line between verse and prose is, of course, up to each individual reader. I do not hear this as verse, for all of the absolute parellism in the phrases, "The dead know nothing, . . . The quick know somewhat." To me, it is prose, with one device of rhythmic repetition, common in verse, present. To you, it may be verse. It is further true that the prose wording consists entirely of emotion-evoking or heart-warming words, welded primarily by native monosyllables or homespun words. But this is true of the best and most effective prose, as well as of poetry.

Our final diagnosis on this effort to write one's sincerest desire toward a definite object is that the result may be squeezed into a metric pattern; or regarded as accent verse, the oldest form of English poetry; or, most naturally of all, treated as free verse. It is probable that the ultimately collective decision will agree with us.

THE RHYTHM OF ACCENT VERSE

We have found that the earliest native English verse had three conventions: four accents to the line, with any desired number of unaccents; a cesura, or bisecting of the line; and at least one instance of alliteration in each half of the line. The latter two of these conventions were abandoned, as unnecessarily unnatural. But the convention of accent verse has been the undercurrent of English verse ever since, no matter what alien meters and devices have been superimposed upon it.

As Coleridge explained accent verse, when he used it in *Christabel,* there is no convention for the repetition of any metric foot whatever. Instead, the sole requirement is that each line shall have so many accented syllables, with the unaccented syllables ranging from none to as many as the poet wishes to insert, placed where he wishes. Thus our line pattern might be any number of accents to the line; and our stanza pattern might consist of 4, 4, 4, 4 accents; or 4, 3, 4, 3; or 4, 3, 3, 4, or whatever we wished.

Suppose you wished to write your heart-tightening delight in the coming of spring in verse, and decided on a 4-accent pattern. Getting the rhythm firmly fixed in the mind, like a drum-beat, BOOM, BOOM, BOOM, BOOM, with the right to place unaccents wherever desired, you might write:

> Spring, spring, spring, spring,
> With the soft greening of the delicate young leaves,
> With flower-buds swelling toward their blossoming,
> With birds passionate with the mating song,
> And with my own heart awakening also
> Toward spring—love—laughter—you!

We need not scan this; the rhythm is too obvious. Note that the second line, for instance, accents these four syllables: *soft, green-, del-, leaves.* The minor accents on certain syllables, i.e., *-cate,*

young, in this line, are ignored. Note that this is not at all difficult to write, but natural, and easy—as easy as writing prose, once
you have keyed your utterance to the proper emotional mood and
height.

If you care to scan this, by natural scansion we have two feet
of four syllables each (*With flower-buds, awakening*), and one of
five (*of the delicate*). But it is all melodious and natural, and
we need no names for these feet, since each has only one accent,
or only one major accent and certain subordinate accents, plus as
many unaccents as are desired.

Suppose we wanted to use the same 4-accent rhythm in a
tribute to autumn, but with couplet rhyme added (1,1; 2,2, etc).
We might get:

> Autumn, crown and peak of the year,
> With the rose in hip and the corn in ear,
> With goldenrod cascading over valley and hill,
> And yet, with its faint hint of chill
> Spreading throughout our golden Paradise,
> Warning of sleet—snow—ice.

Note the speed and crowded movement of the third and fifth
lines (the accented syllables here being *gol-*, *-cad-*, *val-*, *hill*; and
spread-, *-out*, *Par-*, *-dise*—the minor accents on *-rod*, *o-* in the
third line and *gol-* in the fifth, being ignored). Note in contrast
the slower movement of the fourth line, the dead march of the
sixth. This was of course intended, and presents no difficulty in
accent verse. And, even with the addition of rhyme, this is still
as easy as writing good prose. One additional element in word-
choice, the identity of certain sounds to constitute the rhymes,
is added; but this presents no more difficulty to experienced versifiers than walking does to the experienced walker.

Let us see what Coleridge does with this in *Christabel,* which
opens:

> 'Tis the middle of night by the castle clock,
> And the owls have awakened the crowing cock,
> Tu—whit!—Tu—whoo!
> And hark, again! the crowing cock,
> How drowsily it crew.

The first three lines here are admirable 4-accent verse. The fourth
line reverts to accurate iambics (ta-TUM, ta-TUM, ta-TUM,

ta-TUM), too monotonous to be natural, except in brief stretches. The fifth line can be accepted, when we substitute a pause for the missing accent.

Later on, this tentative essay in a revival of accent verse reverts increasingly to the more usual iambic or some other metric pattern, as in:

> The Baron rose, and while he prest
> His gentle daughter to his breast,
> With cheerful wonder in his eyes
> The Lady Geraldine espies,
> And gave such welcome to the same
> As might beseem so bright a dame.

This is execrable versification, judged by any standard. It is too regular, tick-tock, too bookishly unnatural; and the rhyme-induced quality of *to the same* (that is, a terminal evoked purely because of the rhyme already made or to come, and not because it is natural utterance) sags it below serious consideration, if the dead prosiness of it had not already done so.

This same convention of accent verse saturates much of *Mother Goose*, that invaluable repository of folk verse of our race. In the examples given, the different accent feet will be separated, to indicate the freedom with which it is used. In addition, certain feet of four syllables each are italicized.

> Hark, / hark,
> The dogs / do bark,
> The beg- / gars are com- / ing to town.

This last line might be divided more naturally into:

> The beggars / are coming / to town.

The specific foot division is immaterial, if the accent pattern is accurately followed.

> Pease / porridge / hot,
> Pease / porridge / cold,
> Pease / porridge / in the / pot
> Nine / days / old. . . .

> Three / blind / mice,
> See / how they / run!
> They all / ran up / to the far- / mer's wife,
> Who cut off / their tails / with a car- / ving knife. . . .

Bat, / bat,
Come un- / der my hat,
And I'll give / you a slice / of bacon. . . .

What / *are little boys'* / made out of?
Snaps / and snails, / and pup- / py dog tails,
And that's / *what little boys'* / *are made out' of.* . . .

Dee'dle, deedle, / dumpling, / my son / John,
He went / to bed / with his stock- / ings on. . . .

Christmas is / coming, the / *geese' are getting* / fat,
Please' to put a / *pen'ny in the* / old man's / hat. . . .

Hinx, / minx, / the old / witch winks,
The fat / begins / to fry;
There's no- / *body at home'* / but jump- / ing Joan,
Fa- / ther, mo- / ther and I.

Of these eight feet consisting of four syllables each—and I have
tended toward metric scansion, and away from natural scansion,
in most cases, to simplify these and make them more intelligible
to those trained in metric scansion—each has one accent and three
unaccents, or unaccents plus minor accents. Four have the accent
on the first of the four syllables; three on the last; and one (*are
made out of*) on the third. Many other combinations are, of
course, possible.

Walter de la Mare, in his magical *The Listeners,* goes further,
using a 3-accent rhythm, BOOM, BOOM, BOOM. Important
lines are—and we start with a simple one, to indicate the accent
pattern most clearly:

Of the for- / est's fern- / y floor;
"Is there an- / ybody there?" / said the Traveller, . . .
And his horse / in the silence / champed the grasses. . . .
And he smote / upon the door again / a second time. . . .
But only / a host / of phantom listeners. . . .
Fell echoing / through the shadowiness / of the still house.

In most of these, the minor accents have been marked as unaccents, to make clearer the location of the major accent. It is even
possible properly to scan the last of these lines as:

Fell ech- / oing through the shadowiness / of the still house,

[114]

which would give the second foot as having eight syllables, with only one accent. Such are the possibilities of accent verse.

All these combinations of feet, other than those metrically named, were called by the classic academicians syzygies, or couplings of metric feet. In accent verse, we do not need to call upon this term. Here we have many four-syllabled feet, as well as five, six, and eight-syllabled feet. The potentialities of accent verse are unlimited, and are always accepted when they follow the natural usages of conversational speech.

My *Antillean,* for all that it includes no foot longer than *And incredible* (⌣ ⌣ ´ ⌣ ⌣), is an effective use of accent verse, on the whole more varied than *The Listeners.* My *Jehovah,* with its norm, the iambic five-foot line tending toward accent verse, achieves music as fresh and surprising as:

> Héavў / wĭth Ĕgýptĭăn / brácelĕts / ŏf réd / góld.

The Glory Road, written with no thought of its rhythm beyond an unconscious 4-accent norm, uses one four-syllabled foot (⌣ ⌣ ⌣ ´) repeatedly:

> Ŏ dĕ Gló- / rў Róad! / Ŏ dĕ Gló- / rў Róad!
>
> Ĭ'm gwĭne tĕr dráp / mў lóad / ŭpŏn dĕ Gló- / rў Róad!. . .
>
> Tĕr ríde / ĕrlóng bĕhín' / mĕ ŭp tŏ Pár- / ădíse. . . .
>
> Ă-báng-/ ĭn' ŏn dĕ crít- / tĕr wĭd hĭs whíp / ăn' góad. . . .
>
> Ăn' bóun' / hĕ gwĭne tĕr kótch / ŭs ŏn dĕ Gló- / rў Róad.

This is how it is always sung; and this is how it was read, before it was sung. It is not properly seven-foot iambic or the later development of the ballad meter:

> Ăn' bóun˚ / hĕ gwíne / tĕr kótch / ŭs ón / dĕ Gló- / ᴾrý / ᴾRóad.

The norm, the 4-accent pattern, reappears constantly and unmistakeable:

> Ăn' cóme / ăn' dwéll / ĭn dĕ Láwd's / ăbóde.

Vachel Lindsay used the same foot repeatedly in *The Congo,* also in 4-accent verse:

Sagged / and reeled / and poun- / dĕd ŏn thĕ táble, . . .
Beat / ăn émptў bár- / rĕl wĭth thĕ hán- / dlĕ ŏf ă bróom.

Its wide usage and popularity preceded the critical isolation of it, as a typical four-syllabled foot widely used today; and, with it, its further extensions in accent verse.

Its popularity comes from its naturalness of rhythm and its permitting a faithfulness to the real desire as it first crystallizes into words, such as no overformalized metric verse, alien in its inception and development, can ever afford. Soon enough, as we shall see, this was corseted into metric verse, by poets saturated with the Renaissance idolatry of all things classic. That they entirely missed the spirit of the scansion of classical verse; that they sought to inflict on English versification a convention unsuitable to the language; that the compromise result was to weaken and over-formalize natural English verse for centuries—these too we will see clearly.

ACCENT VERSE, PROSE, AND FREE VERSE

But, since all three of these—accent verse, prose, and free verse—call for foot-division based merely upon one major accent and any number of unaccents and minor accents, is there any distinction between them? Are not accent verse and free verse really prose, and is not prose properly accent verse, when scanned?

Here is a typical prose sentence:

> The Declaration of Independence was enacted
> on the fourth day of July.

Treating it for its rhythm, in natural scansion without foot division, this would give:

> The Declaratiŏn ŏf Indĕpéndĕnce wăs ĕnácted
> ŏn thĕ fóurth dáy ŏf Júlý.

In this, minor accents are indicated by (/). When we come to divide this into feet, by natural scansion, with no preconceived pattern, we get:

> The Declaration / of Independence / was enacted /
> on the fourth / day of July.

Here we have five natural feet: 5, 5, 4, 3 and 4 syllables to the foot, respectively. This is certainly prose. It would be hard to regard it even as free verse; though, with a wide pattern involving the repetition of these rhythms, it might come, so used, under that category. But let us start with a 4-accent pattern, BOOM, BOOM, BOOM, BOOM, and chant it, with a tune or without, and we could get:

The Dec- / laration / of In- / dependence

Was enacted / on the fourth / day / of July.

Poetry or not, this would be accent verse. The whole difference is in the preconceived pattern. This brings up the whole matter of the run-on quality of prose, without preconceived pattern limited to so many accents to the line. With such a pattern, prose can be made to coincide with accent verse. It then ceases to be prose. As ordinarily written, prose is not accent verse—not even faintly akin to it. It may be squeezed at any time into an accent pattern; thereby ceasing to be prose. Prose can be set to music by the same process.

It should be pointed out here that the essence of poetry can never lie in artificial line-division. Accordingly, much that is set up as verse has no quality of verse; except an artificial preconceived pattern of so many accents to the line, or so many syllables to the line. Where the content does not fit at all into this artificial pattern, it is in reality prose set up as verse. This applies to much offered as iambic 5-foot blank verse, and to other metric forms. Rhyme cannot make verse. Mere line division cannot make verse. An actual rhythmic pattern in the presentation of it is essential. Where this is lacking, we have prose.

THE RHYTHMS OF CLASSICAL VERSE

Greek rhythm, from Homer onward, was based upon quantity: that is, upon whether the time involved in pronouncing a syllable was *long* or *short*. The convention was that a long syllable took twice as long to pronounce as a short one. A syllable was (1) long by nature, when it contained a long vowel, of which there were five, or a diphthong, of which there were eleven or more. It was (2) long by position, when its vowel was followed by two consonants, or by a double consonant, even if one of these opened the next word. But if (3) the two consonants were a mute and a liquid, it might be long or short. And there are complicated extensions of the rules. This strange basic convention becomes all the more surprising when it is remembered that the Greek language had accent, as well: an accent originally raising the musical tone of the syllable, somewhat as in intoned Chinese speech; and, as the language evolved, gradually shifting to a stress accent, such as English has.

This wholly artificial convention, at least when applied to spoken and written words, proceeded to conquer Latin verse, and drive underground the original accent verse. For long it dominated certain Romance languages, especially French, where accent is so unimportant; but the tendency in all of these was for the native accent verse to break through the rigid quantity patterns, and restore verse to something more natural to the speech. It entered English verse just before the time of Chaucer, and has intermittently been revived since. In an altered form, metric verse, with accents replacing quantities, it is still dominant in English verse, although increasingly battling against a return to the native accent verse. Where did this unnatural convention come from, and why, and wherein does its complete inappropriateness to poetry and verse consist?

Let us dig into quantity verse a little further, to get the picture more clearly. The unit of quantitative verse was called the *mora:* an ordinary short syllable, represented by an eighth note (♪) in music. A long syllable consisted of two morae, or a quarter note (♩). An iamb (◡—), and a trochee (—◡) each consisting of a long and a short, had a length of three morae each. An anapest (◡◡—), a dactyl (—◡◡), an amphibrach (◡—◡) and a spondee (╱ ╱) consisted of four morae each. But any of these, especially the first, second, and fourth, could be used in iambic or trochaic verse, by halving the time of the short syllables: making each a half-mora, or sixteenth note (♬). They were then called cyclic, and took the time of only three morae; and they were indicated especially in the complicated classic scansion. Here are some of the symbols used in classic prosody, with such explanations as they seem to require:

/ ictus, or accent
· secondary accent
| division between feet
◡ short syllable, equal to 1 mora or ♪
– long syllable, equal to 2 morae or ♩
‿ two syllables, equal together to 1 mora, or ♫
ᴗ two syllables, equal together to 1½ morae, or ♩.♩.
◡◡ or –ᴗ a cyclic dactyl
◡‿ or ᴗ– a cyclic anapest
– – a spondee
–ᴗ a trochaic dactyl
◡̄ or ◡̲ a variable syllable, the lower syllable being the more usual
ᒪ protraction of a syllable to 3 morae; a triseme
ᑌ protraction of a syllable to 4 morae; a tetraseme
〉 an irrational syllable
⋮ anacrusis (one or two unstressed syllables prefixed to a verse properly beginning on a long or stressed syllable)
‖ cesura
dieresis
∧ a pause of one mora
∧ a pause of two morae

The poems of Homer, which, as finally crystallized in the *Iliad* and the *Odyssey*, poured Greek verse into a mold as rigid as a castiron sow, were probably composed about 1200 B.C. About 550 B.C., these two poems for the first time were heard of, and were reduced to writing, using the standard dactylic hexameter or 6-foot line, with this unbreakable requirement: the fifth foot must be a dactyl; the first four might be dactyls, or might have spondees substituted; the sixth must be a spondee or trochee. Here is the metric pattern:

– ◡◡ | – ◡◡ | – ◡◡ | – ◡◡ | – ◡◡ | – ◡

To achieve this, for centuries the primitive Homeric poetry was tinkered with, with infinite revision and indeed perversion of the language itself, so that the language finally was cut to fit the poetry; instead of the poetry consisting of language used naturally. As G. G. A. Murray words it in the *Encyclopaedia Britannica,* Homer's Greek was—

shaped and twisted to an extent probably without parallel in literature, by the needs and conveniences of the epic hexameter. . . . Liberties are taken both with accidence and with syntax, in order to ob-
tain forms that are metrically convenient.

This has even led to the suggestion that "the hexameter must
be a foreign metre, made to suit a language other than Greek."
But no such source language has been found.

We can thus trace the excessively artificial convention of
quantity rhythm to Homer, in a language with the facilities for
accent rhythm which English employs. Homer's use of it fixed
and rigidified it to such an extent that it still dictates our metric
vocabulary, and gives rise to constant movements for a return
to it, to replace accent meter and accent verse. Why was this convention adopted, instead of the more natural and logical one of
accent verse? It turned the creation of a poetic line into something
resembling a crossword puzzle, where the requirement was that
words had to be substituted or mutilated to make the product,
verse or poetry—an extraordinary demand.

The answer is obvious; the facts already before us furnish it.
Quantity meter was never a natural requirement of poetry as we
know it: poetry to be spoken, or to be written down. But it was
a natural requirement of poetry to be sung. It did not apply to
the words and syllables that entered into poetry; it applied to
the words and syllables only when they were sung. As long as
every line was to be sung—and the epics started and continued so,
and the dramas started and long continued so—this was a natural
and logical convention for words to be sung to notes of a definite
length. The moment the poetry was regarded as poetry to be
spoken or read, the convention became illogical, absurd, impossible. The words no longer fitted the convention; the convention no longer fitted the words. Our composers do precisely
the same thing with words to be sung, making them long, or
short, with infinitely more variations than the Greek composers
used. But we do not make the mistake of thinking that this convention can be carried over from song with a tune to poetry to
be spoken or read.

But the Greek mind moved slowly, and never emerged from the error that this convention applied logically to words and syllables, rather than merely to musical tunes and the words and syllables sung to them. We do not have to follow this primitive error.

So potent was this sacrosanct dactylic hexameter, with a musical notation to be sung, and not spoken or read, that Greek prosody progressed little beyond it. To lighten it, a lighter form, later named the elegiac couplet by the academic prosodists, was invented: a dactylic hexameter followed by a pentameter. We will come to it in time. This was at first used in war songs and love songs, and not in what we call elegies. The earliest fragments of these are those of Callinus of Ephesus, 7th century B.C. The Athenian Solon and the great Tyrtaeus preferred this form. Athens invented also the iambic (shooting or darting) meter, which the authorities describe as more natural, and closer to prose; but it also was based on a convention suitable only to a song with music. Archilochus of Paros, about 650 B.C., and Hipponac of Ephesus, a century later, its most famous users, wrote especially in satire. Lesbos developed the personal lyric and ode, under Sappho, Alcaeus, and the later Anacreon. Then came the dramas, reverting to the dactylic hexameter—which, indeed, with its quantity convention based on a musical notation, dominated all Greek poetry, and still harms our versification.

Latin verse began independently with what is called the Saturnian meter, the crude irregular measures of the oldest Latin songs. Its scansion is said to be six accent iambs, broken by a cesura after the third one. Macaulay, planning his *Lays of Ancient Rome* in a similar pattern, said that the English equivalent was:

The Queen was in her parlor, / eating bread and honey.

There was much license in the scansion of Saturnian meter, and the verse was described as light and vivacious. There are, of course, certain academic prosodists who hold that it depended on quantity, not accent; and they may be correct, if it had a musical basis. But Roman conquest of Greece, and the use of the cultured Greeks as tutors, poets and teachers, brought the miasma of Greek quantity verse into tremendous esteem. Plautus and Terence be-

[121]

gan the introduction of the quantity dactylic hexameter; Ennius and Lucilius brought in iambic and trochaic verse; and Ennius and the greater Lucretius riveted the artificial alien convention on Latin verse. Rome's provincial attitude toward Greece is not without its modern parallels.

In spite of the temporary reverence paid to it, quantity verse died, of its very unnaturalness, throughout Europe, and in England, where it never took real foothold. Sir Edmund Gosse says of it: "The substitution of stress for quantity as the basis of meter . . . corresponded to a change of enunciation which set in in the late classical period." Thus he falls under the spell of the ancient error. For there was never a time when *quantity* was a natural convention of spoken or written poetry, verse or speech; nor was enunciation ever based upon it—except in words sung or chanted to a tune. Incidentally, even French verse, in a language where accent plays an insignificant part, abandoned the unnatural form, and adopted as a convention, instead, just so many syllables to the line, precisely as the remote Japanese did independently. Then, far more accurately, Gosse proceeds: "The prosodies of Provence, France, Italy and Spain were derived from popular accentual Latin verse." The victory of the unnatural quantity meters was not permanent; a popular revolt brought verse toward actual speech, with its accent basis.

THE EMERGENCE OF MODERN ENGLISH VERSE

Thus Latin verse started accentual; yielded to the quantity corrosion of Greek prosody; and finally returned to accent. It offered itself to medieval Europe equipped with one other device, rhyming. We shall find later how this was unknown to classical verse, and originated about the age of Tertullian, in the church Latin (especially in the churches in Africa), as an ingenious device to make the unfamiliar Latin language of the church ritual more easily remembered and understood by the alien worshippers. By the fourth century A.D., this had reached perfection enough to produce the *Stabat Mater* and the *Dies Irae,* still used in Catholic services.

English verse started with its three native conventions: four accents to the line; cesura (bisection, sometimes called section);

and alliteration. But French had been the court language, predominantly, since the time of William the Conqueror (1066 A.D.); and Geoffrey Chaucer (c. 1340-1440) visited France and Italy, became enthusiastic over their verse conventions, and returned to England, as translator and evangel, to convert his native land to these overseas ways. French verse had already largely abandoned quantity verse; instead, its norm was ten syllables to the line; later, twelve; and finally, eight, in the early plays and the fabliaux—not even accent verse, for theoretically the French language omits accent in speech, while retaining accent symbols on many words. All these early conventional French verses were to be sung, and music may well have dictated the rigid French rules in versification. Of course, music permits far more time-variations than either classic prosody or French verse. Even English accent verse went beyond either, as in:

*Dee'*dle deedle / *dump'*ling, / *my'* son / *John'*,

and many other examples equally familiar.

The corrosion of this Greek oversimplification of rhythm dominated the French, and to a lesser extent the Italian, sources of Chaucer; notably it influenced his friend Guillaume Machault, from whom Chaucer borrowed his 10-syllable verse for couplet use—usually letting it reappear as eleven syllables, with an extra unaccent at the end. For all that Chaucer was saturated as well with Dante, Petrarch and Boccaccio, with ottava rima and the sonnet, he ignored these in the main for the French convention of so many syllables to the line; and *Canterbury Tales* and his other gusty works set the unnatural and recognized English standard as verse whose major convention was so many syllables to the line. But, from the start, the convention was shifted toward the native English accent pattern, and was interpreted as requiring so many syllables with so many accents.

The French devices, rhyme and so many syllables to the line, did not win without an immediate struggle. In Langland's *Vision of Piers the Plowman,* the earlier native verse made an effort to regain its lost domain. But the northern device of alliteration, itself unnatural in speech when formalized, failed to conquer the more pleasing southern novelty, rhyme. In folk verse and the ballad, however, accent verse became predominant, with the addition of the alien novelty.

Chaucer had failed to bring in the sonnet and heroic blank verse, as well as the intricate chant royal. A hundred and fifty years later, the Renaissance reached a reawakened England, filtered again through Italy and France. The Elizabethan age lifted to the peak the borrowed and vastly improved heroic blank verse and sonnet, in the former especially, as Shakespeare's progress in versification showed, letting accent verse gradually reassume its sway. The glorious lyric prose, often an unrecognized free or accent verse, of the King James translation of the Bible worked subtly in the direction of molding the language toward the earlier beauty and naturalness of accent verse.

The movement against rhyme first gained force when blank verse took the center of the stage. Gabriel Harvey, a pedantic grammarian of Cambridge, in 1579 commenced a movement to abandon the alien "ornament" of rhyme, and return to the quantitative classical measures. Spenser briefly subscribed to this reactionary and misguided movement, and wrote in unrhymed accented hexameters and trimeters. Thomas Campion, one of the most melodious of English lyricists, in his 1602 *Observations in the Art of English Poesie,* slashed vigorously into rhyme, calling it a "childish titillation"; but, after a brief divorce from it, he welcomed it again into his poetry. He is remembered for his rhymed songs. Later echoes of this opposition occur in Milton's introduction to *Paradise Lost,* Shelley's preface to *The Revolt of Islam,* Whitman, and clear down to the Imagists and later groups.

Rhyme and English metric verse are still predominant in English versification. But the careers of our leading poets have moved in the direction of the abandonment or at least the demotion of rhyme, and the liberalization of meter, in the direction of the freer and more natural accent verse. Shakespeare, Shelley, Keats, Whitman and Frost are outstanding examples of this tendency. The same tendency has been shown strongly in versification as a whole. The spirit of native natural English verse, based on accent, and unrhymed, still persist; it constantly struggles to free itself from the artificial chains of rhyme and strict meter, and constantly succeeds. This must be kept in mind, to understand the increasing variations from the strict rules of prosody that have been used, permitted, and encouraged, to the constant betterment of English verse. This will be reverted to, after the various metric feet have been considered.

SCANSION AND METER

Scansion, of verse or prose, is its division into its rhythmical units, called feet, with appropriate marks to distinguish accented from unaccented syllables, or long from short syllables, etc. *Natural scansion* is this division, based upon the normal division of words into foot-groups as used in good conversation. *Pattern scansion* is this division dictated by a preconceived rhythmical pattern. *Meter* is that attribute of verse by which its rhythm consists of a repeated formalized arrangement of specific rhythmical feet.

METRIC FEET IN ENGLISH

The common metric feet in English are five in number, two of them two-syllabled, and three of them three-syllabled. The names are taken directly from the Greek, where they stood for quantity verse, and not for accent meter, as in English. These feet are:

Foot	Accent Symbol	Quantity Symbol	Examples
Two-Syllabled Feet			
Iamb or iambus	⌣ /	⌣ −	alert; to go
Trochee	/ ⌣	− ⌣	going; see the
Three-Syllabled Feet			
Anapest	⌣ ⌣ /	⌣ ⌣ −	entertain; to the end
Dactyl	/ ⌣ ⌣	− ⌣ ⌣	wavering; fight to the
Amphibrach	⌣ / ⌣	⌣ − ⌣	delighted; an eagle

In these, the mark (/) stands for an accented syllable; (⌣) for an unaccented syllable, or a short syllable; and (−) for a long one.

Three other feet are commonly employed in English, to substitute in other meters—the amphimacer being especially common in anapestic and dactylic verse:

Spondee	/ /	− −	blitzkrieg; white hope
Pyrrhic	⌣ ⌣	⌣ ⌣	of the
Amphimacer	/ ⌣ /	− ⌣ −	anti-war; hit the deck

Other Greek feet, at times used in English verse, usually without recognition or especial nomenclature, are:

Tribrach	⌣ ⌣ ⌣	⌣ ⌣ ⌣	and in the
Molossus	/ / /	— — —	Great White Chief
Bacchius	⌣ / /	⌣ — —	a huge bear
Antibacchius	/ / ⌣	— — ⌣	flatfooted, God struck the
Ditrochee (two tro- chees as a com- pound foot)	/ ⌣ / ⌣	— ⌣ — ⌣	Alabama, strike a level
Paeon	/ ⌣ ⌣ ⌣	— ⌣ ⌣ ⌣	shadowiness
Choriamb	/ ⌣ ⌣ /	— ⌣ ⌣ —	Kalamazoo
Epitrite, 1st class	⌣ / / /	⌣ — — —	to kill ten men
Epitrite, 2nd class	/ ⌣ / /	— ⌣ — —	hit the White Hope
Epitrite, 3rd class	/ / ⌣ /	— — ⌣ —	Tom kissed a girl
Epitrite, 4th class	/ / / ⌣	— — — ⌣	Ten girls missing

And this by no means exhausts all the ingenuity of classical prosody.

This may look complicated, and sound complicated. It is far simpler and more obvious, once you have mastered its meaning, than the multiplication tables in arithmetic, or the opening moves in chess or checkers. It is quite as easy to use as it is to understand. All your life, you have been using such rhythmic feet in your ordinary speech. If you think the effort of calling so many of these feet by their first names is unnecessary—and I am inclined to agree with you—remember the simpler ones, realize that the others exist and can be looked up, and go on about the more serious business of writing verse and poetry.

Henceforth, we shall ignore the quantity origin of these feet, and treat them as English versification ordinarily uses them, as accent feet.

1. TWO-SYLLABLED FEET: THE IAMB

The commonest metric foot in English verse is the iamb (⌣ /). It has two syllables, the first unaccented, the second accented. The rhythm might be indicated thus, to make it a mental metric pattern:

Rhythm of the iamb: ta TUM

The popularity of this foot grew out of the essential nature of the English language, which has approximately as many accented syllables (including minor accents) as unaccented syllables. It is true that a far larger number of individual words in English are trochees (/ ⌣), TUM ta:

tension, shaken, lightning, Janet, bedspread, rapture

Most of these consist of a root-stem with a suffix, as *-ing, -sion, -en, -ning,* etc. But such trochaic dissyllables in English are ordinarily immediately preceded by an unaccented article, preposition, conjunction, or an unaccented syllable of the preceding word:

while giving, a tension, for Janet, a little vixen

and this gives what is called the iambic character to our speech. In English verse, the line most usually opens with an unaccented one-syllabled word, followed by a word accented on the first syllable, and with alternate accents and unaccents thereafter; and this gives the iambic effect.

IAMBIC WORDS AND FEET

There are quite a number of words in English that constitute complete iambic feet, including:

above, abuse, acquaint, agape, antique, array, attack, behind, below, beneath, betray, collect, compete, confront, debris, declare, decree, delay, delight, dismount, distract, domain, engage, erupt, evoke, fatigue, garotte, gossoon, impale, intrigue, Japan, Jeannette, malign, maroon, moustache, opaque, prorogue, renew, restore, retard, salaam, salute, taboo, unique, unite, veneer, withhold, within

Most of these either commence with an unaccented prefix, or are direct foreign importations.

Iambic feet are constantly constructed from such combinations of words as:

and those, an owl, a ship, as she, but now, by luck, for love, he ate, it runs, she says, the sea, to Rome, we know, with you

IAMBIC LINES

A line of verse or poetry is called technically a verse. But *verse* has three other acceptable meanings: the collective name for the product of versification; a numbered division of a chapter of the Bible; and colloquially, for a group of lines or verses more properly called a stanza, as in, "The first verse of this song." The word *line* is less ambiguous, and should regain favor.

Lines of metric verse are described by the name of the foot, plus the number of feet: monometer or one-foot, dimeter or two-foot, trimeter or three-foot, tetrameter or four-foot, pentameter or five-foot, hexameter or six-foot, heptameter or seven-foot, octometer or eight-foot, and so on. The English nomenclature is simpler and more generally understood.

Typical one-foot iambic lines would be:

Then come. . . .
Ahoy! . . .
We left.

Typical two-foot iambic lines would be:

Then come, my love. . . .
The night is young. . . .
Delight is brief.

Typical three-foot iambic lines would be:

Then come, my love, to me. . . .
The glory of his death. . . .
The last immortal noon. . . .
Inconsequential chat.

Note that a trochee like *glory,* an amphibrach like *immortal,* a five-syllabled word like *inconsequential,* fit perfectly into the iambic pattern; and of course lend pleasing variety to the verse. Typical four-foot iambic lines would be:

Then come, my love, to me, and sing! . . .
Forget inconsequential chat. . . .
Incontrovertibility. . . .
Distinguish good from evil things.

Typical five-foot iambic lines are:

Then come, my love, to me, and sing your song. . . .
For beauty has no lease of settled date. . . .
Not marble, nor the gilded monuments. . . .
The lovely springtide wakens trembling buds.

Notice that in this last line there are four words that are complete trochees in themselves. We shall soon discover how interchangeable the various metric feet are. In the iambic five-foot or pentameter line, we have reached the dominant line in English versification: the line of the heroic blank verse of Shakespeare, Milton, Browning, Robinson, and Frost; of the heroic couplets of Dryden and Pope; of the sonnet, and of other varied uses.

Longer iambic lines may be composed without difficulty.

MASCULINE AND FEMININE ENDINGS

A line ending on an accented syllable is said to have a strong or *masculine ending;* one ending with an unaccented syllable, a weak or *feminine ending*. The phrase is especially applied to an unaccent added after a foot ending on an accent, as an iamb or an anapest. Rhymes on masculine endings are called masculine rhymes; those on feminine endings, feminine rhymes. It is always permitted, in iambic verse, to append an extra unaccented syllable: and the same practice applies to any foot ending on an accent. Thus a stanza of iambic lines, with a pattern of 1, 2, 3, 4 and 5 feet to the lines, could be:

The ocean,
Forever sighing,
Assails the golden beaches
With mad insatiable passion
To make them one with her eternal being.

This is described as iambic verse with feminine endings; and, in scansion, the extra unaccented syllable is added to the iamb, without presumably changing its iambic nature:

T˘he óceăn

But this stops us abruptly. We have had this same foot (˘/˘) described as an amphibrach. Thus an iamb with feminine ending is really an amphibrach. With slight changes, the whole could be written in amphibrachs:

The ocean,
Forever lamenting,
Assailing the gold-gleaming beaches
With hungry importunate longing and passion
To make them all one with her infinite magical being.

We will come soon to the interchangeability of metric feet.

THE IAMB IN ENGLISH VERSE

Iambic verse is found down the whole stretch of English poetry, from Chaucer's *Merciles Beauté:*

Your eyes two wol slee me sodenly,
I may the beauté of hem not sustene,
So woundeth hit through-out my herte kene.

Do not forget that *eyes* and *herte* are dissyllables here.

Forget not yet the tried intent
Of such a truth as I have meant;
My great travail so gladly spent,
Forget not yet!
Forget Not Yet, SIR THOMAS WYATT

If music be the food of love, play on.
Give me excess of it, that, surfeiting,
The appetite may sicken and so die.
Twelfth Night, I, i, WILLIAM SHAKESPEARE

Not only is the iambic five-foot line the norm of English poetic drama, John Milton made it the English epic norm as well:

All in a moment through the gloom were seen
Ten thousand banners rise into the air
With orient colors waving: with them rose
A forest huge of spears: and thronging helms
Appear'd, and serried shields in thick array.
Paradise Lost, I, 544-548.

It appeared in late editions of the ballads, where accent verse had largely been smoothed out; and may, of course, have appeared in some early ballads as well:

O Willy's large o' limb and lith,*
And come o' high degree;
And he is gone to Earl Richard
To serve for meat and fee.
The Birth of Robin Hood, ANONYMOUS

* Joint.

It became the norm for the sonnet:

Mysterious Night! when our first parent knew
Thee from report divine, and heard thy name,
Did he not tremble for this lovely frame,
This glorious canopy of light and blue? . . .
Why do we then shun Death with anxious strife?
If Light can thus deceive, wherefore not Life?
Night and Death, BLANCO WHITE

[130]

Herrick could use it for his lightest trifles:

> Give me the food that satisfies a Guest;
> Kisses are but dry banquets to a Feast.
>> *Kisses,* ROBERT HERRICK

Browning used it in many of his effective dramatic monologs:

> God's works—paint any one, and count it crime
> To let a truth slip. Don't object, "His works
> Are here already; nature is complete;
> Suppose you reproduce her—(which you can't)
> There's no advantage! you must beat her, then."
>> FRA LIPPO LIPPI

It is the dominant foot used in hymns and stately poems:

> God of our fathers, known of old,
> Lord of the far-flung battle-line,
> Beneath whose awful hand we hold
> Dominion over palm and pine,
> Lord God of Hosts, be with us yet,
> Lest we forget, lest we forget.
>> *Recessional,* RUDYARD KIPLING

You may recognize it in hundreds of your favorite poems, in moods ranging from sublimity to:

> My darling wife was always glum.
> I drowned her in a cask of rum,
> And so made sure that she would stay
> In better spirits night and day.

WRITING IAMBIC VERSE

Speech and thought in English do not normally come in perfect iambics—unaccent, accent, unaccent, accent—with never a variation. They come, when unemotional, in the diffuse rhythm of prose; and, in proportion as the speech and thought become emotional, tend toward the regularity of free verse or accent verse. Yet superimposed upon this are so many centuries of iamb-worship among English-speaking people, that the construction of iambs, dictated by the inner tune remembered from Shakespeare or sonnets or other iambic verse, is the essence of simplicity.

As the simplest of metrical exercises, it is easy to write unending iambics, or indeed verses of any other specified metric foot, on any chosen subject. This breeds certainty and deftness in the use of the various metric feet. The ideal pure iambic verse starts off with an unaccented syllable, and thereafter alternates accented and unaccented syllables, except where feminine endings are added at the ends of lines, as pleasing grace-notes. The product of such exercises is as a rule not poetry; but it is technically verse, and not prose. It is well first to write down your iambic pattern, and then fit your syllables beneath the scansion symbols as you write them:

$$\smile \diagup \mid \smile \diagup \mid \smile \diagup \mid \smile \diagup$$
$$\smile \diagup \mid \smile \diagup \mid \smile \diagup \mid \smile \diagup$$
$$\smile \diagup \mid \smile \diagup \mid \smile \diagup \mid \smile \diagup$$
$$\smile \diagup \mid \smile \diagup \mid \smile \diagup \mid \smile \diagup$$

Mentally repeat to yourself this patter,

ta TUM / ta TUM / ta TUM / ta TUM

Then choose a theme, such as sunset seen from a mountain, and proceed to write:

> The sky is stained a vivid red,
> With flecks of gold and purple hue.
> The clouds that drowse across its face
> Display these tints to wake the white.
> The crimson ball that is the sun
> Approaches near the crimsoned earth,
> And throws a ruddy glow across
> The darkened trees, the jagged rocks.

Scansion establishes that you have not varied your pattern so far.

Yet variety is essential to life and vigor in verse, to prevent withering monotony. Now determine to vary the pattern, by putting a trochee in each first foot:

TUM ta / ta TUM / ta TUM / ta TUM

This would be achieved by slight changes:

> Here where the sky grows vivid red,
> Flecked with its gold and purple hue,
> Lighted by clouds across its face.

Or place the trochee in the second foot:

ta TUM / TUM ta / ta TUM / ta TUM

> The sky glowing with vivid red,
> With flecked golden and purple hues,
> And clouds drowsing across its face.

Similarly, the trochee can be inserted in any position in each line. Or it can be shifted as you please, as in four lines, where it occurs first in line one, second in line two, and so on:

> *Here where* the sky glows vivid red,
> With flecked *golden* and purple hues,
> And clouds that drowse *gently* along,
> Display these tints to glow *wildly*.

Now do the same thing, inserting an anapest in each instance instead of a trochee. When we have arrived at the final pattern, with one anapest to each line, in positions 1, 2, 3 and 4, respectively, in the four lines, we might get:

> *Where the sky* is stained a vivid red,
> With flecks *of empur*pled golden hue,
> The clouds that drowse *in its glowing* face
> Display these tints to brigh*ten the white*.

Thus you have inserted a number of ta ta TUM's instead of ta TUM's, and found that the writing automatically clicks into the meter desired, once you have it mentally fixed. Under the treatment of Variations we will discuss how the masters vary the iambic pattern, and how you may do this with most effectiveness.

So far, the versifier has been writing this down. Now learn to improvise iambics, or iambics with any variations desired, without writing them down, speaking them as naturally as you would speak prose. Soon enough you can determine your scheme mentally, and practice the form with all possible variations at great speed and with unfailing accuracy. Even if you have, at times, to warp proper order or even create a neologism, remember: The Greek language was warped incredibly more to fit it to the regular dactylic hexameters of Homer. Such practice is sure to improve your versification in meter.

THE INTERCHANGEABILITY OF METRIC FEET

Thomas Campion, writing in 1602, observed that the trochee was merely the iamb standing on its head, or reversed. That is, any normal iambic line, such as Housman's:

> And malt / does more / than Mil- / ton can

can be turned into accurate trochaic verse, by adding a syllable at the beginning, and dropping one at the end:

> Knów that / mált does / móre than / Mílton

Or a syllable could have been dropped at the beginning, with an added one at the end, or a syllable dropped there:

> Mált does / móre than / Mílton / éver

Similarly, a line of accurate trochees,

> Thén the / wrínkled / óld No- / kómis

can be made accurate iambics, by adding an unaccent before or dropping an accent there; plus adding an accent at the end, or dropping an unaccent there; or by any combination of these:

> The wrín- / kled óld / Noko- / mis sáid
> And thén / the wrín- / kled óld / one sáid

Or take an iambic line with feminine ending:

> In sum- / mertíme / on Brédon

This becomes accurate trochaic verse by merely adding an accent, or cutting off the unaccent:

> Nów in / súmmer- / time ón / Brédon
> Súmmer- / time ón / Brédon

Similarly, trochaic verse that is lacking an unaccented syllable at the end, called catalectic by the Grecian prosodists, of this pattern:

> Térence, / thís is / stúpid / stúff

can become accurate iambic verse by adding an unaccent at the beginning, or eliminating the accent there:

> Now, Tér- / ence, thís / is stu- / pid stúff
> But thís / is stú- / pid stúff, / my fríend

A composer could set this to music requiring a dactylic movement, by adding pauses after each trochee:

> Térence, (P̆) / thís is (P̆) / stúpid (P̆) / stúff (P̆).

Similarly, of course, iambs could be set as anapests. Dactyls could be set to trochaic time by doubling up the speed of the unaccented syllables—that is, halving the notes; and anapests could be set as iambs similarly. If we wanted to change this trochaic line to dactyls, an unaccented syllable would have to be added to each foot:

Terence, but / this is the / stupidest / stuff!

An iambic line could be changed to anapests by adding an unaccent to each foot. Thus, taking our first example:

And this malt / can do more / than John Mil- / ton could do

Or an iambic line could be changed to amphibrachs by adding an unaccent to each foot except the first one: commencing the last line with "And malt," and proceeding to the original ending:

And malt can / do more than / John Milton / could ever

Similarly, trochaic verse can be shifted to amphibrach, by adding an unaccent before it, and an unaccent in each foot:

Now Terence, / but this is / the stupid- / est nonsense

It is clear that anapests, dactyls, and amphibrachs are similarly interchangeable, by merely making sure that we commence with two unaccents for anapests, one for amphibrachs, and none for dactyls, and thereafter having one accent each time followed by two unaccents.

Since this is so—since iamb and trochee are the same, alternating accent and unaccent, the difference merely being whether we commence with the unaccent or not; and since anapest, amphibrach and dactyl are the same—a succession of one accent followed by two unaccents, the difference being merely whether two, one or no unaccents precedes the first accent—what is the value of the differentiations? Or have they any value?

In a matter like this, logic will not save us. The language has developed illogically in many directions. It is not surprising that prosody has made differentiations without great importance, and has stressed these all out of proportion to their real significance. It is enough for us to know that iamb and trochee are interchangeable, at any place in the pattern of either; and that the same is true of the three three-syllabled feet. And that, further-more, a three syllabled foot can always be inserted in place of a two-syllabled one, by quickening the speed of the reading, that is, by treating the two unaccents as an unaccent and a gracenote; and a two-syllabled foot may always be inserted for a three-syllabled one, by permitting a brief pause to replace the missing unaccent.

All this is in the direction of accent verse. It is the common and increasing practice of the masters in versification, and lends variety and beauty to the rhythm of English versification.

TURNING PROSE INTO IAMBIC VERSE

As a mnemonic or memory device, primitive and later people turned their list of the months of the year, the rulers of many countries, and such other prosy matter into verse. An admirable exercise is to take any prose, and turn it into acceptable iambics, or any other specified metric foot. Let us take again the opening of *The Outline of Man's Knowledge,* already scanned, and see how easy it is to turn it into acceptable iambics. What is the least number of changes we will have to make, to transmogrify the first four sentences into iambic verse? First, we give it natural scansion:

Mén and wómen have béen groúped endúringly into the quíck and so on. Now, remembering our ta TUM ta TUM ta TUM iambic pattern, we go to work, and produce:

Áll mèn/ and wóm- / én hàve / béen groúped / foréver
Ínto / the quíck / and ( ) déad. / The déad / knòw nóthing,
Ór whàt / knówledge / they háve / is déad. / The quíck
Knòw sóme- / whàt, and / *they* séek / to gáth- / er móre.
In *this* / accél- / erát- / ed tém- / po of
Our mòd- / ern lív- / ing, ( ) quíck / *ones réal-* / ly húnger
And thírst / áfter / knówledge.

Ten small changes, in thirty-three feet, make the transformation: uninterrupted iambics, except for the permissible trochees. So simple is the exercise. The same prose, or any other, may be turned as easily into trochees; or, with more added unaccents, into anapests, dactyls or amphibrachs.

2. TROCHAIC VERSE

The second of the two-syllabled feet, and the second most common foot in English verse, is the trochee ($/$ $\smile$) . It has two syllables, the first accented, the second unaccented. The rhythm might be indicated thus:

Rhythm of the trochee: TUM ta

It is thus the reverse of the iamb. Commencing with accented syllables, contrary to the common usage of our speech, it gives a more staccato or abrupt effect to the verses, as if one dashed into the meat of the matter, without an introductory unaccented syllable. The most familiar use of it in a long poem in English is Longfellow's *Hiawatha*.

TROCHAIC WORDS AND FEET

The great majority of two-syllabled words in English are perfect trochees:

Adam, agate, arrant, atom, avid, bated, belly, bitten, bottom, caitiff, cattle, cavil, dastard, digging, double, elvish, fatal, frightened, garish, growing, gullah, harbor, hateful, hoary, inner, jaunty, kennel, laughter, longer, mastiff, mated, natal, nuisance, opal, pastime, peasant, queenly, rattle, royal, timber, total, value

Many of these are word-stems with a suffix added, which is not commonly accented: such as *-ant, -ed, -y, -en, -iff, -ing, -ish, -er, -est,* etc.

Perfect trochees are also constructed from such word combinations as:

boy and, for a, let a, men as, throw the, went to, when the, wild as

TROCHAIC LINES

Typical trochaic one-foot lines or monometers would be:

Let him! . . .
Deathless. . . .
England!

[137]

Typical trochaic two-foot lines or dimeters would be:

> Let him try it! . . .
> For it's snowing. . . .
> And the blowing
> Says, get going!

Typical three-foot trochaic lines or trimeters would be:

> Let him try it, brothers! . . .
> When the day is ended,
> Then will come the splendid
> Sunset in the skyway,
> Gilding field and highway.

Typical four-foot trochaic lines, or trochaic tetrameters, would be—let Longfellow give them:

> Should you ask me, whence these stories,
> Whence these legends and traditions,
> With the odors of the forest,
> With the dew and damp of meadows.

Note the natural scansion of the last two lines, to see how variety is added to poetry, by fitting into pattern scansion unaccents or minor accents as if they were major:

> With the odors / of the forest,
>
> With the dew / and damp / of meadows.

Yet, even at that, there is a soporific quality to it. If it were rhymed, it might snap us back to attention oftener:

> Older than your first unrest
>
> Is this / stark pine / on the crest.
>
> Younger than your latest spite
>
> Are the buds that spring tonight.
>
> When your / last smoke / thins and dies,
>
> These pines / still will / brush these / skies,
>
> When your / fire's last / song is sung,
>
> These old / stars will still be young.

> *Birmingham, iii,* CLEMENT WOOD

The use of the italicized spondees also adds to the variety of this use of the pattern. In this example, the final unaccented syllable is omitted throughout, making the verse terminally catalectic. This is always permissible in trochaic verse in English, and is usually given preference, since masculine rhymes are preferred, as a rule, to the less acceptable feminine ones.

It might be asked, following our discussion of the interchangeability of the metric feet, why not call this iambic verse, with the first unaccented syllable uniformly omitted? There is no logical reason for having a separate name for it; least of all a Grecian name referring to quantity verse, not accented meter. But the practice is to let the opening foot in the line, or the dominant foot of the first line or some repeated key meter, determine the naming of the meter. It is hence customary to call such verse trochaic, with the omission of the final unaccent; rather than iambic, with the omission of the initial unaccent.

A famous use of trochaics is in the incantation and other witch scenes in *Macbeth*, with this abrupt and vigorous movement, the catalectic termination of most of the lines adding to the staccato effect:

> Round about the caldron go;
> In the poison'd entrails throw;
> Toad, that under cold stone
> Days and nights hath thirty-one
> Swelter'd venom sleeping got,
> Boil thou first i' the charmed pot!
>
> *All.* Double, double, toil and trouble,
> Fire, burn; and caldron, bubble.

Note the masterly variations in the third and sixth lines. The third line is usually scanned one of these two ways:

> Toad, that / under / cold / stone
> Toad, that / under / co-old / stone

The second of these, involving the pronunciation of *cold* as a dissyllable, was the one probably preferred in Shakespeare's day; similar to his famous line, where *fire* is pronounced first as a dissyllable and then as a monosyllable:

> As fi- / re drives / out fire, / so pi- / ty pity.

In modern practice, the pause (indicated by P) would probably be used instead. In the sixth line,

$$\text{Boil thŏu / fírst ĭ' thĕ / chármeŭ / pót}$$

Charmed, if pronounced as a monosyllable, would, in this and verse for the next two hundred years, have been written *charm'd;* as written *charmed,* it was a dissyllable. This practice is not followed today. Modern versifiers could only use such a word as a dissyllable by the unnatural warping of the language called poetic license, avoided increasingly by the greater poets down the ages. Versifiers should take pains to differentiate between -ed terminations which are pronounced, and those which are not:

Dissyllables: all stems ending in -*d* (including -*ld,* -*nd,* -*rd*) or -*t* (including -*ct,* -*ft,* -*lt,* -*nt,* -*rt,* -*st*), as, *added, scolded, banded, guarded, fitted, directed, gifted, salted, punted, carted, listed;* also *wicked,* meaning evil; *wretched;* and *aged,* as in *an aged man.*

Monosyllables: all other preterites ending in -*d* or -*ed,* including *retched, wicked* when applied to a candle, *aged* in the wood, etc.

It is unnecessary to give examples of five-foot, six-foot, and longer trochaic lines. They can be formed without difficulty.

THE TROCHEE IN ENGLISH VERSE

The famous song, *Summer Is I-Comen In,* from the dawn of English poetry, is primarily in trochees, with the final unaccent missing—that is, catalectic:

> Summer is i-comen in,
> Loud (P) sing cuckoo!
> Groweth seed, and bloweth mead,
> And springeth the wood new—
>   Sing cuckoo!
> Ewe bleateth after lamb,
> Loweth after calve cow;
> Bullock starteth, bucke verteth,
> Merry sing cuckoo!

Note the pause in the second line; and the pronounced syllables of *ewe, calve,* and *bucke,* needed to complete the meter. The unaccent commencing the fourth line, following an accent termi-

nating the preceding line, is a device often used in English versification. It is regarded that, with the proceeding line, the whole
constitutes so many accurate trochees, dactyls, etc.:

mead, and / springeth / the wood / (P) new.

The use of this carry-over unaccent, commencing the new line,
is shown in verse of the general pattern of:

Let me / welcome / spring,
And / all the / flowers' faces,—
Birds up- / on the / wing,
In / unex- / pected / places;
Sap within the bole
Of ancient tree grown mellow;
Love within the soul
Of lucky lass and fellow!

Here intentionally the rhyme for the even-numbered lines is
feminine, the normal for rhymed trochees; while the rhyme of
the odd-numbered lines is masculine, while the missing unaccents
here appear as the initial unaccents, without rhyme, of the even-
numbered lines. The whole may be regarded complete six-foot
trochees, divided into a new line after the fifth syllable in each
instance. Such devices are open to any versifier.

The famous song of Shakespeare's,

Crabbed Age and Youth
Cannot live together

is a memorable lyric in trochees, as are "Where the bee sucks,
there suck I," "Full fathom five thy father lies"—note the rever-
sion to early English alliteration!—"Take, O take those lips
away," "Fear no more the heat o' the sun," Ben Jonson's *Hymn
to Diana*, George Wither's "Shall I, wasting in despair," Thomas
Carew "He that loves a rosy cheek," Sir John Suckling's "Why so
pale and wan, fond lover?" The roll of trochaic lyrics and verses
continues to the present. The abrupt beginning gives it somewhat the effect of a stunt in words, and prevents the wide popularity that the iambic opening has.

We have already quoted Shelley's famous lyric, "Music, when
soft voices die," obviously with a trochaic movement. Here is the

complete scansion. We encounter no especial trouble until we reach the sixth and seventh lines, which, taken independently, seem to be iambic in movement. But, when the formal movement is trochaic, and an unaccent is inserted at the beginning of the line, it is customary to describe this as trochaic verse with an added initial unaccent: anacrusis, to use the term of the Greek prosodists. This gives us:

> Músĭc, / whĕn sóft / vóicĕs / díe,
>
> Víbrătes / ĭn thĕ / mémŏ- / rȳ—
>
> Ódŏurs, / whĕn swéet / víolĕts / síckĕn,
>
> Líve wĭth- / ĭn thĕ / sénse thĕy / quíckĕn.
>
> Róse leáves, / whĕn thĕ / róse ĭs / déad,
>
> Ăre heáped fŏr / thĕ bĕ- / lóvĕd's / bĕd;
>
> Ănd só thȳ / thóughts, whĕn / Thŏu árt / gŏne
>
> Lŏve ĭt- / sélf shăll / slúmbĕr / ón.

Of these eight lines, only the eighth is pure trochees. Line one contains an iamb; line two, a pyrrhic; line three, an iamb followed by a cyclic dactyl; line four, a pyrrhic; line five, spondee followed by pyrrhic; line six and seven, with anacrusis opening, have respectively a pyrrhic, and a spondee following the anacrusis —that strange foot called a bacchius. Nor is this excessive irregularity, when we come to actual poetry as written by the masters. Their inner ear dictates that the variations have more beauty than regularity could possibly have; and the variations fit naturally into what they really mean to say.

It must be made clear that the reader need never know that there is a variation present, or the names of any of them. This analysis is for the versifier alone, as a guidestone toward his own practice. If this had been flawless trochees, it would have been more juvenile, more unnatural, more remote from natural speech and its variety of rhythm-pattern. Its one possible excuse would have been an overpowering passion, that demanded a rhythm as regular as pounding heart-beats. But this is a reflective lyric, not a directly passionate one; and such regularity would have been entirely out of place in it.

DOUBLE RHYME IN TROCHAIC AND OTHER VERSE

Shelley here only once uses a feminine rhyme (*sicken, quicken*), which would be required by the strict trochaic pattern. Double rhymes, as a dominant, tend to be a trifle weak in English verse. The custom of English speech is to end a large proportion of sentences in an accented syllable. It is a strain to hear or read too many feminine endings. There are far more two-syllabled rhymes than single-syllabled ones in English; but a long succession of them, especially in short lines, gluts, and makes the verse tend to be over-sweet or over-pretty. Coleridge, always hacking toward accuracy, asserted:

> Double and trisyllable rhymes form a lower species of wit, and, attended to exclusively for their own sake, may become a source of momentary amusement.

This may come from the fact that we are more used to single rhymes, perhaps because the ingenuity of versifiers in English hears them far more easily than double or triple rhymes. It is entirely the reverse in Italian and other Romance languages.

It is quite as true that a long succession of masculine, accent-syllabled or single rhymes tends to become monotonous, and that an occasional double rhyme lends grace and fluidity to the rhyming movement. This is splendidly brought out in Shakespeare's sonnets, where the double rhymes almost always lend beauty:

> Yet in these thoughts myself almost despising,
> Haply I think on thee,—and then my state
> (Like to the lark at break of day arising
> From sullen earth) sings hymns at heaven's gate.
> For thy sweet love remember'd such wealth brings,
> That then I scorn to change my state with kings.
>
> *xxix*

WRITING TROCHAIC VERSE

Writing trochaic verse as a metrical exercise is as simple as writing iambic verse. Once get the trochaic pattern firmly fixed in the mind, TUM ta, TUM ta, TUM ta, TUM ta, and the trochees simply ripple out:

> Writing pure trochaic verse
> Is the method to rehearse,
> If you'd ultimately see
> Real prosodic mastery.

Or, if you wish the feminine ending,

> Writing bright trochaic verses
> Hardly fills the poets' purses;
> Better far write prose like Plato's,
> Or raise chickens or potatoes.

This was done automatically in rhyme, without intention; for rhyme can become as much of a habit as meter or walking. The exercise is far easier if rhyme is omitted:

> Let the supple trochees ripple
> In a gay cascading torrent,
> Till in utter desperation
> We exclaim: "No more—it's cloying!"

We have already found out that iambic verse can be turned into trochaic by omitting the opening unaccented syllable of each line:

> Curfews toll the knell of parting day;
> Lowing herds wind slowly o'er the lea;
> Plowmen homeward plod their weary way. . . .
> Leave the world to darkness and to me!

Prose can be altered into trochaic verse as simply. The example given, of prose turned into iambic verse, can be shifted promptly into trochees, by omitting the opening unaccents, as was done in the case of Gray's *Elegy*, just above.

3. OTHER TWO-SYLLABLED FEET

The spondee (/ /) consists of two accented syllables. Its rhythm is TUM TUM. It is used to vary iambic, trochaic, and especially any of the three-syllabled feet. Examples are:

Iambic: *Bright star,* / that shines / within / our sky

Trochaic: *Rose leaves,* / when the / rose is / dead

Anapestic: And he killed / *ten men* / ere he fell / to the earth.

Dactylic: High o'er the / *huge hill,* / watching the / meteors

Amphibrachic: One watching / *stars fall,* / one counting / the planets

The pyrrhic (⌣⌣) consist of two unaccented syllables. This is so unnatural in English, that no word can with certainty be given as an exact example. Such preposition as *into, upon,* may be used without accent in a line, and constitute pyrrhics; but each has an accent, in normal speech. Combinations like *of the, and a,* have no accent by themselves, but often are fitted into iambic or trochaic verse as if they possessed an accent. Examples of the use of the pyrrhic are:

Iambic: The slings / and ar- / *rows of* / outra- / geous for-
        tune

Trochaic: Vibrates / *in the* / memo- / ry.

4. THREE-SYLLABLED FEET: THE ANAPEST

The anapest (⌣⌣/) is a foot consisting of two unaccented syllables, followed by one accented one. It is in structure an iamb with an extra initial unaccent. Its rhythm might be indicated thus:

Rhythm of the anapest: ta ta TUM

ANAPESTIC WORDS AND FEET

Examples of three-syllabled words which may be used as pure anapests in English are not numerous:

   appertain, coalesce, disinter, disaffirm, insecure, inter-
   dict, interfere, introduce, supercede, uncontrolled

Since all these have, in actual speech, at least a minor accent on the first syllable, they tend to be amphimacers (/⌣/) in reality. It should be noted that all these begin with a two-syllabled prefix, or with two prefixes, all lacking major accents. Anapests made from a group of words come closer to the pattern:

   a la mode, at the end, for the flag, into Rome, having
   died, in Japan, to beware, to Ostend, with a shout

ANAPESTIC LINES

Typical anapestic lines are not difficult to write. Here is a group to the stanza pattern of 1, 2, 3, 4, 5 anapests to the line:

> At the end
> Of the fight for the flag,
> Let the heavens resound with the crash
> Of the shattering roar of applauding delight,
> And the utter tempestuous screams of the passionate mob.

Note how words that are iambs (*resound, delight*), trochees (*heavens, utter*), amphibrachs (*applauding*), dactyls (*passionate*), as well as the unnamed four-syllabled word *tempestuous,* fit smoothly into the anapestic pattern.

Examples of perfect anapestic verses are not common in English. *The Solitude of Alexander Selkirk,* by William Cowper, comes close to the expected pattern; for all that, in the stanza below, the second, fifth, sixth and eighth lines are initially catalectic, that is, lack an unaccented syllable in the beginning:

> I am mon- / arch of all / I survey;
> My right / there is none / to dispute;
> From the cen- / tre all round / to the sea
> I am lord of the fowl and the brute.
> O Solitude! where are the charms
> That sages have seen in thy face!
> Better dwell in the midst of alarms,
> Than reign in this horrible place.

It would not strain logic to classify this as amphibrachic verse, with an additional initial unaccent in some of the lines, and the concluding unaccent omitted, as is permissible. Indeed, many verses intended to be anapestic are properly amphibrachic, invariably omitting one unaccent in the opening of each line. This merely reminds us how close the various feet are to each other in structure.

WRITING ANAPESTIC VERSE

Get the meter firmly fixed, ta ta TUM, ta ta TUM, ta ta TUM, in your mind, and proceed:

> When the end of the day is at hand,
> And the cattle are penned for the night,
> When the darkness possesses the land,
> And the lamp, with its wavery light,
> Is a beacon to summon us home
> From the hill or the vale or the foam, . . .

This is, of course, far easier to write without rhyme, until rhyme becomes habitual. The result is almost invariably verse, rather than poetry.

As ordinarily written, do not be surprised if unexpected accents crop up at unexpected places; or omitted accents, even internal ones, as in Cowper's *The Poplar Field*. Let us scan carefully the first stanza, the norm line being:

Of my fa- / vorite field, / and the bank / where they grew

which is accurate enough. Here it is:

The pop- / lars are felled, / farewell / to the shade

And the whis- / pering sound / of the cool / colonnade;

The winds / play no lon- / ger and sing / in the leaves,

Nor Ouse / on his bos- / om their im- / age receives.

There are three iambs here: a spondee or trochee preceded by a pause; and at least one molossus. Even more variations than this are typical of most anapestic verse.

Byron's *The Destruction of Sennacherib* is in vigorous anapests. Some anapestic verses have an unaccent missing from the first line of the first stanza. This opening leads us to expect an amphibrachic movement, and is a bit misleading. It is better, as Byron does here, to commence with a norm or pattern line (both in rhythm and in mosaic rhyming), and follow this with any variations. But there is no law for poets, except such laws as they themselves make.

> The Assyrian came down like the wolf on the fold,
> And his cohorts were gleaming in purple and gold;
> And the sheen of their spears was like stars on the sea,
> When the blue wave rolls nightly on deep Galilee.

Here the second foot of the last line consists of three accents (*wave rolls night-*), an unusual foot called molossus by the Greeks. The name need not concern us.

We have already learned how dactyls and amphibrachs may be turned into anapests by altering the opening number of unaccents. Iambs and trochees may be turned into anapests (or dactyls, or amphibrachs) by adding unaccents. Prose may be turned into any of the three-syllabled feet by a similar process to that used in turning it into iambic and trochaic verse. In proportion as the three-syllabled feet are unusual in English, this exercise becomes less and less important.

BLENDING THREE-SYLLABLED FEET

A pleasing effect may be obtained by the varied use of anapests, dactyls and amphibrachs. Francis Miles Finch, in *The Blue and the Gray*, succeeds in such a mixed usage:

> By the flow / of the in- / land river,
>   Whence the fleets of iron have fled,
> Where the blades of the grave-grass quiver,
>   Asleep are the ranks of the dead:
>   Under the / sod and the / dew,
>   Waiting the Judgment Day,
>   Under the one, the Blue;
>   Under the other, the Gray.

This may have been intended as anapestic throughout, with both unaccents omitted in the four opening lines of the refrain. But this refrain is in reality dactylic. It should be noted that the author goes further, and uses an iamb (*-land river, grass quiver,* both with feminine endings), and a trochee (*Judgment, one the*) when it suits his purpose. But these variations come in too regularly to let the whole be regarded as accent verse. This is a skilled preconceived use of variations in meter, and is highly successful.

Anapests, amphibrachs and dactyls may be regarded as parts of an unending tape of this rhythm:

˘ ˘ ´ / ˘ ˘ ´ / ˘ ˘ ´ / ˘ ˘ ´ / ˘ ˘ ´ / ˘ ˘ ´ / ˘ ˘ ´ / ˘ ˘ ´ /

So far, we have no division into feet. If we start with two unaccents, we call the result anapestic. If we start with an accent, we call the result dactyls. If we start with one unaccent, it is usual to call the result anapestic or dactylic (with an unaccent added at the beginning). But this is really amphibrachic. There is the same difference in the type of opening that there is in the use of iamb and trochee to open: the iamb being natural, the trochee abrupt. So the anapest and amphibrach are natural, and the dactyl abrupt. When we add to this that, especially for purposes of rhyming, any of these lines can be terminated with no unaccents, or only one, it becomes clearer how close they are to each other.

The skillful mingling of these, based on their effect when measured against the usual patterns of conversational speech, should be utilized by the adept in versification.

5. DACTYLIC VERSE

The dactyl (╱◡◡) is a foot consisting of three syllables, the first accented, the next two unaccented. It is in structure a trochee with an extra unaccent appended at the end. Its rhythm might be indicated thus:

Rhythm of the dactyl: TUM ta ta

DACTYLIC WORDS AND FEET

There are many perfect dactylic words in the language—the proportion to anapests being almost similar to that of trochees to iambs:

> antonym, battlement, carrying, carnival, canticle, dastardly, deviltry, edible, enema, esculent, fascinate, folio, glimmering, gluttony, happily, lazily, loveliest, merriment, realty, royalist

Many of the words which tend to be amphimacers, with a minor accent on first or last syllables, are used interchangeably as dactyls or anapests:

> introduce, attitude, Samarcand, Michigan

Many combinations of words give perfect dactyls:

> beauty is, fighting a, fly to the, march into, out of the, over the, under the, where in the

DACTYLIC LINES

Typical dactylic lines are not difficult to write. Remembering the rhythm TUM ta ta TUM ta ta, we might get:

> Out of the dusk and the glittering
> Splendor of stars and of nebulae,
> Out of the night with its magical
> Breath of the wind from the galaxy.

More commonly, one final unaccent is regularly omitted:

> Out of the dusk and the glitter,

or even both:

> Out of the dusk and the night. . . .
> Under the sod and the dew.

Thomas Hood's famous *The Bridge of Sighs* is predominantly dactylic:

> One more Unfortunate
> Weary of breath
> Rashly importunate,
> Gone to her death!
>
> Take her up tenderly,
> Lift her with care;
> Fashion'd so slenderly,
> Young, and so fair!

Of the seventeen stanzas, all but two open with dactyls, and these two use amphibrachs. In the main, the poem is strictly dactylic throughout; with a rare use of amphibrachs and even anapests as line-openers. Remember that the readers of this poem, who from the start have enshrined it as a magnificent and courageous defense of the lot of what Victorians called a "fallen woman," merely felt that the meter was unfamiliar and at times a little bumpy; but they had no knowledge of the names of any of the three metric feet involved, or of Hood's dexterity in the use of them. The names of metric feet are for practicing versifiers; they are no concern of the reader or listener. Thus a cabinet-maker may use a peen-hammer, a hand-drill, a spirit-level, a lathe and other tools, familiar to him; but the public is only interested in the finished product, the chest of drawers, the table, the chair, never thinking to ask what tools and precise materials went into its makeup. It is so with a poem. It is the versifier's business to know his tools and his materials as well as a cabinet-maker knows his, and to use them at least as well. The product thereafter is judged from its emotional effect as a whole.

Thus the poetry-loving world a half century ago fell beneath the spell of Elizabeth Akers Allen's *Rock Me to Sleep, Mother*,

> Mother, dear mother! the years have been long
> Since last I listened your lullaby song;
> Sing, then, and unto my soul it shall seem

> Womanhood's years have been only a dream.
> Clasped to your heart in a loving embrace,
> With your light lashes just sweeping my face,
> Never hereafter to wake or to sleep—
> Rock me to sleep, mother, rock me to sleep.

But it was the emotional appeal that won the readers, not the knowledge that this was an example of dactylic verse handled effectively. The author cannot resist an occasional amphimacer (/ ◡ /, as in *Mother, dear; with your light*) or antibacchius (/ / ◡, as in *Since last I; sleep, mother*). But the proportion of these is small, in view of the difficulty of writing natural dactyls in English.

Tennyson's *The Charge of the Light Brigade* was at least equally popular; and the problem of writing this in dactyls, based on a great early English battle song in dactyls, *Agincourt,* was not handled by him nearly so happily. Since many of his lines ended on full dactyls, he avoided the need for discovering triple rhymes in many ingenious ways. At times he let a repetition of the two unaccented syllables replace rhyme entirely:

> Cannon to / right of them,
> Cannon to / left of them,
> Cannon in / front of them
> Volleyed and / thundered.

Here these first three lines rhyme no more than *right, left* and *front* rhyme; the repetition of the unaccented *of them* is a pleasing and inconspicuous substitute. Again, he swung into terminal amphimacers, rhyming only the concluding syllables:

> Stormed at with / shot and *shell,*
> Boldly they / fought, and *well.*

This clearly runs counter to the dactylic pattern. But the readers never guess it, and treasure the poem for what it has to say, not for the rhyme-induced departures from the dactylic pattern.

WRITING DACTYLIC VERSE

With the meter, TUM ta ta, TUM ta ta, firmly fixed in mind, it is possible to write unending dactyls, especially if done without the added requirement of rhyme:

> Out of the dark of prehistory
> Man has emerged, in his impotence,
> Seeking to solve the incredible
> Problems of life and reality.

To show how fully we are conditioned by the habit of rhyming, it is difficult to avoid ending line 2, or some later line, with *mystery,* the obvious rhyme for *history.* If rhyme is desired, this is not essentially more difficult:

> This is the song of the katydid
> Flung in his passion and eagerness:
> "Yes," he insisted—I'll state he did!
> "Life is for plenty, not meagreness!
> Life is for rapture and jolliness,
> Never for dull melancholiness."

ALTERING PROSE AND VERSE INTO DACTYLS

Prose can be turned into acceptable dactyls, by the method already learned for turning prose into iambs and other feet. Anapests, as:

> Let us fly to the hills when the hurricane blows!

are shifted to dactyls by omitting the first two unaccented syllables, adding two at the end; or by adding an accent at the beginning, and lopping off the last accent, or adding two unaccents to it:

> Fly to the hills when the hurricane fulminates! . . .
> Ho, let us fly to the hills from the hurricane!

In the case of amphibrachs, only one unaccent need be shifted. Iambs and trochees require the addition of one internal unaccent to each foot, as well as the proper treatment of the first and last foot, to become dactyls.

6. AMPHIBRACHIC VERSE

The amphibrach ($\smile\,/\,\smile$) is a foot of three syllables, the first and third unaccented, the second accented. It is not usually known or named in English versification, being misdescribed as a mutilated anapest or dactyl, with an excrescence at one end or the other. Since it is as useful a device as any three-syllabled metric foot, the adept at versification will understand it, practice it, and make its use habitual. Its rhythm might be indicated thus:

Rhythm of the amphibrach: ta TUM ta

AMPHIBRACHIC WORDS AND FEET

There is a large number of perfect amphibrachic words in English, including:

advancement, Alaska, alertness, angelic, belated, caresses, collected, cohering, dactylic, decided, departure, detritus, dividing, dominion, dramatic, endearment, erosion, iambic, Jehovah, libation, momentum, O'Kelly, oxalic, Pindaric, religious

Many of these consist of an unaccented prefix, an accented monosyllabic word-stem, and an unaccented suffix to end with: as, *intruding*. It is easy to combine words into a perfect amphibrach:

at ending, in Samos, the fall of, to hit him, we wander.

AMPHIBRACHIC LINES

The dominant music in Lady Nairn's *The Land o' the Leal* is amphibrachic, however laxly used later in the song:

I'm wearing awa', Jean,
Like snaw when it's thaw, Jean,
I'm wearing awa'
To the land o' the leal.

The Bucket, by Samuel Woodworth—familiar to generations as *The Old Oaken Bucket*—moves in strict amphibrachs throughout:

How dear to this heart are the scenes of my childhood,
When fond recollection presents them to view!
The orchard, the meadow, the deep-tangled wild-wood,
And every loved spot which my infancy knew.

The faulty double rhyme, *childhood—wildwood,* ĬLD'HŎOD, ĬLD'WŎOD, is unimportant to the reader, since it possesses enough repetitional elements to be accepted. The adept versifier would avoid it. John Howard Payne, in his opera *Clari,* sang a song predominantly in amphibrachs, which is even more familiar:

To thee I'll return, overburdened with care;
The heart's deepest solace will smile on me there;
No more from that cottage again will I roam;
Be it ever so humble, there's no place like home.
    Home! Home! sweet, sweet Home!
There's no place like Home! there's no place like Home!

Three perfect lines of amphibrachs, rhymed wisely on the masculine ending, with the terminal unaccent omitted—catalectic, to give it its classical name. The fourth line starts with, and continues as, anapestic. The refrain swings into accent verse:

P / P   P / P   P / P   ⌣   / P
Home! / Home! / sweet, / sweet Home!

The concluding line returns to amphibrachic movement, but with permissible variations. This was universally accepted for its message; nor did the reader ever bother with the name of the feet, or the technical skill or lack of it in their use.

In the same stirring meter, with a rare initial anapest, moves Byron's *Stanzas Written on the Road Between Florence and Pisa:*

Oh, talk not to me of a name great in story;
The days of our youth are the days of our glory;
And the mrytles and ivy of sweet two-and-twenty
Are worth all your laurels, though ever so plenty.

For a more accurate use of amphibrachs, in a poem marked by precise use of the more unusual metrical feet, see the song in *The Blood Doom*, in my *Jehovah:*

All this you shall conquer with swordmen and spearmen;
The spear and the sword shall not cease from their labor,
Nor spare man nor woman nor child in their killing,
Till all things that breathe you have slain for my glory!

WRITING EMPHIBRACHIC VERSE

Once riveting the rhythm, ta TUM ta, ta TUM ta, on the memory, it is easy to improvise in amphibrachs—as easy as in any of the other meters:

Away to the woodlands, away to the mountains,
To fields that are blazing with russet and gold;
To valleys that tinkle with song of the fountains,
An Eden to dwell in, a joy to behold!

Prose may be turned into amphibrachs, as easily as into the other meters. This too furnishes an excellent exercise in versification. We have already treated the interchangeability of amphibrachs with anapests and dactyls: the internal music being ⁄‿‿ ‿‿ throughout, with the dactyl starting on an accent; the amphibrach on one unaccent and an accent; the anapest, on two unaccents and an accent.

7. THE AMPHIMACER

The amphimacer is a foot of three syllables, accent, unaccent, accent (⁄‿⁄). Its rhythm is TUM ta TUM. It is less usual than the other three-syllabled feet in English, a language with a relative equality between accented and unaccented syllables.

Typical words which are or which can be used as amphimacers are:

attitude, introduce, contraband, Samarcand

Groups of words easily form amphimacers:

word of God, fight the man, passion's end, love's delight

There is an overtone of the amphimacer in Swinburne's *Hertha*, in spite of its anapestic movement, as in:

I am that / which began. . . .

Out of me / God and man. . . .

I the mouth / that is kissed.

In general, the amphimacer is rare in English.

The same may be said of the other classical feet already listed.

VARIATIONS IN ENGLISH VERSE

When we regard English versification as built upon an immense substructure of accent verse, upon which an alien metric pattern was superimposed, we need not be surprised that variations from meter are rather the norm than the exception: so potent is the underlying native tendency to accent verse.

Three main streams of versifications stemmed out of the early affixing of rigid meter to English.

The first sought to abandon meter altogether, in favor of free verse or polyrhythmic poetry. This was strongly expressed in certain parts of the King James Bible; in the poems of Ossian, Walt Whitman, Adah Isaacs Menken, Stephen Crane, William Ernest Henley, Edgar Lee Masters, Carl Sandburg, Ezra Pound and the Imagists, and many more modern practitioners. Free verse differs from accent verse in that it has no preconceived accent pattern (so many accents to the line) whatever. In this, it resembles prose, differing only in a subtle use of repetition in rhythm which prose avoids. The trap constantly in free verse is an unconscious return to meter, due to the long training in it that the race has undergone. This is increasingly illustrated in Whitman's later poetry (and less markedly throughout), and in all of Masters.

The second stream of versification aimed directly at accent verse, avoiding meter entirely. Most of the early ballads were of this type. Coleridge arrived at this accent verse independently and theoretically in *Christabel,* marked by too great a metric influence throughout; and he was influenced by the ballad use of it in *The Rime of the Ancient Mariner.* Walter de la Mare reached a peak of it in *The Listeners.* My *Antillean* is in the same category. It is heard in Chesterton's *Lepanto,* in *The Glory Road,* in much of Vachel Lindsay's work, and in thousands of lesser poems.

The third stream of versification accepts meter, and thereafter is open to an increasing use of liberties within the metric pattern, in the direction of accent verse. This includes many of the greatest names in English poetry. Dryden and Pope strictly limited the variations they took in iambic meter, for all that the spondee was welcomed as a persistent variation, as in:

Glad cháins, / wárm fúrs, / bróad ban- / nérs and / bróad fáces,
The Dunciad, POPE

with three spondees followed by a pyrrhic and a terminal antibacchius—in verse presumably iambic! Even the familiar quotations at times surprisingly show anapests substituted for iambs, a grace-note usage illustrated in:

A little learning is / ă dán- / gĕroŭs thíng;

Drink deep, or taste not the / Píe- / riăn spring.
Essay on Criticism, POPE

VARIATIONS IN SHAKESPEARE'S IAMBS

But Shakespeare, long before, had slowly developed a supple strength and variety in the iambic pattern, by the use of variations, all in the direction of accent verse—a treatment that has never been bettered in extent by any later poet, Robert Frost being the one possible homely exception. Shakespeare began with a comparatively rigid pattern, as to both the succession of iambs and the *end-stopped* quality of his verse: that is, the meaning coming to a natural end or rest at the end of each line:

> Proceed, Solinus, to procure my fall,
> And, by the doom of death, end woes and all.
> *The Comedy of Errors, I, i.*

> From fairest creatures we desire increase,
> That thereby beauty's rose might never die.
> *Sonnets, ix*

In the *Sonnets,* he soon mounts to lines as varied as:

> And stretch- / ed me- / tre of / an an- / tique song,
> *xvii*

with its unexpected pyrrhics and spondee. Allowing one accent to each foot, this would in reality give us something like:

> And stretch- / ed metre of / an antique / song.
> Suns of / the world / may stain, / when heav- / en's sun staineth.
> *xxxiii*

the last foot here has four syllables—an anapest with a feminine ending, or extra syllable. Here is a line opening with four accents (two spondees):

> These poor / rude lines / of thy deceased lover.
> *xxxii*

Here is an opening we can only describe as a pyrrhic followed by a spondee, and then a trochee:

> Of the / wide world, / dreaming / on things to come.
> *cvii*

The sonnets, an early rather than a late flowering of Shakespeare's genius (approximately 1593-98), show already this audacious use of variation from the iambic norm. The plays mount successively toward the variational peak of *Pericles, The Tempest, Cymbeline,* and *The Winter's Tale,* with a rhythm like the following (and here the scansion used will be the natural one, rather than the artificial iambic pattern scansion) :

> For the flowers now, / that, frighted, / thou lett'st fall
>
> From Dis's / waggon. / Daf- / odils
> That come before the swallow dares, and take
>
> The winds / of March / with beau- / ty; vi- / olets dim,
> But sweeter than the lids of Juno's eyes
>
> Or Cyth- / ere- / a's breath; / pale / primroses,
> That die unmarried ere they can behold
>
> Bright Phoe- / bus in his strength,— / a mal- / ady
>
> Most in- / cident / to maids; / bold ox- / lips, and
>
> The crown- / impe- / rial; lil- / lies of / all kinds,
>
> The flow- / er-de-luce / being one!— / O, these / I lack,
>
> To make / you gar- / lands of; and, / my sweet friend,
> To strew him o'er and o'er!

In lines 10-12, we have 6 iambs; 4 anapests—one of them extremely strained (*lands of; and,*); 2 spondees, 1 pyrrhic, and 1 molussus! There are respectively 11, 12, and 10 syllables to these 3 lines—no uniformity there. There is not even the definite flow of accent verse; the spondaic movement spoils that. It is merely rhythm tending strongly toward free verse—and this is versification, in the presumed iambic metric pattern, in the hands of the race's master versifier!

VARIATIONS IN OTHER IAMBIC LINES

Other outstanding masters of technique show variations as marked.

> Not so / much life / as on / a sum- / mer's day
> Robs not / one light / seed from / the feath- / ered grass.
>
> *Hyperion,* JOHN KEATS

—two spondees opening each line; in the second line these being followed by a trochee. And here is a line from the same poem, presumably iambic, consisting of five trochees:

Thea! Thea! Thea! where is Saturn?

Such a complete departure from the pattern is entirely permissible, in poetry. It is not poetic license; it is acceptable and admired technique. It reminds us afresh that poetry is written by poets, who follow their own inner music; and only thereafter do the academicians lay down their petty ordinances, which the living poets of the past naturally never heard of, and did not observe, and which the living poets of today and tomorrow will consider as of no more weight than dandelion fluff strawed by the wind.

Edna St. Vincent Millay is as masterly. Using the same five-foot iambic pattern, she achieves:

Fishes / would drown; / and the / all gov- / erning reins
Would tangle in the frantic hands of God
And the / world gal- / lop head- / long to / destruction.

Robert Frost goes further in the direction of variation within the pattern. Here are typical lines, scanned naturally:

And spread / her a- / pron to / it. She put / out her hand. . . .
Strange how / such in- / no-cence / gets its / own way. . . .
And the / saw snarled / and rat- / tled, snarled / and rattled. . . .
So. / ᴾ / But the hand / was gone / already.

Here the accented *So*, a foot by itself, is followed by a pause long enough to account for an unaccented syllable, plus the whole foot following it.

Little— / less— ᴾ / nothing! / And that / ended it.

It is this quality of veering toward the natural conversational rhythm, inside a vague skeleton of metric design, that makes Frost's verse far more living than that of most of his contemporaries. The same liberty is open to any versifier, the inner touchstone being that the natural rhythm of the language is faithfully reflected.

In metric poetry or verse, here is an important thing to remember: *Flawlessness in meter is the greatest flaw; perfection, the chief imperfection.* The pattern scansion is of course regular; but the natural scansion of the words superimposed upon the pattern must vary constantly from it. It might almost be said that the naturalness and vitality of the poetry is in direct proportion to the amount of this variance. Natural scansion should leave pattern scansion far below, like a butterfly leaving its wingless cocoon.

This is the constant practice of all able versifiers. Often the simplest lines show its subtle use. Thus W. H. Davies wrote, in *Margery,* the lovely lyric line,

> The butterfly loves mignonette.

Only scansion can show how deftly his natural rhythm departs from his pattern. For the natural scansion, with the accented syllables marked, is:

> The but'terfly / loves' / mignonette'.

But, since the pattern scansion is iambic tetrameter, this would give us:

> The but- / terfly / loves mi- / gnonette.

To fit the pattern, two syllables (-fly, mi-), which are unaccented, receive artificial accents; while one (loves) either goes unaccented, or retains its accent only as a part of a spondee. In this opening of a sonnet by Shakespeare,

> Let me not to the marriage of true minds
> Admit impediments. Love is not love
> Which alters when it alteration finds,
> Or bends with the remover to remove.
>
> *cxvi*

the pattern scansion is, of course,

> ta TUM / ta TUM / ta TUM / ta TUM / ta TUM

The natural scansion of the first line comes closest to:

> TUM TUM TUM / ta ta TUM ta / ta TUM TUM

[160]

and, for the last,

> ta TUM / ta ta ta TUM ta / ta ta TUM

By natural scansion, each of these lines has only three feet, instead of five; at the same time, the first line has six accents, while the fourth line has only three!

A thousand thousand instances could be given, all merely amplifying the necessity of having the natural scansion vary constantly from the goose-step of the pattern scansion. Scan your own verses, and make sure that this variance is usual in them. If you cleave always toward natural phrasing, it is inevitable.

COMBINATIONS OF METERS

We have spoken of the graceful interweaving of anapests, amphibrachs, and dactyls; and have seen examples of a similar use of iambs and trochees together. This can be made a regular alternation in either case. Here is a deft use of dactylic movement, with a counter-tune playing against it within the lines:

> God for King Charles! / Pym and such carles
> To the Devil that prompts 'em their treasonous parles!
>
> Cavaliers, up! / Lips from the cup,
> Hands from the pasty, nor bite take nor sup
> Till you're
>
> *Chorus.*—Marching along, / fifty-score strong,
> Great-hearted gentlemen, singing this song.
> *Cavalier Tunes : Marching Along,* ROBERT BROWNING

This can of course be scanned as anapests with pauses; or dactyls with pauses; or a mixture of both. But the actual fact is that this four-syllabled movement, *God for King Charles,* more accurately given in *Lips from the cup,* reappears six times in twelve possible places; and it really dominates, rather than the straight anapest or the dactyl. It is a dipody (or two feet) or syzygy (joining of meters) consisting of a trochee followed by an iamb, or accent, unaccent, unaccent, accent. It was called a choriamb, in Greek prosody, and dominates the whole movement.

Browning might have written this throughout as choriambs (or trochee, iamb), permitting the occasional spondees:

> God for King Charles! Pymn and such carles,
> Strike them all dead,—treachery's parles!
>
> Cavaliers, up! Lips from the cup,
> Hands from the bread, bite not nor sup,
> Marching along, fifty-score strong,
> Great-hearted knights, singing this song!

Or this first line could have been used, with a trochaic or iambic background thereafter. Browning preferred his own use: a dactylo-anapestic background, with this four-syllable dipody predominant.

Many of the old ballads, in their use of accent verse, tend to the alternation of iambs and anapests:

> Ŏ Ál- / ĭsŏn Gróss, / thăt lives / ĭn yŏn tówĕr.

But the ballads were primarily accent verse, and did not sustain such an alternating device. It could be used effectively:

> O Alison Gross, that lives in yon tower,
> The ugliest witch from here to the sea,
> She lured me one day to come to her bower,
> And many a promise made unto me.

Anapest followed by iamb appeared in Browning's *Home-Thoughts, from Abroad,* a fascinating medley of lyric rhythms:

> Thăt thĕ lów- / ĕst boŭghs / ănd thĕ brúsh- / wŏod shéaf
> Round the elm-tree bole are in tiny leaf,
> While the chaffinch sings in the orchard bough
> In England—now!

My *Salvatore's Dead,* dated 1915, alternated trochaic lines, for the trudge of the funeral march, with anapests, to indicate the subtropical gaiety of the dead man's spirit:

> Salvă- / tŏre's / dĕad; ă / gáp
> Whĕre hĕ wórked / ĭn thĕ dítch- / ĕdge, shŏv- / ĕllĭng múd;
> Slanting brow. A head mayhap
> Rather small, like a bullet. Hot Southern blood.
> Surly, now, now riotous
> With the flow of his joy. And his hovel bare,
> As his whole life is to us—
> A stone in his belly the whole of his share.

> Body starved; but the soul secure—
> Masses to save it from Purgatory,
> And to dwell with the Son and the Virgin pure—
> Lucky Salvatore!

This indicates how the versifier can utilize any combination of rhythms—alternating in each line, various meters in alternating lines, or any combination of these.

There are many instances of definite combinations of meters in familiar poetry. Such a poem as Browning's *Evelyn Hope* may be considered as dominantly a blend of dactyl and trochee:

> Beautiful / Evelyn / Hope is / dead.

This rhythm may be described in many ways; it is, in all probability, accent verse. We find the same type of rhythm in Elizabeth Barrett Browning's *A Musical Instrument:*

> What was he doing, the great god Pan,
> Down in the reeds by the river?
> Spreading ruin and scattering ban.

The first line contains a dactyl, a trochee, an iamb, and a spondee in the fourth foot. But the third line evidently opens with a trochee: it is impossible to regard *Spreading* as either dactyl or spondee. In Matthew Arnold's *The Forsaken Merman,*

> Come, dear children, let us away,
> Down and away below!
> Now my brothers call from the bay.

Trochee (or spondee), trochee, dactyl, accent, for the first line; dactyl, trochee, accent for the second; trochee, trochee, dactyl, accent in the third—unless we call it a hodge-podge of trochees and iambs; or, possibly best of all, accent verse.

James Thomson, in the title line and throughout *Give a Man a Horse He Can Ride,* employs a like blending of rhythms. It is increasingly being used. Robert Frost's dedicatory *The Road Not Taken* being a memorable example:

> Two roads diverged in a yellow wood,
> And sorry I could not travel both
> And be one traveller, long I stood
> And looked down one as far as I could
> To where it bent in the undergrowth.

Spondee, iamb, anapest, iamb for line one; iamb, anapest, iamb, iamb, for the second—so the actual metric patterns are used in something more like accent verse than anything permitted to metric verse. This definitely becomes accent verse in my *The Path:*

> I guess the little folk must use it,
> Whatever there is that lives in woods,
> Bowling the crimson partridge berries,
> Playing leapfrog on toadstool hoods.

For all that this is accent verse, it and similar examples are usually planned and written as patterned metric verse, with an extreme right of variations within the metric pattern. In verses like these, the metric and accent verse tend to meet and coalesce. As loosely used today, metric verse has allowed the impulse of accent verse to flow into it, until accent verse is the frequent result.

The versifier still has full right to formal alternation and inter-weaving of metric feet, within the same line, or alternate lines, couplets or stanzas. But the irregular use of combined metric feet produces a result more accurately described as accent verse.

THE RHYTHM OF FREE VERSE
(Continued)

In our study of the rhythms of versification, we started with free verse, and dealt with it briefly. From this we passed into accent verse, the native convention in English. We then traced the development of classic quantity meters: their conquest of more natural native rhythms, the constant revolts against their artificiality, and their final adoption as the supposed norm of English poetry. Out of a discussion of the variations permitted within the various metric patterns, and the combinations of feet within these patterns, we were brought face to face with the fact that we had arived at accent verse again, by a different route.

But we have not dealt sufficiently with free verse or poly-rhythmic poetry, the least conventionalized of all these forms. Research in this field is still too young to have arrived at any widely accepted conclusions. All that can be done is to indicate some of the trends; analyze them; and see if certain conclusions can be arrived at, which may be of value toward a future final survey of the field, and a widening comprehension of the value and use of free verse.

This discussion must be as accurate and precise as it is possible to make it; for only so can it be of real benefit. Let us, then, assail the problem first by adopting the policy of limiting it to its precise boundaries—an exclusion policy that will leave us, in the end, nothing but free verse to consider. Here are four "Dont's" to remember, in writing free verse:

I. *Don't write metric verse, and think that you are writing free verse.*

In 1870 Whitman published this lovely lyric:

> Joy! shipmate—joy!
> (Pleas'd to my Soul at death I cry;)
> Our life is closed—our life begins;
> The long, long anchorage we leave,
> The ship is clear at last—she leaps!
> She swiftly courses from the shore;
> Joy! shipmate—joy!

Excluding the opening and closing refrain line, this is in regular four-foot iambics. There are eighteen actual iambics, to the one opening trochee and one spondee: a greater regularity than we have so far encountered. Whitman should have written it just as he did; but he should not have labored under the misapprehension that it was free verse, when it wasn't. The master of versification should be able to use any device of versification with equal facility: free verse, accent verse, metric verse; but he should know what he is using. Toward the end, the aging Whitman thought that he was still writing free verse, when he had slumped back into iambics, primarily pentameter, no matter how he sawed his lines up into irregular lengths, to make them resemble superficially the free verse he had once written. Instances multiply, in Whitman's later work: as in this complete poem, *The Untold Want:*

> The untold want, by life and death ne'er granted,
> Now, Voyager, sail thou forth, to seek and find.

This has, in addition to fairly regular iambics, the very faults that Whitman had once boasted he had rigorously excluded from his verse: the stock poeticisms, such as *ne'er* for *never,* and the solemn style *sail thou.* Similarly his *Song of the Redwood Tree* includes *'mid, unreck'd, know I, befitting, yield we, ye, valleys grand:* the frayed echoes of a style two centuries dead, for all that it still appears, to deaden the verses containing it. In any kind of verse, it is inexcusable. And, in free verse, such metric lines and passages as Whitman descended to toward the end are inexcusable.

Much of the work of Edgar Lee Masters, even in *Spoon River Anthology,* sags into iambics, as plodding and unexciting as Gray's *Elegy Written in a Country Churchyard.* The last seven lines of *Elmer Karr,* for instance, have this goosestep rhythm:

> Toward me who wronged the bed of Thomas Merritt.
> Oh, loving hearts that took me in again
> When I returned from fourteen years in prison. . . .
> Repent, ye living ones, and rest with Jesus.

There is every reason why Masters should have written just this, if it was what he wanted to say; but he should have been technique-conscious, and not regarded it as free verse. If he was aware, most of the critics were not. The chief harm was that this, offered as or received as free verse by so many, tended unnecessarily to hobble the genuine technique of free verse, and lead to its misunderstanding and misdefinition.

II. *Don't write accent verse, and think that you are writing free verse.*

An effective poem in *Drum-Taps* moves with a six-accent beat in the main. In the following lines, the probable accents are marked:

> Beat!' beat!' drums!'— / blow!' bu'gles! blow!'
> Through' the win'dows—through doors'— / burst' like a ruth'less force'.
> In'to the sol'emn church' / and scat'ter the con'grega'tion,
> In'to' the school'room / where' the schol'ar is stud'ying;
> Leave' not the bride'groom qui'et— / no hap'piness must he have now' with his bride'.

This last line has a rhythm as tricky as one from de la Mare's *The Listeners.* The foot accented on *now* must have from four to six syllables altogether, and this would be appropriate for either free verse or accent verse. But de la Mare goes as far and further, in definite accent verse; and Whitman himself sets the accent pattern here, in the drum-beat of the opening. Accent verse can best be understood, by beating out the accents to it first in a kind of drumbeat. Whitman should have written these lines just so; but he would have gained in effective expression if he had known what device of versification he was adopting, instead of imagining that, since this clearly was not accepted metric verse, it must be free verse.

Note that Whitman here adopted the ancient convention of dividing each line into two halves or hemistiches—a device developed in classic prosody by the use of the cesura, and in early English verse by a split accompanied by a pause, called bisection or section. This device is as open to free verse as to accent or metric verse.

Whitman repeatedly uses the device of accent verse, in passages whose convention is a numbered group of accents to each line. Take the first eight lines of *Song of the Banner at Daybreak,* which have this number of accents: 4, 7, 4, 8, 4, 4, 4, 4. Scansion of some of these 4-accent lines reveals how completely this is the device that Coleridge rediscovered in *Christabel:*

> Ō a new / song, / a free / song. . . .
> By the wind's / voice / and that / of the drum. . . .
> Low / on the ground / and high / in the air,
> On the ground / where fa- / ther and child / stand.

There was every reason for Whitman to use just this device. But it is not, in its nature, the freedom of free verse; it is as natural, but with the differing convention of so many accents to each line.

The carol of the bird, from *Out of the Cradle Endlessly Rocking,* may be construed as metric verse:

> Winds blow south, or winds blow north,
> Day come white, or night come black,
> Home, or rivers and mountains from home,
> Singing all time, minding no time,
> While we two keep together.

This is more probably admirable accent verse. No lover of Whitman would have a word of it changed. But it would have strengthened his command of his technique if he had recognized it for what it was, and not treated it merely as some mysterious type of free verse. The versifier should have all of the devices of his art at his finger-tips, and use and blend them as he pleases. But he should do this as one aware of what he is doing.

III. *Don't write prose, and think that you are writing free verse.*

The charge is commonly leveled against Whitman that most of his product is merely chopped-up prose. Analysis does not bear this out. Here is as "prosy" a passage as I can discover, from the standpoint of rhythm:

I saw the marriage of the trapper in the open air in the far west—the
    bride was a red girl;
Her father and his friends sat near, cross-legged and dumbly smoking
    —they had moccasins to their feet, and large thick blankets hang-
    ing from their shoulders.
On a bank lounged the trapper—he was drest mostly in skins—his
    luxuriant beard and curls protected his neck—he held his bride
    by the hand.

Except as part of the tremendous sweep of *Song of Myself,* from which this comes, it is not especially emotion-arousing. Yet if it has the regularity tendency of verse, rather than the variety of prose, it is verse, and not poetry to us. Analysis and scansion reveal that it has a definite regularity-tendency. Note the relative parallelism of these parts of it:

> I saw the marriage of the trapper
> in the open air in the far west. . . .
> Her father and his friends sat near,
> cross-legged and dumbly smoking—
> they had moccasins to their feet. . . .
> blankets hanging from their shoulders.
> On a bank lounged the trapper—
> he was dressed mostly in skins— . . .
> curls protected his neck—
> he held his bride by the hand.

These excerpts indicate that this passage, which on first glance seemed to be prose, is in reality dominantly accent verse, with three accents to most of the unit passages. It is definitely verse, whether regarded as free verse or accent verse—for Whitman's inner ear was attuned to an ingrown sense of that rhythm-repetition which constitutes verse, and he weighed each line for its rhythm, weighing it both against the variety of prose and, equally, against the tom-tom regularity of metric verse, which he had tried first, with no success. We cannot find examples of prose easily in Whitman.

But here, in my collected poems, *The Glory Road,* is an experimental passage that is definite prose, and is meant as such:

Let's talk turkey, Tom Benton. Go make toothpaste, if you want three squares a day!

Squidjum Toothpaste, manufactured by the Thomas H. Benton Company, Rump-rump-rump-rump, Indiana and New York, one billion tubes a year, made from the youngest leaves of the finest tobacco grown, containing vitamins A to Z, nature's supreme laxative, and that cooling 5-out-of-every-5 menthol and NO CARBON KNOCKS! One billion tubes a year. On every tube a toll, a penny, almost a penny, a billion pennies a year, for income tax that makes, Christ. . . .

This is not imbedded in light verse, but in bitter satire, in an experimental form which a creator has a right to devise, whether it succeeds or not. There are passages in Stephen Vincent Benet's *John Brown's Body* that are intentional prose. Other experimental verse is apparently prose, and not verse. Thus Walter Conrad Arensberg's *Ing:*

> Ing? Is it possible to mean *ing?*
> Suppose
> > for the termination in *g*
> > > a disoriented
> > > series
> > of the simple fractures
> > > in sleep
> > > > Soporific
> > has accordingly a value for soap
> > > so present to
> > > sew pieces.
> > > And *p* says: peace is.

Mina Loy's *Love Song* is technically prose:

> Spawn of fantasies
> Sitting the appraisable
> Pig Cupid   his rosy snout
> Rooting erotic garbage
> "Once upon a time"
> Pulls a weed   white star-topped
> Among wild oats sown in mucous membrane.

Marianne Moore is famous for her device of setting prose in formal, indented stanza form, a device applauded by some. E. E. Cummings certainly can achieve the variety of prose in some of his lines:

> a: crimbflitteringish is arefloatsis ing-
> fallall! mil, shy milbrightlions
> my (hurl flicker handful
> in) dodging are shybrigHteyes is crum bs (111) if, ey Es

And he has furnished extremer examples. It is enough to say that all this use of prose is legitimate enough, as a device whose effectiveness depends upon its reception. But it should never be confounded with verse.

If the product is not meter, accent verse, or prose, it is free verse. This at least limits our terrain.

The best springboard for an understanding of the subject is a few classic examples. But first, one final warning:

IV. *Don't be misled by false definitions of free verse, making its requirements more difficult than other poetry.*

The latest *Britannica* says of free verse: "The theory upon which it rests is that poetry depends upon the substance rather than the form. The free verse writer seeks to isolate the essential, and convey it to the reader stripped and absolute. The result will be differentiated from prose not so much by its quality of song as by reality captured in a lightning-flash." With all due respect to Humbert Wolfe, who wrote this, it no more differentiates free verse from other verse than it distinguishes lightning-flashes from stale Stilton. It is true of certain limited groups of free verse writers, or so they state. It has been true of certain esoteric groups of metric practitioners. The free-verse writer seeks these factors—namely, an isolated essential, and its conveyance to the reader stripped and absolute—no more and no less than other poets. An epic in free verse, a conceivable and potentially effective product, would hardly require a succession of unintermittent lightning-flashes. Free verse is merely poetry freed of certain precise rhythmic conventions. Remembering this will make the task of writing it far easier.

It would be more accurate to say that free verse is poetry without formalized rhythmic ornamentation. Its advocates hold, not

without reason, that the use of any and every formalized ornament to that extent alters, warps and dilutes the original flow of
poetic inspiration: the actual thing the poet wished to say. No
matter how attractive the formalized ornaments may be, advocates of free verse say that the added accuracy and unwarped utterance of the free verse more than makes up for the lack of formalized ornamentation.

Since the verse lacks the gauds and trinkets of other poetry, it
must make up for this by a deeper sincerity and importance, or a
more pleasing emotional appeal in some other way, in any mood
ranging from the lightest flippancy to the heaviest tragedy. Shelley
said of heroic blank verse that it was no shelter for mediocrity.
This is even truer of free verse. It is no shelter for anything;
it is an opportunity for the direct utterance of pure poetry, in
any mood.

THE RHYTHM OF NOTABLE FREE VERSE

As an aid to rhythmic analysis, scansion is indispensable. To
arrive at the actual rhythm of free verse, however, the result of
the scansion may have to be surveyed from a new slant, a larger
vista, since the repetition element may have some far wider basis
than a mere repetition of ta TUM, ta TUM or TUM ta ta, TUM
ta ta, or even BOOM, BOOM, BOOM, BOOM. It may be a repetition of larger rhythmic units, or some subtle repetition within
the scansion scheme. It may elude us at first, but ultimately it
will tend to become clear.

Here is the opening of Whitman's *Out of the Cradle Endlessly
Rocking,* its very title a poem:

> Out of the cradle, endlessly rocking,
> Out of the mockingbird's throat, the musical shuttle,
> Out of the Ninth-month midnight,
> Over the sterile sands and the fields beyond.

For scansion, not wholly natural, but in the direction of metric
feet, this might give:

> Out of the / cradle, / endlessly / rocking,
>
> Out of the / mockingbird's / throat, the / musical / shuttle,
>
> Out of the / Ninth-month / midnight,
>
> Over the / sterile / sands and the / fields be- / yond,

Eight dactyls; seven trochees, which fit always with dactyls, since both progress from accent to unaccent; one spondee, always interchangeable with either; one catalectic trochee or dactyl at the end: this is verse beyond all argument. Its actual dominant device is a repetition of a definite rhythmic group:

> out of the cradle   endlessly rocking
> Out of the mocking   musical shuttle
> out of the Ninth-month   over the sterile

Out of the sixteen feet, twelve (six groups of two each) follow this precise pattern, except for the spondee in *Ninth-month*. Thus is a usage comparable to Browning's repetition of the rhythm of *Lips to the cup* (choriamb or trochee-iamb) in *Cavalier Tunes,* already quoted. Moreover, the foot count per line is: 3,5,3,5—more regularity. This should properly be described as accent verse, or as metric verse with the permissible variation of using dactyl or trochee at will. It is not free verse.

We have already found out that the bird's carol, from the same poem, is either loose metric verse or excellent accent verse. Thus two dominant portions of this poem are not free verse. It may be used in other portions, but the outstanding parts of the poem are not free verse.

Take the opening of *When Lilacs Last in the Dooryard Bloomed,* the great Lincoln threnody:

When li- / lacs last / in the door / yard bloom'd,

And the great / star ear- / ly droop'd / in the wes- / tern sky / in the
    night,

I mourn'd, / and yet / shall mourn / with ev- / er return- / ing spring.

This is an utterly different rhythm: eight iambs, five anapests (which are akin to iambs, in moving from unaccent toward accent), and three spondees, interchangeable with either. The feet per line are 4,6,6—a definite uniformity. Again we have less accent verse than a permissible variation in metric verse, the *ad lib* interweaving of iambs and anapests in any order the poet prefers. But it is not free verse. It is a tight repetition of elements moving from unaccent to accent, just as the first example was of one moving from accent to unaccent.

Now let us take the natural scansion of the opening of Hamlet's most famous soliloquy. The one device of reading that you should remember, is that a word repeated soon after its first appearance (*be*), when used unemphatically, does not receive an accent. This would give us:

> To bé, / or nót tŏ bĕ. / Thát / ĭs thĕ quéstiŏn.
>
> Whéthĕr / 'tĭs nóblĕr / ĭn thĕ mínd / tŏ súffĕr
>
> Thĕ slíngs / ănd árrŏws / ŏf ŏutrágeŏus / fórtŭne,
>
> Ŏr tŏ táke árms / ăgáinst / ă séa / ŏf tróublĕs. . . .

This is far freer than either example from Whitman. It is opened by seven different types of feet—a feat in itself. Here we have, instead of the 20 iambs promised by the pattern, 4 iambs, 4 amphibrachs, 1 anapest, 2 trochees, 1 single-accented syllable, and 4-syllabled feet, unnamed in classic prosody: 16 feet, where 20 were promised. There is one definite regularity unmentioned. Each line has precisely eleven syllables. But this no more makes verse than prose written with the same convention: except in France and Japan, where it is a convention of verse. This is free verse. And it is written by Shakespeare, not Whitman. It might be loosely called accent verse (for evidently the submerged accent verse helps motivate such excessive variation); but the absence of end-stopped lines, and the absence of any definite pattern of so many beats to the line, forbids our calling it this properly. No, it is free verse.

The essence of free verse, technically, is a verse more regular in rhythm than prose, that does not have a definite accent pattern (so many accents to the line) or a definite metric pattern, with such variations and alternations and interweavings of metric feet as metric prosody and use permits. The lines from Shakespeare qualify; the lines from Whitman do not. We must apply this test to each example offered as free verse, to see whether or not it comes within that category; and, when it does, we must then try to ascertain just how this variation in rhythm, more regular than prose, less regular than accent or metric verse, is arrived at.

Here is the opening of Carl Sandburg's *Chicago*, naturally scanned:

Hog Butcher / for the world,

Tool Maker, / Stacker / of Wheat,

Player / with Railroads / and the Nation's / Freight Handler,

Stormy, / husky, / brawling,

City / of the Big / Shoulders:

Here we have 7 trochees, 3 antibacchiuses, 2 anapests, 1 iamb, 1 amphibrach, 1 unnamed 4-syllabled foot. It is not trochaic verse with metric variations; for these variations exceed any limits that metric prosody permits. Four lines have 3 accents each; yet the vital central one has 5; and it is doubtful if it would be accurate to call it accent verse, though that is permissible, once the scansion is understood. This may properly be called free verse. It should be noticed that the fourth line consists of three natural trochees. This sort of usage is as much at home in free verse as it is in good prose.

How exquisitely different is his gemlike *Fog:*

It sits / looking

over the harbor / and city

on silent / haunches

and then / moves on.

Two accents to each line, yes: this may have been the poet's intended convention. This would make it accent verse. There seems small reason to deny its being called free verse, if that is your decision. Where used with complete naturalness, there are cases where the poem seems to fit accurately into either category. For all the freedom of rhythm here, complete accuracy would list this as accent verse.

Many of Sandburg's best liked poems furnish rich food for study in the fluid rhythms possible to free verse, and at times to accent verse. He can use the forms for the softest and most melting music, as in *Cool Tombs:*

Pocahontas' body, lovely as a poplar, sweet as a red haw in November or a paw-paw in May, did she wonder, does she remember? . . . in the dust, in the cool tombs?

He can strengthen to any desired extent, as in *Prayers of Steel:*

Lay me on an anvil, O God!
Beat me and hammer me into a steel spike.
Drive me into the girders that hold a skyscraper together.
Take red-hot rivets and fasten me into the central girders.
Let me be the great nail holding a skyscraper through blue nights into
    white stars.

He can swing into biting slang, as in *Cahoots:*

Play it across the table.
What if we steal this city blind?
If they want anything let 'em nail it down.

Nothin' ever sticks to my fingers, nah, nah, nothin' like that,
But there ain't a law we got to wear mittens—huh?—is there?
Mittens, that's a good one—mittens!
There oughta be a law everybody wears mittens.

Rhythmically, this is free verse, rather than prose. Yet the poet, once he understands his technique, may intersperse prose with his verse, wherever it suits his purpose and clarifies his meaning.

Here is a soft lyric, my *Springpiece:*

The strayed cherry tree,
Bewildered by red-brick walls,
In the lost bystreet,
Is dusted with green.

Its white blossoms push
Long and scented fingers
Into the liquid air.

Clouds of white butterflies
Silently drift,
Like loosened and breathing petals
Seeking the sun.

This is definitely free verse. It illustrates a device more common in free verse than in accent verse, and impossible in precise metric verse: the occurrence of two or more accents together (*stráyed chér-, réd-brick wálls, lóst bý-, white blós-.*) It is, of course, used in metric verse as a permissible variation.

This and similar devices open to free verse can be learned only through much scansion and analysis. So long as verse has more regularity than the rhythm of prose, and lacks the definite accent or metric pattern, it is technically free verse.

LINE LENGTH IN VERSE

There is a plausible theory, which Arthur Guiterman has ably advocated, that the normal line length of any culture or period is based upon the normal breath exhaled by the reader or chanter of poetry, before inhaling again. According to this, the Grecian norm, which the Latins adopted, was the full six-foot dactylic line, and this indicates that the norm was arrived at by a race of full-chested warrior chanters or rhapsodes. The lyric poets, less full-chested, invented the briefer lines—this indicating their less Herculean physiques. The alliterative 4-accent line of the Anglo-Saxons and their successors, the early English, was less lengthy than the Greeks; which should mean that the bards or reciters of these races were less full-chested than the Greeks. At this, we look sceptical. As before, briefer lyric lines came in. The ballad was originally in the briefer 4-accent meter, and developed into the 4,3 lines: not a 7-accent line, as incorrectly assumed by later commentators; for, if it had been so, by this theory there would have been established a sudden increase in chest-expansion measurement among the British after the early period, and history gives no indication of, or reason for, any such thoractic enlargement. The norm in English versification became fixed, about the time of the Elizabethan Age, by the 5-foot iambic line; and this continues the norm down to today. With Walt Whitman, a vaster line length than any yet encountered is reached, which would indicate a huge chest expansion in the perigrinating Long Island carpenter and printer. A modern tendency shows a more narrow-chested norm than any of these:

> The noose draws tighter;
> This is the end;
> I'm a good fighter,
> But a bad friend;
> I've played the traitor
> Over and over;
> I'm a good hater,
> But a bad lover.
> *Peregrine,* ELINOR WYLIE

Elinor Wylie said precisely this too often in passionate prose, for us to doubt its authentic self-portraiture.

This theory overlooks one important element appearing early

and widely, and reappearing constantly, in the development of our versification: the pause, cesura, division into hemistiches, or section of the line, found definitely in classic verse and Anglo-Saxon and old English alliterative verse; and less formally in early English iambic pentameters. This pause should indicate a breathing-space, and tends to negative or at least half the entire theory.

Line-length in verse depended originally upon the group of musical bars taken as the norm of the tune. When poetry divorced itself from music, the old normal line remained, as a vestige or hangover: a venerable practice continued for its venerability, although the reason for it had vanished. What, then, is to determine the line-length of verse as written today, primarily to be read or spoken, rather than sung?

Shakespeare, a typical example, commenced with a vestigial line-length of ten or eleven syllables, unaccent-accent in pattern, of the general movement of:

> Let me play the fool:
> With mirth and laughter let old wrinkles come,
> And let my liver rather heat with wine
> Than my heart cool with mortifying groans.
> Why should a man, whose blood is warm within,
> Sit like his grandsire carved in alabaster?
> *The Merchant of Venice, I, i*

Soon enough he had matured into:

> A malady most incident to maids;
> Bold oxlips and the crown imperial;
> Lilies of all kinds, the flower-de-luce being one.

But by this time he was in revolt against the vestigial convention, and he lined this:

> A malady
> Most incident to maids; bold oxlips and
> The crown imperial; lilies of all kinds,
> The flower-de-luce being one.

This is not to be read by the actor as it is printed. The printing is a mere skeleton of the metric pattern, and the actual speech pattern slashes boldly across it, approximating the former version of these lines. There is clearly no gain in a line-division which is illogical and not intended to be followed in reading or speaking. What, then, *is* the logical line-division?

The problem of line-length in free verse is an accentuated phrasing of the more general problem. For free verse throws overboard all such conventions as unnatural line-division, and leaves the poet free to terminate his lines where he chooses.

The answer should depend upon the poet's objective. If this is to give the poem the natural rhythm of speech, the line will end where there is a natural pause. This is the general practice of Whitman, Sandburg, James Oppenheim, and so many more. In *Cool Tombs,* Sandburg sets up his entire stanza as one prose paragraph, leaving the reader to divide it into briefer sections (comparable to lines) where the rhythms of speech naturally find a pause. Read this naturally:

I had visited her often; long had sought, with vain endeavor, her obdurate heart to soften; but she answered, "Never, never." Then it softened and ran widely, like an ink-drop on a blotter. I ceased labor, tasted idly, found it bitter, and forgot her.

Read this naturally, and then divide it into lines where the natural conversational rhythm conditions a pause. The rhyme, in this instance, merely corroborates the otherwise natural division. As so read, we must have:

> I had visited her often,
> Long had sought, with vain endeavor,
> Her obdurate heart to soften;
> But she answered, "Never, never."
>
> Then it softened and ran widely,
> Like an ink-drop on a blotter.
> I ceased labor, tasted idly,
> Found it bitter and forgot her.

And so we have one of Gamaliel Bradford's sharp little lyrics, lined logically, as he lined it. Note that it is poetry in either typography; it is not the line division which makes it poetry or verse. This was merely the poet's convenient skeletonizing method of reminding himself of stanza form, rhyme demands, and so on. Here we have metric verse with end-stop lines. The preferred practice of free verse is to let the lines be end-stopped, if line-division be used; instead of the more natural typography found in *Cool Tombs, The Glory Road* collection, and most prose. Break your line, then, if you seek the natural effect, where the natural pause in the poem comes. This will give you, as a rule, an irregular line-length, permissible and indeed to be expected in good free verse.

Another convention permits line-breaks wherever the poet's whim dictates, or for some especial reason of emphasis or the like. At times, this means line-division at an unnatural place in the meaning. An extreme example is Marianne Moore's *My Apish Cousins:*

> Winked too much and were afraid of snakes. The zebras,
> supreme in
> Their abnormality; the elephants with their fog-colored skin
> And strictly practical appendages
> Were there, the small cats and the parrakeet,
> Trivial and humdrum on examination, destroying
> Bark and portions of the food it could not eat.

It is Miss Moore's prerogative to make such line divisions, if she desires. It is any reader's prerogative to dislike them, as illogical and unbeneficial. Alfred Kreymborg in *Old Manuscript* uses an astringent line-division, presumably for emphasis:

> The sky
> is that beautiful old parchment
> in which the sun
> and moon
> keep their diary.

There is at least logic in this, even if it is a logic that the reader may not like. It is a chestnut that such line-division comes from the magazine custom of paying so much per line. It is more to the point that, when periodical publication is desired, there are certain conventions of line-division which editors prefer: usually pat little lyrics, with not more than three or four feet to the lines, with not more than a dozen to two dozen lines, and with a definite rhyme scheme, deftly handled. Where the periodical market is aimed for, this should be taken into account.

The right method is the method which will convey the effect the versifier desires. The natural typography of prose, the natural line-division or word-division of speech, or some artificial varia-tion, for some personal reason of the poet's—all three are open to the writer of free verse, and indeed of all verse.

WRITING FREE VERSE

In writing free verse, the prohibitions are more emphatic than the commands. It must not have a definite accent nor metric pattern, nor the rhythmic variety of prose. With these areas walled off, the poet or versifier is at liberty to produce whatever his inner music and inspiration dictate. Whether inspiration be a wind blowing from without or, as psychologists state, the speech of the unconscious, more or less altered by the consciousness, the result, if the three walled areas are avoided, will be free verse; and, if the emotions are tapped deeply enough, it will also be poetry.

This may seem the hardest goal in versification that has yet been given, because of its indefiniteness. Consider for a moment that prose is as indefinite in rhythm as free verse; it is nevertheless true that writing prose is not a difficult chore. Once the technique of writing free verse becomes habitual, it is easier to write than any of the other forms of verse; and the product should rise above verse to poetry quite as often. And if, in spite of the effort to avoid turning out prose, accent verse, or metric verse, the result should be classifiable under one of these three, it is still good as that sort of product. There is no simpler and more definite way of wording the method of writing free verse. Avoid the other domains, and write ahead; and the result should be free verse, either verse or poetry.

Take any theme, to be done in free verse—say a longing to return home. Let the verse come as naturally as the heart desires this return:

> Out of the long agony of separation,
> Out of the bleak years split from the home nest,
> Drawn by the bright glow from its ancient summons,
> I have returned,
> And life sings again.

This was improvised, and is at least free verse.

Master this form, as an exercise at least, before returning to the more artificial forms. If it presents difficulties, choose definite examples of free verse, and parody them naturally, syllable by syllable, until the technique tends to be habitual. The time comes to every poet when no artificiality is desired, so imperative is the bald, stark word that must be spoken. Be prepared against that hour.

RHYME IN FREE VERSE

The poet or versifier is at liberty to rhyme free verse, as much as any other verse. Its innate naturalness may be regarded as an argument against adding the artificiality of rhyme. There are no famous users of rhyme in free verse, so far. In every such instance, the choice belongs to the individual versifier.

IV

RHYME AND OTHER SOUND-REPETITION DEVICES

SOUND-REPETITION DEVICES IN VERSIFICATION

THE repetition element appearing in the rhythm of verse is a natural result of increased emotion; and rhythm tends to grow more and more repetitive as the emotions mount toward the boiling-point. Later, repetition in verse formalized into various conventions, based upon simple fundamentals of psychology: What one likes, one wants to have repeated. Repetition of what one likes is intensifiedly pleasing. What one likes is remembered. What one likes and is repeated is intensifiedly remembered. Repetition was thus natural; emotionally satisfying; and a mnemonic device.

Repetition is entirely natural. Nature moves in relatively repetitional rhythms. Bird songs and animal cries tend to use repetition. Heartbeats and other natural rhythms use it.

The repetition so far considered has related to rhythm: the flow of the pattern of accented and unaccented sounds, or of sounds based on quantity, number of syllables, bisection of each line unit, parallellism in meaning, or some other phenomenon not primarily differentiating between the sounds themselves. But this ignores that vital consideration, the sounds themselves. It was inevitable that the principle of repetition should be applied to the sounds themselves, which constituted the words.

The first and most obvious type of sound repetition is of complete words, and then of phrases, clauses, sentences, and so on. The echo, in nature, does this unemotionally; but man's emotions automatically use it.

I'm calling on you to fight for liberty, liberty, liberty! . . .

Englande!—Englande!—Englande!—Englande!

Marchaunt Adventurers, ALFRED NOYES

[182]

> Then I wish I was in Dixie, away, away!
> In Dixie land I'll take my stand,
> To live and die in Dixie;
> Away, away, away down South in Dixie!
> Away, away, away down South in Dixie!

So far, this sound repetition has been without planning. In actual speech and verse, various parts or elements of words happened to be repeated, in other words; and those repetitions that were found emotionally or esthetically pleasing were retained and elaborated. The two sound elements in words are vowels and consonants. Which of these do you hear most clearly; or do you hear both with equal facility?

You may test this, just as you may test which eye you focus with. Which of the following four groups of words seem most pleasing, when you read them or read them aloud?

ping-pong, Peter Piper, put your pet in the pink parlor,

hate, flame, shape, laid, Dane, raise, brazen, hating, fated,

ant, saint, went, hint, pint, appoint, canter, hunter, winter,

keep, heap, sleep, creep, weep, keeping, sleeping, weeping

The first and third of these, called respectively *alliteration* and *consonance,* became formalized conventions in lands where consonants were heard more clearly than vowels: that is, in the more northerly lands, which accentuate and clip off consonantal endings on words, due no doubt to the long periods of chill air. The second, called *assonance,* became a formalized convention in lands where vowels were heard more clearly than consonants: in meridional or sub-tropical lands, where the tendency is to keep the mouth open after every consonant, for a terminal vowel: "I tell-a you, Mr. Police-a, I make-a no fight-a." The fourth of these, called *rhyme,* flourishes most widely where both consonants and vowels are heard relatively equally.

It must be emphasized that these conventions grew up naturally, culled from word-usages found pleasing, depending on the locality. Speakers automatically and without preconception first coupled *weal and woe, life and liberty, bag and baggage,* before this became so generally appreciated that it crystallized into the convention of alliteration. Intermittent use bred repeated use,

[183]

and then a usage elaborated into a rigid convention of verse. The same was true of assonance, consonance and rhyme. In general, such conventions could only be transplanted to a new locality if its natural speech stressed the sound-elements used in the repetition. Thus assonance could never flourish in a region which heard vowels only lightly; or alliteration or consonance in the easy-going tropics, where consonants were things to sigh over and forget.

The formalized types of sound repetition are five in number:

1. Direct repetition of words, phrases, clauses, sentences, etc., or of these only slightly changed.
2. Repetition of the letters introducing accented syllables, or alliteration. Out of this grew repetition of non-accented initial consonantal sounds, and of consonantal sounds closely related, called phonetic syzygy.
3. Repetition of the dominant vowel in words, assonance.
4. Repetition of the dominant terminal consonants in words, or consonance.
5. Repetition of the dominant vowels and terminal consonants, or rhyme.

1. DIRECT REPETITION OF WORDS, PHRASES, ETC.

It may be surprising that there is a large body of familiar songs, which most of us may assume contain rhyme, but which are entirely unrhymed: that is, they are blank verse, in the technical sense. These are the bulk of the Negro spirituals and shout-songs. In these, the element of repetition of words and groups of words is so omnipresent, that our ears, accustomed to rhyme, find nothing missing in them. A typical example is *Standing in the Need of Prayer:*

> It's me, it's me, it's me, O Lord,
> And I'm standing in the need of prayer,
> > O Lord,
> It's me, it's me, it's me, O Lord,
> And I'm standing in the need of prayer.
>
> 'Tain't my brother nor my sister, but it's me, O Lord,
> Standing in the need of prayer,
> > O Lord,
> 'Tain't my brother nor my sister, but it's me, O Lord,
> And I'm standing in the need of prayer.

Examples could be multiplied indefinitely:

> Sometimes I feel like a motherless child,
> Sometimes I feel like a motherless child,
> Sometimes I feel like a motherless child,
>> A long way from home,
>> A long way from home.
>
> True believer, true believer,
>> A long way from home.
>
> Sometimes I feel like an eagle in the air, etc.

Or this delightful Creole mellow, from Kennedy's collection:

> I don't want to be buried in a storm,
>> O Lordie,
> Don't want to be buried in a storm,
> O Angel, O Angel,
> I don't want to be buried in a storm.
>
> Dig my grave with a golden spoon,
>> O Lordie, etc.

These can rise to the utmost elaboration, as in *Done Found My Lost Sheep, Somebody's Knocking at Your Door.* Other familiar examples are: *I Couldn't Hear Nobody Pray, You May Bury Me in the East, I'm So Glad Trouble Don't Last Always, Crucifixion, Were You There?, Stand Still Jordan, Roll Jordan Roll, Inch Song. Scandalize My Name* nears rhyme, in the stanzas only—mating *hand, name:* neither assonance or consonance, yet with a vowel and consonantal syzygy too definite to be accidental.

These spirituals were written by Negroes in an alien language, under the influence of alien rhymed songs—the Episcopalian and other Protestant hymns of the English-speaking masters. The central section alone of *Deep River* shows one rhyming coupling: *feas'* (for *feast*) and *peace. Follow Me,* for all of its symphonic elaboration, has only one similar rhyming couplet in the chorus: *land, hand.* To the contrary, *Swing Low Sweet Chariot* and quite a few more have unrhymed choruses, and a couplet rhyme in the stanzas: *see, me; do, too; down, boun'* (for *bound*) in successive stanzas. *Joshua Fit the Battle of Jericho* and *Nobody Knows the Trouble I've Seen* are two more in the same pattern. It is not easy to find an authentic spiritual or shout-song with rhyme appearing in both stanza and chorus. The norm is mere word or phrase repetition; and this satisfies the hearer as fully as if rhyme were present.

We found the same device in Tennyson's *Charge of the Light Brigade:*

> Cannon to right of them,
> Cannon to left of them,
> Cannon in front of them
> Volleyed and thundered.

Here there is no attempt at rhyme; for *right, left,* and *front* do not rhyme; nor can the addition of the unaccented *of them* to each word alter its essential non-rhyming nature. We can go much further back in English poetry, and find the device a familiar one. In the lush Elizabethan period, Bartholomew Griffin constructed a super-sonnet of fifteen lines, every one ending on the sound *more:*

> Yea, let me sigh, weepe, waile, crye evermore;
> For she doth pitie my complaints no more
> Than cruell Pagan, or the savadge Moore;
> But still doth add unto my torments more,

and so on. Another of his sonnets ends every one of its fourteen lines on *heart.* But these are mere eccentricities on a form using another repetition convention, rhyme; and found few imitators.

When we come to *Mother Goose,* we find repetition as prominent as rhyme. Remove it, and much of the charm of the glorious old collection would be lost. It is impossible to do more than list a few of the familiar favorites where it is dominant: *Hark, Hark, the Dogs Do Bark;*

> Pease porridge hot,
> Pease porridge cold,
> Pease porridge in the pot
> Nine days old.
> Some like it hot,
> Some like it cold,
> Some like it in the pot
> Nine days old.

This has alliteration, as well; but the two need not be joined:

> If I'd as much money as I could spend,
> I never would cry old chairs to mend,
> Old chairs to mend, old chairs to mend,
> I never would cry old chairs to mend.

*Sing, Sing, What Shall I Sing?; Curly Locks, Curly Locks, Wilt
Thou Be Mine; There Was a Crooked Man, and He Went a
Crooked Mile;*

> I love sixpence, pretty little sixpence,
> I love sixpence better than my life;
> I spent a penny of it, I spent another,
> And I took fourpence home to my wife.

*Dance to Your Daddie; There Was a Little Man, and He Had a
Little Gun; What Are Little Boys Made Out Of?; Old Mother
Hubbard* throughout saturated with it;

> Hot Cross Buns!
> Hot Cross Buns!
> One a penny, two a penny,
> Hot Cross Buns!

*A Man of Words and Not of Deeds; A Frog He Would a Wooing
Go; Who Killed Cock Robin?; This Is the House that Jack Built,*
and other accretion rhymes and stories; *Taffy Was a Welshman;
As I Was Going to St. Ives;*

> Needles and pins, needles and pins,
> When a man marries, his trouble begins;

the structure of the rhymed alphabets; *Robin the Bobbin; Simple
Simon; To Market, To Market, to Buy a Fat Pig; The Lion and
the Unicorn; Sing a Song of Sixpence; There Was an Old Woman,*
ending—

> Home went the old woman all in the dark,
> Tra, la, la-la-la-la-la.
> Up got the little dog, and he began to bark,
> Tra, la, etc.
> He began to bark, and she began to cry,
> Tra, la, etc.
> "Dearie me, O dearie me, this is none of I!"
> Tra, la, la-la-la-la-la.

All the singing games, *London Bridge Is Falling Down, Here We
Go Round the Mulberry Bush, Looby Lou, Oats Peas Beans and
Barley Grow* and the familiar rest of them. Here is every sort of
repetition: of words, phrases, constructions, sentences, meaningless refrains. In *Mother Goose,* it was commonly used with rhyme,
though not always; but we have found that rhyme is not essential
for its efficacy. The device became almost universal in English

popular verse of this type; but remained so varied that it never became a formula, as it did in such formal verse as the triolet, rondeau, villanelle, ballade and the like. Repetition of words and groups of words was effective; that was enough.

English lyric poetry came in with *Summer Is I-Comen In,* with its significant refrain "Loud sing cuckoo!" The ballad refrains, perhaps commencing with tags of Latin whose meaning was not familiar to the people, soon was secularized into meaningless syllables: *Tra, la, la-la-la-la; Binnorie, O Binnorie; Fol de rol* with countless variants; *Heigh-ho, Says Rowley.* Remember the significant use of the repetition refrains in the ballad *Edward, Edward,* in the tendency toward refrains with meaning. Much of this, as was to be expected, bears the overtone of something to be sung: as if the refrain were to be sung by the chorus, and the progressive development by the soloist. This is typical of many of the Negro spirituals we have already considered. The use of a repeated chorus, or refrain to songs, rose at times from a mere repetition to a repeated or slightly altering chorus that carried on the story, as in *Heaven Will Protect the Working Girl, The Rose Bush,* and so many more. At its jolliest, the refrain is largely meaningless, as in *Camptown Races,* by Stephen Foster:

> Camptown ladies sing this song,
>   Doodah, doodah,
> Camptown racetrack five miles long,
>   O doodah day.
> Went down there with my hat caved in,
>   Doodah, doodah,
> Come back home with my pocket full of tin,
>   O doodah day.
>
> *Chorus:* Gwine to run all night,
>   Gwine to run all day,
> Bet my money on the bobtailed nag,
>   Who's gwineter bet on the gray?

Here, as often, the internal structure bears incremental repetition, which progresses in meaning: "Gwine to run all" being of this nature, with the progression in *night,* followed by *day.* The repetition of the chorus in songs now marks most popular songs, and many of the concert, upper-bracket type.

Formal French verse, which we will come to later, adopted an elaborate use of the refrain—that is, of direct repetition of words and word-groups—often with development in meaning. Compare the refrain,

> A pitcher of mignonette
> In a tenement's highest casement,

in the triolet by H. C. Bunner, reappearing as the fourth, seventh and eighth lines—the triolet pattern. Rondel, rondeau and roundel are starred by refrain use and elaboration. The villanelle uses two lines as its refrains, together, twice alternating, brought together at the end. The rondeau redoublé and the glose use a refrain of four lines cleverly repeated. The sestina, even when unrhymed, has as its device the repetition in 39 lines of 6 terminal words, each appearing in 7 specified places. The ballade and its offspring fling one line back at us with high effectiveness: "Into the night go one and all." And these, commencing as verses to be sung, soon developed into verses to be read or recited primarily. Such Italian forms as the crown of sonnets and the sonnet redoublé use, respectively, the last line of each sonnet for the first line of the next, terminating the seventh in the first form with line 1 of the first; and, in the second form, letting lines 1 through 14 of the first sonnet reappear as the terminal lines of the next fourteen sonnets. Such are the intricate uses to which direct repetition of words and groups of words has been put.

The uses of less formalized word repetition are too multifold and widespread to be more than commented on. Lines like—

> Break, break, break,
> On thy cold gray stones, O sea.
> > *Song, from The Princess,* ALFRED TENNYSON

> Thea, Thea, Thea, where is Saturn?
> > *Hyperion,* KEATS

> A tree's head snaps—and there, there, there, there, there—
> > *Caliban upon Setebos,* ROBERT BROWNING

> Tomorrow and tomorrow and tomorrow
> > *Macbeth,* SHAKESPEARE

> And tomorrow and tomorrow and tomorrow and tomorrow
> > EDNA ST. VINCENT MILLAY

> Stitch, stitch, stitch,
> In poverty, hunger and dirt.
> > *The Song of the Shirt,* THOMAS HOOD

It was Din! Din! Din!
You rascal, where the devil have you been?

Gunga Din, RUDYARD KIPLING

Bryan, Bryan, Bryan, Bryan.

VACHEL LINDSAY

—these and countless others merely indicate how direct repetition still holds its effectiveness.

The intricacy of the repetition can rise through:

O de Glory Road! O de Glory Road!
I'm gwineter drap my load upon de Glory Road! . . .

Cannon to right of them,
Cannon to left of them,
Cannon in front of them
Volleyed and thundered; . . .
Into the jaws of Death,
Into the mouth of Hell
Rode the Six Hundred.

The Charge of the Light Brigade, ALFRED TENNYSON

Ship after ship, the whole night long, their high-built galleons came,
Ship after ship, the whole night long, with her battle-thunder and flame,
Ship after ship, the whole night long, drew back with her dead and her shame.

The Revenge, ALFRED TENNYSON

Listen to the creepy proclamation
Blown through the lairs of the forest nation,
Blown past the white-ants' hill of clay,
Blown past the marsh where the butterflies play,
"Be careful what you do,
Or Mumbo-Jumbo, God of the Congo,
And all of the other Gods of the Congo,
Mumbo-Jumbo will hoo-doo you,
Mumbo-Jumbo will hoo-doo you,
Mumbo-Jumbo will hoo-doo you."

The Congo, VACHEL LINDSAY

They rush in red and purple from the red clouds of the morn,
From temples where the yellow gods shut up their eyes in scorn;
They rise in green robes roaring from the green hells of the sea,
Where fallen skies and evil hues and eyeless creatures be; . . .
They swell in sapphire smoke out of the blue cracks of the ground,
They gather and they wonder and give worship to Mahound.

Lepanto, G. K. CHESTERTON

Then star nor sun shall waken,
Nor any change of light,

> Nor sound of waters shaken,
>   Nor any sound or sight;
> Nor wintry leaves nor vernal,
> Nor days nor things diurnal;
> Only the sleep eternal
>   In an eternal night.
> *The Garden of Proserpine,* ALGERNON SWINBURNE

clear up to the overpowering thunder of:

> Keeping time, time, time,
> In a sort of Runic rhyme,
>   To the throbbing of the bells,
>   Of the bells, bells, bells,
>   To the sobbing of the bells;
> Keeping time, time, time,
>   As he knells, knells, knells,
> In a happy Runic rhyme,
>   To the rolling of the bells,
>   Of the bells, bells, bells,
>   To the tolling of the bells,
>   Of the bells, bells, bells, bells,
>   Bells, bells, bells,
> To the moaning and the groaning of the bells.
> *The Bells,* EDGAR A. POE

The importance of direct repetition of words and groups of words in versification cannot be exaggerated. It can assume any form that the poet's inner ear dictates; and, so long as it is done naturally, it may be enormously effective.

2. REPETITION OF INTRODUCTORY CONSONANTS: ALLITERATION

Alliteration is the repetition of the same sound or sounds at the beginning of two or more words or accented syllables near each other. It could only arise as a convention in a land which put its major emphasis on consonants, rather than on vowels: that is, in a north temperate land, or one further north. The Anglo-Saxon speech developed formal alliteration as one of their three conventions for poetry: the other two being the 4-accent line, and its section or mid-division. When this speech was transplanted into England, it found suitable soil for further growth; and it entered into and flourished in old English verse, as we have seen fully in studying the origin of the ballad and of accent verse in English.

More than this, it entered into the very *warp and woof* of the language: *w*arp and *w*oof being an excellent example of its deep-rooted nature in English. This use of alliteration extends beyond verse into the domain of prose as well. A few of such colloquial alliterative couplings are:

bag and baggage, bed and board, bigger and better, black and blue, cash and carry, do and dare, fire and fury, half and half, hale and hearty, heart and hand, heaven and hell, to have and to hold, in and out, Jack and Jill, might and main, paper and pencil, poet and peasant, right and wrong, rod and reel, shot and shell, stars and stripes, separately and severally, spick and span, time and tide, tried and true, thick and thin, weal or woe; as well as the slogan, Rum, Romanism and Rebellion.

Similes frequently call upon "apt alliteration's artful aid":

blind as a bat, brown as a berry, busy as a bee, clear as crystal, dead as a doornail, dull as dishwater, fit as a fiddle, good as gold, green as grass, hot as Hades, plain as a pikestaff, plump as a partridge, pretty as a picture, proud as a peacock, red as a rose, sweet as sugar, thick as thieves.

Alliteration has even entered into the formation of many words, which have emerged from nonsense or slang into acceptable usage:

chit-chat, dilly-dally, fiddle-faddle, flimflam, flip-flop, knick-knack, pitter-patter, shilly-shally, snickersnee, scrimble-scramble, tick-tock, tittle-tattle, topsy-turvy, wishy-washy.

The ballads, emerging out of the alliterative Old English verse, are naturally packed with vestigial alliteration:

> Child Waters in his *s*table *s*tood
> And *s*troked his milk-white *s*teed;
> To him came a fair yong lady
> As ever did *w*ear *w*oman's *w*eed.
> *Child Waters,* ANONYMOUS

> In *s*ummer when the *sh*aws * be *sh*een **
> And *l*eaves be *l*arge and *l*ong,
> It is *f*ull merry in *f*air *f*orest
> To hear the *f*owlès song.
> *Robin Hood and the Monk,* ANONYMOUS

* Woods.
** Bright.

> As it fell one *h*oly-day, *h*ay-down,
> As *m*any be in the *y*ear,
> When *y*oung *m*en and *m*aids together did go
> Their *m*atins and *m*ass to hear.
> *Lord Musgrave and Lady Barnard,* Anonymous

> "*B*ut wha will *b*ake my *b*ridal *b*read
> Or *b*rew my *b*ridal ale?
> And *wh*a *w*ill *w*elcome my *b*risk *b*ride,
> That I bring o'er the dale?"
> *Fair Annie,* Anonymous

In many of these, the restraint used in earlier verse as to alliteration is gone; if anything, the device is overused.

Alliteration became a tongue-twisting game in *Mother Goose,* as in *Peter Piper Picked a Peck of Pickled Peppers; When a Twister a-Twisting, Will Twist Him a Twist;* and—

> Swan swam over the sea;
> Swan swam back again.
> Swim, swan, swim;
> Well swum, swan.

In addition to others of this type, alliteration appeared often as part of the rhymes:

> Goosey, goosey gander. . . .
> Pease porridge in the pot. . . .
> Malisons, malisons, mair than ten. . . .
> Daffy-down-dilly has come up to town. . . .
> Wee Willie Winkie runs through the town. . . .
> Around the green gravel the grass grows green. . . .
> Deedle deedle dumpling, my Son John. . . .
> One misty moisty morning. . . .
> Georgie, Porgie, pudding and pie. . . .

> This is the cock that crowed in the morn,
> That waked the priest all shaven and shorn,
> That married the man all tattered and torn.
> *The House that Jack Built*

There is one famous stunt poem in English, in which the words in each successive line begin successively with the letters of the alphabet, the one commencing:

> An Austrian army, awfully arrayed,
> Boldly by battery besieged Belgrade.

Truly the ancient device sank in deep.

[193]

ALLITERATION IN SHAKESPEARE

Alliteration has continued prominent in our poetry, since Anglo-Saxon times. Shakespeare's *Sonnets* are full of it:

> A woman's face, with nature's own hand *p*ainted,
> Hast thou, the *m*aster-*m*istress of my *p*assion.
>
> *xx*

> *L*ike to the *l*ark at break of day arising
> From *s*ullen earth, *s*ings *h*ymns at *h*eaven's gate.
>
> *xxix*

> When to the *s*essions of *sw*eet *s*ilent thought. . . .
> And with old *w*oes new *w*ail my dear time's *w*aste.
>
> *xxx*

> *Ful*l many a glorious *m*orning have I seen
> *Fl*atter the *m*ountain-tops with sovereign eye,
> Kissing with *g*olden face the meadows *g*reen.
>
> *xxxiii*

> How careful was I when I *t*ook my way
> Each *tr*ifle under *tr*uest bars to *thr*ust.
>
> *xlviii*

> Tir'd with all these, for restful death I cry,—
> As, to *b*ehold desert a *b*eggar *b*orn,
> And *n*eedy *n*othing trimm'd in jollity,
> And purest *f*aith unhappily *f*orsworn.
>
> *lxvi*

> Give *w*arning to the *w*orld that I am fled
> From this vile *w*orld, with vilest *w*orms to dwell.
>
> *lxxi*

> Upon those *b*oughs which shake against the cold,
> *B*are ruin'd choirs, where late the sweet *b*irds sang.
>
> *xci*

Here, of course, we find the device used more subtly and sparingly than in the obvious folk-verse of *Mother Goose*. The plays never forget the device:

> *G*all of *g*oat, and *sl*ips of yew
> *Sl*iver'd in the moon's eclipse,
> Nose of *T*urk, and *T*artar's lips,
> Finger of *b*irth-strangled *b*abe
> Ditch-*d*eliver'd by a *d*rab.
>
> *Macbeth, IV, i*

The earliest plays, of course, are most surcharged with this venerable device. Thus *The Comedy of Errors* opens:

> *Proceed, Solinus, to procure my fall,*
> *And, by the doom of death, end woes and all.*

The Prologue to *Romeo and Juliet* contains:

> *From forth the fatal loins of these two foes*
> *A pair of star-crossed lovers take their life.*

The ringing rhetoric of the choruses of *Henry V* are full of it:

> *Can this cockpit hold*
> *The vasty fields of France? or may we cram*
> *Within this wooden Q the very casques*
> *That did affright the air at Agincourt?*

So with its rousing speeches:

> *But when the blast of war blows in our ears, . . .*
> *Stiffen the sinews, summon up the blood, . . .*
> *Swilled with the wild and wasteful ocean.*

With typical mastery, Shakespeare satirized the popular fondness for over-alliteration in the delicious parody in *A Midsummer Night's Dream:*

> *Whereat with blade, with bloody baleful blade,*
> *He bravely broach'd his boiling bloody breast. . . .*
> *What dreadful dole is here? . . .*
> *O dainty duck! O dear!*

This is a timely reminder that the unnatural and forced use of alliteration, as of any convention, is destructive to poetic naturalness and effectiveness.

ALLITERATION IN OTHER ENGLISH POETRY

It is unnecessary to run down the gamut of English poetry, to show how ample the use of this device in versification has been. Milton, in the pastoral artificiality of the elegy *Lycidas,* used it:

> *He must not float upon his watery bier*
> *Unwept, and welter to the parching wind.*

Paradise Lost does not disdain it:

> *Of Man's first disobedience, and the fruit*
> *Of that forbidden tree whose mortal taste*
> *Brought death into the World, and all our woe.*

The odes of Keats and Shelley do not scorn it:

> Season of *m*ists and *m*ellow fruitfulness!
> Close bosom-friend of the *m*aturing sun,
> > *To Autumn,* JOHN KEATS

> O *w*ild *W*est *w*ind, thou *b*reath of Autumn's *b*eing!
> > *Ode to the West Wind,* SHELLEY

Another noted example is:

> Where Alph, the sacred *r*iver, *r*an
> Through caverns *m*easureless to *m*an
> > Down to a *s*unless *s*ea. . . .
> As e'er beneath a *w*aning moon was haunted
> By *w*oman *w*ailing for her demon lover. . . .
> Five *m*iles *m*eandering with a *m*azy *m*otion.
> > *Kubla Khan,* SAMUEL TAYLOR COLERIDGE

The famous examples are innumerable:

> And the *s*ilken *s*ad un*c*ertain rustling of each purple *c*urtain
> Thrilled me, *f*illed me with *f*antastic *t*errors never *f*elt be*f*ore.
> > *The Raven,* EDGAR ALLAN POE

> In my sleep I was *f*ain of their *f*ellowship, *f*ain
> Of the liveoak, the *m*arsh and the *m*ain.
> > *The Marshes of Glyn,* SIDNEY LANIER

> When earth's last *p*icture is *p*ainted,
> > And the *t*ubes are *t*wisted and dried,
> When the oldest *c*olor has faded,
> > And the youngest *c*ritic has died.
> > *L'Envoi,* RUDYARD KIPLING

> The *s*plendor falls on castle walls,
> > And *s*nowy *s*ummits old in *s*tory;
> The bright *l*ight shakes across the *l*akes,
> > And the wild cataract *l*eaps in glory.
> > *Song from the Princess,* ALFRED TENNYSON

With Swinburne, alliteration becomes almost a disease—Max Nordau omits the *almost*, and calls it echolalia—so insistently and meltingly does he use it:

> O *g*hastly *g*lories of saints, dead limbs of *g*ibbeted *g*ods! . . .
> *W*aste *w*ater *w*ashes, and tall ships founder, and *d*eep *d*eath waits. . . .
> Rolls, under the *wh*itening *w*ind of the future, the *w*ave of the world.
> > *Hymn to Proserpine*

> > O *g*arment not *g*olden but *g*ilded. . . .

> > O *l*ips full of *l*ust and of *l*aughter. . . .

> All thine the new wine of desire,
>   The *f*ruit of *f*our lips as they clung
> Till the hair and the eyelids took *f*ire,
>   The *f*oam of a serpen*t*ine *t*ongue,
> The *f*roth of the *s*erpents of pleasure,
>   More *s*alt than the *f*oam of the *s*ea,
> Now *f*elt as a *f*lame, now at leisure
>   As wine shed for me. . . .
>
> On the *l*ips and the *l*imbs of thy *l*overs. . . .
>
> The *l*ilies and *l*anguors of *v*irtue,
>   For the *r*oses and *r*aptures of *v*ice.
>
> > > > *Dolores*

Here the combination of singing sounds, alliteration, monotonous rhythmic mastery, have a soporific quality that in the end shrinks the stature of the poet below major ranking. Over and over again his verse is so ornamented that it loses beauty:

> The *m*other of *m*onths in *m*eadow or plain. . . .
>
> With *l*isp of *l*eaves and *r*ipple of *r*ain. . . .
> The *f*aint *f*resh *f*lame of the *y*oung *y*ear *f*lushes
>   From leaf to *f*lower and *f*lower to *f*ruit.
> > > *Chorus from Atalanta in Calydon*
>
> *W*elling *w*ater's *w*insome *w*ord,
>   *W*ind in *w*arm *w*an *w*eather.
> > > *A Child's Laughter*
>
> *B*ird of the *b*itter *b*right gray golden morn,
>   Scarce risen upon the *d*usk of *d*olorous years. . . .
> *Sh*ame *s*oiled thy *s*ong, and *s*ong assoiled thy *sh*ame.
> > > *A Ballade of François Villon*

The device is only valuable, when used with more restraint. Emily Dickinson as a rule used it successfully and naturally:

> > Parting in all we *kn*ow of *h*eaven,
> > And all we *n*eed of *h*ell.

This is the precise interweaving of alliterations, *n,h,n,h,* that we found at the opening of *Beowulf*.

> > In*e*briate of *ai*r am *I*,
> > And *d*ebauchee of *d*ew.

The first of these two lines is interesting. It should be noted that alliteration consists of the identity of consonant sounds, or the absence of any: that is, vowel openings, in alliteration, are used

> > > > [197]

interchangeably. This line has all four syllables vowel-opened, and hence in alliteration: *-e-, -ate, air, I;* but three of the unaccents, *in-, of* and *am,* also start with vowels. Thus seven out of the eight syllables start, from the standpoint of alliteration, with the same sound. Yet we do not get the effect of overuse, as from Swinburne.

Edna St. Vincent Millay is a deft user of it:

> And all but *c*ry with *c*olour! That gaunt *c*rag
> To *c*rush! To *l*ift the *l*ean of that *b*lack *b*luff!

Elinor Wylie's tight-reined passion utilized the device:

> His lustrous *b*ricks are *b*righter than *b*lood,
> His smoking mortar whiter than *b*one. . . .
>
> When *fl*ocks are *f*olded warm,
> And herds to shelter run,
> He *s*ails above the *st*orm,
> He *st*ares into the *s*un.

Rose O'Neill, with her Elizabethan word-music, uses it as naturally as Campion:

> I bring this weight of *s*avage *s*inging here,
> *F*itting for you who *f*east upon *f*ierce things,
> Like to one running *f*rom a wood in *f*ear
> And *t*riumph *t*errible, who strongly *b*rings
> A *b*right *b*east held beneath his rended *b*reast.

Alliteration is a valuable ornament to verse, if it is used naturally and sparingly. Swinburne's overuse of it should be a warning. Its value is in proportion as it fits into the speech-idiom of the language; and hence such devices as interweaving and alternating it, known since Anglo-Saxon versification, are often better than overuse.

DEVICES SIMILAR TO ALLITERATION

Some of these instances of alliteration contain subtler repetitions of consonantal sounds. The one from Shakespeare's Sonnet *xxxiii* couples *full, flatter.* The *Midsummer Night's Dream* example included *bloody, baleful, boiling.* The one from *Paradise Lost* included *first, fruit, forbidden.* The one from *Dolores* coupled *fruit, four, fire, froth;* and *felt, flame.* The second Elinor

Wylie quotation includes *folded, flocks*. These examples are not merely of alliterative repetitions of initial *f, b, f* in the last four. The first one is varied uses of *f* and *l;* the others of *b-l, f-r, f-r, f-l* and *f-l*. The Swinburne example first given, for instance, could have mated *fruit, frore, friar, froth:* obvious alliteration. But notice how he places the consonantal sounds: FRuit, FouR, FiRe, FRoth. It is as if the intermediate vowel was forgotten entirely —and we recall that our analysis indicated that alliteration arose where consonants were emphasized, and vowels unemphasized, and perhaps unnoticed and comparatively unheard; or was slurred over, to permit the expected consonantal coupling. But this is a definite extension of alliteration. This might be called a sort of mosaic alliteration.

The example from Shakespeare's *lxvith* sonnet included:

> As, to *b*ehold desert a *b*eggar *b*orn, . . .
> And purest *f*aith unhappily *f*orsworn.

But the *b* in *behold* is not on an accented syllable, and hence falls outside the strict old rule for alliteration, that it applied only to accented syllables. The same is true of the *f* in *forsworn*. Yet these usages are evidently deliberate, and give an off-accent alliteration that is as subtle and effective as off-accent rhyme. The same is true of the line,

> That did *a*ffright the *a*ir at *A*gincourt.
> *Henry V,* Chorus to *Act I*

where the *a* in *affright* is a similar off-accent alliteration. Poe's "Thrilled me, *f*illed me with *f*antastic terrors" illustrates the same thing; in *fantastic,* the *t* (coupled with the *t* in *terrors*) is the alliteration on the accent; the *f,* coupled with *filled,* is off-accent.

Added to mosaic alliteration and off-accent alliteration, we have yet another usage in some of these lines that must be noted:

> *D*affy-*d*own-*d*illy has come up to *t*own. . . .
> How careful was I when I *t*ook my way
> Each *t*rifle under *t*ruest bars to *t*hrust. . . .
> *T*ired with all *t*hese, for restful *d*eath I cry.

And, in the quotation from *Paradise Lost,* *d*isobedience, *t*hat, *t*ree, *t*aste, *d*eath.

> With *l*isp of *l*eaves and *r*ipple of *r*ain.

Here we have couplings of *d* and *t; t, tr* and *thr; t, th,* and *d;* and *l* and *r.* We are now in a field which is not quite alliteration, and yet partakes of its nature. For this is a repetition of kindred consonantal sounds; and it is subtly satisfying, in cultures where the emphasis is upon the consonants, rather than on the vowels.

We need not delve too deeply into this; for the experts on phonics themselves shift their classifications of consonantal sounds constantly, and this need not trouble the versifier. But there is definite kinship among the sounds in the following groups—with no guarantee that the naming of them clicks with the latest pronouncement in phonics:

Dentals: d, t, th (as in *thin*), TH (as in *though*)
Labials: b, p. (*M* is sometimes added.)
Gutturals or velars: g, k, ng
Labiodentals: f, v
Sibilants: s, z, sh, zh, ch, j
Nasals: m, n, ng
Liquids: l, r

Sidney Lanier gives, as an admirable example of such sound-couplings, this line from one of Daniel's sonnets:

The *d*aily *t*ormen*t* of un*truth.*

Such sound-couplings add, to alliteration, the identities at the beginnings of words or unaccented syllables, as well as sounds at the end (junction consonants) or in the body of words. Here we have a terminal *t* and *th* coupled with the initial *d, t* and *t* in *tr.* The most famous example of this is Tennyson's:

The *m*oan of doves in i*mmem*orial el*m*s,
And *m*ur*m*uring of in*num*erable bees.

For this and the other types of word-couplings, mosaic alliteration and off-accent alliteration, Lanier recommends Sylvester's name, *phonetic syzygy*—taken from Greek words meaning sound-coupling. The simpler English term is certainly more generally comprehensible.

Such sound-couplings will appear, without planning, intermittently in the verse of anyone who writes naturally. They will sound pleasantly in the ear accustomed to emphasizing consonants and the differentiations in their sounds; and, even without knowledge of the precise kinships, they will tend to be preserved by the critical mind. Once they are understood, they may be used as intentionally and successfully as Tennyson did, in the couplet last quoted.

3. REPETITION OF VOWEL SOUNDS: ASSONANCE

In cultures which emphasize vowel sounds rather than consonants—and these include roughly all those grouped around the equator and the nearby subtropical regions—a usage in versification that first appeared intermittently and naturally was singled out for appreciation and formalization: the repetition of important vowel-sounds. So came assonance, which may be defined: *Assonance is the repetition of the last accented vowel (sometimes with all subsequent vowel sounds in the word), in two or more words, with a difference in the consonantal sounds after them.* At first, since there was no emphasis on the consonants, this was not differentiated from rhyme—the same vowel-repetition, with identity of the consonant sounds that followed. But rhyme, of course, is far more limiting than assonance; and so the cultures that emphasized vowels only in the end formalized assonance as identity of the vowel sounds, with differences in the consonantal sounds that followed. Assonance is sometimes called *vowel rhyme*.

It appeared alike in Provençe, early France, and Spain, apparently preceding rhyme in several European languages. There was no tendency, at first, to make the convention any more rigid than was necessary. It is especially notable in French poetry before the twelfth century, culminating in the *Chanson de Roland,* in which all the lines in a *laisse* or stanza had to terminate with the same vowel sound. After 1120, rhyme generally replaced it in France; for the pattern was set by northern France, where the emphasis was chiefly on consonantal sounds. Assonance held its place longer in Provençe; is still far more dominant than rhyme in Spanish poetry; and it is also important in Portuguese, Italian and other Romantic languages. In Irish (Gaelic) poetry it is as important; and this explains why Irish poets writing in English so often automatically use it.

The *Encyclopaedia Britannica* suggests that the Romance languages tend to prefer the correspondence of vowels; the Teutonic languages, of consonants. But this authority fails to understand how inevitable this is, from the influence of geography upon speech. Among the northerly Teutons, where the climate is harsher and colder, the tendency is to shorten the vowels and shut off the words with abrupt explosive consonants; and here we find alliteration and the appearance of that form of consonant-repetition called *consonance,* which we will reach next. Among the races emanating from, or transplanted to, a warmer clime, the tendency is to speak with the mouth relatively open, lazily dwelling on the vowels; and here assonance, or identity in vowels, became the norm, with the consonants regarded as relatively unimportant.

Popular verse in English has long accepted assonance. This may be due in part to the Celtic strain in the race; or this, coupled with a dullness of ear-perception, that fails to observe that rhyme requires a strict identity of consonants following corresponding vowels. Examples from the ballads are:

The Three Ravens: mate, take; feet, keep.
The Twa Sisters: dam, swan.
Lord Thomas and Fair Annet: alane, hame; name, wame (womb).
Fair Margaret and Sweet William: sleep, sheet; ring, in.
Young Waters: feet, deep.
Child Waters: broom, shoon; chin, swim; street, sleep; gates, make.
Robin Hood ballads: thing, behind; gallow, arrow; line, time; Hood, gold; face, was; broom, pound; win, it; ring, in; room, run, noon.

This was certainly not faulty rhyming, in its inception; it was a convention of assonance, or assonance coupled with consonance (some vague repetition of some sound or other being all that was required), which was at first universally followed, by a race to whom rhyme itself was a novelty.

Thus Merrythought, in Beaumont and Fletcher's *The Knight of the Burning Pestle,* sings the famous old song:

> Nutmeg and ginger, cinnamon and cloves,
> And they gave thee thy jolly red nose!

The French language is noted for blurring out consonantal sounds it regards as non-euphonious. In English, we see the tendency in the common pronunciation of *clothes* as if it were *close;* the dropping of the aspirated guttural in *might* and the like, of

the interal *l* in *would* and similar words, and in countless other
examples. The same spirit, which placed the emphasis upon vowels rather than consonants, accounts for the persistence of
assonance in English verse.

   Mother Goose is, as we should have expected, full of examples:

> Goosey, goosey, gander,
> Where shall I wander,
> Upstairs, downstairs,
> In my lady's chamber.

The *gander-wander* coupling have identical terminal consonants
and differing vowels; we will find that called *consonance*. But the
addition of *chamber* is more complicated. As we pronounce it,
the vowel sound is different; hence it is not assonance; and it is
not consonance, for the *-nd* and *-mb* differ. Yet the two are a
definite sound-coupling, the sort of mating that preceded formalized assonance, consonance and rhyme. It is possible, of course,
that, at the time this was first composed, *chamber* was pronounced
similar to the French *chambre;* and this would give us accurate
assonance. Certain couplings, given above, from the Robin Hood
ballads (Hood, gold; face, was; broom, pound; room, run, noon)
are mere sound-couplings, of the cruder type that preceded both
assonance and consonance. Incidentally, Emily Dickinson similarly couples, in place of rhyme:

   pearl, alcohol; inch, experience; death, earth; unmoved, God

These are identical neither in vowel nor in consonants; and yet
the subtle kinship of sound is as obvious to us as it was to this
poet. One of my students once "rhymed," as she thought, *anguish*
and *Flatbush*. Perhaps this goes beyond the bourne of the
pleasing.

   To return to *Mother Goose,* the following are instances of
assonance or the earlier word-couplings from it:

Ride a Cock-Horse: cross, horse
Little Tommie Tittlemouse: fishes, ditches
The Man in the Moon: Norwish, porridge
The North Wind Doth Blow: barn, warm
Pippin Hill: dirty, curtsey
Tom, Tom, the Piper's Son: son, young
Lady-Bird, Lady-Bird: home, gone
Who Killed Cock Robin?:   eagle, needle
Little Tommie Tucker: Tucker, supper, butter.

But, after all, these are not many examples, in a collection so varied and, in the best sense, vulgar. The modern Village Milton often packs his volume with assonances; and in many cases he imagines that these are rhymes, and is quite indignant when he is told that his rhymes are faulty. Thus *Love Among the Mistletoe, and Poems,* by James Byron Elmore, couples:

> gold, soul; street, cheek; Rome, bone; form, born; slope, broke; sweep, meets; wine, unkind; worst, mirth; ve-hemy, Athene, arena, gleamy

One famous quatrain indicates this usage:

> Alcohol is like a snake,
> It can't be kept in bounds;
> It makes of one a perfect wreck,
> A wandering vagrant hound.

Julia A. Moore, the "Sweet Singer of Michigan," perpetrates these rhyming mésalliances, which in essence are assonances or the earlier coupling type:

> abound, town; rhyme, mine; one, home; health, French; received, grieve; send, again; haste, late; out, South; enlist, Wilderness; Infantry, siege; nation, waving; gained it, maintain it,

among hundreds of similar examples. Mary Ann O'Byrne, of Watervliet, New York, in her ten pamphlet volumes before me, couples:

> extreme, seen; stand, damned; gain, claim; sin, them; learn, harm; own, roam; mouth, about; them, men; sing, men; nude, good,

and many more. As attempted rhyme, this is execrable; if used intelligently as assonance—and as a rule not intermixed with perfect rhymes—it is, of course, in most instances acceptable. Yet Edna St. Vincent Millay, in her exquisite *The Poet and His Book,* adds to her rhymes and consonances:

> cupboard, upward; only, homely,

which is assonance used by a master.

George Eliot, in her *Song of Joan* in *The Spanish Gipsy,* sought to reintroduce and popularize assonance in English:

> Maiden crowned with glossy blackness,
> Lithe as panther forest roaming,
> Long-armed naead, when she dances
> On the stream of ether floating,
> Bright, O bright Fedalma!

The device was not well received in English versification, and has had no distinguished followers. It is still prevalent in many songs of the Tin Pan Alley variety, from the hour of Emmett's famous *Dixie,*

> I wish I was in the land of cot*ton,*
> Cinnamon-seed and sandy bot*tom,*

through such combinations as *wicked—ticket* in *Climbing up the Golden Stair, Norfolk—war-talk,* in George M. Cohan's *I Was Born in Virginia,* down to more modern examples of the general tenor of:

> floor, for; shame, rain; girl, world; kissed, this; tune, perfume; childhood, wildwood; love-nest, dove-rest; yes*ter*day-bound, play 'round.

If any versifier desires to use accurate assonance, he would select typical single or masculine assonantal groups following these models:

> bat, slap, ran, sham, hang, grab, crack
> mate, shape, name, gain, tale, wade, take
> head, neck, them, men, step, pet
> need, seek, steam, clean, cheap, meet

With double or feminine endings, we would have such groups as:

> thinning, women, livid, insipid, dizzies
> shopping, bodies, rotting, cottage, knocker
> hoary, hoping, gloaming, moaning, doting
> blackness, trances, hackneyed, mattress, patted, slapping

The device consists in identity of the last accented vowel sound and later vowel sounds; with the consonantal sounds following the last accented vowel sound differing. It does not easily acclimatize itself in English versification, because of our emphasis upon consonantal sounds.

[205]

4. REPETITION OF TERMINAL CONSONANT SOUNDS: CONSONANCE

In our English culture, the emphasis from the start was placed upon consonantal sounds. It is possible that consonance came in independently, as a pleasing device: the repetition of consonantal sounds after the last accented vowel, with a difference in the vowels. But it is more probable that it dated from the efforts of Chaucer and his contemporaries to introduce rhyme from the French, and from the fact that the popular ear, hearing rhyme, did not notice the essential identity of the accented vowels, but assumed that mere identity of consonantal sounds *after* the accented vowels was enough. If this is so, at first consonance and rhyme were used indiscriminately. Soon enough accurate rhyme was isolated by the prosodists, leaving the wider field of consonance to be looked down upon, until its heartening recent revival.

For a definition, we have: *Consonance is the repetition of all consonantal and other sounds after the last accented vowel in two or more words, with a difference in the sound of the accented vowels.* Consonance is also at times called off-rhyme, sour rhyme, and analyzed rhyme. These terms are not appropriate. Consonance appeared slightly more frequently than assonance in the old ballads. From half a dozen of these ballads, we take these examples:

> back, lake; mass, grace; grass, chess; stane, in, son; fast, burst; man, groan, begone; hair, near; queen, syne; smock, work; good, blood; cradle, saddle; middle, girdle.

Three of these, containing in each instance an *r*, are accurately of the cruder sound-coupling that preceded conventionalized consonance. From three of the Robin Hood ballads, we find far more examples:

> hand, found, unbound; knave, have; small, vale, ale; hang, king; had, slade; speak, break; near, briar; tree, high; mean, line; be, they; twin, run; Gisborne, turn; gone, down; two, woe; sod, Hood; foot, boot, shoot; John, stone, gone; steven, heaven.

Consonance fell from popular favor, and for centuries remained an outcast, with two exceptions: so-called "eye-rhymes,"

[206]

which are not rhymes at all, since rhyme is a matter of sound, but which are, of course, acceptable consonance:

> forth, north; earth, hearth; wind, behind; bare, are;

as well as a few, such as *real, steal,* whose negligible eye-rhyme status is indisputable, but which fail completely, because the first is a dissyllable; and the second a monosyllable. The second exception is a group of consonances accepted, because of the rhyming paucity of the language: these applying to important words:

> woman, human; heaven, given; spirit, inherit; bosom, blossom; shadow, meadow; God, road; war, more.

There was also the assonance *is—bliss,* and the more ancient coupling *was—grass,* both permitted for the same reason. It is to be noted that this use of consonance was narrowly limited, and would not have included, for instance, such a consonance as *haven—cloven* to go with the *heaven—given* which was permitted. Yet at any time a poet would use a novel "eye-rhyme" (*oven, cloven*), or even a consonance, if he chose to. For poems are written by poets, not by prosodic rule-makers.

Consonance first emerged, in modern times, in the poems of Emily Dickinson, with tremendous effectiveness:

> Unmoved, she notes the chariot's pausing
> At her low gate;
> Unmoved, an emperor is kneeling
> Upon her mat.
>
> I've seen her from an ample nation
> Choose one;
> Then shut the valves of her attention
> Like stone.

The coupling of *nation* and *attention,* of the more ancient type that preceded both consonance and assonance, indicates that a similar coupling is intended with *pausing* and *kneeling,* which have no identity beyond that of the final unaccented syllable. Crude rhymesters often make this coupling, under the mistaken notion that this constitutes rhyme. Miss Dickinson used it, knowing fully that it was a subtle repetition device, not formalized, yet pleasing. Here are other examples:

> I taste a liquor never brewed
> From tankards scooped in pearl;
> Not all the vats upon the Rhine
> Yield such an alcohol! . . .
>
> I knew not but the next
> Would be my final inch,—
> This gave me that precarious gait
> Some call experience.

Again, we have the subtler earlier coupling, the only identities being of the *-n* and the differing sibilants:

> Forever cherished be the tree,
> Whose apple, Winter warm,
> Enticed to breakfast from the sky
> Two Gabriels yestermorn.
>
> They registered in Nature's book
> As Robin—Sire and Son,
> But angels have that modest way
> To screen them from renown.

Or this:

> What fortitude the soul contains,
> That it can so endure
> The accent of a coming foot,
> The opening of a door!

Note here that both of the consonance terminals open with a *d* sound: *endure* (DYUR) and *door* (DOR). In consonance, initial consonants may be identical—a right forbiden to rhyme. Thus *bait* may be paired with *beat, boot, bite, bit,* etc. In rhyming, identities in opening consonants produce identities, not rhymes.

Emily Dickinson was a careful craftsman, not a careless one. Deliberately she achieved two things in such usage: to cleave closer to her precise inspiration in both visioning and unaltered wording; and to increase and freshen the rhyming facilities of the language, by popularizing this kindred repetition device, consonance. The focal word *death,* for instance, has only the following true rhymes:

breath, saith
proper names like *Seth, Macbeth*
minor accent words like *shibboleth, twentieth,* etc., *Ashtoreth, Elizabeth*
archaic verb forms like *answereth, astonisheth,* etc.

There is here only one universally applicable rhyme, *breath*. Yet death, as Freud points out, is the object of the original instinct, and hence centers a tremendous bulk of poetry; and accordingly, in rhymed verse, must have ample rhyming mates. When consonance is called upon, it at once adds:

faith, wraith, etc.
aftermath, bath, lath, path, wrath, etc.
beneath, heath, sheath, teeth, wreath, etc.
myth, with, pith, smith, etc.
growth, betroth, both, loath, oath, sloth, etc.
Ashtaroth, broth, cloth, Goth, wroth, etc.
booth, sleuth, tooth, truth, youth, uncouth, etc.

There are also sound-couplings such as *lithe, blithe,* with definite sound identities. Thus consonance furnishes a vast addition to the available facilities of rhyming, and makes verse with consonance used as well as rhyme infinitely more fluid than verse with rhyme alone.

Here is a song by Don Marquis, *Sapphics,* using consonance throughout:

Leaps the little river, and laughs at fetters;
Through the pebbled channel it flutes and flutters;
Dances down the rapids where Autumn scatters
     Gold on the waters;

Something bends the sedge and the rushes over,
Something moves and gleams where the grasses waver,—
Can it be a nymph that has taken cover,
     Couched by the river?

May it be a naiad with breasts that glimmer,
Chased of satyrs, dreading their hoofed clamor,
Finding strange delight in the fears that claim her,
     Joy in the tremor?

It is important, in using straight consonance like this, to avoid rhyme altogether. Each new consonance surprises and delights. It will be many years before the novelty of this rediscovered device wears off.

Golden Willow, from *The Glory Road,* is a more extended poem with a similar use of the device, containing such groups of words in consonance as:

willow, shallow, hollow, mellow
airy, very, starry, glory

unceasing, lacing, hissing, caressing
meadow, shadow, credo, tornado
softer, after, left her, drift her

When Chokeberries Hang in Burgundy Clusters, from the same
volume, has these words coupled in consonance:

clusters, asters; glitter, flutter; shining, leaning; panting, wanting; bareness, nearness; morning, returning.

O Hills, My Hills formally blends internal consonance and terminal rhyme:

O hills that the sun-wide green trees *cover*
Over and *over* the lifting loam,
Where the sly breeze whispers to leaves that *shiver*
And doubtfully *waver* to leave their home;
Where blue lakes throb to his careless *passing,*
And rise to his *kissing* with crinkled lips. . . .
And the night awakes like a far voice *singing*
Of hidden *longing* and pain's eclipse,—

O hills, my hills, it was you that bore me,
And lifted for me a rigid breast.
My blood is red with your iron redness.
Your granite gladness, your heaving zest
To grope for the sky with long green fingers,
Out of the hungers that wrench your soul—
This is the breath my life is breathing:
Without you, nothing; and with you, whole.

Those who were dropped in plain or valley
Are never wholly at heart's ease.
Their lowland hearts lose pulse and shiver,
When the sky roars over the last bent trees.
They scuttle for walls and a hut's stooped ceiling,
They cringe from the flailing, crest-leaping storm.
But only above the crag's last dolmen
Is the heart of the hillmen at ease, and warm!

O hills, my hills, it is you will shield me,
And quietly fold me again to your breast,
When my heart is done at last with the valley,
And I look to the hilly heights for rest.
Bright at the end of a long tired groping
The hour for sleeping, and you the bed,
With the sun-wide green of the trees to cover
Over and over the quiet head.

Edna St. Vincent Millay, in her haunting *The Poet and His
Book,* has these instances of consonance:

worry, bury, withered, gathered; cluttered, spattered; quarrel, laurel; hunters, winter's; valleys, bellies.

Here she usually uses rhyme, with occasional inserted consonance or assonance:

> Boys and girls that steal
> From the shocking laughter
> Of the old, to kneel
> By a dripping rafter,
> Under the discolored eaves,
> Out of trunks with hingeless covers
> Lifting tales of saints and lovers,
> Travelers, goblins, thieves,
>
> Suns that shine by night,
> Mountains made from valleys,—
> Bear me to the light,
> Flat upon your bellies
> By the webby window lie,
> Where the little flies are crawling,—
> Read me, margin me with scrawling,
> Do not let me die!

Elinor Wylie achieved much effective consonance in her second volume:

woman, human (a coupling used also by Poe and earlier poets); pussy-fur, Lucifer; ovens, province; pantries, gentry's; rustics, acrostics; bloody, body; people, ripple; mourner, corner; primer, dreamer; standard, pondered; noble, trouble; music, physic; Circe, hearsay; Vulcan, falcon; languish, distinguish.

By her third volume, she had reached a rare use of similar masculine or one-syllabled consonances:

lost, ghost; sword, lord; suns, bronze, once; wins, prince.

Here the last of these is true assonance; while *once, bronze* and *ovens, province* belong to the sound-couplings that preceded formalized consonance and assonance. The rustic lyricist W. W. Christman furnishes effective uses of consonance:

hammer, amour; apple, tipple; spiral, laurel; current, torrent; brood, good; bar, fare; Lord, board; whorls, curls; gather, weather; sterile, squirrel; chords, bards; pasture, vesture; fluted, goat-footed; gentle, lintel; scatters, daughters; poured, heard; wool, gull; mocker, walker; ebon, ribbon; maple, apple; sparrow, morrow; heaven, woven; rustling, nestling.

His first volume contained this exquisite *Song of a Summer Night:*

> The hills and valleys day made ardent
> Are veiled and hid from sight;
> A broad winged bird with cries discordant
> Drives through the falling night.
>
> Somewhere I hear a stray lamb bleating,
> Lost in the dark dew,
> And there's a lonely owl repeating
> His faint, far-off halloo.
>
> The brook pours over the ledges, frothing,
> And hurries fast away;
> A sparrow wakes and sings for nothing,—
> He cannot wait till day.
>
> Oh, wide and high the heaven arches,
> And steep the road that runs
> Out of the holy hill where marches
> Arcturus with his sons.

This etching of a Bozenkill night illustrates how skilful consonance can freshen and add delight to rhyme.

Marjorie Meeker exults in such couplets in consonance as:

mothless, deathless; garden, burden; sever, over; wharves, curves; walked, wrecked; sail, bell; gleam, limn; risen, frozen; drifter, after; angry, hungry; cynic, ironic.

Note that there is a freshness in the recognition of the hitherto untapped possibilities in each of these couplings.

Consonance is a device increasing in popularity, for the two reasons given. It permits the poet to hew closer to his original meaning, since it gives him a far wider choice of words to select from than precise rhyme; and it vastly increases the terminal possibilities of the language in rhyme-and-consonance verse. It is in harmony with the Teutonic genius, the basis of our speech, which throws its emphasis on consonants, instead of on vowels, as is the tendency in the Romance and Celtic languages. The masters of the past have increasingly shown a tendency toward consonance; Shakespeare, Keats, Shelley, Burns, with his immortal

Tam o' Shanter packed with the very consonance to which the
more elegant poets of his time felt superior:

> Johnie, crony; clatter, better; gracious, precious; rustle,
> whistle; key-stane, beast in; swallow'd, bellow'd; ford,
> smoor'd; evil, devil; flainen, linen; shot, boat; harn,
> worn; scanty, vauntie,

clear to:

> Ah, Tam! Ah, Tam! thou'll get thy fairin!
> In hell they'll roast thee like a herrin!
> In vain thy Kate awaits thy comin!
> Kate soon will be a woefu' woman!
> Now, do thy speedy utmost, Meg,
> To win the key-stane o' the brig—

to the final couplet,

> Think ye may buy the joys o'er dear;
> Remember Tam o' Shanter's mare.

It took a hundred years for consonance, with its naturalness
and enlargement of the possibilities of rhyme, to become a custom in our versification. But the time has now come.

WRITING VERSE WITH CONSONANCE

Naturally, a rhyming dictionary does not give directly the
rich possibilities in consonance that are open to the versifier. It
is enough that it gives the full rhyming potentialities of the
language. But it gives indirectly all the available consonances,
once the method of arriving at these is discovered.

The best rhyming dictionaries list the words in phonetic
groups. Each of the three major divisions, one-syllabled rhymes,
two-syllabled rhymes, and three-syllabled ones, is divided into five
groups, the A, E, I, O and U rhymes. Each of these vowel groups
progresses through the various consonantal terminals in the
alphabet:

A, AB, AD, AF, AG, AJ, AK, etc.

and each of these in turn has exhausted every possible A sound: as,

ĀB, ĂB, ÄB and ȦB together;

and the same with the other letters. Suppose we want to use the rhyming dictionary to find all the possible consonances for such a word as *grab,* listed under ĂB. We would find two groups of these in the AB neighborhood, ĀB and ÄB; and also under the EB's, IB's, OB's, and UB's. Thus:

ĀB: astrolabe, babe, etc.

ÄB: squab, swab, etc.

ĒB: glebe, grebe

ĔB: cobweb, ebb, etc.

ĪB: ascribe, bribe, diatribe, gibe, etc.

ĬB: ad lib, bib, crib, fib, glib, etc.

ŌB: disrobe, globe, Job, lobe, etc.

ÔB: daub, etc.

ŎB: athrob, cob, fob, hob, job, etc.

ŪB: cube, tube, etc.

ŬB: chub, club, cub, drub, dub, etc.

We will also have looked for OIB, OŎB, and OUB, and found no words. And that is all.

The same process will establish the possible consonance mates for any word, whether one-, two-, or three-syllabled. The process takes more time than does the looking up of a mere rhyme; but it is, after all, intrinsically simple. And, once the habit of writing in consonance is arrived at, the rhyming dictionary (except in excessively formal and light verse) will no more be needed, except in revision, in the case of consonance than in the case of rhyme.

5. REPETITION OF ACCENTED VOWEL AND SUBSEQUENT SOUNDS: RHYME

The flowering of sound repetition in English versification is that alien importation, rhyme. It may be defined: *Rhyme is the identity in sound of an accented vowel in each of two or more words, usually the last vowel accented, together with identity of all of the sounds following; while the consonantal sounds imme-*

diately preceding differ. Rhyme can only flourish in cultures which hear both consonants and vowels with clarity, and can distinguish between differences in the sounds in both. Examples of perfect rhymes are:

Eat. Sound, ĒT. Rhymes: beat, Crete, suite, elite, mete, greet, conceit, Lafitte, etc.

Playing. Sound, Ā'ing. Rhymes: baying, inveighing, surveying, straying, etc.

Pierian. Sound, ĒR'i-an. Rhymes: Algerian, Shakespearean, Valkyrian, Siberian, etc.

The spelling makes no difference; the sole determinant is the pronunciation. Accordingly, rhyming dictionaries based upon groups of words spelled alike are defective. For, to look up the rhymes to *eat,* in such a dictionary you would have to find the *-eat* group, and also the *-ete, -uite, -ite, -eet, -eit, -itte* groups, etc.; and even then you might find that you had missed certain groups. The rhyming dictionary of greatest use is one based upon phonetic groupings.

For all that rhyme originated in late Latin, probably among the priests of the African church, and spread through Italy and France to England, it is so deeply embedded in the language, that it has passed into colloquial rhyming couplings, at home in prose as in verse:

> hook or crook; high and dry; wear and tear; pluck and luck; wedded and bedded; as snug as a bug in a rug; lock, stock and barrel; might makes right; June moon.

The language is rich in rhyming doublets, or words which involve rhyming elements: some of them recent, and ranging down to the latest slang:

> abracadabra; bow-wow; choo-choo; chow-chow; chuck-a-luck; harum-scarum; helter-skelter; higgledy-piggledy; hocus-pocus; hodge-podge; hotsy-totsy; humdrum; Humpty Dumpty; hurdy-gurdy; hurly-burly; itsy-bitsy; Jeepers Creepers; lah-de-dah; loco-foco; mumbo-jumbo; namby-pamby; razzle-dazzle; roly-poly; rub-a-dub-dub; teensy-weensy; teeny-weeny; willy-nilly.

Since the device has thus entered into the core of the language, its use may be, and should be, as natural as these words are.

One-Syllable, Single or Masculine Rhymes

One-syllabled rhymes are called single or masculine rhymes. Examples are:

> day, assegai, they, au fait, auto-da-fé, sleigh, bouquet, Bordelais, Chevalier, corvée, entremets, etc.
> bet, met, regret, aigrette, Barnett, debt, minuet, etc.
> admit, counterfeit, mitt, opposite, etc.
> alone, groan, mown, Boulogne, sewn, etc.
> abuse, adduce, caboose, deuce, douce, Roos, Russ, juice, Zeus, etc.

Two-Syllabled, Double or Feminine Rhymes

Two-syllabled rhymes are called double or feminine rhymes. Examples are:

> airy, Mary, epistolary, prairie, etc. Cf. where he.
> rector, collector, spectre, subjecter, etc. Cf. wrecked her.
> chided, guided, provided, fly did, etc.
> blowing, hoeing, helloing, foreknowing, etc.
> ruddy, study, bloody, etc. Cf. mud, he.

Rhymes of two or more syllables may be composed of two or more words or parts of words: *where he, wrecked her, fly did,* etc. They are then called mosaic rhymes. These will be discussed later.

Three-Syllabled, or Triple Rhymes

Three-syllabled rhymes are called triple rhymes. Examples are:

> breakable, implacable, mistakeable, etc.
> ascendancy, dependency, etc.
> hideous, invidious, Phidias, etc.
> acrimonious, erroneous, etc.
> crest of it, best of it, west of it, etc.
> cheating him, beating him, etc.
> deep into, sleep into, etc.

One warning is needed in the use of three- and more-syllabled rhymes: the foot-count at the end of the line ends with the accented syllable where the rhyme starts, and not with the end of the word. Thus, in a sonnet, where five feet are required, each line of the following terminal couplet lacks a foot:

> I know I have the sure ability
> To do my mission with facility.

Scanned by the iambic pattern, this would apparently give:

I know / I have / the sure / abil- / ity.

But this would require the last foot to be *-ity,* with the rhyme on the sound *-ty;* and since both lines end with this sound, we would have single-rhyme identity here, according to the five-foot pattern; and this means no rhyme at all, in the five-foot pattern. It constitutes a triple rhyme (-bility, -cility) in a four-foot pattern.

Hence, in sonnet usage, these lines would have to follow the pattern of:

I know that I possess the sure ability
To consummate my mission with facility.

Here the five-foot iambic pattern would give us,

I know / that I / possess / the sure / ability.

This gives us a terminal iamb with two added unaccented syllables as grace-notes; and this is how triple rhyme is counted.

The same word, *ability,* properly single-rhymed in a couplet to terminate a sonnet, might give us:

I know / I have / the sure / abil- / ity
To show a love as ample as the sea.

For here we have obvious single rhymes (-ty, sea), and the foot-count is correct.

Rhymes of More than Three Syllables

Rhymes of three and more syllables are, as a rule, more suitable in English to light verse than to serious poetry. Yet Browning, as in *Of Pacchiarotto, and How He Worked in Distemper*— as serious in intent as any of his poems—used rhymes like:

contemporaneous, extraneous; prelude, hell-hued; sides of it, wide so fit; distemperer, emperor; pooh-poohed it is, lewd ditties; conventional, mention all; Pheidipides, Euripides.

This matter is left to the individual versifier.

It is possible, especially in light verse, to rhyme far more than three syllables. Usually this is done by mosaic rhymes—a group of words or parts of words; yet an amusing effect can come, at the right place, by long single-word rhymes of many syllables.

Do not forget the important warning that the main accented rhyme-syllable must fit into your rhythm pattern as its last foot. Thus, if your pattern were three feet to the line, this would be wrong:

> Rhyme, in its proper place,
> Lends dignity and grace;
> It's unmistakable,
> If not too breakable.

For, since your pattern is three feet to the line, you have no rhyme here: only the identities *-ble, -ble* on the third feet, where the rhyming syllables are due. This would be correct:

> Rhyme, in its proper place,
> Lends dignity and grace;
> It's truly unmistakable,
> With grace that is unbreakable.

For here the third feet have the rhymes *-takeable, -breakable,* which are perfect triple rhymes. Let your major rhyming syllable come in its proper place in the rhythm pattern, and regard the syllables thereafter as mere added gracenotes.

Groups of words constituting four-syllabled rhymes include:

> feloniously, erroneously, acrimoniously, etc.
> effectually, intellectually.
> ecstatically, erratically, emphatically, etc.
> cynically, clinically, finically, etc.
> gloriously, victoriously, uproariously, etc.
> lyrically, satirically, empirically.

These rhymes can be arrived at by looking up, in the three-syllabled rhymes, such ones as will take suffixes like *-ly, -ness,* etc. Mosaic rhymes of four-syllables include:

> completed the task, repeated the task, defeated the task, etc.
> away with them all, play with them all, gay with them all, etc.
> love for a night, turtle-dove for a night, etc.
> mad with delight, glad with delight, etc.

Five-syllabled rhymes include:

> luminosity, acumenosity, bitumenosity, etc.
> boreality, marmoreality, No! reality, etc.

oratoricality, allegoricality, etc.
pedestrianating, equestrianating.
agility with it, possibility with it.
back to my cabin, track to my cabin.
story of it all, glory of it all.

Six-syllabled rhymes include:

attitudinizing, platitudinizing.
work till the end of it, shirk till the end of it.
fight to the bitter end, smite to the bitter end.
June and a night of love, moon and a night of love.

Seven-syllabled rhymes include:

attitudinizingly, platitudinizingly.
attitudinarian, platitudinarian.
song full of my love for you, all along full of my love
    for you, etc.

Minor Accent Rhymes

An early and pleasing device in rhyming is to rhyme a word's
major accent with the minor accent of another word. This tends
to avoid the cloying nature of too obvious rhyme, and quickens
the mind to more alert attention. Shakespeare uses this commonly, as in his sonnets:

> That thereby beauty's rose might never die. . . .
> His tender heir might bear his memory.
>
> *i*

Memory, properly a triple rhyme with the proper name *Emory*
or with *tremory*, is not even given a secondary accent on the last
syllable by the dictionaries. Yet it is so pronounced; and this
usage from Shakespeare is a popular one. As usually used today,
however, the terminal *-y*'s are rhymed with the long *e* sound
heard in *sea*. Thus, from *xvi* in my *The White Peacock*,

> Let death and pain come lonely to us; we
> Must float together into ecstasy.

To return to Shakespeare's sonnets, here are other instances of
minor accent rhymes:

> And only herald to the gaudy spring. . . .
> And, tender churl, mak'st waste in niggarding.
>
> *i*

[219]

To place the major accent rhyme first, followed by the minor one, makes certain that the latter is properly pronounced, with a faint overtone of accent; otherwise, the ear might expect a triple rhyme—even if the major accent in the word (*niggarding*, in this instance) occurs in the fourth foot, instead of the fifth, where it should be. Yet this precaution is ignored by the masters, when it suits better what they have to say.

Such rhymes can be composed entirely of minor accents, as in this quatrain doubly illustrating it:

> Were it aught to me I bore the canopy,
> With my extern the outward honouring,
> Or laid great bases for eternity,
> Which prove more short than waste or ruining?
>
> *cxxv*

Other examples of minor accent rhyme in the sonnets include:

> And many maiden gardens, yet unset. . . .
> Much liker than your painted counterfeit.
>
> *xvi*

According to modern usage, *counterfeit* (final syllable pronounced *-fit*) would be rhymed with *it, bit, wit,* etc.

> Thou art more lovely and more temperate. . . .
> And summer's lease hath all too short a date.
>
> *xviii*

Modern pronunciation gives the last syllable of *temperate* as ĭt. Nevertheless, it is today used as often, or more often, in the manner that Shakespeare used it; a sort of consonance, based upon the illogical excuse of "eye-rhymes," or words terminally identical in spelling. Here is another example of a similar usage:

> Had my friend's muse grown with this growing age, . . .
> To march in ranks of better equipage.
>
> *xxxii*

In most cases, the pronunciations have not changed:

> How can my muse want subject to invent, . . .
> Thine own sweet argument, too excellent.
>
> *xxxviii*

> Some say thy fault is youth, some wantonness. . . .
> Both grace and faults are lov'd of more and less.
>
> *xcvi*

This device, of minor accent rhyming, is effective in proportion as the minor accent is unheard in ordinary speech. Preterites of verbs with -*ed* pronounced, already listed, and participles ending in -*ing*, are very effective when so used:

> Of all the things I once inherited;
> Come back, and give me life, who now am dead! . . .

> To jest at Winter's bleakest withering,
> To die, and be born again some cursed Spring!
> *Eagle Sonnets*, CLEMENT WOOD, *xxviii*

These examples are sufficient to indicate to the versifier the use of minor accents with major accents, or with other minor accents.

Rhyming with Misplaced Accents

The early ballads furnish many examples of words rhymed on syllables not ordinarily accented, with the accents removed from their normal positions for the purpose of the rhyming. Louise Pound suggests with good reason that this was due to the influence of French pronunciation so dominant at court. Examples are:

> The miller quickly drew the dam,
> An' there he found a drown'd woman.
> *The Twa Sisters*, ANONYMOUS

> Both here and beyond the sea. . . .
> To bring them to my brother, King Jamie.
> *Sir Andrew Barton*, ANONYMOUS

> And shake the green leaves off the tree, . . .
> For of my life I am weary.
> *Waly, Waly, but Love Be Bonny*, ANONYMOUS

> Far into the north countree; . . .
> Ellen, must go with me.
> *Child Waters*, ANONYMOUS

> "Stand you still, master," quoth Little John,
> "Under this trusty tree,
> And I will go to yond wight yeomán,
> To know his meaning truly."
> *Robin Hood and Guy of Gisborne*, ANONYMOUS

This last example is from a stanza pattern rhyming 1,2,1,2; that is, *John* rhymes with yeo*man*, as well as *tree* with tru*ly*. With this example, it is needless to quote further from the ballads.

The modern use of misplaced accent rhyme does not come from any alien influence, but is primarily an attempt to enlarge the rhyming possibilities of the language. It is hence akin in spirit to the modern popularity of consonance, and has the same subtle effectiveness. It is well used in W. W. Christman's fine *The Pines,* moving from:

> I give, bequeath, devote, devise
> Shelter to every bird that flies;
> Harbor to all that walk or creep;
> To the red fox a bed for sleep;
> Table and roof for every guest,
> And place for dove and thrush to nest.
>
> Years hence, some boy driving tranquil
> Slow cattle up the pasture hill. . . .

Clearly, this is not to be pronounced *tran´quil,* with no accent on the second syllable; for the pattern requires here a rhyme for *hill.* Just as clearly, it is not to be artificialized into *tran-quil´,* with its only accent on the second syllable; for good reading no less than good poetry must be suffused with the naturalness of the best colloquial rhythms. Some mean halfway between these two should be arrived at: almost as if this were a spondee, *tran´quil´:* or, even better, like the natural pronunciation, but with the syllable lingered on long enough to make sure that the rhyme will be heard, with about the effect of a minor accent rhyme.

Examples of this device from *The Glory Road* include this use, in *The Ballad of Fritz Duquesne:*

> Death gives no life to the ravished dead;
> But for this your soul has been appointed,
> And, till honor rots and right is vain,
> They will not net you, Fritz Duquesne.

The natural scansion of this,

> But for this / your soul / has been appointed

clearly gives us no rhyme for *dead.* Hence the spoken rhythm must transfer some of the accent on *-point-* to each of the subordinate syllables of the word, giving the word two minor accents flanking the major one. The same device is used in *Blind Mary,* another instance from accent verse:

> The throb within life, the smile within death,
> The stars that blaze with their singing breath,
> The choiring angels—and the vast anguish
> That tore her soul when she won her wish.

Here clearly *an'guish* would be definitely wrong; *an-guish'* would be definitely artificial; and only the treatment with major and minor accent, *an'guish"*, brings out the undertone of rhyme with the same effect of naturalness that rhyme on a minor accent affords.

The same device may be used effectively in dialect verse, as in *Judgment Day:*

> Dey hang my Jesus, 'cause he spoke de trufe:
> You can't jail God under no church's roof!
> You can't ketch God wid no fly-paper—
> But my boy Jesus caught de Lawd wid prayer!

When a minor accent is given to the last syllable of *fly'pa'per* the result is acceptable consonance, with a freshness that accurate rhyming could never give. *Sugar Plum* uses the same device:

> Sugar Plum,
> You says yes, I buys a ring;
> You 'n' me has a church wedding.

The last foot must be read with a minor accent on *-ding.* Since this poem is in tight trochees, and not accent verse, it would tend to wreck the rhythm to have a trochaic dissyllable before *wedding,* as "You 'n' me has a happy wedding." The use of the strong monosyllable here drains some of the accent out of the first syllable of *wedding,* and prepares for the rhyme of the nature of a minor accent rhyme.

Sonnet *xiii* in *The White Peacock* furnishes another example:

> Barred Eden, when I had tossed the angel there
> The cates and comfits that would bribe his sting,
> And the beloved dupe and the dear lover
> Could dwell forever in this Judas spring.

Here a minor accent on the last syllable of *lover* gives it the proper effect of consonance with *there.*

This device, when read with a minor accent on the unaccent to be used as rhyme, is refreshing, quietly startling, and widens the range of rhyming possibilities. It is, of course, helpful to the reader to put the major accent first. Yet three of the six examples given plunge right in with the misplaced accent, and none of them fails. When read correctly, there is naturally no obstacle to understanding the presence of the rhyme; and, if one in reading the poems to himself stumbles over one of these rhymes, a moment's rereading should set him right. An added element of value to the device is the faint overtone of a practice familiar in the dawn of modern English verse, the hour of the popular ballad, and since abandoned for four centuries; which gives it the status of an old but neglected friend.

The minor accent added gives definite additional emphasis to the word so treated; and, in all the cases given, the words deserve this added emphasis. So far, misplaced accent rhyme and consonance have been used only once in each poem quoted from. Ultimately some versifier will go further, even to the extent of making each rhyme in a poem of this nature.

Synthetic Rhymes

At times, words are artificially lengthened, altered or constructed, to suit the rhythm scheme, or, more commonly, the rhyme scheme. When Autolycus sings, in *The Winter's Tale,*

> Jog on, jog on, the footpath way,
> And merrily hent the stile-a:
> A merry heart goes all the day,
> Your sad tires in a mile-a,
>
> *IV, ii*

the added suffixes to *stile* and *mile* are needed for the rhythmic or musical pattern of the song. At times, synthetic rhymes are similarly created:

> There was an unfortunate fellow
> Whose nose was unable to smell-o.
> He was easy to please,
> For a Limberger cheese
> He'd insist had an odor quite swell-o.

This device is never to be recommended, except in verse intentionally folksy, or as deliberately used in light verse by Ogden Nash:

> In January everything freezes.
> We have two children. Both are she'ses.
> *One Third of a Calendar,* OGDEN NASH

> In every twelve months
> It comes but onths. . . .

> Ah, happy apathy.
> Ah, may this Yuletide indeed turn out to be the
> Yuletide without mishapathy.
>
> *April Yule, Daddy,* OGDEN NASH

Mosaic Rhymes: Rhymes of Two and More Words

The only rule for accurate mosaic rhymes, or rhymes composed of two or more words or parts of words, is that all the sounds, consonantal and vocal, following the accented syllables to be rhymed, must be identical, even as to accent. In other words, this is the rule implicit in the definition of rhyme. Thus *satin* and *that in* may rhyme:

> And for my gown of satin,
> Be sure that you put that in!

This is because *that* receives a natural accent, as *sat-* does. If there is any uncertainty, to avoid mispronunciation that would wreck the rhyme, italicize the uncertain syllable:

> Be sure that you put *that* in!

But in this usage,

> I always dress in satin.
> I always buy two gowns, that in
> Emergencies, one tearing,
> The other I'd be wearing,

there is an accent on *gowns,* preceding *that,* which makes the accent on *that* extremely unnatural and undesirable. This would be even more definite, if the line read:

> I always purchase two, that in
> Emergencies, etc.

Here we have a succession of iambs, and the preceding foot, *-chase, two,* makes it almost impossible to read *that in* as a trochee, even if the *that* were italicized: since the word has no natural emphasis whatever. Yet note how easily this could be cured:

> I always purchase two, so that in

Here the rhythm of the iambs hints that *so that* is another iamb, and tends to throw a natural accent, at least a minor one, on *that.*

Or the whole line could be altered to one equivalent to the first
in rhythm,

> I love to dress in satin,
> And buy two dresses, that in
> Emergencies, one tearing,
> The other I'd be wearing.

Where mosaic rhymes are to be used, and accent emphasis must
be thrown on one syllable to constitute the rhyme, this sort of
pains must be taken, to be sure that a perfect rhyme is finally
arrived at.

Similarly, making sure that the accent falls properly, *Quentin*
can be made to rhyme with *went in; aided* with *play did; needed*
with *he did; carded* with *star did*. In several of these, the unaccented syllables apparently differ in vocal sounds. But in speech
these unaccented vowels are slurred over and tend to blur into
identity: as the terminal syllables in disposi*tion*, physi*cian;* outra-
geous, conta*gious,* etc.

Again, the position of the consonants in the later syllables may
differ, so long as the actual succession of sounds is identical. Examples are *pray tin, hate in; ask it, pass-kit*. In one poem, Browning achieves these rhyming couplings:

we know, Bernardino;	*not* owe, Giotto;
helmet, well met;	Hades, paid ease, ladies;
tax him, maxim;	prince meet, mincemeat;
Pontiff, won't if;	conventional, mention all;
not half! a bet!, alphabet;	there's X, Fair Sex;
trumpets, dumb pets;	few venal!, Juvenal;
outside, louts eyed;	mortar, sort are;
tractable, fact, able;	company, lump any;
especially, fresh ally;	Poverty, covert tie;
essayed, "Yes" said;	lambdas, damned ass;
ill able, dissyllable;	stubborn, cub born;
monkey, one key;	reared in, mere din;
person, her son;	structure, tucked your;
cue be, booby, ruby;	sides of it, wide so fit;

pooh-poohed it is, lewd ditties, nudities

Some of these succeed, and some do not: the failure being due
to some difference in the sound. A good sample of the failure is
not half! a bet, coupled with *alphabet*. He is apparently misled
by the presence of the *l* in *half;* but it is not pronounced here.

He could rhyme *Ralph, a bet!* with *alphabet,* assuming he indicated the accent properly; but *half* wrecks it. Other failures, and their reasons, are:

> there's X, Fair Sex—*z* in the first pair, *s* in the second
> trumpets, dumb pets: impossible to hurry the 2nd *m* like the first
> few venal!, Juvenal—the *e* in the last word is not long
> especially, fresh ally—the last *y* is long *i;* the first not
> Poverty, covert tie: the second group has 2 *t*'s; the first, one
> essayed, "Yes" said—the first word has long *a;* second, short *e*
> lambdas, damned ass: the *a* in *ass* differs from the 2nd *a* in lambdas; there is also *z* in the first, *s* in the second
> stubborn, cub born: a 2nd *b* in the second missing in the first
>
> monkey, one key: monkey is MŬNGK'i; one key, WŬN'kĔ. These differ completely
> sides of it, wide so fit: the *f* in *of* is pronounced *v; z* in the first, *s* in the second; the *o* is short *u* in the first, long *o* in the second.

I can imagine that Browning had a magnificent time coupling these mosaic rhymes together. But he let spelling rule, instead of sound, and one who aims at accurate rhyming cannot do that. For Browning, he succeeded admirably. An adept at versification will avoid these types of sound mésalliances, unless he is deliberately clowning, and seeking to get rhymes as faulty as possible.

If we wanted to generalize from these examples, we would say that among the chief things to guard against in making mosaic rhymes are: using the *z* sound of *s,* found in plurals, coupled with an *s;* inserting an *h,* which should be pronounced (*rector, expect her*)—though this is a minor blemish; pronouncing a consonant once in one rhyme, and twice in the other—*poverty, covert tie;* failing to observe the actual sounds, as pronounced, of vowels—especially unaccented ones; and missing the NGK sound heard in words like *monkey, thanks,* etc.

There is one warning for mosaic rhymes: the rhyming must give the effect of utter naturalness, or it will furnish an obstacle to the easy flow of your verse. Here are three famous examples, which succeed:

O ye lords of ladies intel*lectual,*
Inform us truly, have they not hen*pecked you all?*
        Don Juan, I, xxii, Lord Byron

Should it even set fire to one's castle and *burn it, you're*
Amply insured for both building and *furniture.*
    Sir Rupert the Fearless, Richard Henry Barham
            (Thomas Ingoldsby)

You haven't the nerve to take bi*chloride;*
You lie up nights till you're gaunt and *sore-eyed.*
Poems in Praise of Practically Nothing, Samuel Hoffenstein

In using such mosaic rhymes, there is some merit in putting the simpler one first, as Byron and Hoffenstein did; and then follow with a group whose pronunciation matches the first. Barham, however, did not hesitate to put *furniture* second. W. S. Gilbert at times uses one method, at times the other, achieving:

> monotony, got any; cerebellum too, tell 'em too; lot o' news, hypotenuse; din afore, Pinafore; strategy, *sat* a gee; wary at, Commisariat.

Guy Wetmore Carryl's equally deft mosaic rhymes are famous:

> did it, he, timidity; curiosity, closet he; any son's, Tennyson's; vehement, see he meant; grotto-like, Watteau-like; nymph, any, symphony; Arcadia, afraid o' yer; abuse of her, Lucifer; mount a sign, countersign; "Drat," he said, "the brat," he said.

The type of cleverness evidenced in many of these rhymes entered the lyrics of popular songs, in part through the influence of the wits who graduated from the Columbia *Jester* about the beginning of this century's first World War; and the practice, so evident in many Tin Pan Alley lyrics today, of using mosaic rhymes, may properly be called Columbia *Jester* rhyming.

In *Dream a Little Dream of Me,* we find:

> above you, love you; kiss me, miss me; on, dear, dawn, dear; find you, behind you.

By now, these have been used so much, that there is little freshness in them; they have entered into the class of clichés, the more so because their mosaic quality makes them conspicuous. Similar clichés, or combinations almost as bad, are:

It is ghastly to hear this sung by some uninspired precisionist, who makes of it:

> Mama throw a nickel,
> And the man will pick
> (Pause) A little tune you love.

It would be as bad to have this turned into a single rhyme:

> Mama throw a nick-
> (Pause) El, and the man will pick
> (Pause) A little tune you love.

For this misses the delicious mosaic double rhyme, utilizing two words and a part of a third, in one instance.

Other examples of successful mosaic rhymes in recent songs are:

> Sing out with gusto,
> And just o-
> Verlorded the place.
> *Johnny One Note,* Lorenz Hart

> Summer journeys to Niagara
> And to other places aggra-
> Vate all our cares.
> *Manhattan,* Lorenz Hart

> Because the sun is much too sultry,
> And they must avoid his ultry-
> Violet ray.
> *Mad Dogs and Englishmen,* Noel Coward

In the instance given from *The Man with the Mandolin,* the single rhyme was erroneous, because the double rhyme was there all the time. With slightly different wording, this could have been a single rhyme, of the type of that given by Gilbert:

> Mama throw a nick-
> El, and the man will pick
> Some little song you love.

All of these examples given have been from light verse. It is probable that Browning, if he had been familiar with the device, would have defiantly inserted it in serious poetry. That privilege is open to any versifier.

Rhymes Involving Splitting Familiar Phrases

C. S. Calverley, that much imitated English master of versification, opens his *Ode to Tobacco* with a subtle rhyming device, in which the mayhem is committed on familiar phrases, instead of on words:

> Thou who, when fears attack,
> Bidst them avaunt, and Black
> Care, at the horseman's back
>   Perching, unseatest;
> Sweet when the morn is gray;
> Sweet, when they've cleared away
> Lunch; and at close of day
>   Possibly sweetest.

Here the familiar phrase "Black Care" is split so that *Black* becomes a terminal rhyme; and "when they've cleared away lunch" is similarly split, to let *away* furnish the terminal rhyme. Here, instead of having the idiomatic rhythm of speech phrases coincide with the rhythm of the rhyme's recurrence, these two are deliberately put at cross currents, which abruptly calls our attention to words otherwise or at least not of supreme importance in the phrase. The famous Ode illustrates this device constantly:

> Yet know I five or six
> Smokers who freely mix
>   Still with their neighbors.

His *Dover to Munich* is full of the same device:

> And the usual evening midge
> Is settling on the bridge
>   Of my nose.

When Oliver Wendell Holmes wrote *The Last Leaf,* using a rhythm similar to this last, he was careful to make his lines end-stopped:

> And if I should live to be
> The last leaf upon the tree
>   In the spring,
> Let them laugh, as I do now,
> At the old forsaken bough
>   Where I cling.

The essence of this light verse device that we are considering is to replace the end-stopped lines with lines deliberately cutting a familiar phrase at some unexpected place, and using this artificial terminal as part of the rhyme-scheme, with unexpected rhyme-emphasis on some interior word in the phrase:

And on the silent river
The floating starbeams quiver;—
And now, the saints deliver
    Us from fleas.

Calverley's *Morning* is uniformly brilliant in its use of this device, climaxed with:

But when breakfast-time hath come,
And he's crunching crust and crumb,
He'll no longer look a glum
    Little dunce;
But be brisk as bees that settle
On a summer rose's petal;
Wherefore, Polly, put the kettle
    On at once.

The familiar phrase, "Polly, put the kettle on," here suffers both a startling fission and an unexpected addendum. Calverley's *Changed* must be quoted in full, as a supreme achievement in this field:

I know not why my soul is rack'd;
    Why I ne'er smile as was my wont;
I only know that, as a fact,
        I don't.
I used to roam o'er glen and glade
    Buoyant and blithe as other folk;
And not infrequently I made
        A joke.

A minstrel's fire within me burn'd.
    I'd sing, as one whose heart must break,
Lay upon lay; I nearly learn'd
        To shake.
All day I sang; of love, of fame,
    Of fights our fathers fought of yore,
Until the thing almost became
        A bore.

I cannot sing the old songs now!
    It is not that I deem them low,
'Tis that I can't remember how
        They go.
I could not range the hills till high
    Above me stood the summer moon:
And as to dancing, I could fly
        As soon.

The sports, to which with boyish glee
    I sprang erewhile, attract no more;
Although I am but sixty-three
        Or four.

> Nay, worse than that, I've seemed of late
> To shrink from happy boyhood—boys
> Have grown so noisy, and I hate
> A noise.
>
> They fright me, when the beech is green,
> By swarming up its stem for eggs;
> They drive their horrid hoops between
> My legs:—
> It's idle to repine, I know;
> I'll tell you what I'll do instead:
> I'll drink my arrowroot, and go
> To bed.

Never forget, in exulting in the restrained mastery of this, to notice how such old conventions, as, for instance, alliteration, constantly reappears:

> glade, glen; buoyant, blithe; lay, learn'd; hills, high; swarming, stem; horrid, hoops; fame, fights, fathers, fought

The more alert of the song lyricists have followed Calverley in the use of this device. Thus Lorenz Hart, in *Manhattan,* constantly makes use of it:

> We'll see Manhattan,
> The Bronx and Staten
> Island too. . . .
>
> Our future babies
> We'll take to Abie's
> Irish rose;
> I hope they live to see it close.

Locations of Rhyme: End Rhyme

End rhyme is rhyme used at the end of lines. In the familiar near-triolet, Leigh Hunt's end-rhymes—alternately masculine and feminine—are italicized:

Jenny kissed me when we *met,*	1
Running to the chair I *sat in.*	2
Time, you thief, who love to *get*	1
Sweets upon your list, put *that in!*	2
Say I'm weary, say I'm *sad,*	3
Say that health and wealth have *missed me;*	4
Say I'm growing old, but *add*—	3
Jenny *kissed me.*	4

The rhyming scheme is indicated by the numbers to the right. Letters are used instead of numbers by some authorities, but they are not so easy to differentiate. Here the odd-numbered lines have the single rhymes, *met, get* (rhyme sound 1); *sad, add* (rhyme 3); the even-numbered lines have the double rhymes, *sat in, that in* (rhyme 2); *missed me, kissed me* (rhyme 4). This is alternate rhyming, indicated by 1,2,1,2,3,4,3,4. We will study the various positions which end rhymes may assume, in dealing with the stanza, or group of lines.

Internal Rhyme

Rhyme is at times used within the line, to give a more emphatic sound-repetitional effectiveness. This may occur midway of a line, or at some other formal position within it; or it may be placed informally wherever the versifier desires. In the poem of Leigh Hunt's, quoted above, line 6 has an informal internal rhyme:

Say that *wealth* and *health* have missed me.

Here *health* and *wealth,* a pair of rhyming words, are used, almost in a folk-saying way, completely native to our language. The same coupling is found in:

Early to bed and early to rise
Makes a man healthy, wealthy and wise.
Mother Goose

Note the various repetitional devices used here:

Word Repetition: early to, early to
Alliteration: *m*akes a *m*an, *w*ealthy and *w*ise
Internal Rhyme: healthy, wealthy
End Rhyme: rise, wise

The internal trochaic rhymes are emphatic, and this adds to their effectiveness. Yet, in this couplet of only fourteen words, we have no feeling of over-ornamentation: merely of vast compression or concentration, and a natural inevitability of expression which makes this, to many, poetically important; and, to all, mnemonically easy to remember.

Here is a passionate passage from Sidney Lanier's *The Symphony:*

"Each *day,* all *day,*" these poor folk *say,*
"In the same old *year-long, drear-long way,*
We *weave* in the *mills* and *heave* in the *kilns,*
We *sieve* mine-meshes under the *hills,*
And *thieve* much gold from the Devil's bank *tills,*
To *relieve,* O God, what manner of *ills?*"

In these six lines, we have these many repetitional devices:

Word Repetition: day, day; We, We; in the, in the
Internal Rhyme: Formal: (Halving a line) day—(say), mills
—(kilns)
Formal: (1st foot of line) weave, sieve,
thieve, relieve
Formal: (3rd foot of line) heave
Informal: year-long, drear-long
Alliteration: say, same; mine-meshes, much, manner
End Rhyme: say, way; kilns, hills, tills, ills

There are even more subtle devices also present:

Assonance, direct or indirect: day, say, same; folk, old, gold;
each, weave, etc.; meshes, Devil's
Consonance, implicit: mine, hills; gold, God. This is rather
the crude convention preceding consonance.

When fully analyzed, effective poetry is often as surcharged with
devices as this.
Let us take the first stanza of Tennyson's song, *The Splendor
Falls on Castle Walls,* for its use of internal rhyme and the other
devices listed:

The splendor falls on castle walls,
And snowy summits old in story;
The long light shakes across the lakes,
And the wild cataract leaps in glory.
Blow, bugles, blow, set the wild echoes flying;
Blow, bugle; answer, echoes, dying, dying, dying.

The repetitional conventions here used include:

Word Repetition: The, The; And, and; Blow, blow, blow;
bugles, bugle; dying, dying, dying; wild, wild
Internal Rhyme, Formal: falls—(walls), shakes—(lakes)
End Rhyme: story, glory; flying, dying
Alliteration: splendor, snowy, summits, story, shakes; long,
light, leaps; walls, wild; blow, bugles

Assonance implicit: snowy, old, story, glory, blow, blow, blow, (heard more softly in echoes); cataract, answer; light, wild, wild, flying, dying

Consonance implicit: falls, old, wild

With a master craftsman like Tennyson, all these elements came naturally. In forty-two words, we have at least fifty-four examples of formal repetition devices! The two stanzas that follow are just as full of repetition devices, differently, and always effectively used. The hearer or reader does not need to identify or know any of these devices; any more than the user of a piece of hardware need know the intricate details of mining, smelting, refining and manufacturing behind the finished product. Its effect is all that he cares for. The same is true of poetry. The emotional effect is all that is important—except to the shaper of the emotional appeal, the poet or versifier. He must know his trade as carefully as any other craftsman; for only so can he shape the crude emotional appeal of his inspiration, as first it occurs to him, to its maximum effectiveness.

Need the beginner in versification, or even the adept, use these devices, once he knows them? This is entirely a voluntary matter. Poems of powerful emotional appeal can be written with not one of these devices consciously put in. As a rule, several of them, notably word repetition and alliteration, will automatically insert themselves where the emotional appeal is strong enough and spontaneous enough; and are always at hand, as intensifiers, if desired.

Thus we have gathered together all our devices involving the repetitions of sound, and find that they blend and cooperate to make the verses increasingly effective.

Writers of light verse add greatly to the effectiveness of their line, in proportion as they master and use these various devices. My *Farewell to Yesterday* illustrates, in light verse, the cumulative effect of these devices:

> Come let us weep for Phyllis dead,
> For lovely Amaryllis dead,
>   For snowy-shouldered Chloë,
>   And for Corydon the fair;
> For vines that once had been the veil
> Of nymphs that lurked within the vale,
>   Whose precious loves enmesh us
>   In the mazes of their hair.

The pipes of Pan are heard no more;
The lilting lyre is stirred no more;
  The lute is mute; the word no more
    From Delphi's cave is spoken.
From now through all eternity
We're going to have modernity:
  A long farewell to Arcady—
  A welcome to Hoboken!

Added to the word repetition, the formal and informal internal rhyme, the end rhyme, the more than twenty instances of alliteration, the assonance, we have here subtle repetitions of things familiar: "Come let us weep," "The pipes of Pan," "A long farewell to—"; and, of course, the mosaic rhymes, so effective in light verse. Such verses justify the effort, and point emphatically to the richness of ornamental devices open to the practitioners of versification in English.

Incorrect Rhymes: Identities

One of the commonest errors in rhyming is seeking to rhyme a full word sound—including preceding consonant—with itself. By the definition of rhyming, there must be a difference in the consonantal sounds preceding the repeated identity of accented vowel or vowels and all subsequent sounds. Spelling does not concern us here; rhyming is a matter exclusively of sound. Identities commonly sought to be rhymed, erroneously, include the following types:

    bay, bey, obey, disobey
    bare, bear, forbear, Baer
    red, read, redd, overread
    lying, underlying, overlying, underlying
    loyalty, reality, possibility, probability, impenetrability
        (The first two are 1-syllabled identities; the last three
        are both 1- and 3-syllabled identities.)
    astrologic, biologic, geologic, pathologic
    arithmetician, partition, mathematician, dentition

The analysis goes by the sounds sought to be rhymed. Thus the rhyming sound in the first group is Ā; and the identities are all BĀ—BĀ, BĀ, o-BĀ′, dis-o-BĀ′. In the 5th group, the identities of the first two with the rhyming sound TĒ (or TĬ), are: loy'al-TĒ', re-al'i-TĒ'. As single rhymes, the third word would be pos'si-bil'i-TĒ. The last three here, considered as triple rhymes, are pos'si-BĬL'ĭ-tĭ, prob'a-BĬL'ĭ-tĭ, im-pen-e-tra-BĬL'ĭ-tĭ. In every case, we have identities, whether of 1, 2 or 3 syllables. These must be rigorously excluded from verse and poetry in English.

False Rhymes: Differing Vowels

The accented vowel sounds must always be identical. Failure in this means no rhyme. The couplings once classed as ear-rhymes fall within this category:

earth, hearth	real, steal
are, bare	flow, allow
north, forth	meet, wet

All but the *real-steal group* constitute acceptable consonance; and they may be used as such, if the writer understands that this is not rhyme, but a differing convention. Train your ear to the accuracy that will distinguish between such mismatings as *north* and *forth*. If they seem to you to rhyme, analyze them:

> *Gnaw* does not rhyme with *foe*. The first is the sound of
> ô heard in talk; the other, the sound of ō heard in folk.
> Adding an -*r* to each, *nor* does not rhyme with *fore* or
> *four*.
> Adding a -*th* to each, *north* does not rhyme with *forth*.

Rhyming sounds for *north* include the baseball player Orth, *swarth,* the archaic *abhorr'th,* etc.; rhymes for *forth* (or *fourth*) include the archaic *pour'th, ador'th,* etc.

As for *real* and *steal,* the first is a dissyllable, the second a monosyllable. They no more rhyme than *dais* and *lais:* dā'is and lāis, *lais* having here the sound of *lays* or *laze. Real* rhymes with *ideal, hymeneal,* etc.; *steal* with *heel, Castille, deshabille, O'Neill,* etc.

FALSE RHYMES: DIFFERING TERMINAL CONSONANTS

This error is as common as the former one (except for eye-rhymes) is uncommon. The following types of words are often matched, under the mistaken idea that they are rhymes:

> main, game
> hate, shape
> feed, sleet, sleep
> blame, games
> miss, kissed
> baker, hater
> comfort, discernment
> silver, deliver
> orange, lozenge

The first three of these, and the sixth, constitute accurate assonance. But assonance is not at home in English versification; it is ordinarily used because the versifier believes that the combinations rhyme, when they do not. If assonance is to be used, it should be the exclusive convention; or used in as masterly a fashion as Edna St. Vincent Millay uses it, in a poem permitting rhyme and consonance also.

Watch out for using plurals or other inflections (as, *games, kissed*) to mate with the ordinary sound of the uninflected word-stem. The *-s* (usually pronounced *z*) or the *-d* makes the sounds following the accented vowel different. Of the type of *comfort, discernment* are such misgroupings as: *sorrow, hallow; passing, running,* where the terminal unaccented identities *-ow,* or *-ing* do not satisfy the definition of rhyme. This type of error is rooted deep in folk-usage, and must be carefully watched for.

Examples of this type of false rhymes are certainly found in the masters. But it is the prerogative of the poet to write as he sees fit; and if his poetry has compensating virtues, the slips are forgiven. Where Byron and Browning slip into such gaucheries, small perfectionists, like Swinburne, Housman, Robinson, Chesterton and Poe, are never guilty of them. A precise use of assonance is an audacious experiment; slovenly rhyming, with assonance appearing where rhyme is expected, is a sure sign of mediocrity in versification. Once the versifier has learned his craft, he can break the rules when and where and how he pleases. Until then, his energy had best go toward learning the rules.

FALSE RHYMES THROUGH MISPRONUNCIATION

Errors of mispronunciation account for quite a number of false rhymes. *Forth—north,* also classified as an "eye-rhyme," is an example of this. Until the versifier has trained his ear to distinguish between the sounds of these two differently pronounced words, he has not reached a real mastery of sound-differentiation.

One common mispronunciation is the omission of the *r*, found among seaboard Southerners and in many other localities. Examples of this error are the effort to rhyme such groups of words as the following:

fork, talk	morn, dawn	mourn, alone
car, ma, pa	report, coat	pork, choke
lord, broad	charm, balm	

stalking, corking	mourning, groaning
morning, dawning	fire, Hezekiah
four, Noah	charming, balming

None of these coupled words rhymes. The *r* makes all the difference. In light and colloquial verse, they can be rhymed, by utilizing the mispronunciation.

The Southern omission of the terminal *d* in words like *behind* causes similar miscouplings:

rind, mine	friend, men	hand, man

The fact that the first three of these are mispronounced rin', han', frien', does not make them accurate rhymes, since the appeal of the verse is not limited to mispronouncing Southerners. They could be used in dialect verse as rin', frien' and han'.

The similar omission of a terminal *g* occurs over a territory far greater than the Southern states. It leads to similar errors:

parting, martin, marten	herding, burden
slighting, whiten	floating, oaten
rioting, quiet in	tatting, satin

In dialect verse, such couplings are, of course, proper. But in verse not using dialect, the *g* in words like *parting* should be as audible as the *g* in *God*.

A rarer case is mispronunciations caused by unfamiliarity with the language as pronounced. This has caused couplings like:

singer, finger, ginger	Natal, fatal
heinous, Venus	Hades, spades

Related to this is a mere ignorance of pronunciation, as in mis-rhymes like:

fete, mete   show, vow

Pronunciation must be mastered, before rhyming can be accurate.

FALSE RHYMES: DOUBLET RHYMES FOR DOUBLE RHYMES

It is entirely proper, as a stunt, to rhyme pairs, triplets or more accented words in phrases, as in these instances:

> I want to find a *long hill,*
> Because I have a *strong will.*

> I love to see *spring rain fall,*
> Before birds on *wing stain all.*

> There is a *sky-blue sprite there,*
> Full of a *high hue, bright, fair.*

But this is a definite rhyming stunt, and should be understood so by the versifier. *Long* rhymes with *strong,* and *hill* with *will;* but *long hill* does not rhyme with *strong will*—instead, it rhymes with *strong hill,* and *strong will* with *long will.* The same is true of the more complicated other groups.

In much careless verse, such groups are considered as a single instance of rhyme; and this violates the definition of rhyme. An example is the familiar:

childhood, wildwood,

where the consonants (*h, w*), introducing the unaccented syllables, differ. Here *child* rhymes with *wild,* and *hood* with *wood.* But *childhood* does not rhyme with *wildwood:* instead, it would rhyme with such a mosaic grouping as *wild hood, mild hood;* and *wild-wood* with *mild wood,* as a *child would,* and the like. George M. Cohan's famous misrhyme, *Norfolk, war talk,* is of this type.

Thus *byway* and *sly play* do not rhyme, though the constituent parts of each do rhyme; nor do *sea-side* and *tree-tied.* Such word groupings are never double rhymes; they are two rhymes, or two pairs of rhymes. Noel Coward similarly misrhymes *inmate* and *in late;* and in *The Love Nest,* that popular favorite, we find *love-nest* and *dove-rest.* As double rhymes, these fail, however much they may be sanctified through their usage by experts in versification. Each one consists of two perfect pairs of rhymes, and, as such, it passes.

RHYME-INDUCED WORDS

Now we come to a far more serious fault in rhyming, which is true of many of the ablest practitioners of versification. The rhyme sound must never be induced or ordered forth by some rhyming mate; it must, instead, fit naturally into the wording— as naturally as if the whole had been spoken in prose. This is a result hard to achieve, but it is essential.

Thus, if your first line is

> We celebrate this merry Christmas,

and you desire couplet rhyming, the only possible complete rhyme is *isthmus,* whose preferred pronunciation omits the *th,* as that of Christmas omits the *t.* For *strabismus,* the only other possibility, is pronounced ĬZ′mus; unless, at that, we go to such a mosaic rhyme as *this* muss, or:

> No mistletoe to let a kiss muss
> A flawless make-up.

It is essential that the reader or hearer never suspect that the coupling *isthmus* was used because of the *Christmas,* and because there was no other rhyming sound available. Thus we might have:

> We celebrate this merry Christmas,
> Exiled here on the narrow isthmus
> Between the rigorous winter cold
> And further snows still to unfold.

Beware of more obvious couplings:

> We celebrate this merry Christmas,
> As sea is split from sea by isthmus.

The same fault of rhyme-induction can come in far simpler rhymes:

> The birds are singing out their hearts
> Because at last the summer starts. . . .
>
> Above us is an airplane—
> Look, you can see it there plain! . . .
>
> The rainbow follows every storm
> To make the hues of heaven warm.

The effort to improvise rhyme-induced couplings is increasingly difficult, the more you are trained to avoid this fault, and let your rhymes always come with the natural order of good conversation. And yet, it is a fault which mars much verse and much poetry.

Browning threw this injunction overboard, as in this rococo passage from the poem about Pacchiarotto, already quoted:

> Long after the last of your number
> Has ceased my front door to encumber,
> While, treading down rose and ranunculus,
> Your *Tommy-make-room-for-your-uncle*-us!
> Troop, all of you man or homunculus,
> Quick march! for Xanthippe, my housemaid,
> If once on your pates she a souse made
> With what, pan or pot, bowl or *skoramis*,
> First comes to her hand—things were more amiss!
> I would not for worlds be your place in—
> Recipient of slops from a basin!

This is an anthology of bad rhyming usages. In direct speech, this would be—assuming the more difficult parts can be understood:

Long after the last of your number has ceased to encumber my front door, while, treading down rose and (ranunculus) buttercup, Your (whatever that phrase means) troops, all of you, man or dwarf, march quickly! For if once Xanthippe, my housemaid, drenched your pates with whatever came first to her hand, pan, pot, bowl, or Grecian container, things would be more amiss! I would not be in your place for worlds—recipient of slops from a basin!

Four inversions, all of them induced by the rhyming; a false rhyme (*ranunculus, uncle-us,* for a long ū is in the former sound); and all thoroughly unnatural in phrasing. Such verbal gymnastics are relished in light verse, providing they are used naturally, which these are not. In serious poetry they are a blemish, since they attract our attention to the perverted virtuosity of the performer, not to what he has to say.

Rhymes should be inserted in the natural order of words used in good conversation. Otherwise rhyming ceases to be an ornament, and becomes a blemish.

The one final warning is to avoid perfect rhymes that have been used so frequently that they have become banal, hackneyed, clichés:

kiss, bliss	love, above, turtle-dove	earth, mirth
June, moon	spring, wing burn, yearn	death, breath

Any of these can be revivified by a new and unexpected usage. Otherwise, find fresher rhyming terminals; or call upon consonance to save you from banality.

Another group of undesirable rhymes is rhymes too similar to their neighboring words, especially neighboring rhymes. For rhymes to be most effective, they should have sharp, clear-cut outlines, and not blur and become confused with nearby words. If your rhyming scheme is 1,2,3,2, this would be an unwise grouping:

> I do not like a stormy night;
> I have no traffic with the rain,
> Playing its silly lashing game
> Against the beaten window-pane.

For here the terminal sound in *game* is so similar to the rhyming pair, *rain-pane,* that the hearer is sure to be bewildered, and probably come to the conclusion that *game* was meant for a rhyme, and turned into a faulty one. It is even more confusing to have such rhymes as the following—the patterns here being 1,2,1,2:

> I find a reassuring charm
> In nights quickened by rain and storm;
> I'm sure they cannot do me harm
> So long as I keep dry and warm. . . .

> Snow is falling deep,
> Intermixed with sleet,
> And the meadows sleep
> 'Neath the chilly sheet. . . .

> Now the night is all serene,
> And the shining candles gleam
> Far across the darkened scene
> With a fascinating beam.

In all of these cases, the too great resemblance of the rhyming sounds is disconcerting, and misleads the ear as to which words rhyme with which. Similar bewildering groups would include *hear, stir, near, fur; hit, his, lit, melodies,* and so on. These are increasingly blurring, as they use the more sonorous vowels and such consonants as *m, n, r, l, t, p,* etc.

Lanier words this warning by saying that such rhyming sounds, nearly resembling each other, are like two shades of red in which one fades the other. It is always wise to choose neighboring rhymes that are quite distinct from each other.

Once the rule is thoroughly understood, it is the prerogative of the poet to violate it, if he desires. At times he will gain a subtle music, especially in thoughtful poetry, by deliberately bringing such similar rhymes into juxtaposition. This is always experimental, and should be weighed carefully before being used.

A warning as to the position of rhymes is that they should not be placed so far apart that the effect of one is forgotten before the second is heard. This warning is given by Lanier; and in *The Revenge of Hamish* he violates it more definitely than any other poem that occurs to mind. This, too, is a prerogative of genius.

TONE COLOR IN THE RHYMES

Of possible rhymes, clearly those are strongest and most effective which have the most sonorous and effective tone color. The long vowels are all effective, for the voice dwells on them; and this includes the *a* heard in *harm.* Since the short vowels, heard in *bat, step, clip, not, but,* are relatively hurried over, from the vowel standpoint they are less desirable in rhyming than the former group. Of the consonants, the more sonorous (incidentally, the easiest to sing) are *r, l, m, n,* and next to these *t, p, d.* Each consonantal sound tends to have a different effect: the sibilant hiss in *s* being very different from the sustained rumble in *m* or *r.* There are times when the thing to be said demands the swifter vowels, the more staccato consonants. Let the thing to be said dictate the type of rhymes that are used. Always, too, saying naturally what is to be said is most important of all. This advice about tone-color in the rhymes applies most definitely when the versifier has a choice between two pairs of rhymes, both equally satisfying from the standpoint of what he has to say.

THE CREATIVE FUNCTION OF RHYME

Rhyming in versification does not merely mean the insertion of rhyming words at various specified places, as if they were meaningless refrains which could be put in or taken out without in any way affecting the rest of the word usage. It is a far more dynamic, creative and shaping thing than that.

Once the poet has decided upon or written down a line which he intends to rhyme, its terminal word assumes control over the terminal word or words that must rhyme with it; and, of course, with all words leading up to and away from this word. The choice of what is to be said next is enormously limited by this terminal word, for its rhyming mates are infinitesimal in number, compared to the word resources of the language. To make this clear, once Shakespeare had written the now familiar line,

> The quality of mercy is not strained,

he could not, in rhymed verse, have gone ahead with:

> It droppeth as the gentle rain from Heaven
> Upon the place beneath. It is twice blessed.
> It blesseth him that gives, and him that takes.

If he had been using couplet rhyming, the second line would have had to rhyme with *strained;* in alternate rhyming, the third line. This means that the terminal word of the second (or third) line must be chosen from the list of rhymes for *strained* in the rhyming dictionary; and they are not infinite in number, all being preterites or past participles of the limited number of verbs rhyming with *strain:*

> abstain, appertain, arraign, ascertain, attain, bestain, brain (used as a verb), cane, campaign, complain, constrain, contain, co-ordain, deign, detain, etc.

Of course, *constrain,* an identity with *strain,* is omitted. Assuming alternate rhyming, as in the opening of an Elizabethan sonnet, our fourth line must now rhyme with *Heaven;* and here our rhymes are far more limited in number, being restricted to:

> eleven, leaven, seven.

And that is all, except where custom (shielding it under the mis-leading name of "poetic license") permitted this limited group of consonances:

> driven, forgiven, given, riven,

and a few more. Let us drive this home: the fact that this is to be rhymed at once vetoes the third and fourth lines as Shakespeare wrote them; and dictates that in place of these lines be put lines terminating with one of the *-ained* preterites and one of the few mates for *Heaven*. Even if the poet did his best, he would have to arrive at something like:

> The quality of mercy is not strained;
> It droppeth as the gentle rain from Heaven
> On earth, with double blessing pre-ordained—
> On him who gives, and him to whom it's given.

Grant that the meaning has not materially suffered, but the nat-uralness—shall I say the beauty?—are all gone and mere tinkling verse replaces the original poetry. And now *blessed* must go out as a terminal, and so must *takes*. Or, if we are to retain these as rhyming terminals, we must drop *strained* and *Heaven* and, doing our best, arrive at:

> The quality of mercy is unjessed:
> It droppeth as a sudden shower breaks
> Upon the place beneath. It is twice blessed.
> It blesseth him that gives and him that takes.

Unjessed, meaning unchained, is Elizabethan; but its meaning is largely forgotten today.

It is clear that, no matter which pair of terminals we retain, we have forced the original free-flowing poetry into a tight con-ventional pattern, with a pitifully limited choice of words; and have chipped and mutilated our original meaning and its spon-taneous expression. To make up for this, we have the tinkle of rhyme: the repetition pleasure from terminal sound-identities. But the pleasure must be indeed extreme to compensate for what we have surrendered. The greater poets, and the great poets as they matured, recognized this, in their more mature products, and turned from rhyme to blank verse of some sort—metric, accent, or free. Certain simple lyrics, even with most of them, still came with the repetition pleasure of rhyme used as an ornament; but the ampler works avoided its artificiality.

Imagine what *Hamlet* or *The Tempest* would have been like, if rhymed throughout! Yet the ages of Dryden and Pope severely blamed the author of those plays for omitting rhyme. As for *Paradise Lost*, let Milton speak his own vigorous words:

> The measure is English heroic verse without rime . . . rime being no necessary adjunct or true ornament of poem or good verse, in longer works especially, but the invention of a barbarous age, to set off wretched matter and lame metre; graced indeed since by the use of some famous modern poets, carried away by custom, but much to their own vexation, hindrance, and constraint to express many things otherwise, and for the most part worse, than else they would have expressed them. . . . (True musical delight . . . consisting) not in the jingling sound of like endings. . . . The troublesome and modern bondage of riming.

Shelley, in his *Preface* to *The Revolt of Islam*, underwrote this fully:

> I have adopted the stanza of Spenser (a measure inexpressibly beautiful) not because I consider it a finer model of poetical harmony than the blank verse of Shakespeare and Milton, but because in the latter there is no shelter for mediocrity; you must either succeed or fail.

It is well for the versifier aspiring to be a poet of authentic and unwarped utterance to ponder these words, and the reality behind them. For purposes of the simple song or ornamental verse, rhyme has its immense and pleasing place; but the ultimate speech of the soul does not naturally flow into it.

Yet, once it has been decided upon, its power must be comprehended, and utilized. This power is by no means purely negative and inspiration-warping. It becomes at once, by a sort of paradox, affirmative, and inspiration-awakening. Not for mere translation of blank verse into rhyme, as in the quatrain from *The Merchant of Venice*—a task as difficult as any translation; but for the actual writing and development of first-rate poetry and verse.

After all, the poet has an infinity of things to say; and at times any stimulus, even an irrelevant and mechanical one, can unlock some utterance, that may be of far more significance than that at first intended. In this deeper sense, the quality of being rhyme-induced (that is, the dictation by a rhyming sound, once chosen, of its mating rhyme and all that leads into it and out of it) may be a distinct benefit, and may be a theme-widener and a verse-beautifier to the poet. Rhyming and its exacting demands are definite brain-stimulants, which may spur on the poetic imagination. It is true that, where the poem is planned or comes unplanned with rounded contours and finality of utterance, the insertion of the requirements of rhyme limits the field, so that only the master achieves in it that finality of natural utterance which is one of the inimitable charms of great poetry. But where there is any vagueness of outline in the poem as it comes, or any uncertainty of utterance, the requirements, themselves, of rhyme may direct the flow of inspiration into more effective utterance than would have been the case without rhyme. The content sterility of much blank verse—metric, accent, and free—is a strong negative proof of this.

A negative example is my *Night Entrance: Isla da Margarita, Venezuela,* which I definitely intended as a sonnet. But the first line came forth spontaneously,

> The cradle moon beyond the creaking cordage,—

At once the versifier knew that there was no rhyming-mate for this; that the line was right, and should not be changed; and that this was no time, with the passion of the tropic night surging through him, in impressions so fugitive that they had to be caught now or never, to ponder an evasion of the rules for the sonnet, or change the planned form. Without thought, he altered the rhyme scheme so that the next three lines rhymed with each other—and with what relief he leapt to a simpler rhyme-sound, full of rhyming-mates!

> The wide road of silver over the sea;
> And, at the side, swishing eternally,
> The lapping water tonguing us hungrily.

Now the potency of that first line came in—negatively, and partially positively. For it dictated that lines five and nine of the sonnet should end in unrhymed trochees, in each instance followed by three lines rhyming with each other:

> Low glow-edged clouds, like breasted incredible mountains.
> Jutting rocks black in the moon's pour.
> The far twinkle of lights on ship and shore,
> And our loosed island rooted to earth once more.

Perhaps it was irritation at the spoiling effect of rhyme on that first line that swung the versifier into a minor accent rhyme and a consonance in the third quatrain:

> The glittering brilliance of the southern heavens,
> With barred Orion wheeling over us,
> And the low golden splendor of Canopus,
> Followed by the all alien Southern Cross;

and then the couplet, to complete a variant sonnet in a form not without merit:

> And the pole star, flickering and very dim,
> Eternally at the horizon's rim.

Perhaps this example will illustrate, better than many another, the subtle influence of the exigencies of rhyming. For here the terminal *cordage* dictated the triplet rhyming of lines 2-4, 6-8, and 10-12; as well as the trochaic endings, unrhymed, of lines 5 and 9, and, by this dictation arbitrarily walled possible words this side or that of its swiftly-erected boundaries, and to the end played a creative part, largely negative but still shaping, down to the very last couplet.

Positive proof of the creative quality of rhyme is more difficult to arrive at. Let us consider one of my recent poems, *The Path*, for analysis in this regard. It is, on the surface, loosely and naturally written. Yet, take the first stanza:

> If I had a path, I'd keep it open,
> I'd keep it open, for people to pass,
> Going to anywhere they wanted,
> Over the straggly weeds and grass.

Here *grass* is definitely rhyme-induced. The versifier had to struggle to get any fourth line that followed naturally after the natural movement of the first two, indeed of the first three lines. The result is, to put it most kindly, no gain; and at worst only a minor blemish. In other words, to revert to the *Merchant of Venice* example, here, as in that case, the meaning stopped with *wanted*, and the fourth line is surplusage, inserted because a 1,2,3,2 rhyme-scheme had been planned. This is no doubt as innocuous a fourth line as could be added; but it is, in essence, padding; and good poetry has as little of that as possible.

In the fifth stanza, however,

> If there's a way opened before you,
> Even a disused woodland track.
> It's something to help you to remember,
> And you always might want to be coming back.

Here the terminal *back* is just as much rhyme-induced as *grass*
was. The difference is in the result. The requirements of rhyme
here suddenly stretched wide the writer's meaning to something
better and more important than he originally had to say. One
of the favorite stanzas in the poem,

> I guess the little folk must use it,
> Whatever there is that lives in woods,

commenced so; and at once the very limitation of possible rhymes
aroused the versifier to the effective and almost inevitable conclusion, considering the language's limited rhyme-supply:

> Bowling the crimson partridge berries,
> Playing leapfrog on toadstool hoods.

> The path is always waiting for you,
> However the grass and the vines may grow,
> If you're berrying or after flowers,
> Or feel that you've simply got to go

> Somewhere out of the indoor tension
> Into a world that's cool and green,
> Where you can walk the bitter mood off,
> And come back taller and serene.

There is nothing rhyme-induced in the stanza following the one
about the little folk. But, in the next stanza, the limited rhyming
facilities for *green* definitely guided the poet into arriving at the
effective "taller and serene."

In the final stanza, the poet determined to end with the couplet he had started with—a device frequently effective. This, of
course, induced the terminal rhyme that preceded it:

> It isn't a path, when no one passes,
> Barred by some silly selfish ass.
> If I had a path, I'd keep it open,
> Always wider, for people to pass.

The change made in this repetend, at the opening of the last line,
was not rhyme-induced and is as effective as the best achievement
that rhyme created. The second line, it must be granted, is weak,

due to the requirements of rhyming. But the broadening device in "always wider" saves the ending. So it is that rhyming functions creatively.

When in the sonnet mood, repeatedly the final line comes first; or, after the first line comes, the final line comes next, as the climax of what is to be said; or, when the whole development is being considered before any words have come, the final line swarms up first out of the nebulosity. Thereupon the poet must shape his whole sonnet toward this last line. Since the result is so often pleasing, it cannot be said that the device is wholly a blemish. It always alters and guides the original inspiration—the matter pushed up by the unconscious; but this alteration may be an improvement quite as often as a deterioration. This definite emotional and mental process has its analogue on the material plane, as when a thin batter is poured into a breadstick iron. The individual molds for the breadsticks correspond to the lines of the sonnet: shaped as to length and number of syllables, and location of accent and unaccent, and even in many cases as to terminal rhyme-sound. The poet may not pour his inspiration forth freely, if he wants a sonnet, any more than the cook pours the batter freely on an iron spider, when he desires breadsticks. But in each case the result justifies the process. In life, some liberties must be surrendered, to retain the maximum of liberty: this is part of the social system. And so the sonnet comes, rhyme-guided throughout, often by its last line, which came first.

An example of a creative last line, which came first, can at times be picked out inerrantly, as, from my *Eagle Sonnets:*

> Beauty is all we know and all we are.
>
> *xviii*

More often, with me, the first line emerges first, and thereafter dictates what follows:

> I have been sure of three things all my life.
>
> *iii*

> I cannot know that other men exist.
>
> *iv*

> O bitter moon, O cold and bitter moon,
>
> *ix*

> When down the windy vistas of the years
>
> *xi*

That which made me was bred of ache and bleeding,

xiv

We are the singing shadows beauty casts,

xx

In most of these cases, however, the last line came long before all the intervening lines had been finished; was jotted down hurriedly at the bottom; and in turn thereafter dictated the gradual mount up to it, as a climax. No doubt the most outstanding example of this, in the sonnets referred to, was the xith, where the last line was:

Its silence sings a dusty song of dust.

Here the creative power of this line not only dictated what led up to it; it commenced the pattern for the ensuing sonnet, as well:

This is the song it sings: that all was dust,
And dust again shall have its regal hour,
When braggart life and breathing beauty must,
As all things must, crumble into its power.

In passing, the wide use of the other sound-repetition devices should be noted here:

Alliteration: silence, sings; dusty, dust; song, sings; braggart, breathing, beauty.
Word repetition: sings, sings; dusty, dust, dust, dust.
Assonance: regal, breathing; dusty, crumble.
Consonance: song, sings.
Phonetic syzygy: braggar*t*, brea*th*ing, beau*t*y, mus*t*, *th*ings, etc.

There are, of course, subtler examples: all coming without planning on the versifier's part—the natural repetitional devices of verse. The same quality of opening sonnet lines, acting as dictators of what follows, appears amply in my *The White Peacock:*

I bring three little gauds for you to wear,

viii

And still the starveling crumbles at your gates,

xii

Ahoy, there, you slim craft with the virgin ensign!

xxii

I'll marry you under a Romany patteran!

xxiii

You are the lock, to which I am the key;

xxxiii

Now you have spread your wings to every wind,

xlviii

Examples of the obvious subsequent shaping quality of last lines from these sonnets appear especially in:

Two of the black gentry, off together!

xxii

Two falling stars . . . but, O my love, two stars!

xxiii

Gloria, my dear mate beyond all knowing.

xlviii

It is, of course, obvious that the two most important lines of a sonnet are the first and the last. At times the white-hot importance of the last line more than excuses a definite rhyme-induced rhyming terminal preceding it:

The will beneath, as rank as swampland fennel,
Lashes dog reason back into his kennel.
The Eagle Sonnets, xvii

When the versifier wrote this, he did not know whether or not there was such a thing as swampland fennel. He still does not know. He had no idea whether it was rank or not, if it did exist. Botany here had to yield to poetic truth: a parlous proceeding, not to be indulged in too far. But here the expected rhyme is inserted; and all the emphasis falls upon the crashing conclusion, which is what is remembered. Shall I explain this as an emergency created by the requirements of rhyme, met by heroic measures? The sonnet succeeds, and the essential last line comes through unaltered. That is the main thing. Here rhyme is not the benevolent despot, but the ruthless dictator. And so used are we to the effectiveness of the sonnet, that few could consider this group of poems more effective, if done without rhyme. Just as few would consider *Othello* as effective if rhyme had been used throughout.

YOUR MENTAL RHYMING DICTIONARY

A score of years ago my *Mental Rhyming Dictionary* was invented, which appears in perfected form in *The Craft of Poetry* and also in *The Complete Rhyming Dictionary and Poet's Craft Book*. It has proved valuable to thousands of poets and versifiers, both as a necessary supplement to the rhyming dictionaries on the market, and in emergencies when no rhyming dictionary is available. A rhyming dictionary is at times needed in the writing or critical revision of rhymed poetry; and it is indispensable in writing light verse and formal verse, such as the ballade, requiring a specified number of perfect rhymes to a given rhyme-sound. We will soon find that the technique of the *Mental Rhyming Dictionary* must be applied to any rhyming dictionary on the market, before it can be of full use to the versifier.

Here is the method. First write down—having memorized them in advance—all the common consonantal sounds in the language. Here is a phonetic division of these sounds, which is rather accurate:

CONSONANTAL SOUNDS

Single	*Double*	*Triple*	*Rare*
(Vowel—no con-sonant)			
B	BL		BW
	BR		
CH			
D	DR		DW
F	FL		
	FR		
G	GL		
	GR		GW
H	HW (what)		
J			
K (C)	KL		
	KR		
	KW (QU)		
L			
M			
N			
P	PL		PW
	PR		
R			
S	SK (SC)	SKR (SCR)	
		SKW (SQU)	
	SL		

CONSONANTAL SOUNDS—*continued*

Single	Double	Triple	Rare
	SM		
	SN		
	SP	SPL	
		SPR	
	ST	STR	SV
	SW		
SH	SHR		
T	TR		
	TW		
th (thin)	thR		
TH (this)			
V			VL
W			
Y			
Z			ZH
			ZL

To remember this more simply:

1. There are 23 single consonantal sounds: None (the vowel opening), B, CH, D, F, G, H, J, K (C), L, M, N, P, R, S, SH, T, th, TH, V, W, Y, and Z.
2. Both L and R are used after 6 sounds: B, F, G, K (C), P, and SP.
3. R without L is used after 6 sounds: D, SK, SH, ST, T and th.
4. W is used commonly after H, K (KW, QU) and T; and rarely after B, D, G and P: 7 instances altogether.
5. S takes after it K (C), L, M, N, P, T, W, KR (CR), PL, PR, TR and KW (Q)—12 sounds.
6. There are four other rare usages: SV, VL, ZH and ZL.

Thus the number of sounds are 23; 7; 6; 6; 12; and 4, a total of 58.

USING THE MENTAL RHYMING DICTIONARY

Suppose you wished to find the possible rhymes for *sea* (pronounced SĒ). The rhyming sound is -Ē. Keeping this in mind, run down the 58 varieties of possible consonantal sounds—remembering to sound mentally words of two or more syllables, accented on the last, which would give us rhymes: as BRĒ in debris. This would give us:

Vowel, ———
B bee, be BL ——— BR debris, Brie
CH Manichee

D Dee, fiddle-de-dee DR heraldry
F fee, apostrophe FL flee, flea FR free
G ghee GL glee GR agree
H he HW whee
J gee, mortgagee
K (C) key, quay KL ———— KR decree KW (QU) soliloquy
L lee, lea, jealousy, etc., jubilee
M me, epitome
N knee, anemone
P pea PL plea, panoply PR ———— PW point d'appui
R Marie, revelry
S see SK (SC) ski SKR ———— SKW (SQ) ————
    SL ———— SM ———— SN snickersnee
    SP ———— SPL ———— SPR spree, esprit
    ST ———— STR ———— SW ————
SH she, debauchee SHR ————
T tee, ability, devotee TR tree TW ————
th sympathy thR three
TH thee
V eau de vie, vis-a-vis
W wee, we, ennui
Y ye, employee
Z Zuyder Zee, bourgeoisie, chimpanzee, devisee

We have found here 38 out of a possible 58 rhymes, a large enough number to satisfy the most exacting formal verse many times over. And more unusual rhymes, including mosaic rhymes made with parts of words, might fill out all or most of the rest.

Naturally the haul is not always so large, when we cast the net of our Mental Rhyming Dictionary into the sea of English words. Suppose we had ended our first line with *huge,* in a form requiring three more words to be rhymed with this. A combing of the *Complete Rhyming Dictionary,* with the results classified by our Mental Rhyming Dictionary technique, would give us only:

B gamboge
F demonifuge, febrifuge, insectifuge, subterfuge, vermifuge
H huge
SKR (SCR) Scrooge, scrouge
ST stooge

Here are only four rhyming possibilities; but they are so uncolloquial and unusual in meaning and usage, in the main, that we might well have to alter our first line, and end with a word that can be more easily rhymed.

Double or feminine rhymes are arrived at in the same way. Suppose we wanted to find possible rhymes for *banded*. By running down the consonantal sounds classified by our Mental Rhyming Dictionary, or by applying this to the harvest baled together in the rhyming dictionary, we arrive at:

B banded, contrabanded, disbanded
BR branded, brandied
D deodanded
H handed, backhanded, clean-handed, forehanded, high-handed, etc.
K (C) candid, candied
L landed, unlanded
M demanded, commanded, countermanded, etc.
P expanded
S sanded, sandied
STR stranded

These are all, until we compose such mosaic rhymes as:

Ann did, man did, catamaran did, a grand id

—*id* being used both in biology and psychoanalysis; or, with a split mosaic rhyme:

You noticed, then, the grand id-
Iotic way he landed.

When we come to triple rhymes, we have to make use of our Mental Rhyming Dictionary the same way, to divide into their proper brackets the rhymes furnished by the best rhyming dictionary so far available. Suppose we wanted the rhymes to *poetical*. Here is what we would find:

Vowel aloetical, noetical, poetical
B alphabetical
J (G) apologetical, energetical, exegetical
K catechetical
L homiletical
M arithmetical, cosmetical, hermetical
N planetical
R anchoretical, emporetical, heretical, theoretical
T dietetical
th aesthetical, antipathetical, antithetical, apathetical, epithetical, hypothetical

And that is all. The rule for using this Mental Rhyming Dictionary, of course, is the essence of simplicity:

Choose only one rhyme out of each group!

Follow that rule, and, provided you have properly applied the Mental Rhyming Dictionary technique, your rhyming will invariably be perfect. In this case, a mosaic rhyme would be more difficult; but it could be done—it can always be done, by ingenuity:

> And do not ever let these petty cal-
> Isthenics make you energetical. . . .
>
> I'm feeling quiet poetical.
> So come out on the jetty, Cal.

The indispensability of this Mental Rhyming Dictionary technique appears—to choose an extreme example—if we desired a triple rhyme to *logical*. *The Complete Rhyming Dictionary* gives 81 words which apparently rhyme with this. Yet the first 68 of these, and the last 13, furnish not a single rhyme! In other words, there are here 80 identities to *logical,* as the Mental Rhyming Dictionary technique establishes:

> L aerological, amphibiological, amphibological, analogical, anthological, anthropological, archaeological, astrological, bibliological, biological, bryological, chronological,

clear down to the final *zymological*. Only one actual rhyme appears in the 82 listed words:

> G synagogical

To this might be added its rhyming identity, *pedagogical*. If we required a third rhyme for *logical,* only a mosaic rhyme would aid us:

> You boast that you are logical.
> You're only pedagogical!
> Just as your body's podgy, Cal,
> Your mind has gotten stodgy, Cal!

Clever light verse often requires such accurate rhyming. Only the technique of the Mental Rhyming Dictionary can give it to us.

RHYMING DICTIONARIES

About 1679, the first rhyming dictionary appeared in English: *English Parnassus, or a Help to English Poesie,* by Joshua Poole, of Clare Hall, Cambridge. It contained a collection of many rhyming monosyllables in English. Edward Bysshe, in 1702, published *The Art of English Poetry,* containing a plentiful "magazine" or dictionary of rhymes, and this remained the standard for half a century. In 1775 Walker's *Rhyming Dictionary* appeared; and, for all of its faults, it remained the standard for years. Other rhyming dictionaries include Dr. Trussler's in 1783, Tom Hood's in 1877, and, best of all so far, Loring's *Rhyming Lexicon;* Burgess Johnson's, about 1935; and my *The Complete Rhyming Dictionary,* 1936, which in turn became the standard.

These may be grouped thus:

1. Those which, like certain editions of Walker, arrange by word terminational spelling only. Thus, the first word group included consists of words ending in *-a:*

    asthma, comma, dogma, drama, era, etc.;

and the last words would be those ending in *-uzz:*

    buzz, fuzz, etc.

The faults of this system are obvious. These rhyming sounds,

    vertebrae, quay, ye, lea, fee, pot-pourri, Brie, debris,
      esprit

would have to be looked for at 9 different places: and others here are omitted, which rhyme perfectly with these. This is the plinth of unhandiness.

2. Those restricted to rhymed monosyllables. For all that monosyllables dominate in serious rhymed English poetry, the first nineteen of Shakespeare's *Sonnets* have thirteen double rhymes; and the xxth alone has seven! Hence, it is clear that the monosyllabic rhyming dictionary is very deficient. Moreover, a typical one of this type—Brewer's with apparent phonetic division, commences:

    A compare ER, OR
    asthma, comma, dogma, era, gala

None of these rhyme with each other. *Asthma* rhymes with *fantasma, plasma,* etc.; *comma,* with *momma; drama* with *Brahma, lama, llama, pajama, panorama,* etc.; *era* with *chimera, Hera, lira,* etc.; *gala* with *shillalah;* or, with Italian *a,* almost with *calla, Allah, Valhalla;* while *dogma* has no rhyming mate. Meanwhile, this list omits practically every authentic *ä* rhyme:

> ah, aha, algebra, bah, camera, eclat, faux-pas, papa, Shah, spa, etc.

3. The first predominantly phonetic rhyming dictionary that became popular was Loring's. But his use of phonetic division was lax; rhymes of the type of *war,* for instance, not being as a rule listed as ÔR rhymes, but tending to appear in the A's. The outstanding phonetic rhyming dictionary is *The Complete Rhyming Dictionary*.

All these, faulty or not, required in actual use, to have the rhyming words regrouped and divided by the Mental Rhyming Dictionary technique. Each poet, in using any of them, either so regrouped the rhyming words, or else ran the risk of using identities, instead of rhymes. "The *Unabridged Rhyming Dictionary* uses this technique, and hence eliminates the otherwise necessary regrouping.

Never forget that, when the Mental Rhyming Dictionary has been applied and the words regrouped, one simple rule will be all that the versifier will have to learn:

Choose only one rhyme out of each group.

This will insure invariable perfect rhyming technique. Like all important inventions, its application is the essence of simplicity.

USING A RHYMING DICTIONARY TO LOCATE CONSONANCES

Consonance is today playing an increasing part in the writing of acceptable poetry and verse. A good rhyming dictionary can be used to arrive at all possible consonances for any given word, and fairly quickly, once the method is understood. Assuming that the use of the rhyming dictionary is understood, we would proceed as follows:

Suppose we desired all possible consonances for *hate*. This has the rhyming sound *AT*. In consonance with it would be all sounds of an accented vowel followed by *T*, providing the vowel differed from the *Ā* in *hate*. Here are the various sounds; and each group would have to be looked up, to arrive at all the possible consonances:

Under AT: ĂT acrobat, at, etc.

ÄT squat, etc.

Under ET: ĒT beat, etc.

ĔT bet, etc.

Under IT: ĪT fight, etc.

ĬT wit, etc.

Under OT: ŌT quote, etc.

ÔT caught, etc.

ŎT hot, etc.

OIT quoit, etc.

O͝OT foot, etc.

OUT bout, etc.

Under UT: ŪT brute, etc.

ŬT but, etc.

There are thus never more than the five major groups to look up; plus the variant sounds OI, OO and OU under the O'S. In actually writing verse, it is rarely necessary to look up more than two or three of these groups, to furnish the word or words in consonance that are desired.

In two-syllabled consonance, the method is the same. Thus, to find words in consonance with *enter,* we would search these five major groups:

Under AN'tur: ĀN'tur (painter), ĂN'tur (canter) .

Under EN'tur: No ĒN'tur words.

Under IN'tur: No ĪN'tur words. ĬN'tur (winter)

Under ON'tur: No ŌN'tur words. ÔN'tur (saunter)

[263]

OIN'tur (pointer). No ŎN'tur words.

OUN'tur (counter). No ŎON'tur words.

Under UN'tur: No ŪN'tur words. ŬN'tur (hunter)

In three-syllabled consonance, the same method would be followed. In view of the scarcity of common three-syllabled rhymes, consonance here is valuable and at times very pleasing. As, for *flattering,* ĂT́ ur-ing,

No ĀT'ur-ing or ÄT'ur-ing words.

ĔT'ur-ing (fettering). No ĒT'ur-ing.

ĬT'ur-ing (glittering) . No ĪT'ur-ing.

ŎT'ur-ing (tottering) . OIT'ur-ing (loitering).

No words commencing ŌT, ÔT, ŎOT, OUT'ur-ing.

ŬT'ur-ing (muttering). No ŪT'ur-ing.

Here we have five groups added, to supplement the limited group of perfect rhymes for *flattering.*

V

STANZA PATTERNS

STANZA DEFINED

A STANZA is one or more lines (or verses) of verse, constituting a division of a poem or verse. It corresponds, in versification, to a paragraph in prose, which may, of course, consist of from one sentence to many sentences. A prose paragraph is indented—that is, set inside, or to the right of, the flush line of the other lines— at its beginning, to set it off from the other paragraphs. A stanza in poetry may be similarly indented; or, as often, separated by additional space from the other stanzas; or otherwise set apart typographically.

Many dictionaries give also a more specialized definition for stanza: a formalized unit of a poem, of two or more (generally of four or more) lines recurrently identical in line-length, metrical structure, and rhyming pattern, where rhyme is used. This is merely a subhead of stanza, as at first defined.

A stanza is, in popular parlance, called a verse. A line is accurately called a verse. These double usages need cause no obscurity.

STANZAS OF ONE LINE

No poem comes to mind with formal stanzas consisting of only one line. A rhymed alphabet or an unrhymed one might be of this type; but usually these are in couplets, or set continuously.

Various examples of one-line stanzas, comparable to simple one-sentence paragraphs in prose, are:

This is the house that Jack built.

Mother Goose

Whoever you are, to you endless announcements! . . .

Democracy! near at hand to you a throat is now inflating itself and joyfully singing. . . .

With me firm holding, yet haste, haste on. . . .
Starting from Paumanok, WALT WHITMAN

You are, then, cold coward. . . .

Aye; but, beloved—
The Black Riders, STEPHEN CRANE

What are we? I know not.
The Monk in the Kitchen, ANNA HEMPSTEAD BRANCH

I don't know what part of the pasture you mean, . . .

He's a thriftier persons than some I could name.
Blueberries, ROBERT FROST

Pocahontas' body, lovely as a poplar, sweet as a red haw in November or a pawpaw in May, did she wonder? does she remember? . . . in the dust, in the cool tombs.
Cool Tombs, CARL SANDBURG

The Queen of Sheba came to see King Solomon. . . .

We were the oxen.
King Solomon and the Queen of Sheba, VACHEL LINDSAY

fathandsbangrag.
Portrait of a Pianist, E. E. CUMMINGS

Shantih   shantih   shantih
The Waste Land, T. S. ELIOT

My heel, at least, shall spare you.
Snake, JOHN RUSSELL McCARTHY

Shut up, you black sow! . . .

The factory girls, they have a pretty good time.
Birmingham, CLEMENT WOOD

These varied examples remind the poet or verse-writer that he is at full liberty to set off one line as a complete stanza by itself, whenever that adds to the effectiveness of his product.

ONE LINE POEMS

It should be remembered that groupings of any number of lines, from one upward, may constitute a complete poem, instead of a stanza. Examples of complete poems in only one line include:

I see in you the estuary that enlarges and spreads itself grandly as it pours into the great sea.
To Old Age, WALT WHITMAN

Of Equality—as if it harm'd me, giving others the same chances
and rights as myself—as if it were not indispensable to my
own rights that others possess the same.
Thought, WALT WHITMAN

Some may carp at regarding this as one line; but Whitman did.
Others may scan it, and proclaim that it is prose. Often both
schools of thought are right, in close matters dealing with versification. From Sidney Lanier's *Poem Outlines* there are a number of
exquisite single line poems:

Birth is but a folding of our wings. . . .

Star-drops lingering after sunlight's rain.

STANZAS OF TWO LINES: THE COUPLET

A stanza or a poem of two lines is called a couplet. In classical
and later prosody it is called a distich. It may be unrhymed:

One's-self I sing, a simple separate person,
Yet utter the word Democratic, the word En-Masse.
One's-Self I Sing, WALT WHITMAN

I am the grass.
Let me work.
Grass, CARL SANDBURG

A young moon deserts the cloudy chase,
And dreams in a garden of stars.
Day's End, GLORIA GODDARD

In classic prosody, an elegiac couplet consisted of a dactylic
hexameter, followed by a so-called dactylic pentameter. Here is
an example in English metric verse based on accent:

In the hexameter rises the fountain's silvery column,
In the pentameter aye falling in melody back.
Translation from Schiller, COLERIDGE

It may be rhymed:

Poems are made by fools like me,   1
But only God can make a tree.   1
Trees, JOYCE KILMER

Rhyming mates are indicated by the same number: 1,1 here.
This is the most obvious rhyming for couplets. However, verse
might be written in couplet stanzas, with the rhyming mates
placed in different couplets. A simple example would be:

[267]

The craze to make new forms in verse   1
Possesses poets everywhere.   2

The theory breathes like a prayer;   2
The practice often is a curse.   1

Just as easily, the couplets might have been rhymed 1,2; 1,2. Or more intricate rhyming schemes could be use: as, 1,2; 1,3; 3,4; 4,2, etc. In couplet stanzas, and indeed in stanzas of any length, the poet has the whole range of free verse, accent verse, and the different meters and combination of them, to choose from; while the lines may be of the same length, or of any desired lengths.

Love took up the glass of Time, and turned it in his glowing hands;
Every moment, lightly shaken, ran itself in golden sands;
                   Locksley Hall, TENNYSON

There will come soft rains and the smell of the ground,   1
And swallows circling with their shimmering sound;   1

And frogs in the pools singing at night,   2
And wild-plum trees in tremulous white;   2

Robins will wear their feathery fire,   3
Whistling their whims on a low fence wire.   3
      There Will Come Soft Rains, SARA TEASDALE

This is admirable 4-accent verse. Note how many minor accents are ignored in the form, or major accents are treated as minor accents: *soft, plum, fence,* etc.

COUPLET RHYMING: HEROIC COUPLETS

The word *couplet* is used in the phrase *couplet rhyming* to describe that device of rhyming in which each pair of lines, usually of the same length and metric or accent pattern, rhyme together; whether such pairs of lines constitute separate stanzas, or not. The rhymed iambic five-foot couplets were introduced by Chaucer:

He wayted after no pompe and reverence,   1
Ne maked him a spyced conscience,   1
But Cristes lore, and his apostles twelve,   2
He taughte, and first he folwed it himselfe.   2
  Prologue to Canterbury Tales, 525-528, CHAUCER

It was used by Spenser; by Marlowe, in *Hero and Leander;* by Donne; by Shakespeare, Fletcher, Ben Jonson and other dramatists. Elizabethan drama was written primarily in heroic blank verse—that is, unrhymed iambic pentameters. But even here the couplet, or two or more couplets, had a definite function. They were often used to announce the entrance of a new character. Thus Lady Macbeth's entrance is cued by this couplet, spoken by her husband:

> Hear it not, Duncan, for it is a knell
> That summons thee to heaven or to hell.
> *Macbeth, II, i*

Even more frequent is the use of the couplet to close a scene, as when Hamlet says:

> Till then sit still, my soul: foul deeds will rise,
> Though all the earth o'erwhelm them, to men's eyes.
> *Hamlet, I, ii*

The use of one or two couplets to close an act, or the play itself, is commonest of all:

> Within my tent his bones tonight shall lie,
> Most like a soldier, order'd honorably.—
> So, call the field to rest; and let's away,
> To part the glories of this happy day.
> *Julius Caesar, V, v.*

Iambic pentameter couplets were the dominant verse form in the ages of Dryden and of Pope, and are called *heroic couplets:*

> Three poets, in three distant ages born,   1
> Greece, Italy and England did adorn.   1
> The first in loftiness of thought surpassed;   2
> The next in majesty; in both, the last.   2
> The force of Nature could no further go: 3
> To make a third she joined the former two.   3
> *Under the Portrait of Milton,* JOHN DRYDEN

> Next, o'er his books his eyes began to roll,
> In pleasing memory of all he stole,
> Now here he supped, now there he plundered snug,
> And sucked all o'er, like an industrious bug.
> Here lay poor Fletcher's half-eat scenes, and here
> The frippery of crucified Moliere;
> There hapless Shakespeare, yet of Tibbald sore,
> Wished he had blotted for himself before.
> *The Dunciad,* ALEXANDER POPE

Heroic couplets have proved of tremendous effectiveness in satiric verse. The couplets, in the strict use, should be end-stopped; and the individual lines tend to be, although the fifth line quoted from Pope is a run-on line. There is tremendous artistry in the variations permitted to be introduced, for all of their limited nature.

Couplet rhyming may be used with lines of any length or metric or accent pattern:

> Good friend, for Jesus' sake forbear
> To dig the dust enclosed here.
> Blest be the man that spares these stones,
> And curst be he that moves my bones.
>
> *Epitaph,* WILLIAM SHAKESPEARE

> Ah, Tam! Ah, Tam! thou'll get thy fairin!
> In hell they'll roast thee like a herrin'!
> In vain thy Kate awaits thy comin!
> Kate soon will be a woefu' woman!
>
> *Tam o' Shanter,* ROBERT BURNS

> For the earth that breeds the trees
> Breeds cities, too, and symphonies.
> Equally her beauty flows
> Into a savior, or a rose—
> Looks down in dream, and from above
> Smiles at herself in Jesus' love.
>
> *Earth,* JOHN HALL WHEELOCK

> You also, laughing one,
> Tosser of balls in the sun,
> Will pillow your bright head
> By the incurious dead.
>
> *A Girl,* BABETTE DEUTSCH

COUPLETS AS COMPLETE POEMS

As in the case of single lines, couplets may constitute complete poems—in which case, of course, they cease to be stanzas:

> Women sit or move to and fro, some old, some young,
> The young are beautiful—but the old are more beautiful than
>   the young.
>
> *Beautiful Women,* WALT WHITMAN

> So pray we to the God we dimly hope
> Against calamities we clearly know.
>
> *Poem Outlines,* SIDNEY LANIER

> The apparition of these faces in the crowd;
> Petals on a wet, black bough.
>
> *In a Station of the Metro,* EZRA POUND

Is it as plainly as our living shown,
By slant and twist, which way the wind hath blown?
On Seeing Weather-Beaten Trees, ADELAIDE CRAPSEY

White is the skimming gull on the somber green of the firtrees,
Black is the soaring gull on a snowy glimmer of cloud.
Standards, CHARLES WHARTON STORK

Till you came—
I was I.
Variation, ALFRED KREYMBORG

STANZAS OF THREE LINES: THE TRIPLET OR TERCET

A group of three lines, whether used as a stanza or as a complete poem, is called a triplet, or tercet. In early Wales and Ireland it was called a triad. The triplet is by no means as common as the couplet or the four-line form, the quatrain. It may be unrhymed and informal, when used as a stanza:

Of life immense in passion, pulse and power,
Cheerful, for freest action form'd under the laws divine,
The Modern Man I sing.
One's-Self I Sing, WALT WHITMAN

I am a man who, sauntering along without fully stopping,
    turns a casual look upon you and then averts his face,
Leaving it to you to prove and define it.
Expecting the main things from you.
Poets to Come, WALT WHITMAN

Shine! shine! shine!
Pour down your warmth, great sun!
While we bask, we two together.
Out of the Cradle Endlessly Rocking, WALT WHITMAN

It may be unrhymed, and yet formal:

I have had playmates, I have had companions,
In my days of childhood, in my joyful school-days;
All, all are gone, the old familiar faces.

I have been laughing, I have been carousing,
Drinking late, sitting late, with my bosom cronies;
All, all are gone, the old familiar faces.
The Old Familiar Faces, CHARLES LAMB

In this poem, Lamb's individual pattern is in the main unrhymed six-foot trochaic, with seven feet in the fifth line here; and with the terminal line of each triplet an unaltered refrain. The poet is always at liberty to create his own pattern, the test of its survival and imitation being popular approval of it. In this case, Lamb was highly successful.

Or our triplet may be rhymed:

> I said, "I toil beneath the curse, 1
> But, knowing not the universe, 1
> I fear to slide from bad to worse. 1
>
> "And that, in seeking to undo 2
> One riddle, and to find the true, 2
> I knit a hundred others new." 2
> *The Two Voices*, ALFRED TENNYSON

Here we have each triplet rhymed in the pattern, 1,1,1. Another common rhyming pattern, 1,2,1, is found in the structure of the villanelle:

> O Singer of Persephone! 1
> In the dim meadows desolate, 2
> Dost thou remember Sicily? 1
>
> Still through the ivy flits the bee, 1
> Where Amaryllis lies in state; 2
> O Singer of Persephone! 1
> *Theocritus*, by OSCAR WILDE

Another rhyming pattern is 1,1,2. The third lines of successive pairs of stanzas may rhyme with each other:

> Spring comes racing down 1
> Over meadow and town, 1
> Waking each of us. 2
>
> Flowers are in bloom, 3
> And the brisk perfume 3
> Is mysterious. 2

The third lines of the successive stanzas need not rhyme with each other, which might give us:

> Flowers are in bloom, 3
> And the brisk perfume 3
> Challenges and rouses. 4

These lines are not indented. It is always proper to eliminate indentation. If indentation is used, to show rhyming mates, as usually, only those lines which rhyme with each other are similarly indented: the third and sixth, in the original example.

The last rhyming possibility, restricted to the triplet itself, is 1,2,2: for there are only four possibilities, 1,1,1; 1,2,1; 1,1,2 and

1,2,2. If we tie up the first lines of successive stanzas by rhymes, we would have:

Where the waters wander	1
By a still lagoon	2
In the drowsy June,	2
Let me linger yonder,	1
Dreaming of an hour	3
When life was a flower.	3

Where there is no such rhyme-interlocking of successive stanzas, our second stanza might be:

There I linger, dreaming	3
Of a vanished hour	4
When life was a flower.	4

As we found in the case of couplets, the lines from various stanzas may be united to each other by various devices of rhyming. There is no limit to the ingenuity that may be thus displayed. Thus we might have 1,2,2; 2,3,3; 3,4,4; 4,5,5, etc.; or 1,2,3; 2,3,4; 3,4,5; 4,5,6, and so on. The poet has full liberty of creation in this regard.

TERZA RIMA

The most famous example of interweaving of rhyming triplets occurs in the form called terza rima: 1,2,1; 2,3,2; 3,4,3; 4,5,4, etc. It is written continuously, not in stanzas. The end of the poem or canto (a major portion of a long poem) is a couplet, using as its rhyme-sound the sound of the central line of the preceding triplet; thus, n-1, n, n-1; n, n. It is a definite form of chain verse, the rhyming forming the link. This is the rhyme-scheme used by Dante in his *Divina Commedia*. The number of lines in each poem or canto is unlimited, providing it is a multiple of three plus two, the two representing the concluding couplet.

Shelley, in his *Ode to the West Wind,* used terza rima in groups of fourteen lines: four tercets, set up as separate stanzas, followed by a concluding couplet:

Make me thy lyre, even as the forest is:	1
What if my leaves are falling like its own!	2
The tumult of thy mighty harmonies	1
Will take from both a deep, autumnal tone,	2
Sweet though in sadness. Be thou, Spirit fierce,	3
My spirit! Be thou me, impetuous one!	2

Drive my dead thoughts over the universe	3
Like withered leaves to quicken a new birth!	4
And, by the incantation of this verse	3
Scatter, as from an unextinguished hearth	4
Ashes and sparks, my words among mankind!	5
Be through my lips to unawakened earth	4
The trumpet of a prophecy! O wind,	5
If Winter comes, can Spring be far behind?	5

Here the rhyming scheme of each individual triplet is 1, 2, 1; but the 2 of each triplet becomes in turn the 1 of the next; and so to the concluding couplet.

Before we leave this, let us study how the sound-repetition devices, in the hands of a master, vary from the requirements of strict rhyme. *Is—harmonies* illustrates a major accent rhyming with a minor one—a subdued instance, because the *is* itself logically receives no emphatic accent. *Tone—one, fierce—universe, hearth—earth, Wind—behind* are consonances, not rhyme: for all that three of them were once excused as "eye-rhymes." *Verse —universe* is an identity, not a rhyme. Only two pairs of rhymes, or four terminal words out of fourteen, fit the rules of rhyming. It is so that actual poetry overleaps all boundaries set up for it by formal rulemakers.

The fourteen-line terza rima is at times used as a separate poem. It constitutes a form not too remote from the Shakespearean sonnet, and is sometimes called a terza rima sonnet.

TRIPLETS AS COMPLETE POEMS

Complete poems in triplet form are at times encountered:

To the States or any of them, or any city of the States,
    Resist much, obey little,
Once unquestioning obedience, once fully enslaved,
Once fully enslaved, no nation, state, city of this earth, ever afterward resumes its liberty.
            To the States, WALT WHITMAN

    A man feared that he might find an assassin;
    Another that he might find a victim.
    One was more wise than the other.
        The Black Riders, lvi, STEPHEN CRANE

      Youth is the happy hour
      When we are still young enough

To choose our own mistakes.
Youth, CLEMENT WOOD

Spring. . . .
Gongula. . . .
Too long.
Papyrus, EZRA POUND

STANZAS OF FOUR LINES: THE QUATRAIN

A stanza or a poem of four lines is called a quatrain. It is the most popular stanza length in English versification. It may be used in informal unrhymed free verse:

Low-hanging moon!
What is that dusky spot in your brown yellow?
O it is the shape, the shape of my mate!
O moon, do not keep her from me any longer.
Out of the Cradle Endlessly Rocking, WALT WHITMAN

Lay me on an anvil, O God!
Beat me and hammer me into a crowbar.
Let me pry loose old walls;
Let me lift and loosen old foundations.
Prayers of Steel, CARL SANDBURG

I, who would be the fire he lavishes
On a dull insensate world,
Must be the chains
That bind him where the vultures gnaw.
Shame, GLORIA GODDARD

The quatrain may be used in more formal unrhymed free or other verse:

I met a seer,
Passing the hues and objects of the world,
The fields of art and learning, pleasure, sense,
To glean eidolons.
Eidolons, WALT WHITMAN

Or it may be used, with lines of any length and meter, in strictly formal unrhymed verse:

Now all is hushed save where the weak-eyed bat
With short shrill shriek flits by on leathern wing,
Or where the beetle winds
His small but sullen horn.
Ode to Evening, WILLIAM COWPER

The chief use of the quatrain stanza is in rhymed versification, with a variety of patterns, many of them familiar. The simplest and most common of these, using only one pair of rhymed words, has been familiar since the time of the early ballads:

> In Scarlet Town, where I was born,   1
> There was a fair maid dwellin',   2
> Made every youth cry well-a-way!   3
> Her name was Barbara Allen.   2
> *Barbara Allen's Cruelty*, ANONYMOUS

This originated as accent verse, 4,3,4,3 feet to the lines; not, as later misunderstood, as a couplet of 7,7 feet. It later developed into loose iambic verse of the same 4,3,4,3 foot pattern. It was called ballad meter, or Service Stanza.

It is clear that, using two unrhymed lines and only one pair of rhymes, there are five other possible rhyme patterns for the quatrain. Three of these place the couplet together—1,1,2,3; 1,2,2,3; 1,2,3,3. The other two let the rhyming mates come first and third (1,2,1,3) or first and fourth (1,2,3,1). None of these is especially common.

Another rhyme-pattern, appearing early in the ballads, is:

> I wish I were where Helen lies   1
> Night and day on me she cries,   1
> I wish I were where Helen lies   1
> On fair Kirconnell Lee.   2
> *Fair Helen of Kirconnell*, ANONYMOUS

This form has three lines rhymed together, instead of only two rhymed lines; and here only the fourth line is unrhymed. This fourth line may be, as in the ballad quoted from, rhymed with the fourth line of successive stanzas: a chain-verse device.

There are three other possible arrangements of four lines so rhymed:

> Ah, Love! could thou and I with Fate conspire   1
> To grasp this sorry Scheme of Things entire,   1
> Would we not shatter it to bits—and then   2
> Remould it nearer to the Heart's Desire!   1
> *The Rubaiyat of Omar Khayyam*, EDWARD FITZGERALD

For all that Sir Philip Sidney used this precise stanza in his *Astrophel and Stella*, the immense popularity of Fitzgerald's *Rubaiyat* caused the stanza to be called the Rubaiyat stanza, and to be imitated to surfeiting. It has been used with four-foot lines, as well as with the five-foot ones that Fitzgerald used.

The other two possible quatrain patterns with three lines rhyming together and one unrhymed line are 1,2,1,1 and 1,2,2,2.

The last group of rhymed quatrain patterns calls for all four of the lines to be rhymed. This may be all on one rhyming sound:

If I'd as much money as I could tell,	1
I never would cry old clothes to sell,	1
Old clothes to sell, old clothes to sell,	1
I never would cry old clothes to sell.	1

Mother Goose

Quatrains with couplet rhyming are simpler and far more popular:

Tiger, tiger, burning bright	1
In the forests of the night,	1
What immortal hand or eye	2
Framed thy fearful symmetry?	2

The Tiger, WILLIAM BLAKE

Except for the first rhyming pattern given, with only one pair of rhymes (1,2,3,2), the most popular rhyming pattern for quatrains is alternate rhymes, 1,2,1,2:

Piping down the valleys wild,	1
Piping songs of pleasant glee,	2
On a cloud I saw a child,	1
And he laughing said to me:	2

A Song of Singing, WILLIAM BLAKE

The four-foot iambic quatrain of this type is more familiar than the trochaic one Blake used, although Longfellow adopted a related stanza for *A Psalm of Life* and other familiar didactic pieces:

Tell me not, in mournful numbers,	1
Life is but an empty dream!—	2
For the soul is dead that slumbers,	1
And things are not what they seem.	2

Here the effect of the double rhyme in the odd-numbered lines tends to tie each up to the even-numbered line which follows— as if we had one long trochaic line of eight feet, broken at the end by a pause, where an unaccented syllable is omitted. Quite as familiar is the statelier five-foot iambic quatrain of this pattern:

Some village Hampden that, with dauntless breast,	1
The little tyrant of his fields withstood,	2
Some mute inglorious Milton here may rest,	1
Some Cromwell guiltless of his country's blood.	2

Elegy Written in a Country Churchyard, THOMAS GRAY

This was formerly called the *elegiac stanza*. Where the stanzaic pattern is 3,3,3,3 iambic feet—

All melancholy lying,	1
Thus wailed she for her dear;	2
Replied each blast with sighing	1
Each billow with a tear.	2

JOHN GAY

this was formerly called Gray's stanza.

The last pattern in which all four lines are rhymed has a couplet in the center:

I hold it truth with one who sings	1
To one clear harp in divers tones,	2
That men may rise on stepping-stones	2
Of their dead selves to higher things.	1

In Memoriam, ALFRED TENNYSON

For all that this stanza had been used trochaically in *The Phoenix and the Turtle,* attributed to Shakespeare; in iambic pentameters by Milton and Coleridge; and in the same iambic tetrameters by Sir Philip Sidney (*Astrophel and Stella,* Song ii) and Ben Jonson (*Elegy,* in *Underwoods*), its familiar use by Tennyson has caused it to be called the In Memoriam stanza.

Three common quatrains found in hymnology—and any rhyming is permissible in all of them—are:

Long Meter: four iambic four-foot lines, usually rhymed 1,2,3,2.

Common Meter: four iambic lines of 4,3,4,3 feet. This, the commonest hymn meter, is the same as ballad meter.

Short Meter: four iambic lines, 3,3,4,3 feet. This corresponded to the couplet of 6,7 iambic feet, so monotonously popular in the 16th century as Poulter's measure.

All three of these can be doubled into doubled quatrains, or eight lines.

These quatrains, and the many hymns written to fit them, bring us close to the method by which the conventions of versification became rigidified, in the beginning. Some early hymn-writers created a tune to each of these three meters, or adapted them from secular music. The tunes, as such, with rigid metric requirements, became popular. Thereafter many other tunes were written to fit these precise meters; and countless other hymns to fit these tunes. Of course, the various hymns in Long Meter are interchangeable, and may be sung to any of the Long Meter tunes; and so may the various Common and Short Meter hymns.

It was thus that Robert Burns and many more composed most of their poems to tunes already extant: the creativeness lying in the pouring of great poetry into familiar metric patterns. It was thus that Shakespeare and his contemporaries, Milton, Shelley, Keats, Browning, Robert Frost, poured their creativeness into the five-foot unrhymed iambic pattern. But, in proportion to their greatness, they tended to vary this toward accent verse, that basic English method of versification. So it is that the conventions of versification come, and develop.

QUATRAINS AS COMPLETE POEMS

There are many quatrains which constitute separate poems. These may be in informal free verse:

Lo, the unbounded sea,
On its breast a ship starting, spreading all sails, carrying even her
    moonsails,
The pennant is flying aloft as she speeds so stately—below emulous
    waves press forward,
They surround the ship with shining, curving motions and foam.
                    The Ship Starting, WALT WHITMAN

November, you old alchemist,
Who would have thought
You could turn the high arrogance of golden-rod
To still plumes of silver?
                Coin of the Year, CLEMENT WOOD

But the general class of quatrain poems contains far more rhymed ones. Certain poets, notably Father Tabb, are at their best in this clipped form, as in:

Into the charnel Hall of Fame
    Only the dead should go;
Then write not there the living name
    Of Edgar Allan Poe!

Father Charles L. O'Donnell is also noted for his quatrains. These rhymed quatrains, of course, can use any of our fourteen possible quatrain rhyme-schemes, and any of the rhythmic devices already discussed.

[279]

He drew a circle that shut me out—
Heretic, rebel, a thing to flout.
But Love and I had the wit to win:
We drew a circle that took him in!
                    Outwitted, EDWIN MARKHAM

I hear the winds, the winds, the river pass,
And toss the fretful book upon the grass.
Poor book, it could not cure my soul of aught—
It has itself the old disease of thought.
                    Out of Doors, WALTER CONRAD ARENSBERG

First Month: "Set down in my cabin, honey!"
Second Month: "Stan' up, my pie!"
Third Month: "You go to wu'k, you wench!
    You well to wu'k as I!"
                    ANONYMOUS NEGRO SECULAR

The famous Little Willies are in rhymed quatrains, of various
patterns:

Willie and two other brats
Licked up all the Rough-on-Rats.
Father said, when mother cried,
"Never mind—they'll die outside."
                    ANONYMOUS

Other notable quatrains include:

I never saw a Purple Cow,
I never hope to see one;
But I can tell you, anyhow,
I'd rather see than be one.
                    The Purple Cow, GELETT BURGESS

When you're away, I'm restless, lonely,
Wretched, bored, dejected; only
Here's the rub, my darling dear,
I feel the same when you are here. . . .

Maid of Gotham, ere we part,
Have a hospitable heart—
Since our own delights must end,
Introduce me to your friend.
Songs in Praise of Practically Nothing, SAMUEL HOFFENSTEIN

And few there are who live, alas,
    And they are far from here,
Who know how young and dear I was
    When I was young and dear.
                    ROSE O'NEILL

The golf links lie so near the mill
That almost every day
The laboring children can look out
And see the men at play.
SARAH N. CLEGHORN

STANZAS OF FIVE LINES: CINQUAINS

A stanza or a poem of five lines is called a cinquain. It was formerly called a quintain. As a stanza, it may, of course, be in free verse; it may be used in formal blank or unrhymed verse:

Tears, idle tears, I know not what they mean,
Tears from the depth of some divine despair
Rise in the heart, and gather to the eyes,
In looking on the happy autumn-fields,
And thinking of the days that are no more.
Song from The Princess, ALFRED TENNYSON

Rhymed cinquains are often used as stanzas. They may be of any rhyme-scheme, and of any type or types of accent or metric verse, as also they may be of any line-length. A few typical examples are:

Go, lovely Rose! 1
Tell her, that wastes her time and me, 2
That now she knows 1
When I resemble her to thee, 2
How sweet and fair she seems to be. 2
The Rose's Message, EDMUND WALLER

Hail to thee, blithe spirit! 1
Bird thou never wert, 2
That from heaven, or near it, 1
Pourest thy full heart 2
In profuse strains of unpremeditated art. 2
To a Skylark, PERCY BYSSHE SHELLEY

The form here is four three-foot trochaic lines, followed by a six-foot iambic. This last line is called an Alexandrine. It appeared in France in the early part of the 12th century; for a century was supplanted by the decasyllabic line; and about the middle of the 16th century came in again, and still dominates French verse. The name probably came from its wide usage in the romances connected with Alexander. In English, Alexandrines were rarely used throughout a whole poem. Alexandrines were used as the first half of Poulter's measure, and to terminate many stately stanzas.

> Where seven sunken Englands   1
>   Lie buried, one by one,   2
> Why should one idle spade, I wonder,   3
> Shake up the dust of thanes like thunder   3
>   To smoke and choke the sun?   2
> *The Ballad of the White Horse,* G. K. CHESTERTON

> The bells they sound on Bredon,   1
>   And still the steeples hum,   2
> "Come all to church, good people,"—   3
>   Oh, noisy bells, be dumb;   2
>   I hear you, I will come.   2
> *Bredon Hill,* A. E. HOUSMAN

In the hands of a master, the form may vary from stanza to stanza, with distinct advantage. Here we will treat each stanza separately, starting each rhyme scheme with 1; although the stanzas are not interlocked by rhyme.

> Helen, thy beauty is to me   1
>   Like those Nicaean barks of yore   2
> That gently, o'er a perfumed sea,   1
>   The weary, wayworn wanderer bore   2
>   To his own native shore.   2

> On desperate seas long wont to roam,   1
>   Thy hyacinth hair, thy classic face,   2
> Thy Naiad airs, have brought me home   1
>   To the glory that was Greece   2
> And the grandeur that was Rome.   1

> Lo! in yon brilliant window-niche   1
>   How statue-like I see thee stand,   2
>   The agate lamp within thy hand!   2
> Ah, Psyche, from the regions which   1
>   Are Holy Land!   2
> *To Helen,* EDGAR A. POE

Each stanza has its own rhyme scheme, differing from each of the others: 1,2,1,2,2; 1,2,1,2,1; 1,2,2,1,2. The number of feet differ as markedly: 4,4,4,4,3; 4,4,4,3,3; 4,4,4,4,2. It is so that actual poetry comes. Mere verse tends to repeat its stanza forms, since the pleasure of recognizing the repetition of the familiar is an ornament, when the subtler pleasure of variety in likeness is not present.

CINQUAINS AS COMPLETE POEMS

A cinquain can constitute a complete poem, in any type of verse. Here is an example in free verse:

> Yes, I have a thousand tongues,
> And nine and ninety-nine lie.
> Though I strive to use the one,
> It will make no melody at my will,
> But is dead in my mouth.
> *The Black Riders, iv,* STEPHEN CRANE

Adelaide Crapsey invented a formal poem-pattern, unrhymed, its five lines containing respectively 1, 2, 3, 4 and 1 feet, all iambics. This specific form is commonly called a *cinquain;* though the term is far wider than her form.

> These be
> Three silent things:
> The falling snow . . . the hour
> Before the dawn . . . the mouth of one
> Just dead.
> *Triad,* ADELAIDE CRAPSEY

This has been widely imitated.

A more famous cinquain is the limerick, which will be taken up under formal verse. A famous example is:

> There was a young man named Achilles   1
> Whose wrongs always gave him the willies.   1
> So he sulked in his tent   2
> Like a half-witted gent—   2
> Say, wasn't them heroes the sillies!   1
> *How Homer Should Have Written the Iliad,* E. M. ROBINSON

STANZAS OF SIX LINES: SESTETS

A stanza or a poem of six lines is called a sestet or sextet. The term is even more familiar, as the name for the concluding six lines of a sonnet. This usage will be dealt with under the treatment of the sonnet.

Sestets can occur as the stanzas of free verse, or of formal unrhymed verse, as in this example of accent verse:

> Gibraltar's steep unyielding ways,
> Or the stabbing beauty of plundered Greece,
> Tossed on a bleakly troubled sea,
> Or lulled by blue Sorrento's hills,

Always our binary bright in the sky,
Always we walk together.
We Walk Together, GLORIA GODDARD

Sestets are often used as stanzas in rhymed poetry, with a multitude of rhyming and rhythmic patterns:

Even as the sun with purple-colour'd face   1
Had ta'en his last leave of the weeping morn,   2
Rose-cheek'd Adonis hied him to the chase;   1
Hunting he loved, but love he laugh'd to scorn;   2
    Sick-thoughted Venus makes amain unto him,   3
    And like a bold-fac'd suitor 'gins to woo him.   3
Venus and Adonis, WILLIAM SHAKESPEARE

In this stanza, with the rhyming pattern, 1,2,1,2,3,3, alternate rhyming followed by a terminal couplet, we have the first elaboration of the simple quatrain rhyming 1,2,1,2, which appears in later ballads and elsewhere, as a favorite form for narrative verse. We will find this development made far more intricate and elaborate in later longer stanzas, cresting in the Shakespearean sonnet.

I wandered lonely as a cloud   1
    That floats on high o'er vales and hills,   2
When all at once I saw a crowd,   1
    A host, of golden daffodils;   2
    Beside the lake, beneath the trees,   3
    Fluttering and dancing in the breeze.   3
I Wandered Lonely as a Cloud, WILLIAM WORDSWORTH

Here we have the same rhyme-scheme as in *Venus and Adonis*, with the use of tetrameters instead of pentameters; but the tempo and mood are light and lyrical, instead of stately and passionate.

She walks in beauty, like the night   1
    Of cloudless climes and starry skies;   2
And all that's best of dark or bright   1
    Meet in her aspect and her eyes;   2
Thus mellowed to that tender light   1
    Which heaven to gaudy day denies.   2
She Walks in Beauty, LORD BYRON

TAIL-RHYME STANZAS

Here is one of the favorite stanzas of Burns:

Wee, sleekit, cow-rin', tim'rous beastie,   1
O what a panic's in thy breastie!   1

Thou need na start awa sae hasty,	1
Wi' bickering brattle!	2
I wad be laith to rin and chase thee	1
Wi' murd'ring pattle!	2

To a Field-Mouse, ROBERT BURNS

This is predominantly iambic, with 4,4,4,2,4,2 as its rhythmic pattern. The characteristic feature of such stanzas is the presence of two or more short lines rhyming together, and serving as "tails" to the various parts of the stanza. It is called tail-rhyme stanza in English, *versus caudati* in medieval Latin, *rime couée* in French, and *Schweifreim* in modern German, all with the same meaning. It is supposed to be a development of the refrain stanza called the *Alleluia hymn form*, shown in

> Laetabundus
> Exultet fidelis chorus,
>   Alleluia!
> Egidio psallat coetus
> Iste laetus,
>   Alleluia!
> *De Nativitate Domini*, ST. BERNARD

It may expand from a sestet:

And if I should live to be	1
The last leaf upon the tree	1
In the spring,	2
Let them laugh, as I do now	3
At the old, forsaken bough	3
Where I cling.	2

The Last Leaf, JOHN GREENLEAF WHITTIER

to far longer tail-rhyme stanzas:

Fair stood the wind for France,	1
When we our sails advance,	1
Nor now to prove our chance	1
Longer not tarry;	2
But putting to the main,	1
At Caux, the mouth of Seine,	1
With all his martial train,	1
Landed King Harry.	2

Agincourt, MICHAEL DRAYTON

The movement of this was used by Tennyson in *The Charge of the Light Brigade*, even with Drayton's method of avoiding the expected triple rhymes on the dactyls, by substituting amphimacers (´ ◡ ´), and rhyming only their last syllables.

Another famous example is Tennyson's *The Lady of Shalott:*

Willows whiten, aspens quiver,	1
Little breezes dusk and shiver,	1
Through the wave that runs for ever	1
By the island in the river	1
Flowing down to Camelot.	2
Four gray walls, and four gray towers,	3
Overlook a space of flowers,	3
And the silent isle embowers	3
The Lady of Shalott.	2

This is predominantly trochaic, 4,4,4,4,3; 4,4,4,3. But any rhythmic foot may be used, with the various parts of the stanzas of any length, and any number of terminal tail-lines, rhyming with each other.

SESTETS AS COMPLETE POEMS

The sestet, and the longer groups of lines to be treated hereafter as stanzas, may in each case constitute separate poems.

A hut, a tree,	1
And a hill for me,	1
And a piece of weedy meadow.	2
I'll ask no thing	3
Of God or king	3
But to clear away his shadow.	2

Diogenes, MAX EASTMAN

A centipede was happy quite,	1
Until a frog, in fun,	2
Said, "Pray, which leg comes after which?"	3
This raised her mind to such a pitch	3
She lay distracted in a ditch,	3
Considering how to run.	2

The Centipede, ANONYMOUS

STANZAS OF SEVEN LINES: SEPTETS

A group of seven lines, constituting a stanza or a poem, is called a septet. It has the same complete liberty of structure that shorter groups of lines have. One of the most famous septet stanzas is that used by Chaucer in some 14,000 lines of his poetry, and now called *rhyme royal*. The form, like the name, was of French origin; and the name is akin to *chant royal* and *ballat royal*, familiar in the nomenclature of court poetry. The name is more commonly derived from its later use by James I of Scotland in his *The Kinges Quhair*. Its introduction into English versification appears from this earlier use:

To you, my purse, and to no other wight   1
Complain I, for ye be my lady dear.   2
I am full sorry now that ye be light,   1
For, certes, ye now make me heavy cheer.   2
Me were as lief-y laid upon a bier   2
For which unto your mercy thus I cry,   3
Be heavy again, or els-e mote I die.   3
The Complaint to His Empty Purse, GEOFFREY CHAUCER

Here the alternately rhymed quatrain, supplemented in the *Venus and Adonis* stanza by a terminal couplet, has a fifth line added before the couplet, rhyming on the 2 sound. The form grows apace. Rhyme royal was later used in a more famous poem:

Thus he replies: "The colour in thy face   1
(That even for anger makes the lily pale,   2
And the red rose blush at her own disgrace)   1
Shall plead for me, and tell my loving tale: 2
Under that colour am I come to scale   2
Thy never-conquer'd fort: the fault is thine,   3
For those thine eyes betray thee unto mine."   3
The Rape of Lucrece, WILLIAM SHAKESPEARE

This stanza was used with much success by Masefield, in *Dauber* and other book-length poems.

The internal couplet had a tendency to interrupt the flow of the narrative; the concluding couplet did this to an even greater degree. In 1920, a stanza appeared which used the same number of rhymes, but eliminated both couplets:

The night's mysterious wings pulsed through the dark,   1
The night's mysterious noises cracked and shivered,   2
And where their fingers met a visible spark   1
Seemed to leap forth at them, and pulsed and quivered   2
Throughout them both. Their thickened tongues were dumb,   3
The pretty words of star-lore undelivered,   2
The pretty words that found no breath would come.   3

Canopus, CLEMENT WOOD

The rhyming device here, which eliminates couplet-rhyming entirely, was hailed by Gamaliel Bradford as the best rhyming stanza for narrative verse ever invented. It may, of course, be used with briefer lines, as four-foot iambics; with longer stanzas; and with other rhythms.

A large number of other septets have been used as stanzas, and there are many more possibilities. A graceful use of tail-rhyme in a septet appears in this form:

Swiftly walk over the western wave,	1
Spirit of Night!	2
Out of the misty eastern cave	1
Where, all the long and lone daylight,	2
Thou wovest dreams of joy and fear,	3
Which make thee terrible and dear,	3
Swift be thy flight!	2

To Night, PERCY BYSSHE SHELLEY

STANZAS OF EIGHT AND MORE LINES: OTTAVA RIMA

In dealing with stanzas or with poems of eight lines (octaves or octets) and more, only those will be selected for especial consideration that have earned a prominent place in English versification. The poet or versifier may at any time use any of the models already invented, or create new patterns, as to rhythm, rhyme-scheme, and line-length, to please himself.

Ottava rima is an Italian stanza, made classic by Ariosto and Tasso, and introduced into England, together with the sonnet and other Italian borrowings, by Sir Thomas Wyatt. It consisted of eight lines, the first six rhyming alternately, with a terminal rhymed couplet. In Italy, it was originally written in hendeca-syllabics (lines of eleven syllables). Milton, Keats, Byron and others usually wrote it in five-foot iambics:

But "why then publish?"—There are no rewards	1
Of fame or profit when the world grows weary.	2
I ask in turn,—Why do you play at cards?	1
Why drink? Why read—To make some hour less dreary.	2
It occupies me to turn back regards	1
On what I've seen or pondered, sad or cheery;	2
And what I write I cast upon the stream	3
To sink or swim—I have had at least my dream.	3

Don Juan, LORD BYRON

The presence of the terminal couplet was sure to endear it to English ears. For the original form of the English ballad was 4-accent rhymed couplets; and the couplet device has a habit of suddenly appearing in the most unexpected places in English versification. James Russell Lowell, objecting to it as to rhyme royal for narrative purposes, said that the rhyming couplet seems "to put on the brakes with a jar."

THE SPENSERIAN STANZA

For his *The Faerie Queene* Edmund Spenser invented a stanza, since named after him, which has long been a favorite in stately verse, especially narrative. It consists of eight five-foot iambic lines, followed by an Alexandrine, or line of six iambic feet: this being an effort to break the monotony of the terminal rhyming five-foot couplet:

Full on this casement shone the wintry moon,	1
And threw warm gules on Madeline's fair breast,	2
As down she knelt for Heaven's grace and boon;	1
Rose-bloom fell on her hands, together prest,	2
And on her silver cross soft amethyst,	2
And on her hair a glory, like a saint;	3
She seem'd a splendid angel, newly drest,	2
Save wings, for heaven:—Porphyro grew faint:	3
She knelt, so pure a thing, so free from mortal taint.	3

The Eve of St. Agnes, JOHN KEATS

Note the unexpected consonance—*prest, amethyst*—replacing rhyme in one couplet. The revival of consonance, that ancient ballad and folk-verse device, commenced early, and proceeded unobtrusively to its recent flowering.

Spenser sustained this stanza form for 3,848 stanzas in his most famous poem. He had many followers in using it. Thomas Chatterton's *Chatterton stanza* grew out of: ten lines, nine of five-foot iambic, the tenth an Alexandrine; rhyming 1,2,1,2,2,3,2,3,4,4.

REFRAIN STANZAS

Many stanza forms include a refrain. This may be repeated from stanza to stanza as a mere appendage, even a meaningless one; or it may be interwoven by rhyme as an integral part of the stanza's rhyming scheme. The Negro spirituals are full of examples:

> I looked over Jordan and what did I see,
> Coming for to carry me home,
> A band of angels coming after me,
> Coming for to carry me home.

Cho.—Swing low, sweet chariot,
 Coming for to carry me home,
Swing low, sweet chariot,
 Coming for to carry me home.

We have dealt with this device from another angle in considering the first sound-repetition employed in versification—repetition of words and groups of words.

The poet and versifier are unlimited in the use to which they can put refrains. A few examples which may suggest various possible uses are given here. Unless obviously otherwise, the refrain line or lines usually close the example:

"Bring out your rubber-tired hearses, bring out your rubber-tired
 hack,
They're taking poor Johnnie to the graveyard, and they ain't a-goin'
 to bring him back,
 He was her man, and he done her wrong!"
      Frankie and Johnnie, ANONYMOUS

  Hark to an exiled son's appeal,
   Maryland!
  My Mother State, to thee I kneel,
   Maryland!
  For life and death, for woe and weal,
  Thy peerless chivalry reveal,
  And gird thy beauteous limbs with steel,
   Maryland, my Maryland!
Maryland, my Maryland, JAMES RYDER RANDALL

"Prophet!" said I, "thing of evil! Prophet still, if saint or devil!
By the heaven that bends above us, by the God we both adore,
Tell this soul with sorrow laden if, within the distant Aidenn,
It shall clasp a radiant maiden whom the angels name Lenore?
Clasp a rare and radiant maiden, nameless here forevermore?"
  Quoth the Raven, "Nevermore!"
       The Raven, EDGAR A. POE

  O sing unto my roundelay,
   O drop the briny tear with me,
  Dance no more at holy-day,
   Like a running river be.
    My love is dead,
    Gone to his death-bed,
    All under the willow-tree.
Minstrel's Roundelay from Aella, THOMAS CHATTERTON

"Ah! what white thing at the door has cross'd,
   Sister Helen?
Ah! what is this that sighs in the frost?"

"A soul that's lost as mine is lost,
            Little brother!"
        (O Mother, Mary Mother,
    Lost, lost, all lost, between Hell and Heaven!)
            Sister Helen, DANTE GABRIEL ROSSETTI

The cataract of the cliff of heaven fell blinding off the brink,
As if it would wash the stars away, as suds go down a sink. . . .
The seven heavens came roaring down for the throats of hell to drink,
And Noah he cocked his eye and said, "It looks like rain, I think;
The water has drowned the Matterhorn as deep as a Mendip mine,
But I don't care where the water goes, if it doesn't get into the wine!"
            Song from The Flying Inn, G. K. CHESTERTON

    South of the Border I rode back one day.
    There in a veil of white by candlelight she knelt to pray;
    The mission bells told me that I mustn't stay
    South of the Border, down Mexico way.
        South of the Border, JIMMY KENNEDY and MICHAEL CARR

STANZAS IN FORMAL ODES

For typical longer formal stanzas in English versification, the odes of Keats furnish an admirable subject for study. *To a Nightingale* has a stanza of ten lines, all iambic: the eighth line three-foot, the rest five-foot. The rhyme scheme is uniform in all eight stanzas:

My heart aches, and a drowsy numbness pains   1
    My sense, as though of hemlock I had drunk   2
Or emptied some dull opiate to the drains   1
    One minute past, and Lethe-wards had sunk: 2
'Tis not through envy of thy happy lot,   3
    But being too happy in thy happiness,—   4
        That thou, light-winged Dryad of the trees,   5
            In some melodious plot   3
Of beechen green, and shadows numberless,   4
    Singest of summer in full-throated ease.   5

Nothing could be simpler than this rhyme scheme: a quatrain rhymed alternately (1,2,1,2), followed by a sestet with one of the accepted rhyme-schemes found in the Italian sonnet (3,4,5,3,4,5); and the regularity of this broken in its fourth line by the omission of two complete feet. There was enough originality here to please, and enough of the accustomed patterns to satisfy.

On Melancholy uses this rhyme-scheme for its first two stanzas, but the eighth line here is five-foot, like all the others. The third stanza makes one minor variation in the order of the rhymes in the

[291]

concluding sestet: 3,4,5,4,3,5. When actual poetry is concerned, such a minor variation is negligible. It could never harm the emotional appeal of the poem, whether read or heard. Only analysis reveals it. The versifier should always remember that such a variation is far better than a strained and unnatural construction.

On a Grecian Urn also has a stanza of ten lines:

Heard melodies are sweet, but those unheard	1
Are sweeter; therefore, ye soft pipes, play on;	2
Not to the sensual ear, but, more endear'd,	1
Pipe to the spirit ditties of no tone:	2
Fair youth, beneath the trees, thou canst not leave	3
Thy song, nor ever can those trees be bare;	4
Bold Lover, never, never canst thou kiss	5
Though winning near the goal—yet, do not grieve;	3
She cannot fade, though thou hast not thy bliss,	5
For ever wilt thou love, and she be fair!	4

Note how indentation, if it is to be used at all, indicates always rhyming mates. Here alternately rhymed quatrains open, followed by sestets whose rhyme-scheme varies from stanza to stanza:

First and fifth stanzas,   3,4,5,4,3,5
Third and fourth stanzas, 3,4,5,3,4,5
Stanza given above,   3,4,5,3,5,4

Note the variations from strict rhyming used in this ode:

Consonance: on, tone; unheard, endear'd; priest, drest; morn, return; pastoral, all.
Minor accent rhymes: shed, unwearied; citadel, tell.
Minor accent with assonance: sacrifice, skies.

It is surprising how often the masters moved away from the strict rules laid down in studies of prosody, and always in the direction of a greater freedom and a more natural and unforced expression.

The rich beauty of *To Autumn* has eleven lines to the stanza, iambic five-foot, with the alternately rhymed quatrain coming first, 1,2,1,2, followed by:

First stanza   3,4,5,4,3,3,5
Stanzas two and three, 3,4,5,3,4,4,5

The device common to all of these odic stanzas is to open them with a quatrain alternately rhymed: 1,2,1,2; and thereafter to use six or seven lines, the rhymes here commencing 3,4,5, and thereafter repeating this or using the same three rhyme-sounds in some other order. The essence of all this is simplicity. Far more complicated rhyme-schemes can be, and have been, invented by many poets.

VARIATIONS IN STANZA PATTERNS

Several different stanza patterns may at times be used in one poem with great effectiveness, where their natural movements are selected to emphasize definite emotional differences in the content of the poem. The simpler method would be to express all the emotional states of the poem in one identical stanza; but this would be less natural than to let the stanza form shift as the emotions dictate. Poe was a master craftsman in this regard, and *To One In Paradise* is an excellent example. Regarding each stanza as a unit, we have:

Thou wast that all to me, love,	1	
For which my soul did pine,		2
A green isle in the sea, love,	1	
A fountain and a shrine,		2
All wreathed with fairy fruits and flowers,		3
And all the flowers were mine.		2
Ah, dream too bright to last!	1	
Ah, starry Hope! that didst arise		2
But to be overcast!	1	
A voice from out the Future cries		2
"On! on!"—but o'er the Past	1	
(Dim gulf!) my spirit hovering lies		2
Mute, motionless, aghast!	1	
For, alas! alas! with me	1	
The light of life is o'er!		2
"No more—no more—no more!—"		2
(Such language holds the solemn sea	1	
To the sands upon the shore,)		2
Shall bloom the thunder-blasted tree,	1	
Or the stricken eagle soar!		2
And all my days are trances,	1	
And all my nightly dreams		2
Are where thy dark eye glances,	1	
And where thy footstep gleams—		2
In what ethereal dances	1	
By what eternal streams.		2

Here the first and last stanzas are comparatively quiet in mood, and roughly similar in their sestet structure: three iambic feet to each line, with the normal rhyming alternately 1,2,1,2,1,2. But the first stanza inserts a four-foot line, out of the rhyme-scheme entirely, as its fifth line: as if prophetic of the turmoil to come.

The second and third stanzas have seven lines each. The first opens with the lines of 3,4,3 feet: the second and third lines having the movement of the *end* of a ballad stanza of 4,3,4,3 feet—definitively in the gentler mood that preceded it. Now follows a quatrain rhymed 2,1,2,1, and with ballad rhythm: 4,3,4,3. The third stanza opens with three more staccato lines of only three feet each—and then a quatrain rhymed 1,2,1,2, with the ballad rhythm, 4,3,4,3, found in the second stanza. Thus the second and third stanzas have an internal symmetry, with differing introductions. And the last stanza returns to the quiet mood of the first. The emotional response produced by such planned artistry is automatic on the part of the reader or hearer, and the art is not wasted.

The Conqueror Worm is as deft in its masterly variations. The first two stanzas move with no symmetrical number of feet to the lines: a device that breeds uneasiness and uncertainty. Here the pattern of feet to the line is: 3,4,4,3,4,3,4,3—with its final quatrain ballad meter; then 4,3,3,4,4,4,4,2—a heavy movement, abruptly broken by the brief final line. Then for two stanzas we shift to doubled ballad meter, as the story mounts to its appalling climax:

But see, amid the mimic rout	1
A crawling shape intrude!	2
A blood-red thing that writhes from out	1
The scenic solitude!	2
It writhes!—it writhes!—with mortal pangs	3
The mimes become its food,	2
And the angels sob at vermin fangs	3
In human gore imbued.	2

This rhyme-scheme has been used throughout the first four stanzas. Suddenly the time quickens to anapests, only three to each line: and the rhyming scheme becomes less formalized, as we come to the end:

Out—out are the lights—out all!	1
And, over each quivering form,	2
The curtain, a funeral pall,	1
Comes down with the rush of a storm,	2

> And the angels, all pallid and wan,   3
>   Uprising, unveiling, affirm   4
> That the play is the tragedy, "Man,"   3
>   And its hero the Conqueror Worm.   4

The stanzaic variations in *The Haunted Palace* are not so formalized as in these two cases, but they are still used with inerrant deftness. The rhyme-scheme is simple and uniform throughout; and every stanza has its short sixth line of only two feet:

> Banners yellow, glorious, golden,   1
>   On its roof did float and flow,   2
> (This—all this—was in the olden   1
>   Time long ago,)   2
> And every gentle air that dallied,   3
>   In that sweet day,   4
> Along the ramparts plumed and pallid,   3
>   A winged odor went away.   4

The number of feet to the line here is 4,4,4,3,4,2,4,4. Note the pauses, similar to accent verse, in the impressive fourth line. The first and third stanzas have all the lines, except the sixth, of four feet each. The last two are the same, except that the eighth line is only three feet. The stanza quoted has only three feet in its fourth line; the fourth stanza has three feet in the second line, as well. Naturally, the reader or hearer does not note these things; only the analyst of versification, including the author, makes sure of them. The last stanza, without a change in meter, alters the mood entirely by a use of words requiring more time to pronounce, as the mood requires:

> And travelers, now, within that valley,
>   Through the red-litten windows see
> Vast forms, that move fantastically
>   To the discordant melody.
> While, like a ghastly rapid river,
>   Through the pale door
> A hideous throng rush out forever
>   And laugh—but smile no more.

It is amazing, on reflection, to realize that the former poem is a poetic sublimation of man's entire existence on the globe, with death as the victor in the end; and that *The Haunted Palace*, depicting the coming of madness to a sane mind, treats with marvelous passion, and ever-present symbolism, such factual details as the human head, brain, breath, eyes, mouth, and even teeth. And, in both instances, at the end is a sudden outburst of realization of the meaning of the whole: a frenzied poetic widening of the matter treated of, until it assumes enormous significance. This same exquisite starburst of poetic widening occurs, for instance, in such vastly different poems as Robert Frost's *The Road Not Taken, Stopping by Woods on a Snowy Evening,* and *Mending Wall,* Edwin Arlington Robinson's *The Mill,* and so many more. It is one of the crowns of poetry.

THE SONNET

The sonnet, equally at home as stanza or complete poem, will be taken up in the next chapter, Poem Patterns.

SPACING RHYMES

An important thing is not to place your rhymes so far apart that the effect of the sound-repetition is lost through forgetfulness. The right way is indicated by Coleridge's famous *The Rime of the Ancient Mariner,* which opens in accent verse with:

It is an ancient Mariner,	1
And he stoppeth one of three:	2
"By thy long gray beard and glittering eye	3
Now wherefore stopp'st thou me?"	2

Here fifteen syllables separate the rhyming sounds *three* and *me.* But consider a typical stanza from Sidney Lanier's magnificent *The Revenge of Hamish:*

And gazed hungrily o'er, and the blood from his back drip- dripped in the brine,	1
And a sea-hawk flung down a skeleton fish as he flew,	2
And the mother stared white on the waste of blue,	2
And the wind drove a cloud to seaward, and the sun began to shine.	1

Between *flew* and *blue* there are only ten syllables, but between the rhyming mates *brine* and *shine* there are forty syllables. This dilutes the repetitional effect of rhyming so thin, that it either is tasted as unappetizing skimmed milk, or the effect is lost entirely. This is an over-refinement of subtlety that is entirely ineffective.

In your stanza rhyme-patterns, then, have your rhyming words close enough together to let their effect reach the ear without straining. Yet there are devices, open both to serious and light verse, by which a rhyming mate can be almost indefinitely postponed, as in the concluding stanza of the White Knight's song from Lewis Carroll's *Through the Looking-Glass:*

> And now, if e'er by chance I put
> My fingers into glue,
> Or madly squeeze a right-hand foot
> Into a left-hand shoe,
> Or if I drop upon my toe   3
> A very heavy weight,   4
> I weep, for it reminds me so   3
> Of that old man I used to know—   3
> Whose look was mild, whose speech was slow   3
> Whose hair was whiter than the snow,   3
> Whose face was very like a crow,   3
> With eyes, like cinders, all aglow,   3
> Who seemed distracted with his woe,   3
> Who rocked his body to and fro,   3
> And muttered mumblingly and low,   3
> As if his mouth were full of dough,   3
> Who snorted like a buffalo—   3
> That summer evening long ago   3
> A-sitting on a gate.   4

Here one hundred and one syllables separate *weight* from its rhyming mate, *gate*. But the build-up and the suspense make us wait for the final rhyme as for rain after a dustbowl drought. The hammer-taps of the Ō-rhymes constantly remind us that something is coming; the very structure of this makes the long wait highly effective.

The general rule is, keep your rhyming words comparatively close together. There are devices that circumvent this.

STANZAS IN LIGHT VERSE

All that has been said of stanza formation and scheme applies to light verse, as well as to serious. C. S. Calverley, W. S. Gilbert, A. A. Milne and many more masters of light verse excel in even more intricate stanzas, with complex rhythm and rhyme interweaving, than we have yet encountered in serious poetry. For here the emphasis is more definitely on the delightful devices than in the case of serious verse, where there is often a gain in keeping the stanza pattern unobtrusive.

The undisputed master of light verse stanzas so far is Guy Wetmore Carryl, famous for his *Fables for the Frivolous, Mother Goose Grown Up,* and *Grimm Tales Made Gay.* Each of his sixty or so light verse masterpieces hews to its stanza form with meticulous accuracy, scorning the variations a mere Keats or Shakespeare might adopt. Several of his typical stanza forms may indicate to the versifier some of the possibilities open before him:

```
Though she was only a shepherdess,          1
    Tending the meekest of sheep,               2
Never was African leopardess                1
    Crosser than Little Bo Peep:                2
Quite apathetic, impassible                 3
    People described her as: "That              4
Wayward, contentious, irascible,            3
    Testy, cantankerous brat!"                  4
         The Blatant Brutality of Little Bo Peep
```

This octave has one of the simplest of all rhyming schemes; but the brilliant use of triple rhyme lifts it into distinction. Here is a more complicated pattern:

```
She was one of those creatures              1
    Whose features                          1
    Are hard beyond any reclaim;                2
And she loved in a hovel                     3
    To grovel,                               3
    And she hadn't a cent to her name.          2
She owned neither gallants                   4
    Nor talents;                             4
    She borrowed extensively, too,              5
From all of her dozens                       6
    Of cousins,                              6
    And never refunded a *sou:*                 5
Yet all they said in abuse of her           7
Was: "She is prouder than Lucifer!"         7
    (That, I must say, without meaning to blame, 8
    Is always the way with that kind of a dame!) 8
    The Commendable Castigation of Old Mother Hubbard
```

This stanza form calls for four pairs of double rhymes, located in adjoining feet and followed by a triple rhyme. Yet the straightforward conversational directness is never altered. This requires mastery in versification. Another famous pattern is:

```
A maiden from the Bosphorus,                1
With eyes as bright as phosphorus,          1
    Once wed the wealthy bailiff                2
```

Of the caliph	2
Of Kelat.	3
Though diligent and zealous, he	4
Became a slave to jealousy.	4
(Considering her beauty,	5
'Twas his duty	5
To be that!)	3

Note the inevitability and the colloquial naturalness of this; and then recall that all verse, serious or light, requires this. The temptation to quote further must be resisted, although there are more than two score other stanza patterns here worth studying.

In our discussion of Rhymes Involving Splitting Familiar Phrases, we have given examples of Calverley's superb handling of stanza forms. The design in *Ode to Tobacco* is simple tail-rhyme:

How they who use fusees	1
All grow by slow degrees	1
Brainless as chimpanzees,	1
Meagre as lizards;	2
Go mad, and beat their wives;	3
Plunge (after shocking lives)	3
Razors and carving knives	3
Into their gizzards.	2

The rhyming device, in this dactylic movement, is the same that we found in Drayton's *Agincourt* and Tennyson's *Charge of the Light Brigade,* substituting an amphimacer ($\prime \smile \prime$) for the final dactyl, and using a masculine rhyme on its last accented syllable. Calverley is fond of tail-rhyme, and always uses it with complete naturalness, as in *Morning:*

'Tis the hour when white-horsed Day	1
Chases Night her mares away;	1
When the Gates of Dawn (they say)	1
Phoebus opes:	2
And I gather that the Queen	3
May be uniformly seen,	3
Should the weather be serene,	3
On the slopes.	2

Here we have simple trochaics. An amusing device is the stately archaic movement of the first four lines, followed by the almost casual modern speech in the second quatrain.

Any of these stanzas can be made more effective by the use of a refrain, as in Edward Lear's *The Owl and the Pussy-Cat:*

The Owl and the Pussy-Cat went to sea	1
In a beautiful pea-green boat:	2
They took some honey, and plenty of money	1
Wrapped up in a five-pound note.	2
The Owl looked up at the stars above,	3
And sang to a small guitar,	4
"O lovely Pussy, O Pussy, my love,	3
What a beautiful pussy you are,	4
You are,	4
You are,	4
What a beautiful Pussy you are!"	4

In this poem, the refrain differs from stanza to stanza, being merely an embroidery of the eighth line of each stanza in the above fashion. Eugene Field's *Wynken, Blynken and Nod* moves from a nine-line stanza to a refrain that reappears after each stanza:

All night long their nets they threw		
To the stars in the twinkling foam,—		
Then down from the skies came the wooden shoe,		
Bringing the fishermen home:		
'Twas all so pretty a sail, it seemed	3	
As if it could never be;	4	
And some folk thought 'twas a dream they dreamed,	3	
Of sailing that beautiful sea:	4	
But I shall name you the fishermen three:	4	
Wynken,		R
Blynken,		R
And Nod.		R

Both of these familiar favorites, it should be noted, revert from the comparative artificiality and stiltedness of metric verse to the more ancient and natural English device of accent verse. A longer refrain device is used by James Whitcomb Riley in *Little Orphan Annie:*

Onc't they was a little boy wouldn't say his prayers,	1
An' when he went to bed at night, away up stairs,	1
His Mammy heerd him holler, an' his Daddy heerd him bawl,	2
An' when they turn't the kivers down, he wasn't there at all!	2
An' they seek'd him in the rafter-room, an' cubbyhole, an' press,	3
An' seek'd him up the chimbly-flue, an' ever'wheres, I guess;	3

But all they ever found was thist his pants an'
  roundabout: 4
An' the Gobble-uns 'll git you
   Ef you   R
    Don't   R R
     Watch   R
      Out!   (R)4

Here we have a seven-foot accent movement, based on the ancient ballad meter. Notice how effectively it appears at the end of line two:

An' when / he went / to bed / at night, / $\smallsmile$ / $\overset{(P)}{}/$ $\overset{(P)}{}/$ stairs
              away up stairs

On of the major masters of rhythmic and stanza pattern inventiveness is W. S. Gilbert. The finale of Act I of his *Iolanthe* shows him at his dexterous technical best. Here is the swift succession of the major novel stanzaic patterns, commencing with tail-rhyme:

Iolanthe	When tempests wreck thy bark,	1
	And all is drear and dark,	1
	If thou shouldst need an arm,	1
	I'll give thee one.	2

Phyllis: What was that?

Lord Tolloller:	I heard the minx remark	1
	She'd meet him after dark	1
	Inside St. James's Park,	1
	And give him one.	2

Then we have the second major movement:

Lord Mount Ararat:	This gentleman is seen	1
	With a main of seventeen,	1
	A-taking of his *dolce far niente;*	2
	And wonders he'd achieve,	1
	For he asks us to believe	1
	She's his mother, and he's nearly	
	five-and-twenty!	2

After the entrance of the Fairies, we have this fine rhythmic movement, with impressive refrains, that surmount in meaning their nonsense originals:

Strephon: The lady of my love has caught me talking to
       another.   1
All: Oh, fie! Strephon is a rogue.   R

Strephon:	I tell her very plainly that the lady is my mother.	1
All:	Taradiddle! taradiddle! tol-lol-lay!	R'
Strephon:	She won't believe my statement, and declares we must be parted	2
	Because on a career of double-dealing I have started;	2
	Then gives her hand to one of these, and leaves me broken-hearted.	2
All:	Taradiddle! taradiddle! tol-lol-lay!	R'

The pauses (a foot and a half in each instance) after *Oh* and *fie* are very effective; as well as the pauses (each representing one unaccent) after *tol, lol* and *lay*. The Lord Chancellor chimes in with astonishing mosaic rhyming:

Go away, madam!	1
I should say, madam,	1
You display, madam,	1
Shocking taste.	2
It is rude, madam,	3
To intrude, madam,	3
With your brood, madam	3
Brazen-faced!	2

The Fairy Queen retorts in a stanza almost like a double limerick, which the Chancellor uses in replying to her:

A plague on this vagary!	1
I'm in a nice quandary:	1
Of hasty tone	2
With dames unknown	2
I ought to be more chary.	1
It seems that she's a fairy	1
From Andersen's library;	1
When I took her for	3
The proprietor	3
Of a ladies' seminary.	1

The ending, the doom spoken by the Fairy Queen, moves from couplets to a delicious mosaically rhymed quatrain:

Hence forth, Strephon, cast away
Crooks and pipes and ribbons so gay,
Flocks and herds that bleat and low;
Into Parliament you go. . . .
He shall prick that annual blister,
Marriage with deceased wife's sister;
He shall offer to the many

```
        Peerages at three a penny. . . .
        Peers shall teem in Christendom,        5
            And a duke's exalted station                6
        Be attainable by com-                    5
            petitive examination.                       6
```

G. K. Chesterton, in his *Song Against Songs* in *The Flying Inn*, moved from jovial satire to a rousing strain, in an effective simple stanza of twelve lines:

The song of the sorrow of Melisande is a weary song and a dreary song,
    The glory of Mariana's grange has got into great decay,
The song of the Raven Never More has never been called a cheery song,
    And the brightest things in Baudelaire are anything else but gay.
        But who will write us a riding song,
        Or a hunting song or a drinking song,
        Fit for those that arose and rode
        When day and the wine were red?
        But bring me a quart of claret out,
        And I will write you a clinking song,
        A song of war and a song of wine
        And a song to wake the dead.

In spite of the line division, the actual movement is 8,7 feet, accent verse, throughout. Thus lines 5, 7, 9, and 11 have no rhyming mates, since they are in reality the ends of half lines which are not supposed to rhyme in this pattern. They are so indicated above. For purposes of emphasis, Chesterton decided to bisect these later lines—the real movement of the whole being that of an octave of alternate 8,7 foot lines, with alternate rhyming.

A. A. Milne carries this matter of line-division much further, in his *When We Were Very Young* and *Now We Are Six*:

```
        The King asked                       –
        The Queen, and                       –
        The Queen asked                      –
        The Dairymaid:                       1
        "Could we have some butter for       –
        The Royal slice of bread?"                  2
        The Queen asked                      –
        The Dairymaid,                       –
        The Dairymaid                        –
        Said, "Certainly,                    3
        I'll go and tell                     –
        The cow                              –
        Now                                  –
        Before she goes to bed."                    2
```

[303]

In spite of the amusing hashing of line-length and the internal rhyme *The cow Now,* the pattern is predominantly 4-accent verse, rhymed 1,2,3,2. The feet range from amphibrachs and amphibrachs with feminine endings ($\smile \diagup \smile \smile$) to wilder feet, with a minor accent as well as a major one. But the sing-song *Mother Goose* quality of the rhythm is apparent throughout. This fascinated readers young and old, as did another familiar tune from the second volume:

Christopher Robin	–
Had wheezles	1
And sneezles,	1
They bundled him	–
Into	–
His bed.	2
They gave him what goes	3
With a cold in the nose,	3
And some more for a cold	–
In the head.	2
They wondered	–
If wheezles	1
Could turn	–
Into measles,	1
If sneezles	1
Would turn	–
Into mumps;	4
They examined his chest	5
For a rash,	–
And the rest	5
Of his body for swellings and lumps.	4

The total is twenty-eight feet of dactylic verse. Each seventh foot has a terminal rhyme (*bed, head; mumps, lumps*); in addition, each seven feet has two (in one instance three) internal rhymes, not always placed in identical positions. And always, the amusing divided lines, the divisions fitting the poet's whim. Such liberties the poet is always entitled to take, leaving it to his public to approve or disapprove.

STANZAS IN POPULAR SONGS

In view of the importance of the song market to the versifier, something should be said about the stanza construction of such as become popular. The best instructor in this regard is the type of song popular at the time the versifier intends to try.

About 1872, when *Silver Threads Among the Gold* was written by Eben E. Rexford, the pattern was simple:

Darling, I am growing old,	1
Silver threads among the gold,	1
Shine upon my brow today,	2
Life is fading fast away.	2
But, my darling, you will be	3
Always young and fair to me.	3

The so called first verse or stanza consisted of these six lines, with the last two used as a refrain to complete the eight-line stanza. The chorus—the refrain repeated, after each stanza—was merely lines one through four. Thomas P. Westendorf's *I'll Take You Home Again, Kathleen,* dating from the same period, had a verse of eight lines of four iambic feet each, rhymed alternately, with a chorus half as long, also rhymed alternately. This simple form still finds a market today.

Drill, Ye Tarriers, Drill, Thomas F. Casey's 1888 offering, had a typical verse of four lines, four accents to each line; but the refrain was more individual: 3,3,4,4,3 feet, with two repeated single feet to close. A few years later, James Thornton's *My Sweetheart's the Man in the Moon,* had a typical quatrain verse of seven feet to the line; but elaborated the chorus into 3,3,2,2,4;3,3,2,2,3-foot lines:

My sweetheart's the man in the moon,	1
I'm going to marry him soon,	1
'Twould fill me with bliss,	2
Just to give him one kiss,	2
But I know that a dozen I never would miss;	2
I'll go up in a great big balloon,	1
And see my sweetheart in the moon,	1
Then behind some dark cloud,	3
Where no one is allowed,	3
I'll make love to the man in the moon.	1

This process of chorus elaboration is still going on.

The same period gave birth to Charles K. Harris's *After the Ball,* still one of the most popular of sob songs. The music required that the verse be sung as eight lines of seven-foot accent verse. The chorus was three accent feet to the line, a double quatrain with the ancient ballad rhyming 1,2,3,2:

> After the ball is over,
> After the break of morn,
> After the dancers' leaving,
> After the stars are gone,
> Many a heart is aching,
> If you could read them all;
> Many the hopes that have vanished,
> After the ball.

The five repetitions of *After the,* the repetition of *Many,* merely point to the perennial popularity of the ancient repetitional devices. For song purposes, the two-foot last line becomes 3-accented:

$$\text{Áf- / ter the / báll.}$$

Of the same vintage is Harry von Tilzer's famous *She's Only a Bird in a Gilded Cage,* with a verse consisting of an octave of 4,3 accent verse, rhymed alternately; and a chorus-octave rhymed more simply, 1,2,3,2; 4,5,6,5—although the 6-line has internal rhyme, a device that seems to have impressed each new lyric-writer with the idea that he had discovered a new planet.

Many modern favorites start as simply, although they may consist of only an elaborated chorus—as *Stormy Weather,* or *South of the Border.* Thus *An Apple for the Teacher* has an octave chorus, 6,7-foot lines, rhymed couplet-wise. The chorus of *The Umbrella Man,* in definite accent verse, is only a quatrain, all rhymed on one sound. With *Ain't Cha Comin' Out* we get a more typically modern elaboration. The first two movements of the chorus proceed:

> Each night at eight,
> Under her window he'd wait,
> He would look up and shout,
> Ain't cha comin' out?

The final line here is repeated twice. This is predominantly dactylic, with 2,3,2,1 for the number of feet. The final line, however, has four unaccents before the concluding accent ($\smile\smile\smile\smile\diagup$). After the second movement, we get:

> He couldn't strum a guitar,
> A banjo or mandolin,
> He couldn't sing Tra-la-la,
> He couldn't whistle or hum,
> He'd just come there and shout,
> Ain't cha comin' out?

A dactylic quatrain, 3,3,3,3, followed by a couplet like the one terminating the first movement, of 2,1 feet—the last single-foot accent line being repeated three times. In many such cases, the lyric—the trade name for words to be set to music—is written to fit a tricky modern tune; in others, the tune to fit a tricky modern lyric.

Are these lines a good example of versification, or less than good? They are at least natural, and singable. As poetry to be read or spoken, they would be rather unimpressive. The rhyming is elementary, in spite of the nice use of internal rhyme (*strum, hum, come*); the second line of the quatrain, ending *mandolin,* for instance, has no rhyming mate. This device, incidentally, is common in popular songs; as if later exigencies of rhyming made the dangling line forgotten. And yet, admirably fitted to a sparkling dance tune, these lines at once became far more welcomed and popular than hundreds of more pretentious lyrics. Incidentally, in the field of popular songs, anything resembling a caste distinction between serious verse and light verse is wiped out: the two stand on an entirely equal footing.

As delightfully formal is *Comes Love,* its first two movements to this pattern:

> Comes a rain storm, put your rubbers on your feet,
> Comes a snow storm, you can get a little heat,
> Comes love (pause), nothing can be done.

The actual accenting of this is:

> Comes a rain / storm (pause) / put your rub- / bers on your feet,

—definitely accent verse, with the second accent falling on the pause, and with four syllables to the fourth foot ($\smile \smile \smile /$). The third line is:

> Comes love / (pause) / (pause) / nothing can / be done.

The third movement is definite four accent throughout:

> Don't / try / hid- / in',
>
> 'Cause there is- / n't an- / y use / (pause),
>
> You'll / start / slid- / in',
>
> When your / heart turns / on the / juice,

[307]

As sung, this consists of a quatrain, alternately rhymed. But *hidin', slidin'* get *two* accents each, not one: a departure as radical as Calverley's in always using amphimacers rhymed on the last syllable to terminate the dactylic lines in *Ode to Tobacco*. The charm of many varied popular choruses today comes from such devices as this.

Ira Gershwin's choruses are always deft, as in this movement from *Do-Do-Do:*

> Do, do, do what you've done, done, done before, (pause), baby, (pause),
> Do, do, do what I do, do, do adore, (pause), baby, (pause),
> Let's try again, sigh again, fly again to heaven,
> Baby, see, it's A, B, C, I love you and you love me.

This is definitely accent verse, 8 accents to the line; with intricate internal rhyming, including the mosaic rhyme *baby, see—A, B, C,* as well as terminal rhyme, when it suits his purpose.

Cole Porter is noted for at least an equal ingenuity in rhyming and stanza pattern, as in this opening movement of the chorus of *It's De-lovely:*

> The night is young, the skies are clear,
> And if you want to go walking, dear,
> It's delightful, (pause), it's delicious, (pause),
> It's delovely. (pause—pause—pause).

The third movement typically varies:

> You can tell at a glance
> What a swell night this is for romance,
> You can hear dear Mother Nature murmuring low,
> "Let yourself go." (pause)

And then comes the return to the first movement, slightly lengthened for a conclusion. The four lines last given really constitute two 8-foot accent lines. In accent verse, it is all-important to mark the accents; but the beginnings and endings of the feet are not nearly so important, since they are boundary marks that may be shifted, in many cases, without affecting the flow of the verse.

Many of the more popular song-lyricists have abandoned metric verse for accent verse, as better fitted to pleasing musical setting and closer to the spirit of English speech and song. This fact is important to all who aim at this important field. And in it, as in all aspects of versification, mastery of the technique is important, both for immediate acceptance and continuing popularity.

CLASSIC LINES AND STANZAS: DACTYLIC HEXAMETERS

The Greek dactylic hexameter, the classic model from the time of Homer onward—as the iambic five-foot line is in classical English versification—has a complicated structure. Of its six feet, the first four are either dactyls or spondees; the fifth must be a dactyl; and the last is a spondee or trochee. If a spondee appears in the fifth line, the verse is called spondaic. By scansion, a dactylic hexameter would be:

⌐ ‿ ‿	— ‿ ‿	— ‿ ‿	— ‿ ‿		— ⌐
or	or	or	or	— ‿ ‿	or
— —	— —	— —	— —		— ‿

In Greek and Latin verse, and in rare examples of English verse, this is written with a quantity basis—long and short syllables, determined by strict rules—as opposed to the English device of accented and unaccented syllables.

Dactylic hexameters may be written in English in accent meter, as in Longfellow's *Evangeline*, which would give:

> This is the / forest pri- / meval, the / murmuring / pines and
> the / hemlocks.

Such a dactylic movement is not especially at home in English, with its relative equality in the number of accented and unaccented syllables in normal speech. And this has no basic similarity to the Greek quantity line. Greek verse, in addition, had elaborate rules for the location of the cesura, or pause, in each line.

Accurate quantity hexameters were written by Sir Philip Sidney in English:

> That to my advancement their wisdoms have me abased,
> Well may a pastor plain*; but alas his plaints be not esteemed,
> Oppressed with ruinous conceits by the aid of an outcry.

* Complain.

To ears trained in English speech, this sounds like unimpressive prose. Yet it satisfies the rigid quantity scansion, as verse, by the classical definition. Notice the scansion of the third line:

Oppress'd / with ruin- / ous con- / ceits by the / aid of an / outcry.

Here *with* must be dwelt on unnecessarily, and the word *ruinous* would be read, if we substituted accent for quantity—and accent is all our ears are trained to hear—*ru-in-ous⁄*, with no accent except at the end. This patently flies in the face of all normal English word-usage.

Those interested in experimental efforts to revive abandoned verse forms from time to time write quantity hexameters in English. The modern ear may continue to hear them as prose.

THE SO-CALLED PENTAMETER: THE ELEGIAC COUPLET

To lighten the ponderous tread of the artificial dactylic hexameters, the elegiac couplet was invented, about the 7th century B.C. This consisted of a dactylic hexameter followed by a so-called pentameter following this pattern:

— ∪ ∪	— ∪ ∪	— ‖ — ∪ ∪	— ∪ ∪	—
or	or		or	or	or
— —	— —		— —	— —	∪

This is really a classic hexameter with half a foot omitted in both the third and sixth feet; and with the privilege of a spondee in the fifth. The familiar example in English accent meter is from Coleridge:

> In the hexameter rises the fountain's silvery column;
> In the pentameter aye falling in melody back.

Tennyson revised this, in an effort to achieve quantity rather than accent meter:

> Up springs hexameter, with might, as a fountain arising,
> Lightly the fountain falls, lightly the pentameter.

The elegiac couplet was at first used in Greece for love-songs, war-songs, and didactic poems, and only later for elegies. In English, it has so far been used only in examples in versification.

CLASSIC HENDECASYLLABICS

Hendecasyllabics or 11-syllabled lines in classic prosody were composed of a spondee, a dactyl, and three trochees. Tennyson lightly did his best in *Hendecasyllabics:*

Ō yōu / chōrŭs ŏf / īndŏ- / lēnt rĕ- / vīewĕrs,

Īrrĕ- / spōnsĭblĕ, / īndŏ- / lēnt rĕ- / vīewĕrs,
Look, I come to the test, a tiny poem,
All composed in a meter of Catullus;
All in quantity, careful of my motion,
Like the skater on ice that hardly bears him,
Lest I fall unawares before the people,
Waking laughter in indolent reviewers.

Since we hear these lines as meter based on accent, it should be noted that the second, fourth, fifth, sixth and eighth fail to give the opening spondaic effect. In English, this remains more of a stunt in versification than a device of poetry.

In modern usage, a hendecasyllabic line is any line of verse containing eleven syllables.

ALCAICS

There are three examples of Alcaic lyric verses, named from Alcaeus of Lesbos, poet friend of Sappho, and their reputed inventor:

(1) Alcaic hendecasyllabic or 11-syllabled:

˘or − ˘ − ˘or − ˘ ˘ − ˘ −or

Tennyson attempted this in English quantitative verse:

Ō mīghtў̆-mōuthĕd īnvēntŏr ŏf hārmŏnĭes.

(2) Alcaic decasyllabic or 10-syllabled:

− ˘ ˘ − ˘ ˘ − ˘ − −or

Tennyson gave this as:

Mīltŏn, ă nāme tŏ rēsōund fŏr āgĕs.

(3) Alcaic enneasyllabic or 9-syllabled:

˘or − ˘ − ˘or − ˘ − −or

[311]

Tennyson's version was:

Ḡod-gĭftĕd ōrgăn vŏice ŏf Ēnglănd.

The Alcaic stanza was a quatrain, two hendecasyllabics followed by a decasyllabic and an enneasyllabic. It was a great favorite with Alcaeus and the Roman Horace. There is much dispute as to how the lines should be divided into feet. Certain authorities describe:

1. The hendecasyllabic, as a spondee or iamb, an iamb, a long syllable, and two dactyls;
2. The decasyllabic as two dactyls, followed by two trochees;
3. Instead of an enneasyllabic, the third line appears as one of these four-foot lines:

(I)	⌣ – – –			
	or			
(II)	– ⌣ – –		_ ⌣ ⌣ ⌣̲	_ ⌣ ⌣ _	⌣ _ ⌣̲
	or	(stress on 1st or 4th syllable)	(stress on 1st or fourth syllable)	(stress on 1st long syllable)
(III)	– – ⌣ –			
	or			
(IV)	– – – ⌣			

The names of the four initial feet here are epitrite: first, second, third or fourth class, depending on the location of the unaccent. This is followed by two choriambi or choriambs, and a bacchius.

In dealing with the Alcaic stanza, these authorities prescribe as first and second, two Alcaic hendecasyllabics, as above; third, a line of nine syllables, iambics but hypercatalectic—catalectic meaning lacking a syllable at the beginning, or terminating in an imperfect foot; fourth, a ten-syllabled Alcaic, as above. Tennyson achieved:

O mighty-mouthed inventor of harmonies,
O skilled to sing of time or eternity,
    God-gifted organ voice of England,
    Milton, a name to resound for ages.

The complete Alcaic poem consisted of several of such strophes or stanzas. The result, in English, is usually acceptable verse, rather than poetry.

SAPPHICS

Sapphics are named after Sappho of Lesbos, so famous in antiquity that she was called The Poetess, as Homer was called

The Poet. A Sapphic line consisted of five equal beats; its central one of three syllables, the others of two each. The original Sapphic stanza was a quatrain with this scansion:

$$- \;\smile \;\Big| \; \text{or} \; \Big| \; - \;\smile\;\smile \; \Big| \; - \;\smile \; \Big| \; \text{or}$$

$$- \;\smile \;\Big| \; \text{or} \; \Big| \; - \;\smile\;\smile \; \Big| \; - \;\smile \; \Big| \; \text{or}$$

$$- \;\smile \;\Big| \; - \;\smile \; \Big| \; - \;\smile\;\smile \; \Big| \; - \;\smile \; \Big| \; \text{or}$$

$$- \;\smile\;\smile \;\Big| \; - \;\smile \; \Big|$$

Swinburne is only one of many English poets who tried to do Sapphics based on quantity in English. Here is a typical stanza:

Saw the / white im- / placable / Aphro- / dite,

Saw the / hair un- / bound and the / feet un- / sandalled

Shine as / fire of / sunset on / western / waters;

Saw the re- / luctant

John Addington Symonds, seeking to translate the famous ode to Aphrodite by Sappho into English, gave us:

> Glittering-throned undying Aphrodite,
> Wile-weaving daughter of high Zeus, I pray thee
> Tame not my soul with heavy woe, dread mistress,
> Nay, nor with anguish,
>
> But hither come, if ever erst of old time
> Thou didst incline, and listenedst to my crying,
> And from thy father's palace down descending
> Camest with golden
>
> Chariot yoked; thee fair swift flying sparrows
> Over dark earth with multitudinous fluttering,
> Pinion on pinion through middle ether
> Down from heaven hurried.

To my scansion, this does not fit either quantity verse or accent meter in English, according to Sappho's model. Nor is it accurate translation. Sappho's plea for winning the love of a girl is altered into a plea for aid in winning a man, by a Victorian convention. My own rendering is:

Jewel-throned immortal one, Aphrodite,
Zeus's daughter, spell-weaver, I beseech you
Never harm me, never subdue with sorrow,
    Goddess, my spirit.

Rather come to aid me, if you have ever
Heard my soft voice summoning from afar, and
Hearkened to it, leaving your father's lofty
    Sun-golden palace,

And with chariot yoked you came near, your lovely
Hurtling birds around all the murky earth, with
Densely whirring pinions, come down from airy
    Heavens through mid-space.

This is still profoundly unsatisfactory. It is adequate verse, but it is not poetry, nor does it catch any of Sappho's real spirit. For what she wrote, in her own words—set to a tune on the lyre, of course, in Greek words, yet meant for our hearts and souls rather than our meter-metronoming ears—was:

Rainbow-throned, immortal Aphrodite,
daughter of Zeus, spell-weaver,
I plead with you, Goddess,
do not wear down my heart
with torturing unfulfilment.

But come to me,
if ever before, at any time,
you have heard my voice from a distance,
and have responded,
leaving your father's golden palace,

and, in your yoked chariot,
toward shadowed earth
the strong wings of your two beautiful swift swans
have drawn you, beating down from high heaven
through mid-air.

Quickly then you came;
and you, O blest Goddess,
with a smile in your immortal eyes,
asked me gently what had upset me this time,
and why I called you,

and what it was
that I throbbed so to achieve
in my frantic heart:
"Whom now must I tempt to give you her passion?
Who is it that spurns you, Sappho?

"For even if she flee you now,
she shall soon follow you;
if she scorn the gift, she soon shall give;
if she love not, she soon shall love,
though she be all unwilling."

Come to me now!
Deliver me from clawing pain,
and win for me
what my heart cries to have won.
Come, you yourself be my aid!

Sapphics in English, with the meter based on accent, are far more successful than any quantitative experiments. In the example already given, Don Marquis adds consonance to the ornaments used in his poem. Sapphics are at least as successful with neither rhyme nor consonance:

I am part of night. In the silent darkness,
When the moon brings balm and a silver rapture,
Let me lift my soul to the starry heavens,
    One with their vastness.

To the dark surrendering all my being,
Let me dream white dreams of my soul's fulfilment,
Spun of old romance and an utter giving
    To the beloved one.

Let no thievish day with its garish glitter
Steal my sleep and dreams that are golden soul-talk;
Night, forever gather me to your bosom,
    Child of my spirit.
                    From *The Deathless Flower*, IDA ELAINE JAMES.

Sapphics can also be used amusingly in light verse, as in George Canning's *The Friend of Humanity and the Needy Knife-Grinder*:

Needy knife-grinder! whither are you going?
Rough is the road; your wheel is out of order—
Bleak blows the blast;—your hat has got a hole in't.
    So have your breeches.

Weary knife-grinder! little think the proud ones
Who in their coaches roll along the turnpike—
Road, what hard work 'tis crying all day, "Knives and
    Scissors to grind O!" . . . .

I give thee sixpence! I will see thee damned first,—
Wretch! whom no sense of wrongs can rouse to vengeance!—
Sordid, unfeeling, reprobate, degraded,
    Spiritless outcast!

ARCHILOCHIAN VERSE

Archilochian verse is named after the Greek satiric poet Archilochus, 7th century B. C. The verse called Archilochian is a dactylic four-foot catalectic—that is, lacking a terminal syllable:

$$- \;\smile\;\smile\; | \;-\;\smile\;\smile\; | \;-\;\smile\;\smile\; | \;-\;\smile\;\wedge$$

The Lesser Archilochian is the same line without the opening dactyl: a dactylic three-foot or trimeter, likewise catalectic:

$$- \;\smile\;\smile\; | \;-\;\smile\;\smile\; | \;\bar{\ }\;\bar{\ }_{\wedge}$$

A composite verse is a dactylic tetrameter acatelectic or complete, plus a trochaic tripody:

$$\begin{matrix} \bar{\ }\bar{\ } \\ \text{or} \\ -\smile\smile \end{matrix} \left| \begin{matrix} \smile\bar{\ } \\ \text{or} \\ -\smile\smile \end{matrix} \right| - \left\| \begin{matrix} \bar{\ } \\ \text{or} \\ \smile\smile \end{matrix} \right| -\smile\smile\ \# \;-\smile\left| -\smile\right| -\smile$$

We are now deep in that gloomy prosodic land where even the words used by the inhabitants flutter helplessly outside our strained comprehension.

The Archilochian strophe is a dactylic hexameter followed by a lesser Archilochian; a dactylic hexameter followed by an iambelegus; an iambic trimeter followed by an elegiambus; or a greater Archilochian followed by an iambic trimeter catalectic.

If you insist on further illumination, an iambelegus is an iambic dimeter followed by half of an iambic pentameter:

$$\smile -\;|\;\smile -\;|\;\smile -\;|\;\smile\;\#\;-\smile\smile\;|\;-\smile\smile\;|\;\#\;\bar{\ }_{\wedge}$$

or a trochaic dimeter catalectic with anacrusis (one or two extra preliminary unstressed syllables), followed by a lesser Archilochian. An elegiambus is half of an elegiac pentameter (two dactyls and a long syllable) with an iambic dimeter:

$$-\smile\smile\;|\;-\smile\smile\;|\;-\;\wedge\;\#\;\smile -\;|\;\smile -\;|\;\smile -\;|\;\smile -$$

Dimeter is here used, not as two feet, but as two dipodies, or four feet.

Compared to the simplicity of English versification, with which this book has been mainly concerned, and compared to the clarity of Shakespeare and *Comes Love,* this is complicated to the point of absurdity. It is clearly impossible that poetry, the essence of the soul's desires, can be intentionally expressed in any such intricate jigsaw puzzling. Verse, yes; amusing verse, if such logometry happens to amuse.

Has our delving into it, then, no value? Poetry comes naturally and spontaneously. In some later lull, prosodists rigidify and
enshrine the original natural usage into adamantine patterns.
Later versifiers, misled by the prosodists as to how poetry came,
squeezed and tortured their inspiration into these straight-jackets;
until some creative pattern-maker broke the old patterns, and
wrote his own poetry as freshly as did the first poets.

Playing the Adam to new and rigid poetic forms did not end
with the coming of the barbarians and the collapse of the first
Roman empire. It mars our own time, too. Important poets have
never bothered to engender, christen and popularize any of these
tortuous new forms. There are forms or stanzas called the Spenserian stanza, the Shakespearean sonnet, the Miltonic sonnet, the
Wordsworthian sonnet, the *In Memoriam* stanza, and the *Rubaiyat* stanza, but they were not named so by their originators.
Campion, Burns, Shelley, Keats, Browning, Poe, Whitman, Robinson, Frost, Chesterton, de la Mare, Elinor Wylie, Edna St. Vincent Millay, never bothered to invent a cinquain, a sonnette, a
triolet redoublé, a glose royal, and baptize it in the waters of
Helicon, and spread its merits through the little poetry magazines,
for the versifying pond-skippers to revere and imitate. Yet, since
such forms mushroom into view constantly, some of the worthier
among them will be included, before this book is ended.

It remains that poetry comes differently, a lovechild, unplanned, unblueprinted, winning its way by no clacque clamor,
no offer of a ribband to wear on the coat. It comes, and stays.
As for the others,

> Rhymes and rhymers pass away, poems distill'd from poems
>   pass away,
> The swarm of reflectors and the polite pass, and leave ashes,
> Admirers, importers, obedient persons, make but the soil of
>   literature. . . .
> He masters whose spirit masters, he tastes sweetest who results
>   sweetest in the long run,
> The blood of the brawn beloved of time is unconstraint.
>   By *Blue Ontario's Shore,* WALT WHITMAN.

MISCELLANEOUS CLASSIC METERS

A choriamb we have found to be a foot of four syllables:
long, short, short, long ($-\cup\cup-$), like a trochee welded to an iamb.

A choriambic line consists of a spondee, three choriambi or choriambs, and an iamb:

$$- - \mid - \smile \smile - \mid - \smile \smile - \mid - \smile \smile - \mid \smile -$$

An example, in English meter based upon accent, would be:

> But look! Speech from the strained soul of the
> flea, squeaking "Revere my stunt!"

Browning used a choriambic movement, with accent instead of quantity, in his familiar *Cavalier Tunes: Marching Along:*

> God for King Charles! / Pym and such carles. . . .
> Cavaliers, up! / Lips from the cup.

A galliambic line is composed of iambs, one of which drops its final accent; the next to the last foot being an anapest. Or it is defined as two iambic dimeters catalectic, the last lacking its final syllable. Or as four Ionic feet *a minore*. An Ionic foot *a minore* is $\smile \smile - -$; four of them would be:

$$\smile \smile - - \mid \smile \smile - - \mid \smile \smile - - \mid \smile \smile - -$$

The former alternative definition would give, regarding dimeter as a dipody:

$$- \smile \mid - \smile \mid - \smile \mid - \smile \parallel - \smile \mid - \smile \mid - \smile \mid -$$

There is no rhythmic correspondence between this first line of sixteen syllables, and the second of fifteen. The definition includes both.

Incidentally, an Ionic greater or *a majore* foot is two longs followed by two shorts, $- - \smile \smile$.

Other terms in classic prosody that may require definition are:

Acatalectic Verse: verse not defective in the last foot; verse complete in the number of syllables.

Arsis: the lighter or unstressed part of a foot, especially in quantitative verse; later, through a misunderstanding, the accented syllable of a foot.

Cesura: A break in a verse caused by the ending of a word within the foot. A *masculine cesura* followed the thesis, or stressed part of the foot; a *feminine cesura* followed the arsis or unstressed part. A *trithemimeral cesura* comes after the third half foot, which means in the second foot; a *penthemimeral cesura,* after the fifth half foot; a *hepthemimeral cesura,* after the seventh half foot; and so on. A *bucolic cesura,* in dactylic hexameter, is a cesura occurring in the fourth foot, especially in pastoral poetry.

Catalectic Verse: Verse lacking a syllable at the beginning, or terminating in an imperfect foot.

Diaeresis, Dieresis: The break caused by the coincidence of the end of a foot with the end of a word. *Bucolic diaeresis,* a diaeresis occurring in the fourth foot, especially in pastoral poetry.

Enjambement: The extension of the sentence beyond the limits of the distich, or couplet.

Ictus: Metrical stress.

Thesis: The heavier or stressed part of a foot in classical prosody, especially in quantitative verse; later, through a misunderstanding, the unaccented syllable or syllables of a verse.

INDENTATION

Indention, or indentation, is setting a line in—that is, to the right of—the margin; setting it inside the flush line of the text. In prose, paragraphs are indented at their beginning; and at times quotations are indented as a whole, that is, set inside the margins on one or both sides. In poetry, there are three proper ways to use indentation:

1. Separate stanzas or parts of a long poem may be indented, precisely as prose is indented. Or the beginning of a short poem may be so indented.

2. Extremely short lines may be set centered inside both margins, for symmetry.

3. Lines which rhyme with each other are indented alike, to show the correspondence in rhyme-terminals.

Nothing shows the untrained amateur—poet, editor, or publisher—more than indenting wrongly. Here are a few Don'ts, under the usage in (3):

(a) Never indent blank verse of any sort: that is, lines which have no rhyme. This is wrong:

> Then the little Hiawatha
>   Said unto the old Nokomis
> "Let us wander to the waters,
>   To the shores of Gitchee-Gummi."

This should, of course, be set up:

> Then the little Hiawatha
> Said unto the old Nokomis,
> "Let us wander to the waters," etc.

(b) Never indent alternately lines which have couplet rhyming. This is wrong:

> Grasshopper, your fairy song
>   And my poem alike belong
> To the dark and silent earth
>   From which all poetry has birth.

This is the commonest misuse of indentation. Of course, this must be set up as:

> Grasshopper, your fairy song
> And my poem alike belong
> To the dark and silent earth
> From which all poetry has birth.
>   *Earth*, JOHN HALL WHEELOCK

(c) Never indent *except* to showing rhyming correspondence: the wrong way being,

> The Moving Finger writes; and, having writ,
>   Moves on; nor all your Piety nor Wit
> Shall lure it back to cancel half a Line,
>   Nor all your Tears wash out one Word of it.

This, of course, must appear in the familiar form, if indentation is used:

> The Moving Finger writes; and, having writ,
> Moves on; nor all your Piety nor Wit
>   Shall lure it back to cancel half a Line,
>   Nor all your Tears wash out one Word of it.
> *The Rubaiyat of Omar Khayyam*, EDWARD FITZGERALD

And there is one positive rule:

(d) Verse need never be indented to show correspondence in rhyming. Unindented verse, verse set flush along the margin all the way, is always correct.

INDENTING THE SONNET

There are two correct ways to indent a Shakespearean sonnet, if indentation is desired; and the first of these is the older, the preferred, and the one dating from Shakespeare's time. There is only one correct way to indent the Italian, Miltonic or Words-worthian sonnet in English, providing indentation is used. Here they are—the numbers standing for the complete lines, rhymed as in these rhyming schemes:

```
Shakespearean Sonnet                Italian Sonnet
(1)        (2)
1          1                    1
2            2                    2
1          1                    2
2            2                  1
3          3                    1
4            4                    2
3          3                    2
4            4                  1
5
6          Space               Space
5          5
6            6                  3          3
  7        5                      4          4
  7          6                      5  or  3
           7                    3            4
           7                      4      3
                                    5          4
```

Where indentation is used throughout the Shakespearean sonnet, it is also proper to set the final couplet to the right of the position of the last (6) rhyme. Where a sonnet is broken in meaning by a full stop, in lines 8 or 9 (or even elsewhere), at times the space appears here, the new sentence starting slightly to the right of the period, after the space. The Italian sonnet may also be indented after each quatrain and each tercet.

THE TYPOGRAPHY OF POETRY

There is a common misconception that lines of formal length, often all of them indented or centered on the page, and usually each beginning with a capital letter, are necessary for poetry. The following is clearly poetry:

My life closed twice before its close; it yet remains to see if Immortality unveil a third event to me, so huge, so hopeless to conceive as these that twice befell.

Parting is all we know of heaven, and all we need of hell.

Parting, EMILY DICKINSON

This is commonly printed, following Emily Dickinson's desire,

> My life closed twice before its close;
> It yet remains to see
> If Immortality unveil
> A third event to me,
>
> So huge, so hopeless to conceive
> As these that twice befell
> Parting is all we know of heaven,
> And all we need of hell.

We are accustomed to the following poetry set up in a format more usual in prose:

1 Lord, thou hast been our dwelling place in all generations.
2 Before the mountains were brought forth, or ever thou hadst formed the earth and the world, even from everlasting to everlasting, thou art God.
3 Thou turnest man to destruction, and sayest, Return, ye children of men.
4 For a thousand years in thy sight are but as yesterday when it is past, and as a watch in the night.

Psalm xc

Certain modern editions of the Bible are setting this up as we expect prose to appear:

Lord, thou hast been our dwelling place in all generations. Before the mountains were brought forth, or ever thou hadst formed the earth and the world, even from everlasting to everlasting, thou art God.

Thou turnest man to destruction, and sayest, Return, ye children of men. For a thousand years in thy sight are but as yesterday when it is past, and as a watch in the night.

Psalm xc

Though I speak with the tongues of men and of angels, and have not charity, I am become as sounding brass, or a tinkling cymbal. And though I have the gift of prophecy, and understand all mysteries, and all knowledge; and though I have all faith, so that I could remove mountains, and have not charity, I am nothing. And though I bestow all my goods to feed the poor, and though I give my body to be burned, and have not charity, it profiteth me nothing.

Charity suffereth long, and is kind; charity envieth not; charity vaunteth not itself, is not puffed up, doth not behave itself unseemly, seeketh not her own, is not easily provoked, thinketh no evil; rejoiceth not in iniquity, but rejoiceth in the truth; beareth all things, believeth all things, hopeth all things, endureth all things.

I Corinthians xiii, 1-7

Fourscore and seven years ago our fathers brought forth upon this continent a new nation, conceived in liberty, and dedicated to the proposition that all men are created equal. Now we are engaged in a great civil war, testing whether that nation, or any nation so conceived and so dedicated, can long endure. We are met upon a great battlefield of that war, etc.

The Gettysburg Speech, ABRAHAM LINCOLN

The damage done by the usual artificial typography of poetry is not small. It repels the large class of readers who are used to and like prose, and, for a variety of reasons—especially the namby-pamby quality of most current verse—have a distinct antipathy to poetry, and prefer never to read it. It thus cuts appreciably into the size of the audience that poetry should reach. Since poetry is the concentrated utterance of man's deepest desires, this is costly to the readers who avoid it, for they are missing man's most passionate and concentrated words; and it is also costly to the poets, who collectively starve from actual neglect, as well as spiritual non-appreciation. Anything that will properly make poetry again vital to the average man and woman should be adopted. The artificial typography, which has become to many a badge, in effect resembling a smallpox sign, should certainly be eliminated, unless there is strong reason for its retention.

The chief reason urged for preserving the present artificial typography of poetry is that we are used to it. How deep does this objection and the reason for it go; and is it a permanent bar to a sane and logical typography for poetry, and a widened audience and appreciation for the poet?

A survey of the history of the typography used for poetry may aid.

All early poetry used the typography or method of writing used for prose. In Egypt, the papyrus, on which both poetry and prose was written, was employed in the form of rolls, with the writing in narrow columns—although the papyrus, which could have roll joined to roll without limit, had no limitation as to size. Four considerations dictated this:

(1) Each line was what the eye could grasp at one glance. The conventionalized width of column was as functional as the width of a newspaper column, or the size of a tabloid newspaper.

(2) The pay of the scribes, so much a line, caused the line's

length to become conventionalized. Galen says that the unit of measurement among the Greeks was the average Homeric line of thirty-six letters, or sixteen syllables. But if a Homeric line had thirty-seven letters, one letter of course was carried over willy-nilly; and thereafter no line corresponded, except by accident, with the line of poetry. At the end of the roll, the number of *stichoi* or *epe*—lines, that is—was written down, to indicate how much the scribe was to receive.

(3) To indicate how much the manuscript was to cost; for the purchaser paid by the *stichos* or line. In Diocletian's time, the scribe received twenty-five denarii for a hundred stichoi of the first quality, and twenty for the second quality.

(4) To prevent any alteration of the sacred text by copyists, especially among the Hebrew sacred writings, the rabbis stipulated the precise number of letters that were to go on each line. There could be no deviation from this, without heavy penalty.

All this naturally applied to prose, as to poetry. Nor were the words divided at all, space between words being as yet uninvented. The separation of words in Latin texts was not completed until the 11th century A. D.; in Greek texts, not until the 15th.

About 170 B. C., Eumenes II of Pergamus, envying the Alexandrian library, determined to excel it. But the Egyptian Ptolemies, who had a monopoly on papyrus, refused to sell any to him. He invented as a substitute parchment (from *pergamentum*, named after his city), the skilfully treated hides of sheep and calves (cf. *vellum*, from the old *veel*, calf; cf. our *veal*). In spite of the larger parchment pages, man's innate conservatism and imitation of the past continued to use the narrow columns familiar on papyrus. The great *Codex Siniaticus* of the Bible, dating from the fourth century A. D., has four narrow columns to each page, or eight columns to a spread of two pages. The *Codex Vaticanus*, of the same century, has three narrow columns to each page. Later on, the number became two; finally, one. Even today we are familiar with books with two columns to the page, and, more rarely, of three; and to periodicals and newspapers of eight or more.

The Vatican palimpsest of Cicero's *De Republica* has precisely eleven letters to each narrow line. It is clear that poetry, so written, would be more hashed than by any writer in the modern artificial fashion.

The oldest literary papyrus containing poetry that has been discovered is the fourth century B. C. *Persae* of Timotheus of Miletus, in which the letters to a line are: 15, 16, 15, 18, 15, 15, 14, etc. No attempt is made to write this with the artificial conventionalized line of poetry, nor to end each word on a line. The papyrus containing the poems of Bacchilides, dated by paleographists the middle of the first century B. C., has 23, 14, 21, 18, 19, 19 letters per line, in one 6-line fragment. This, too, was written as we are accustomed to seeing prose written, as was the first century B. C. *Odyssey* fragment—with an average of 22 letters to the line—as well as the second century A. D. *Iliad* fragment, found at Tebtunus, averaging 16 letters to the line. The oldest literary Latin papyrus, a fragment of a poem on the battle of Actium, first century A. D., is similarly set as prose would be, averaging 18 letters to the line.

In contrast to these, there is a first century A. D. fragment of the *Odyssey,* and a second century A. D. *Iliad* fragment, in both of which the artificial conventionalized poetic line-division appears. It was, then, at about the beginning of the Christian era, some 1,900 years ago, that the present method of writing or printing poetry for permanent record came into being. Yet Hebrew and other Oriental poems, written long after the fifth century A. D., were written continuously, like prose. This may still be found in some Hebrew poetry today.

It is probable that the poet, when he skeletonized each line for its scansion, set it up artificially, to test its accuracy of versification: very possibly with scansion marks, as well. It is clear that, when a copy was furnished to a singer (and poems at first were written to be sung or chanted), the correspondence of syllable to note should be indicated, for the convenience of the singer. Thus one of the musical versions of my *The Glory Road* opens:

> O de Glo-ry Road! O de Glo-ry Road!
> I'm gwine ter drap my load up-on de Glo-ry Road!
>
> I lay on my bed on-tell one er-clock,
> An' de Lawd come call-in' all His faith-ful flock.
> An' He call "Whoo-ee," an' He call "Whoo-ee,"
> An' I knowed dat de Sab-ior wuz er-call-in' me, etc.

This is the syllabified version required by the singer. It would be kindergartenish, if furnished so to the matured reader. As the poem appeared in *The Independent* in 1917, and in *The Earth Turns South* two years later, it used the line-division written down for the poet for his own guidance, as to line-length and rhyme-scheme:

> O de Glory Road! O de Glory Road!
> I'm gwine ter drap mah load upon de Glory Road.
>
> I lay on mah bed ontell one erclock,
> An' de Lawd come callin' all His faithful flock.
> An' He call "Whoo-ee," an' he call "Whoo-ee,"
> An' I knowed dat de Sabior wuz er-callin' me, etc.

As it appeared in my collected poems, *The Glory Road*, in 1936, it was set up logically, for the reader's understanding and enjoyment:

> O de Glory Road! O de Glory Road! I'm gwine tuh drap mah load upon de Glory Road!
>
> I lay on mah bed ontell one erclock, an' de Lawd come callin' all his faithful flock. An' He call "Whoo-ee," an' He call "Whoo-ee," an' I knowed dat de Sabior wuz er-callin' me, etc.

It is for the poet and publisher of the future to determine which of these three forms will most commend itself to the widest audience of intelligent readers. It is clear that mere artificial brief line division cannot transmogrify prose into poetry:

> It is for the poet and publisher
> Of the future to determine which
> Of these three forms will most
> Commend itself to the widest audience
>
> Of intelligent readers. It is clear
> That mere artificial brief line
> Division can not transmogrify prose
> Into poetry, etc.

This remains the prose it was, in spite of its meaningless artificial line-division. Poetry remains the poetry it is, no matter what its line-division. Let, then, the understanding and appreciation of the reader, the audience, determine the form in which it is to be presented to him in the future. Already poets are kicking at the pricks of the stiff artificial usual convention . . . by omitting the artificial capital letters at the beginning of lines of verse; and, in the cases of such widely-differing versifiers as Walt Whitman, Carl Sandburg, Walt Mason, and others, increasingly setting up verse in the direction of the logical typography familiar in prose. Several volumes have already adopted this device throughout. There will be others.

VI

POEM PATTERNS

A CONSIDERABLE number of poems have the pattern of the whole poem dictated as rigorously as the requirements for a Rubaiyat quatrain, rhyme royal, or the Spenserian stanza. These include such familiar examples as the sonnet, the limerick, the triolet, and the ballade, as well as many not so well known. Before we turn to these, a word should be said about the poem regarded as a whole, instead of as a mere collection of individual stanzas.

From the standpoint of stanzaic structure, the two classes are the poems that, having once selected a stanza to begin with, use it undeviatingly throughout; and those that vary the stanza form, or lack formal stanzas or stanza division entirely. Many of your favorite poems come within the former category: including Gray's *The Elegy Written in a Country Churchyard,* Tennyson's *In Memoriam,* Fitzgerald's *The Rubaiyat of Omar Khayyam,* Shakespeare's two long narrative poems, Byron's *Don Juan,* most of Swinburne, clear down to almost all of the poems in E. A. Housman's *The Shropshire Lad.* In all these poems, unless the whole poem is to be regarded as a mere collection of unset jewels, there must be a unity to the poem, a definite development from beginning up to its major climax, and on to the end. Even *The Rubaiyat,* in its Persian original a mere collection of quatrains unrelated and regarded as individual poems in the main, is held by Fitzgerald's genius to a coherent and united development of a hedonistic and fatalistic philosophy; and this pervading unity added enough to the appeal of its separate quatrains to make it the theme-song of a generation.

Where the poet does not vary his stanzaic structure for the

length of the poem, in proportion to the length and sweep of the poem must be the fluidity, in word usage and the subtler emotion-arousing variations, of his treatment of his uniform stanza. The stanza chosen must be used differently, to respond to each demand made upon it in the development of the theme as a whole; and the parts must always be subordinated to the total effect, so that the intrinsic unity and uninterrupted development of the poem throughout are not marred, even by irrelevant flashes of beauty, impressive enough when taken alone, but flaws in the larger scheme. After its completion, the poem must be surveyed critically as a whole, and made most effective by excision, no less than by improvement and addition. By this rigid test, the last brief stanza of Lepanto is probably a blemish, and might with benefit be eliminated; and the final sixteen lines of *lxii* in *A Shropshire Lad,* "Terence, this is stupid stuff," for all that it is a not irrelevant amplification, had best be forgotten. If the masters nod, it behooves us to be on guard.

A large group of poems vary the stanza itself, to meet the differing demands of the poem's development. The old ballads often added at will a line, a couplet, or even three lines, when the story to be told required it. Coleridge's *The Rime of the Ancient Mariner,* based upon this simple stanzaic norm,

> All in a hot a copper sky,
> The bloody Sun, at noon,
> Right up above the mast did stand,
> No bigger than the Moon,

expands into stanzas of five, six, and even one of nine lines. G. K. Chesterton's *The Ballad of the White Horse,* with the same norm, includes many stanzas of five and six, and two of seven lines. Tennyson's *The Charge of the Light Brigade,* in tail-rhyme verse, has stanzas varying from six to twelve lines in length. Yet the effect is as unified as if the stanzas were identical in length. The same poet's stirring sea ballad, *The Revenge,* has stanzas ranging from five to twenty-one lines; yet the effect is natural, cumulative, uniform—just as a story in prose need not have paragraphs of the same number of words, or sentences, or of the same length. Even as formal a poem as Wordsworth's *Ode on the Intimations of Immortality from Early Childhood* has stanzas or divisions ranging from eight to thirty-nine lines. We have studied certain specific poems for their variations in stanza structure; and examples multiply in English poetry. Always the proper test is the artistic and emotional integrity and unity of the whole.

A third method is to have two or more types of formal stanzas, appearing at regular or irregular intervals in the poem. Thus my *Gwine to Heaven* has an identical opening and closing stanza pattern:

> Gwine to Hebb'n! Gwine to Hebb'n!
> I'm gonter go, I'm gonter go, I'm gonter leave dis world of woe,
> Pack an' trabbel, pack an' trabbel
> To de kingdom of my Lawd;
> Howdy sebb'n! Come elebb'n!
> I'm goin' there, I'm goin' there, I'm gonter climb de golden stair,
> Leave de debbil, an' his rabble,
> For to claim my soul's reward.

Stanzas two and four use a differing pattern, to describe the arrived goal:

> Dar dey'll wash me white as snow,
> In Jerusalem land.
> Dar dose honey ribbers flow,
> In Jerusalem land.
> I go, you go, all of us go,
> To de Lawd's bap*tizin'*, I know—
> Wash me white as de dribb'n snow,
> In Jerusalem land.

The central stanza is only six lines long, and arrives at the climax of the poem in its own way. This device, of opening and closing with a definite stanza, and inserting a differing pattern or patterns within, is effective through its own symmetry. It is especially pleasing when set to music. *Aphrodite Enoikia* and *The Poem*, from the same volume (*The Earth Turns South*), are even more complicated developments of symmetrical stanzaic progression and return.

While, however, the singer is at liberty to change his tune or stanza pattern when and where he pleases, there is one warning. A poem predominantly of one pattern, which shifts without reason at one or more places, often gives the effect of crude and sloppy workmanship. The poet's inner ear must be the determinant, in an effort to reflect that presentation of the poem's material which will be unifiedly most effective.

Even as variation of the stanza or within the stanza places

more of a creative burden upon the poet than the use of a uniform stanza, development without formal stanza—such as is found in most examples of free verse, and so many other poems—puts the greatest burden of all upon him, especially of eliminating surplusage and stripping the poem to only such lines as conduce rigorously to the result aimed at.

After the poem is written, it should always be surveyed as a whole, and its totality of pattern studied. For it is the pattern of the whole poem that you present to your reader or hearer; and you must in the end rise or fall by your own innate and developed powers of selectiveness.

And now for those poems and light verse, native and imported, where the pattern of the whole poem is laid down in advance for the poet.

THE SONNET: THE ITALIAN OR PETRARCHAN SONNET

The sonnet is a poem or stanza of fourteen iambic pentameter lines, with a rigidly prescribed rhyme-scheme. There are two main types, the Italian (or Petrarchan) and the Shakespearean (or English); and many minor varieties.

The first sonnet that emerged out of the long prior period of Italian experimentation is ascribed to Piero delle Vigne, chancellor of Frederick II of Sicily, who died in 1249. Its precise ancestry is obscure: while some trace it to the *canzone* strophe, or some other Italian or French formal stanza, the most plausible hypothesis sees in it an extended *ottava rima* (1,2,1,2,1,2,3,3). This would call for the complete rearrangement of the octave rhymes, and the addition of a formalized sestet, changes so extreme that the theory rather shrinks in importance.

Most authorities regard the founder of the form as Guittone of Aerzzo, who died forty-five years later. He firmly established the laws of the construction of the sonnet. He first laid down that there must be an octave, rhymed 1,2,2,1; 1,2,2,1; followed by a sestet permitting certain variations in rhyming, but vigorously excluding a final couplet. The octave, in turn, was divided into two quatrains; and the sestet into two tercets. The subject matter of a sonnet should consist of one idea, or one emotion continuously elaborated throughout, and complete in itself. The four portions of a sonnet should progress in this manner:

The first quatrain should state the principal idea.

The second quatrain should illustrate and elaborate it.

The first tercet, after an intervening pause, should treat it differently.

The final tercet should treat it still differently, and must have at least the dignity of the opening, with some epigrammatic force.

Guittone insisted most of all upon the unified nature of the whole. In the hands of Dante and especially Petrarch, this became the model for Italy and much of Europe.

As an example or a pure Italian or Petrarchan sonnet, here is James Y. Gibson's rendition of Lope de Vega's *Sonnet on The Sonnet:*

To write a sonnet doth my Julia press me.	1
I've never found me in such stress or pain.	2
A sonnet numbers fourteen lines, 'tis plain,	2
And three are gone ere I can say, God bless me!	1
I thought that spinning lines would sore oppress me,	1
Yet here I'm midway in the last quatrain!	2
And if the foremost tercet I attain,	2
The quatrains need not any more distress me.	1
To the first tercet I have got at last,	3
And travel through it with such right good will,	4
That with this line I've finished it, I ween.	5
I'm in the second now, and see how fast	3
The thirteenth line comes tripping from my quill.	4
Hurrah! 'tis done! Count if there be fourteen.	5

This example is given, in spite of its archaisms, because it is not easy to find, in English, an Italian sonnet following the strict model throughout, especially as regards the development from quatrain to quatrain, to tercet and so to the concluding tercet.

There is only one permissible rhyme-scheme for the octave of the Italian sonnet: 1,2,2,1; 1,2,2,1. This includes three contiguous couplet rhymes, which makes it all the stranger that a terminal couplet is forbidden. The sonnet given has one of the two permissible rhyme schemes for the sestet: 3,4,5; 3,4,5. There is one other, 3,4,3; 4,3,4. Here is a more notable sonnet following this second pattern—*On First Looking into Chapman's Homer,* by Keats, flawless except for its run-on between the tercets:

Much have I travell'd in the realms of gold,	1
And many goodly states and kingdoms seen:	2
Round many western islands have I been	2
Which bards in fealty to Apollo hold.	1
Oft of one wide expanse had I been told	1
That deep-browed Homer ruled as his demesne:	2
Yet never did I breathe its pure serene	2
Till I heard Chapman speak out loud and bold.	1
—Then felt I like some watcher of the skies	3
When a new planet swims within his ken;	4
Or like stout Cortez—when with eagle eyes	3
He stared at the Pacific—and all his men	4
Look'd at each other with a wild surmise—	3
Silent, upon a peak in Darien.	4

By the strict technical requirement, line 11 must be end-stopped. In this sonnet, Keats wrote otherwise.

Professor L. T. Weeks examined 6,283 sonnets for their rhyme schemes, and established that the three-rhyme terminal had appeared in these arrangements in them:

3,4,5;	3,4,5	3,4,5; 4,5,3
3,4,5;	4,3,5	3,4,3; 5,4,5
3,4,5;	3,5,4	3,4,3; 5,5,4
3,4,5;	5,3,4	3,3,4; 5,5,4
3,4,5;	5,4,3	3,4,4; 5,3,5

besides these two, forbidden because of the terminal couplet:

3,4,3; 4,5,5   3,4,4; 3,5,5.

Variants of the two-rhyme sestet included:

3,4,4; 3,3,4   3,4,3; 4,4,3
3,4,4; 3,4,3   3,4,3; 3,4,3

besides this one, forbidden for its terminal couplet:

3,4,3; 3,4,4.

And there are other possible variations. Yet, if a strict Italian or Petrarchan sonnet is to be written, it is best to choose between the two permissible sestet rhyme-schemes, 3,4,5; 3,4,5 and 3,4,3; 4,3,4, and let the strict progression involving quatrains and tercets rule.

Sharp, in his introduction to *Sonnets of This Century*, made certain additional stipulations, some of them valuable. He sought to limit each line to ten syllables, which would forbid the feminine ending, as well as the use of a cyclic anapest or dactyl. He forbade any internal rhymes; and provided that the rhyme-sounds of the octave should be harmoniously at variance, and those of the sestet distinct in intonation from those of the octave. He demanded continuous sonority throughout, with an end more impressive than the commencement. There can be small quarrel with the last four of these requirements.

There is one minor warning, in writing Italian sonnets with the sestet rhyming on two sounds only. There is a tendency to write this as three end-stopped couplets, 3,4; 3,4; 3,4. It must never be forgotten that the only accurate Italian form calls instead for two end-stopped tercets, 3,4,3; 4,3,4.

THE MILTONIC SONNET

When Milton turned to the sonnet, he became most famous for this type:

When I consider how my light is spent,	1
Ere half my days in this dark world and wide,	2
And that one talent which is death to hide	2
Lodged with me useless, though my soul more bent	1
To serve therewith my Maker, and present	1
My true account, lest He returning chide,	2
"Doth God exact day-labor, light denied?"	2
I fondly ask. But Patience, to prevent	1
That murmur, soon replies, "God doth not need	3
Either man's work or His own gifts. Who best	4
Bears His mild yoke, they serve Him best. His state	5
Is kingly; thousands at His bidding speed,	3
And post o'er land and ocean without rest;	4
They also serve who only stand and wait.	5

On His Blindness

The rhyming here is accurate. But, instead of the expected full stop, pause and break in the direction at the end of the octave, we have a device sometimes indicated by a stanzaic division here:

> "Doth God exact day-labor, light denied?"
> I fondly ask.

> But Patience, to prevent
> That murmur, soon replies, "God doth not need
> Either man's work," etc.

In the celebrated sonnet, *On the Late Massacre in Piedmont,* lines 8-10 are:

> Mother with infant down the rocks. Their moans
> The vales redoubled to the hills, and they
> To heaven. Their martyred blood and ashes sow, etc.

A sonnet with this device—no full pause after the octave, but a carry on, which may be accompanied by a full stop within the eighth (or sometimes the ninth) line, is called a Miltonic sonnet.

Milton wrote nineteen sonnets in English: only six of them fully use this device. At least eight have end-stopped octaves, in the Italian manner. From the rest, we must generalize as we can, realizing how experimental Milton was in the sonnet. Always his octaves follow the 1,2,2,1; 1,2,2,1 pattern. But his sestets have seven using the 3,4,3; 4,3,4 pattern; six using the 3,4,5,3,4,5; and also the following:

> 3,4,5; 4,3,5 (two)   3,4,4; 3,4,3 (two)
> 3,4,4; 3,5,5   3,4,3; 5,5,4

The sonnet *On the New Forces of Conscience Under the Long Parliament* is *caudated* or *tailed* by this addition, after the fourteenth line:

> That so the Parliament   5
> May with their wholesome and preventive shears   6
> Clip your phylacteries, though balk your ears,   6
> And succour our just fears,   6
> When they shall read this clearly in your charge,   7
> New Presbyter is but old Priest writ large.   7

This device he also derived from the Italian. Other forms of the tail are used, including forms as short as a couplet.

THE WORDSWORTHIAN SONNET

Wordsworth wrote approximately five hundred sonnets, and is hailed as one of the more important sonneteers in English. While it is difficult to isolate any single type as the one he preferred, this sonnet shows typical variations:

> Scorn not the Sonnet; Critic, you have frowned   1
> Mindless of its just honors; with this key   2
> Shakespeare unlocked his heart; the melody   2
> Of this small lute gave ease to Petrarch's wound;   1

A thousand times this pipe did Tasso sound;   1
  With it Camoens soothed an exile's grief;   3
  The Sonnet glittered a gay myrtle leaf   3
Amid the cypress with which Dante crowned   1
His visionary brow: a glow-worm lamp,   4
  It cheered mild Spenser, called from Faery-land   5
To struggle through dark ways; and, when a damp   4
Fell round the path of Milton, in his hand   5
  The Thing became a trumpet, whence he blew   6
  Soul-animating strains—alas, too few!   6

This alteration of the sestet to 1,2,2,1; 1,3,3,1 is typical of many of his more important sonnets. He tended more to break the meaning in the ninth line than the eighth:

The world is too much with us; late and soon,   1
  Getting and spending, we lay waste our powers: 2
  Little we see in Nature that is ours;   2
We have given our hearts away, a sordid boon!   1
This sea that bares her bosom to the moon,   1
  The winds that will be howling at all hours,   2
  And are up-gathered now like sleeping flowers;   2
For this, for everything, we are out of tune;   1
It moves us not.—Great God! I'd rather be   3
  A Pagan suckled in a creed outworn;   4
So might I, standing on this pleasant lea,   3
  Have glimpses that would make me less forlorn;   4
Have sight of Proteus rising from the sea,   3
  Or hear old Triton blow his wreathed horn.   4

In a letter to Dyce, written in 1833, Wordsworth said that, to him, the sonnet was not architectural, but as "an orbicular body —a sphere or a dewdrop," whose excellence consisted mainly in a pervading sense of unity—which, after all, was also the Italian objective.

When sonnets are described as Miltonic or Wordsworthian, care should be taken to indicate which precise variations from the strict Italian form are used, or are to be used. In general, the extreme variation in the sestet, even to the use of a concluding couplet, as in the first Wordsworthian sonnet quoted, and the octave variation, 1,2,2,1—1,3,3,1, are typically Wordsworthian.

THE SPENSERIAN SONNET

The Spenserian stanza, which Spenser invented for *The Faerie Queene*, had this rhyme-scheme: 1,2,1,2; 2,3,2,3; 3, the concluding line being an Alexandrine. Soon after Wyatt and Surrey transplanted the sonnet to England, Spenser began to write sonnets, with this rhyme-scheme, related to that of his preferred stanza:

1,2,1,2; 2,3,2,3; 3,4,3,4; 5,5.

We have here three quatrains with chain-rhyme linking, also reminiscent of terza rima; and the concluding couplet is akin to the device used by terza rima to conclude poems or cantos. This sonnet found few imitators. But it was a transition form to the most popular and English of all sonnet forms.

THE WYATTIAN SONNET

It is still a mystery why Chaucer, with his familiarity with Italian poetic forms, failed to introduce the sonnet into English. It may have been that he was uninterested in so short a type of poem. Sir Thomas Wyatt, who shared with Henry Howard, Earl of Surrey, the introduction of the sonnet into England, in the ebullient Elizabethan age, wrote fairly close to the strict Italian model. But his sestets tended to be of the 3,4,4; 3,5,5 type, ending on the banned couplet. The name Wyattian sonnet is applied to a form he occasionally used:

1,2,2,1; 1,2,2,1; 3,3,4,4,5,5.

This sonnet, ending on three couplets, was not especially popular during his lifetime, and has been largely ignored since.

THE SHAKESPEAREAN OR ENGLISH SONNET

In *Tottel's Miscellany,* which in 1557 first made England sonnet-conscious, Surrey wrote one sonnet ("The soote season that bud and bloom forth brings,") on only two rhymes, in a transitional rhyme-scheme stricter than Spenser's:

1,2,1,2; 1,2,1,2; 1,2,1,2; 1,1.

As in the case of Spenser, this consists of three quatrains with a concluding couplet: the difference being that the interlinking of stanzas by one rhyme-sound has been replaced by a limitation of the whole sonnet to two rhyming sounds.

In the same collection, we encounter one of his sonnets, which is the earliest one with the familiar Shakespearean pattern:

Set me whereas the sun doth parch the green,	1
Or where his beams do not dissolve the ice;	2
In temperate heat, where he is felt and seen;	1
In presence prest of people mad or wise;	2
Set me in high, or yet in low degree;	3
In longest night, or in the shortest day;	4
In clearest sky, or where clouds thickest be;	3
In lusty youth, or when my hairs are gray;	4
Set me in heaven, in earth, or else in hell,	5
In hill, or dale, or in the foaming flood;	6
Thrall, or at large, alive whereso I dwell,	5
Sick, or in health, in evil fame or good,	6
Hers will I be; and only with this thought	7
Content myself, although my chance be nought.	7

The development of this form was inevitable. The popular pattern in English balladry was 1,2,3,2, at times polished to 1,2,1,2. The *Venus and Adonis* stanza was 1,2,1,2,3,3. Rhyme royal, popular since Chaucer, progressed to 1,2,1,2,2,3,3. The Spenserian stanza moved 1,2,1,2; 2,3,2,3,3. The quatrain, with second and fourth lines rhymed, or with alternate rhyming, was rooted deepest in English versification. The other stanzas mentioned commenced with an alternately rhymed quatrain, the Spenserian stanza using two of these, and ended with a couplet. The sonnet that Surrey first used, now called the Shakespearean sonnet, of three quatrains alternately rhymed followed by a couplet, was the natural flowering of all these.

After Surrey's initial use of the form, we have seen what Spenser did with it, influenced by his own pet stanza. Drummond preferred that his octave have two rhyming sounds only; although at times he arranged these in quatrains rhymed alternately. But the sestet terminated by a couplet, 3,4,3,4; 5,5, had come to stay, altering the whole tercet-arrangement of the Italian sonnet. Daniel preferred the Shakespearean form; although in several sonnets he interlinked one rhyme from each quatrain into the succeeding one, somewhat as Spenser had done. So did Sylvester and Constable. Habington sought to popularize a sonnet of seven couplets; but this *Habington sonnet* failed of imitation.

With Shakespeare, the pattern became firmly fixed. Here is the enduring model:

When in disgrace with fortune and men's eyes,	1
I all alone beweep my outcast state,	2
And trouble deaf Heaven with my bootless cries,	1
And look upon myself, and curse my fate,	2
Wishing me like to one more rich in hope,	3
Featur'd like him, like him with friends possess'd,	4
Desiring this man's art, and that man's scope,	3
With what I most enjoy contented least,	4
Yet in these thoughts myself almost despising,	5
Haply I think on thee—and then my state	6
(Like to the lark at break of day arising	5
From sullen earth) sings hymns at heaven's gate;	6
For thy sweet love remember'd such wealth brings,	7
That then I scorn to change my state with kings.	7

We have dealt already with the rhythmic variations which Shakespeare introduced into the sonnet. Note, in line 1 here, the trochaic opening, the spondaic conclusion; the anapest in line 3; the trochaic opening of line 5, and also of line 6; the same in line 9, where we also find a double or feminine rhyme introduced, a graceful variation to break the monotony of too many masculine rhymes; clear to the two spondees in line 13. It is so that the sonnet is written, in the hands of a master.

For modern Shakespearean sonnets of the highest distinction, many of those by Masefield, Chesterton, Robinson, Arthur Davison Ficke, Edna St. Vincent Millay, David Morton, and my *Eagle Sonnets,* repay study. The colloquial sonnets of John V. A. Weaver are an indication of an effective novel use to which the form may be put.

THE SONNET AS A STANZA

The sonnet may be used as a stanza, in what is called a *sonnet sequence,* instead of as a complete poem. As a stanza, it may be used formally or informally.

One formal use is in the *Crown of Sonnets.* This was first written in medieval Italy, and consisted of seven Italian sonnets. The last line of the first six of these became the first line of the ensuing sonnet; the last line of the seventh was a repetition of the first line of the first. Since the poem was regarded as a whole, no rhyming sound once used in any sonnet could be repeated thereafter during the Crown, except in the formal repetition of the lines already mentioned. John Donne, in his *Holy Sonnets,* wrote such a sequence, *La Corona,* using the Italian sonnet.

The Crown of Sonnets may of course be written in the more natural Shakespearean sonnet. The same care should be taken in avoiding any repetition of a rhyming sound once used. There is no logical reason why a Crown of Sonnets should be restricted to precisely seven sonnets, for the chain-verse device permits of a lesser or greater number.

The *Sonnet Redoublé,* as awkwardly named as the rondeau redoublé, consists of fifteen sonnets, interlocked in rhyming by the type of device used in the villanelle, the rondeau redoublé, and the glose. The fourteen final lines of the last fourteen sonnets are, in order, the lines of the first, text, or crown sonnet. No rhyming sound, once used, may thereafter be repeated in the sonnet redoublé, except in the formal repetition of a line already referred to. This was originally written with Italian sonnets, but would gain in naturalness if Shakespearean sonnets were used. The whole sequence must have a definite unity and progression throughout. There is a variation of the sonnet redoublé in which the fourteen lines of the text sonnet are used, in order, not as the concluding lines of the next fourteen sonnets, but as their initial lines. There is no noteworthy example of either form in English.

Informal sequences of sonnets in English have been as successful as the formal sequences have been unimpressive. Elizabeth Barrett Browning's forty-four *Sonnets from the Portuguese,* using the Italian rhyme-scheme but not the Italian strictness of development, are famous as a sequence of love-poems. Dante Gabriel Rossetti's *House of Life,* a sequence of a hundred and one Italian sonnets, is regarded as the best 19th century example of the form. Arthur Davison Ficke's *Sonnets of a Portrait Painter* is one of the outstanding American sonnet sequences, marked always by a sonorous beauty. Masefield's and Miss Millay's sequences are also important. The eighty-six *Eagle Sonnets* (*The Flight of The Eagle,* in *The Glory Road*), are also a tightly knit sequence.

Some of the interlocking devices used in this last named sequence are worthy of mention. The first and second sonnets of the sequence, in reverse order and development, are repeated as the last two, framing the whole. There is definite development in the group of sonnets dealing with agriculture, the mechanical age, the war-makers, the leisure class, with the poets as the resplendent climax. The sequence of seasons, commencing "Break out in fire, my hill, at autumn's calling," are closely tied together by theme development. The five sonnets commencing "A little tune," dealing with the poet's themes, are linked together by their direct repetition in the openings. The six groups following, culminating with the seven sonnets to beauty, are linked together by the repetition of the opening "We cling to life, because—." There are other interlinking devices as definite. And these barely tap the possibilities open to the poet.

COMBINED AND IRREGULAR SONNETS

The preferred French sonnet is the Italian octave, which contains internally three couplets; with a sestet based upon three rhymes, commencing with a couplet: 3,3,4,5,4,5 or 3,3,4,5,5,4. This has not yet become naturalized in English. A common liberty here is that used by Wordsworth, of introducing a third rhyme in the Italian octave: 1,2,2,1; 1,3,3,1. The sonnet already quoted from Wordsworth, *Scorn Not the Sonnet,* as we have noted, combined this variant Italian opening with a Shakespearean conclusion: 4,5,4,5,6,6.

Even more common is the use of a Shakespearean octave as an opening, followed by one of the accepted Italian sestets, as in this famous war sonnet by Rupert Brooke:

If I should die, think only this of me:	1	
That there's some corner of a foreign field		2
That is for ever England. There shall be	1	
In that rich earth a richer dust concealed;		2
A dust whom England bore, shaped, made aware,	3	
Gave, once, her flowers to love, her ways to roam,		4
A body of England's, breathing English air,	3	
Washed by the rivers, blest by suns of home.		4

And think, this heart, all evil shed away,	5		
A pulse in the eternal mind, no less		6	
Gives back somewhere the thoughts by England given,			7
Her sights and sounds; dreams happy as her day;	5		
And laughter, learnt of friends; and gentleness,		6	
In hearts at peace, under an English heaven.			7

It is always possible that such combination sonnets come because the poet is familiar with both sonnet forms, and takes at will from one or the other, from a superfluity of riches, or from an alternation of mood, even induced by fogginess at the moment of creation. Such combined forms may move with the full flow of poetry to the end; and remind us anew that poems are written by poets, who make their own patterns.

At the same time, as Watts-Dunton pointed out in his treatment of the sonnet in the 11th edition of *The Encyclopaedia Britannica*, the charm of this and other fixed forms, to the sophisticate, comes from familiarity in advance with the rhyme scheme to be followed; and this charm is subtly dissipated, when any break in the expected rhyme-scheme occurs. We feel somehow as if we were listening to a limerick with an extra foot or an extra line: a sense of surprise, its pleasure being doubtful, unless the lines themselves compensate for the shock caused by the disappointed expectations, by additional and unexpected poetic delight. As a rule, it is wiser to follow the accepted forms, unless there is an inner necessity in the poem itself that compels a deviation.

Among irregularities not to be commended in principle is such a sonnet as Celia Thaxter's *Beethoven,* with its opening Italian quatrain, followed by ten lines of Shakespearean sonnet: 1,2,2,1; 3,4,3,4; 5,6,5,6; 7,7. Yet here is an irregular sonnet which clearly ranks among the masterpieces of English poetry:

I met a traveler from an antique land	1		
Who said: Two vast and trunkless legs of stone	2		
Stand in the desert. Near them, on the sand,	1		
Half sunk, a shattered visage lies, whose frown	2		
And wrinkled lip and sneer of cold command	1		
Tell that its sculptor well those passions read		3	
Which yet survive, stamped on these lifeless things,			4
The hand that mocked them and the heart that fed;		3	
And on the pedestal these words appear:				5
"My name is Ozymandias, king of kings:			4
Look on my works, ye Mighty, and despair!"				5
Nothing beside remains. Round the decay					6
Of that colossal wreck, boundless and bare,				5
The lone and level sands stretch far away.					6

There are several ways of regarding this rhyme-scheme. It might be seen as an alternately rhymed quatrain to open—the typical Shakespearean sonnet opening; with the same type of quatrain to close; and, between these, 1,3,4,3,5,4, which, as a rhyme-scheme, has no sensible pattern at all. But Shelley, as his *Ode to the West Wind* established, tended toward terza rima. After his opening couplet, 1,2, Shelley here has 1,2,1; 3,4,3; 5,4,5; 6,5,6: not quite a faithful following of the terza rima pattern, yet close enough to indicate its influence.

Is this a sonnet, or not?

We come back to our original definition of sonnet: "a poem or stanza of fourteen iambic pentameter lines, with a rigidly pre-scribed rhyme-scheme." Who is to prescribe the rhyme-scheme? Shelley here preferred to prescribe his own. If this had been widely copied, by now it would no doubt have been called the Shelleyan sonnet. Let us give him his full poet's prerogative. As a poem, this will certainly endure.

We have already seen the tailed or caudated sonnet ripping through the boundary restricting the sonnet to fourteen lines. At least one Elizabethan ignored the requirement of rhyme alto-gether. Bartholomew Griffin ended every line of a fifteen line "sonnet" on the rhyming sound *more;* while his *xxiiird* sonnet, for all that it preserved the length-limit of fourteen lines, ended each one of them on *heart,* and with great effectiveness, as he addresses his poem:

> And I must die, if thou have not her heart.
> Thy bed (if thou rest well) must be her heart:
> He hath the best part sure that hath the heart;
> What have I not, if I have but the heart?

One of my *Gloria* sonnets, coming after this terminal line of another, "Come back, and give me life, who now am dead!", uses a more staccato and peremptory iambic four-foot line, instead of the expected pentameter:

> Come back. . . Or I shall know the sun
> Holds but a scanted tenancy;
> That star-faint sky and riding moon
> Have already gone from me. . . .
> That the red petals of my days
> Have lost each jewelled nectar line,
> And each shrivels, dulls, decays,
> And mold furs all that was mine.
> Gone the spring and the wind-flowers swaying,
> The white yarrow and the red,

The autumn's crown of tansy glowing.
There is only that hour when the dead
Stir in their slumber, dream they're awake.
And will you, against this death, come back?

Here are three instances of consonance, as well. No injunction
will lie to prevent such experimental divagations. There is always
safety in following the prescribed rules.

WRITING THE SONNET

In writing the sonnet—and this applies even more strongly
to writing any of the elaborate fixed forms given hereafter—until
the poet has the form thoroughly memorized, it will aid to write
down your rhyme-scheme in advance. As you arrive at the first
sound for each of your rhyming groups, it is well to write this
sound at the top of a blank column, numbered according to the
number of the rhyme-sound in your rhyme-scheme. Then, as the
lines are written, or at any stage during the writing of them,
it is wise to write down in each column the initial consonant
sounds already used, to make sure that you will not repeat a rhyming sound, which would be identity, and not rhyme. This is not
so necessary with the straightforward Shakespearean sonnet, with
quatrain alternate rhyming, followed by a couplet; though even
here the skeleton rhyme scheme will aid. But when you come to
an Italian sonnet, say with 1,2,2,1; 1,2,2,1 for the octave, and 3,4,3;
4,3,4 for the sestet, this becomes valuable, as insurance against
repeating a rhyming sound.

If aggressive old John Milton had used this method in writing
his sonnet *On the Detraction Which Followed Upon My Writing
Certain Treatises,* which is surprising light verse from him, he
would have written down first the second column, *Rhyme Scheme;*
filled in the four successive rhyme-sounds as he first hit upon
them; and, as the sonnet progressed, would have added the consonantal opening sounds in these four columns, as the sonnet
itself grew in column one. His complete notebook page would
then have looked like this:

	Rhyme Scheme	(1) ÔR'don	(2) ĪL	(3) ÄSP	(4) ĒK
A book was writ of late called *Tetrachordon,*	1	K			
And woven close, both matter, form, and style;	2		ST		
The subject grew; it walked the town a while,	2		HW		
Numbering good intellects; now seldom pored on.	1	P			
Cries the stall-reader, "Bless us! what a word on	1	W			
A title-page is this!"; and some in file	2		F		
Stand spelling false, while one might walk to Mile—	2		M		
End Green. Why, is it harder, sirs,	1	G			
than *Gordon,*	3			L	
Colkitto, or *Macdonnel,* or *Galasp?*					
Those rugged names to our like mouths grow sleek,	4				SL
That would have made Quintilian stare and gasp.	3			G	
Thy age, like ours, O soul of Sir John Cheek,	4				CH
Hated not learning worse than toad or asp,	3			Vowel	
When thou taught'st Cambridge and King Edward Greek.	4				GR

By this check, the poet used, for the various rhyme-sounds, the following:

(1) ÔR'don: k, p, w, g

(2) ĪL: st, hw, f, m

(3) ÄSP: l, g, and the unconsonanted vowel

(4) ĒK: sl, ch, and gr.

No identities; rhyme throughout. From a standpoint of technical rhyming, this has no flaws. When used during the writing of the Italian sonnet or an elaborate formal poem, this device gives a check before the verses are done, and may save much rewriting.

THE CINQUAIN

This unrhymed formal cinquain, invented by Adelaide Crapsey, has already been treated under five-line stanzas.

THE LIMERICK

The limerick, as Brander Matthews points out, is the only fixed form indigenous to the English language. We find in *Mother Goose* (*Songs for the Nursery, or, Mother Goose's Melodies for Children,* published by Elizabeth Goose, formerly Vertigoose, married to Thomas Fleet, a Boston printer, and first appearing in 1719) limericks illustrating all three stages of the development of the form. The first stage opened and closed with a nonsense line:

Hickory, dickory, dock!	1
The mouse ran up the clock.	1
The clock struck one—	2
The mouse ran down,	2
Hickory, dickory, dock!	1

Langford Reed, historian of limericks as well as collector, quotes this French limerick of about the same period:

> Digerie, Digerie, Doge,
> La souris ascend l'horloge;
> L'horloge frappé,
> La souris s'éschappé,
> Digerie, Digerie, Doge.

He quotes also from the *Menagiana* this epigram in limerick form, quoted in Boswell's *Life of Johnson,* on a young lady who appeared at a masquerade dressed as a Jesuit, during the conflict between the followers of Molinos and Jansenius:

> On s'étonne ici que Caliste
> Ait pris l'habit de Moliniste;
> Puisque cette jeune beauté
> Ôte à chacun sa liberté
> N'est-ce pas une Janseniste?

Even granting the antiquity of these, it is still probable that the form originated in England, and that the first French example given is a translation. For the *Mother Goose* rhymes, many of them, are far older than their compilation. The name *limerick* may well have come from the custom of singing a chorus, "Won't

you come up to Limerick?" after impromptu verses composed to
the limerick pattern at convivial parties; as today several tunes,
including the one with the chorus "Sweet violets," are used at
modern parties for the same purpose.

Of the same type, in *Mother Goose,* as "Hickory, dickory,
dock!" are "Diddledy, diddledy, dumpty, The cat ran up the
plumtree"; "Dickery, dickery, dare, The pig flew up in the aur,"
and the most charming of all:

> Danty baby diddy,
> What can a mammy do wid 'ee,
> But sit in a lap
> And give 'un a pap,
> Sing danty, baby, diddy?

The famous anonymous *Tom-a-Bedlam Song,* discovered in
Giles Earle's Songbook in the British Museum, suggests this pattern, in doubled form:

> I know more than Apollo,
> For oft, when he lies sleeping,
> I see the stars
> At bloody wars
> In the wounded welkin weeping;
> The moon embrace her shepherd,
> And the queen of love her warrior,
> While the first doth horn
> The star of morn,
> And the next the heavenly farrier.

Ben Jonson, in his masque, *The Gipsies Metamorphosed,* uses
the same meter in his song, "The wheel of fortune guide you."
Shakespeare and other Elizabethans used stanza-patterns varying
only slightly from it. The *Mother Goose* collection has many
rhymes which approach the pattern, including "Pussy ate the
dumplings, the dumplings,"

> What are little boys made out of, out of,
> What are little boys made out of?
> Snaps and snails
> And puppy-dogs' tails,
> And that's what little boys are made out of.

Three of them, one only four lines long, progress to the third
stage of the limerick, where the last line reaches a climax in the
action:

> The barber shaved the mason,
>   As I suppose,
>   Cut off his nose,
> And popped it in a basin. . . . .,

> Doodle doodle doo,
> The Princess lost her shoe; '
>   Her Highness hopped.
>   The fiddler stopped,
> Not knowing what to do.

These two, and "Good Queen Bess was a glorious dame," hint already the flowering of the form.

The second stage of the limerick, the one used by Edward Lear, ended the first and fifth lines with the same word, usually a geographical name, at times these lines being identical. Here is an example from *Mother Goose:*

> As I was going to Bonner,
> Upon my word of honor,
>   I met a pig
>   Without a wig,
> As I was going to Bonner.

The third and final stage of the limerick has a new rhyming word in the fifth line, instead of mere repetition; and this line usually becomes the climax of the whole. Here are two classic examples from *Mother Goose:*

> There was an old man of Tobago,
> Who lived on rice, gruel, and sago;
>   Till, much to his bliss,
>   His physician said this—
> "To a leg, sir, of mutton you may go."

> There was an old soldier of Bister
> Went walking one day with his sister,
>   When a cow at one poke
>   Tossed her into an oak,
> Before the old gentleman missed her.

The limerick never attained popularity until Edward Lear, then a tutor in the family of the Earl of Derby at Knowsley, composed, about 1834, a group of them to amuse the little grandchildren of his employer. When these were published in 1846, in quatrain typography, they became immense favorites:

> There was an Old Man of Cape Horn,
> Who wished he had never been born;

So he sat on a Chair till he died of despair,
That dolorous man of Cape Horn.

There was a young lady of Greenwich,
Whose garments were border'd with Spinach;
But a large spotty Calf bit her shawl quite in half,
Which alarmed that young lady of Greenwich.

There was an old person of Ealing,
Who was wholly devoid of good feeling;
He drove a small gig, with three Owls and a Pig,
Which distressed all the people of Ealing.

The first result was to awaken the English wits to parodies of these; and, from this, to use the form, with rhymes as deft as Lear's. The rhythmic and rhyming scheme of the limerick appears from this classic:

There was / a young la- / dy of Niger,   1
Who smiled / as she rode / on a tiger.   1
  They came back / from the ride   2
  With the la- / dy inside   2
And the smile / on the face / of the tiger.   1

More Limericks, COSMO MONKHOUSE

The movement is anapestic, here with the permissible omission of an unaccented syllable from each of the first two lines, and with feminine ending. This could be described as amphibrachic; but the fifth line usually, as here, is anapestic throughout, and indicates that this is the better name for the meter. The metric pattern is 3,3,2,2,3 feet to the lines; the rhyme-scheme, 1,1,2,2,1. In the example given, the identity in lines 2 and 5 (*tiger—tiger*) cannot spoil the charm of this; although the pure pattern would avoid it.

To write a limerick, familiarize yourself with the metric pattern:

ta TUM/ ta ta TUM / ta ta TUM ta,
ta TUM/ ta ta TUM / ta ta TUM ta,
  ta ta TUM / ta ta TUM
  ta ta TUM / ta ta TUM,
ta ta TUM / ta ta TUM / ta ta TUM ta.

Any of the five feet opening the lines can omit the first unaccented syllable. The conclusion can be single-rhymed, or rhymed on two, three or more syllables.

It was Arnold Bennett who observed that all the best limericks are unquotable. But this still leaves a plethora of clever masterpieces. There is no type of word ingenuity that has been omitted. Here is one where the proper pronunciation of the first abbreviation is a guide to the rhyme:

> An amorous M. A.
> Says that Cupid, that C. D.,
>   Doesn't care for his health,
>   But is rolling in wealth;
> He's the John-Jaco-B. H.
> ANONYMOUS

This must be read by pronouncing M. A. "master of arts," and the corresponding terminals to rhyme with it: "caster of darts" and "John Jacob Astor of hearts." Here is a famous tongue-twister, which should be spoken rapidly, to be most effective:

> A tutor who tooted the flute
> Tried to teach two young tooters to toot.
>   Said the two to the tutor,
>   "Is it harder to toot, or
> To tutor two tooters to toot?"
> *Four Limericks*, CAROLYN WELLS

There is an unexpected denouement to:

> There was a young lady of Diss,
> Who said, "Now I think skating bliss!"
>   This no more will she state,
>   For a wheel off her skate
> Made her finish up something like this!

Among other classics are:

> There was an old man of Calcutta
> Who had an unfortunate stutter.
>   "I would like," he once said,
>   "Some b-b-b-b-bread,
> And some b-b-b-b-b-b-butter."
> ANONYMOUS

> I'd rather have Fingers than Toes;
> I'd rather have Ears than a Nose;
>   And as for my Hair,

I'm glad it's all there;
I'll be awfully sad, when it goes.

GELETT BURGESS

There was a young girl of Australia
Who went to a dance as a dahlia.
   When the petals uncurled,
   It revealed to the world
That the dress, as a dress, was a failure.

ANONYMOUS

There was a young woman named Bright,
Whose speed was much faster than light.
   She set out one day,
   In a relative way,
And returned on the previous night.

ANONYMOUS

There was an old person from Tring
Who, when somebody asked her to sing,
   Replied, "Isn't it odd?
   I can never tell '*God
Save the Weasel*' from '*Pop Goes the King!*' "

ANONYMOUS

A young man very fond of pajamas
Had a pair from the hair of the llamas;
   But their feminine air
   Made his friends all declare
They were made from a pair of his mamma's.

ANONYMOUS

There once was a sculptor named Phidias,
Whose knowledge of art was invidious.
   He carved Aphrodite
   Without any nightie,
Thus shocking the ultra-fastidious.

ANONYMOUS

Last Line Contests involving limericks are intermittently popular. In this, only the first four lines of a new limerick are printed, and the fifth is left blank. Prizes as high as $2,250 a word have been offered in England in such contests. When competing in such contests, list from the Rhyming Dictionary all possible rhymes to the rhyme-sound appearing in lines 1 and 2; mark them with their initial consonant sounds, to be sure you do not give an identity to either of the rhymes in the first two lines; and then call all your ingenuity and naturalness of speech to bear on the task.

[351]

LITTLE WILLIES

Any verse form can become, almost overnight, a favorite with light verse writers. A dozen years ago, some college wit wrote and published this rhyme, in his college paper:

> Tobacco is a filthy weed—
>   I like it.
> It satisfies no normal need—
>   I like it.
> It makes you thin, it makes you lean,
> It takes the hair right off your bean;
> It's the worst darned stuff I've ever seen.
>   I like it.

The form caught on. At once most newspaper columnists and professional and amateur versifiers chronicled a similar like or dislike. Similarly, any of the practically unknown fixed forms might suddenly achieve a mushroom popularity.

In 1902 appeared Col. D. Streamer's (Harry Graham's) *Ruthless Rhymes for Heartless Homes,* containing *Tender-Heartedness:*

> Billy, in one of his nice new sashes
> Fell in the fire and was burnt to ashes;
> Now, although the room grows chilly,
> I haven't the heart to poke poor Billy.

This skyrocketed across the land, for all that it was not featured in the book, being most popular in this anonymous revision:

> Little Willie, in bows and sashes,   1
> Fell in the fire and got burned to ashes.   1
> In the winter, when the weather is chilly,   2
> No one likes to stir up Willie.   2

This quatrain had couplet rhyming, and was accent verse, with four accents to the line. The appeal of it and accompanying quatrains of the same type, ever since miscellaneously grouped as Little Willies, lay in the frank sadism and unblushing misanthropy, especially toward members of the family group. Here are a few more masterpieces from the same volume:

> Father heard his Children scream,
> So he threw them in the stream,
> Saying, as he drowned the third,
> "Children should be seen, *not* heard!"
>   *The Stern Parent*

Baby in the caldron fell,— 1
  See the grief on Mother's brow; 2
Mother loved her darling well,— 1
  Darling's quite hard-boiled by now. 2
                      Baby

Making toast at the fireside,
Nurse fell in the fire and died;
And, what makes it ten times worse,
All the toast was burned *with* nurse.
      Misfortunes Never Come Singly

Late last night I slew my wife,
  Stretched her on the parquet flooring;
I was loath to take her life,
  But I *had* to stop her snoring.
               Necessity

Sam had spirits naught could check,
  And today, at breakfast, he
Broke his baby sister's neck,
  So he shan't have jam for tea!
        Impetuous Samuel

An Angel bore dear Uncle Joe
  To rest beyond the stars.
I miss him, oh! I miss him so,—
  He had such good cigars.

Here are some of later vintage, most of them following the couplet rhyming of the original Little Willie, and as a rule unfortunately anonymous:

Dr. Jones fell in the well,
  And died without a moan.
He should have tended to the sick,
  And let the well alone. . . .

Pity now poor Mary Ames,
Blinded by her brother James.
Red hot nails in her eyes he poked—
I never saw Mary more provoked! . . . .

Willie poisoned Auntie's tea.
Auntie died in agony.
Uncle came and looked quite vexed.
"Really, Will," he said, "what next?" . . . .

Little Willie hung his sister.
She was dead before we missed her.
"Willie's always up to tricks.
Ain't he cute! He's only six!" . . . .

[353]

Willie fell down the elevator—
Wasn't found till six days later.
Then the neighbors sniffed, "Gee whizz!
What a spoiled child Willie is!"

The model for a Little Willie, with its sadistic slant and its trick
last line, can easily be acquired from these examples.

FORMAL VERSE: PROVENÇE AND ELSEWHERE

Poets and versifiers writing in English have at their disposal
a large number of foreign verse forms, especially adapted, in
English, to light verse and occasional verse—that is, verse written for a special occasion. A brief survey of the background and
development of these forms will aid our understanding and use
of them.

The culture called Provençal extended from the mouth of the
Gironde to Lyons, on the north, and included the southern part
of France, as well as Aragon, Valencia, Catalonia, and the Balearic
Islands of Spain; all using the Langue d'Oc, a Romance language
no more akin to French than it was to Spanish or Italian. A
hothoused culture appeared here, from the eleventh century to
its extermination in the religious crusades against the Albigen-
sians and other groups, before the fourteenth century. Patronized
by premature Renaissance magnificoes almost illiterate, and quite
unlearned in the classics, and no more literate themselves, the
troubadours, or composers of songs and music, and the glittering
jongleurs, who composed or performed them, for two hundred
years dazzled in a rhyming Court of Love as fantastic as if Gilbert
and Sullivan had invented, peopled and tuned it. Their themes
were largely limited to three: the agonies of the masculine lover;
formalized warfare; and a late admission of religious subjects.
Descriptions of nature, of the lover's sufferings, of warfare, had to
be as stiff and formalized as if taken from a conventionalized
tapestry. The verse forms were more rigid than the laws of Hitler
and Stalin, including always a requirement for perpetual minor
recombination of the shopworn conceits. Identical rhyme-schemes
for each stanza, complicated rhyming patterns, word-play, alliteration, forced constructions, difficulties tending toward making
the product unintelligible: these were demanded. And, naturally,
poetry was as surely exiled from their product as truth from the

debates of the medieval schoolmen. Here were their chief accepted verse forms:

1. The *vers:* octosyllabic lines arranged in stanzas.

2. The *canso* or *canzo,* which developed from it: five to seven stanzas, with interlacing rhymes; later requiring the interlacing of masculine and feminine rhymes. This was restricted to themes of love and gallantry.

3. The *sirventesc* or *sirvente,* composed of short stanzas, with a simple identical rhyme scheme; used for moral, political and religious subjects, serious or satirical.

4. The *tenso,* an improvising contest between two poets, the second taking the opposite side of any argument propounded by the stanza of the first, and using the identical rhyme and rhythm pattern.

5. The *alba,* a farewell at morning. This and the three following ones are classified primarily by theme.

6. The *serena,* an evening song.

7. The *pastorella,* devoted to pastoral themes.

8. The *planh,* a lament for the death of the poet's patron or lady-love.

9. The *breu-doble* (double short), a 14 line poem with 3 rhymes, two of them repeated twice in the three quatrains, and given once in a concluding couplet; while the third finished each quatrain. There is one of the germs of the later sonnet here.

10. The *retroensa,* with refrain more than one line long.

11. The *balada,* a song accompanying the dance. It has no resemblance to the latter ballade.

12. The *ley,* which altered into the *lai* in northern France.

13. The *sestina,* an intricately patterned unrhymed poem, which alone survived. See its treatment later.

This dialogue by Aimeric de Pegulhan illustrates the mood of Provençal love poetry:

> "Lady, for you great torment must I bear."
> "Sir, you are foolish, for I do not care."
> "Lady, for heaven's sake to me be kind."
> "Sir, quite in vain your empty prayers you'll find."
> "Good lady, I do love you faithfully."
> "Good sir, and I dislike you utterly."
> "Lady, my heart is therefore in distress."
> "Sir, mine is ever light with happiness."

There are four more stanzas of this, the last one ending:

"Love, do not think my heart from her to lure."
"Friend, then resolve in patience to endure."
"Love, may I hope my happiness to gain?"
"Friend, yes! at last, through service and through pain."

Bernart de Ventadorn, most famous of the singers of courtly lady-service, sings thus, in a poem of seven well-knit stanzas, with three-line envoy:

She whom I love with faithful mind
    Is best and fairest, yet my eyes
    Are filled with tears, my heart with sighs;
Too much I love—my hurt I find.
Helpless, Love takes me prisoner,
    And in his prison I must sit;
    No key but pity opens it,
And pity is not found in her. . . .

Good lady, this alone I ask,
    As vassal take me; service due,
    As to a lord, I'll pay to you,
Though no reward should crown my task.
Behold me here at your command,
    Frank, humble, courteous, bold and gay;
    Would you, like bear or lion, slay
One who thus yields him to your hand.

These translations, quoted by Lewis F. Mott, with much reason omit the tight rhyming of the original.

Bertran de Born, most famous of the laureates of courtly war, wrote thus, most probably when Richard Coeur de Leon and Alfonso of Castile were about to unite against the French monarch, in a vigorous sirventesc:

If honor and if courage do not melt
    From the two kings, we soon shall see the fields
    With fragments strewn of swords and helms and shields
And men cut through the body to the belt;
In fury we shall see steeds charging past,
    And many a lance through bosom and through thigh,
    And joy and tear, moan and exultant cry:
Vast is the loss, the gain surpassing vast.

Pennant and flag, trumpet and beating drum,
    Insignia and chargers of the best,
    We soon shall see; for wealth we then will wrest
From usurers, so that good times will come.

No beast of burden safely can proceed
  Upon our roads, nor townsman free from fear,
  Nor merchants come from France to traffic here—
Rich will those be who seize the goods they need.

This freebooting attitude can hardly shock us today. Yet there is an end to those that live by the sword.

With the ending of Provençal culture, except for a recent revival, similar in some respects to the neo-Gaelic movement in Ireland, the sun of culture moved to the north. Eustache Deschamps (1328-1415), a friend of Chaucer, left more than 1,175 ballades, as well as rondeaus, virelais, and other formal verses. The chronicler Jean Froissart, Guillaume de Machault, Charles d'Orléans, famous for his rondels, and François Villon, prince of ballade-makers, made the forms enduring. The rules for the forms were rigidified in *L'art et science de rhetorique pour faire rigmes et ballades* (1403), by Henri de Croi. In the mid-17th century, Voiture and others revived the rondeau and other forms resplendently. Chaucer and his contemporaries introduced the ballade and other forms into England. Then these forms passed into a long eclipse, until their revival almost at the end of the nineteenth century.

ON THE RULES OF THE VARIOUS FORMS

The rules for the fixed forms are stricter, in English, than in French. Here is the major law as to rhyming:

1. No syllable or group of syllables, once used as a rhyme, can be used in the same poem as a rhyme, even if spelled differently, nor if the whole world is altered by a prefix. Identities are strictly forbidden.

In French, words of the same sound and spelling may be used to rhyme, if the meaning differs. In the most famous French ballade, *Des Dames du Temps Jadis* (commonly rendered with the refrain, "But where are the snows of yesteryear?"), Villon couples, as rhymes:

Rommaine, germaine, maine, qu'humaine, morne,
  Maine, sepmaine, remaine
royne, seraine, Lorraine
Rouan, an
lis, Allis

These would be identities, to us; and this usage is strictly forbidden in English. This bars such identities, in English, as:

> *Ruth,* a girl's name, and *ruth,* pity
> *bear,* an animal; *bear,* to support; *bare; forbear*
> sale, sail.
> claim, declaim, disclaim, reclaim
> (single rhyme) tea, manatee, imbecility, impossibility,
>   sanity
> (triple rhyme) facility, imbecility

With the *Mental Rhyming Dictionary* technique applied to the possible rhymes, or using a rhyming dictionary which adopts it and divides its rhymes by initial consonantal sounds, the rule is: Use only one rhyme from each group introduced by a differing consonantal sound.

2. The refrain must not be a meaningless repetition of sounds, as in many ballads, songs, and jingles; it must aid in the progression of the thought; must come in naturally; and must be repeated in all its sounds, without any change of sound.

Slipshod versifiers alter the refrain by changing the introductory word, as by using *an* in the refrain when first used, and thereafter *the, but, if,* and so on. The rule requires the repetition of the same sounds throughout. Punctuation may be changed, or spelling, or meaning, even by the use of a pun. Thus these are permissible:

> It's meat, this sale; it meet, this sail.
> Gray day; Grayed aye; Grade A.

JAPANESE FORMS

The Hokku.—The Japanese forms, the tanka and the hokku, follow Japanese poetry (*tanka* or *uta*) in having alternate verses of five and seven syllables.

The hokku or haikai consists of only three lines, of 5, 7, and 5 syllables, or seventeen in all. There is no stipulation or requirement as to rhythm or rhyme. An example is:

> More fleeting than the
> Flash of withered windblown leaf,
> This thing men call life.

The Tanka.—The Japanese tanka ordinarily has thirty-one syllables, consisting of five lines, with respectively 5,7,5,7,7 syllables. An example is:

> The rippling sea-swell,
> Curling upon the gold sand,
> And, curving over,
> A bough of cherry blossoms,—
> Youth shielding eternal age.

Longer Japanese poems may be constructed in the tanka form, with the invariable alternation of 5 and 7 syllables to the line, terminating in an added 7-syllabled line. This is more closely akin to poetry of our culture than is generally recognized. French poetry long stipulated so many syllables to the line. English poetry has at times included it, derived from the French. Thus the final use of so-called heroic blank verse, supposedly iambic pentameter, as exemplified in Shakespeare, came to be either ten or eleven syllables to the line, with the matter of accent largely disregarded: a form approaching the Japanese.

THE KYRIELLE

This is the simplest of all French forms; so simple that it is used by many poets in English, without the faintest idea that they are using a named French form. The word is apparently a diminutive for *Kyrie,* short for *Kyrie eleison,* the Greek prayer "Lord, have mercy upon us," so common in the Christian ritual; and points to a religious origin for the form.

A kyrielle is a poem in quatrains, with eight syllables to the lines, and with the last line of each stanza repeated as a refrain. Christian hymnbooks contain many examples of this.

In the tent the lamps were bright;	1
Out beyond the summer night	1
Thrilled and quivered like a star:	2
We beneath were left so far.	2 (R)
From the depths of blue profound	3
Never any sight or sound	3
Came our loneliness to mar:	2
We beneath were left so far.	2 (R)
But against the summer sky	4
Only you stood out and I;	4

From all other things that are	2
We beneath were left so far.	2(R)

The Pavilion, A. MARY F. ROBINSON

2(R) is, of course, the refrain line, rhyming with (2).

Many other examples, written otherwise in the kyrielle pattern, contain less or more than eight syllables to the line. The famous hymn *Just as I Am*, by Charlotte Elliott, with the repeated fourth line "O Lamb of God, I come, I come," is a kyrielle, using the rhyme-scheme 1,1,1,2(R). The device is employed constantly, with lines of any chosen length.

CHAIN RHYME AND VERSE

We have seen the use of chain rhyme in terza rima, with the tercets linked by rhyme thus:

1,2,1; 2,3,2; 3,4,3; 4,5,4; 5,6,5, etc.

There could be similarly linked quatrains:

1,1,2,1; 2,2,3,2; 3,3,4,3; 4,4,5,4, etc.,

or using any other stanza pattern, providing rhyming sounds linked stanza to stanza. This process could mount to a chain of sonnets, with the final rhyme in each sonnet repeated as the opening rhyme sound of the next: a less rigid pattern than the Crown of Sonnets.

The link may be only of the rhyming sound; or it may include a word, a phrase, a line, or even more. The French chain rhyme (*La rime Enchâinée*) requires that one word and one only grow from each line into the next:

Dieu des Amans, de mort me garde
Me gardant donne-moi bonheur,
Et me le donnant prend ta darde
Et la prenant navre son coeur
Et le navrant me tiendias seur.

CLÉMENT MAROT

In one type of chain verse, the link is the final word or group of words in each line, as this opening stanza of an anonymous poem uses:

Nerve thy soul with doctrines noble,
Noble in the walks of time,
Time that leads to an eternal,
An eternal life sublime.

[360]

Similarly, phrases may be interlocked:

> The rarer seen, the less in mind,
> The less in mind, the lesser pain,
> The lesser pain, less grief I find,
> The lesser grief, the greater gain,
> The greater gain, the merrier I,
> Therefore I wish thy sight to fly.
>
> BARNABY GOOGE

This device, which here tends to grow monotonous, has a more natural and expanded use in this familiar *Mother Goose* chain verse:

> A man of words and not of deeds
> Is like a garden full of weeds;
> And when the weeds begin to grow,
> It's like a garden full of snow;
> And when the snow begins to fall,
> It's like a bird upon the wall;
> And when the bird away doth fly,
> It's like an eagle in the sky;
> And when the sky begins to roar,
> It's like a lion at the door;
> And when the door begins to crack,
> It's like a stick across your back;
> And when your back begins to smart,
> It's like a penknife in your heart;
> And when your heart begins to bleed,
> You're dead, and dead, and dead indeed.

In this chain verse of John Byrom's, the last line of each quatrain becomes the first of the next—the usage we found in the *Crown of Sonnets:*

> My spirit longeth for Thee
> Within my troubled breast,
> Although I be unworthy
> Of so divine a Guest.
>
> Of so divine a Guest,
> Unworthy though I be,
> Yet has my heart no rest,
> Unless it comes from Thee.
>
> Unless it comes from Thee,
> In vain I look around;
> In all that I can see
> No rest is to be found.
>
> No rest is to be found,
> But in Thy blessed love,

and so on.

THE PANTOUM

A more elaborate type of chain verse is the Malayan pantoum, introduced into French verse by Ernest Fouinet, and popularized by Victor Hugo in the *Orientales*. It is written in quatrains, and the second and fourth lines of each stanza become the first and third of the next. In the last stanza, the second and fourth lines are the third and first of the first quatrain; so that the opening and closing lines of the pantoum are identical. The rhyme-scheme would then be:

1,2,1,2; 2,3,2,3; 3,4,3,4; 4,5,4,5; . . . n,1,n,1.

And the arrangement of the complete lines would be the same, with the one reversal in the last stanza already explained. Here is the method, in English:

Here we are riding the rail,	1
Gliding from out of the station;	2
Man though I am, I am pale,	1
Certain of heat and vexation.	2
Gliding from out of the station,	2
Out from the city we thrust;	3
Certain of heat and vexation,	2
Sure to be covered with dust.	3
Out from the city we thrust:	3
Rattling we run o'er the bridges:	4
Sure to be covered with dust,	3
Stung by a thousand of midges.	4
Rattling we run o'er the bridges,	4
Rushing we dash o'er the plain;	5
Stung by a thousand of midges,	4
Certain precursors of rain.	5
Rushing we dash o'er the plain,	5
Watching the clouds darkly lowering,	6
Certain precursors of rain;	5
Fields about here need a showering,	6

And so to the final quatrain, ending with the original first line:

Ears are on edge at the rattle,	14
Man though I am, I am pale,	1
Sounds like the noise of a battle,	14
Here we are riding the rail.	1

En Route, Brander Matthews

[362]

As Dr. Matthews pointed out, the effort here has been to make the constant repetitions more than tolerable: to make them subservient to the monotonously recurrent sound of the rattle and strain of the cars. Even in formal verse, the air of naturalness is one of the highest achievements to aim for.

THE LAI GROUP

The Lai.—The French lai grew out of the Provençal ley. The form has been largely abandoned since the time of early French poetry. In the French usage, the lai was composed of couplets of five-syllabled lines, all on the same rhyme, separated by single lines of two syllables, on a different rhyme. The complete stanza thus contained only two rhymes. The number of lines per stanza was not fixed; nor the number of stanzas per poem. Here is the only ancient French example, first printed by Père Mourgues in his *Traité de la Poésie:*

> Sue l'appui du Monde
> Que faut-il qu'on fonde
> D'espoir?
> Cette mer profonde
> Et débris féconde
> Fair voir
> Calme au matin l'onde;
> Et l'orage y gronde
> Le Soir.

A curious old tradition is preserved in the lai, of starting the short lines, not centered, but flush with the longer ones. This detail was called *Arbre fourchu* (a forked tree), from its supposed resemblance to a trunk with bare branches projecting from it.

In the lai each fresh stanza has its own two rhyme sounds, without reference to preceding stanzas. An example in English is:

> Summer heat today
> In its torrid way,
> I see,
> With its awful ray
> Sears till it must slay
> Poor me,
> Tree and grass and clay.
> It's the bay—the spray
> For me!

Ho for leaping foam!
Leave the sandy loam,
To leap
In the waves, and roam
Our ancestral home,
The deep!

But a squall of rain
Drives us once again
To shore.
Clothes are drenched. We strain
Wildly to regain
Once more
The returning train.
A rheumatic pain
Of yore
Drives me near insane.
Bays are, it is plain,
A bore!
Holiday Lai, ALVIN WINSTON

The Virelai Ancien.—The virelai ancien curtails the liberty of shifting rhymes in the various stanzas of the lai, and requires that the long lines of each stanza take their rhyme from the short lines of the preceding one, thus bringing the form within the classification of chain verse. The word comes from *virer,* to turn, plus *lai.* The example quoted above in French is said to have been a mere fragment of a virelai, which proceeds by "veering" the two rhymes from stanza to stanza.

Thus, in a twelve line stanza, the virelai rhyme-scheme would be:

1,1,2,1,1,2,1,1,2,1,1,2; 2,2,3,2,2,3,2,2,3,2,2,3; and so on until the last stanza rhymed n,n,1,n,n,1,n,n,1,n,n,1.

Thus the last stanza returns to the opening (1) rhyme. Each rhyme sound appears twice: once in the longer couplets, and once in the short lines. John Payne's virelai ancien, *Spring Sadness,* proceeds:

As I sat sorrowing,
Love came and bade me sing
A joyous song and meet,
For see (said he) each thing
Is merry for the Spring,
And every bird doth greet
The break of blossoming
That all the woodlands ring
Unto the young hours' feet.

Wherefore put off defeat
And rouse thee to repeat
   The chimes of merles that go,
With flutings shrill and sweet,
In every green retreat,
   The tune of streams that flow
And mark the fair hours' beat,
With running ripples fleet
   And breezes soft and low.

For who should have, I trow,
Such joyance in the flow
   And sadness of the May,—

and so on. The ninth and final stanza is:

So for the sad soul's ease
Remembrance treasures these
   Against time's harvesting,
That so, when mild Death frees
The soul from Life's disease
   Of strife and sorrowing,
In glass of memories
The new hope looks and sees
   Through Death a brighter Spring.

Thus the rhyme has returned to the (1) of the first stanza. It is a pity that Payne failed to differentiate between the long lines and the short lines, as required by the French form.

The Virelai Nouveau.—The virelai nouveau is a more formalized simplification of the lai; but it is closer akin to the villanelle and the rondeau redoublé than to the virelai ancien, just as the rondeau redoublé departs from the rondeau in the direction of the glose. The virelai nouveau is written throughout on two rhymes. It opens with a couplet which serves thereafter as a refrain—the villanelle using the first and third lines of the opening tercet similarly, and the rondeau redoublé and glose using the four lines of the opening quatrain as terminal refrain lines. The two refrain lines of the virelai nouveau are used to close alternate stanzas until the last, when both are used, but in reverse order.

This sounds complicated. An example will show how simple it is:

Good-bye to the Town!—good-bye!   1 (R)
Hurrah! for the sea and the sky!   1 (R′)

In the street the flower-girls cry;	1
In the street the water-carts ply;	1
And a fluter, with features awry,	1
Plays fitfully, "Scots, wha hae"—	2
And the throat of the fluter is dry;	1
Good-bye to the Town!—good-bye!	1(R)

And over the roof-tops nigh	1
Comes a waft like a dream of the May;	2
And a lady-bird lit on my tie;	1
And a cock-chafer came with the tray;	2
And a butterfly (no one knows why)	1
Mistook my Aunt's cap for a spray;	2
And "next door" and "over the way"	2
The neighbors take wing and fly:	1
Hurrah! for the sea and the sky!	1(R')

Here 1(R) and 1(R') are, of course, the two refrain lines. Succeeding stanzas proceed: 1,1,2,1,2,1,2,1,1(R) and

$$1,2,1,2,1,2,1,2,1,1,1,1,1,1,1(R').$$

The conclusion is:

So Phyllis, the fawn-footed, hie	1
For a hansom. Ere close of the day,	2
Between us a "world" must lie,—	1
Hurrah! for the sea and the sky!	1(R')
Good-bye to the Town!—GOOD-BYE!	1(R)

July, AUSTIN DOBSON

There is no stipulation as to the number of lines to a stanza. The rules are simple: the rhyming restricted throughout to only two rhymes, and the use of the refrain lines alternately to terminate the stanzas, and both in reverse order to terminate the final stanza. The form is light, amusing, and easy to write.

THE SICILIAN OCTAVE

The Sicilian octave consists of eight 5-foot iambic lines, rhymed alternately on two sounds: 1,2,1,2,1,2,1,2. It is sometimes used as a fixed form for a complete poem. An example is:

The wind of poetry blows high and strong,	1
But not of its own choice in alien meter.	2
Instead of miles of formalized ding-dong	1
Preferred by some super-involved frog-eater,	2
Exotic as Kanchatka or Hong Kong,	1
Give us the homely strain of *Peter, Peter*	2
The Pumpkin-Eater for our festive song:	1
The taste is homelier by far, and sweeter.	2

THE RISPETTO

The rispetto is an Italian form, with inter-rhyming lines ranging from six to ten in number, although not usually exceeding eight. Used rarely in English, the rhyming is 1,2,1,2; 3,3,4,4. It is at times divided into two stanzas.

A multitude of formalized designs	1
Offends the very soul of poetry.	2
Why not have candid and spontaneous lines,	1
To picture what our souls would have life be?	2
Why fritter away the energy of the Muse	3
In lais and rondels and such trifling brews?	3
But I forget Light Verse, with trifling crowned:	4
These, lightsome queen, shall be *your* stamping-ground.	4

TEMA CON VARIAZIONI

Lewis Carroll, in *Rhyme? and Reason?*, offered this delightful form, which has been used since by a number of poets. In tema con variazioni, a familiar stanza—a quatrain by Thomas Moore, in Carroll's example—is served up line by line, each line opening a new stanza, which is completed by the new versifier in the same stanza form. The possible variations in the use of this device are unlimited, since the original text may have any chosen rhyme or rhythm scheme. It is best to keep the variations in the same pattern as the texte. Here is Carroll's example:

I never loved a dear Gazelle—	1 (T)
Nor anything that cost me much:	2
High prices profit those who sell,	1
But why should *I* be fond of such?	2
To glad me with his soft black eye	3 (T)
My son comes trotting home from school:	4
He's had a fight, but can't tell why—	3
He always was a little fool!	4
But, when he came to know me well,	1 (T)
He kicked me out, her testy Sire:	5
And when I stained my hair, that Belle	1
Might note the change, and thus admire	5
And love me, it was sure to dye	3 (T)
A muddy green or staring blue:	6
While one might trace, with half an eye,	3
The still triumphant carrot through.	6

In this, Carroll embroiders three or possibly four different thumbnail stories out of the original texte. It might be more effective as used by others, in which all of the variations relate to the same theme or story.

A number of these forms are akin to that ancient process called jazzing or swinging the classics or some familiar tune in music, recently revived, amid the teeth-gnashing of many lovers of the older music. These constitute an admirable vehicle for light verse. They may yet establish themselves in serious poetry, especially in an answer to some familiar expression in poetry with which the answerer disagrees.

THE RONDEAU REDOUBLÉ

The rondeau redoublé was devised by Jean de la Fontaine (1624-1695), the famous French writer of fables. It is a Theme With Variations, akin to the glose, consisting of twenty-five lines: five quatrains followed by a concluding quatrain, which is tailed by the first half or some portion of the first line, as the concluding unrhymed refrain. Moreover, the four lines of the first quatrain appear successively as the terminal lines of the second, third, fourth and fifth quatrains. The scheme then is:

1(R),2(R),1(R′),2(R′); 2,1,2,1(R); 1,2,1,2(R);
2,1,2,1(R′); 1,2,1,2(R′); 2,1,2,1,R.

Here is *A Daughter of the North,* by Gelett Burgess:

Who wins my hand must do these three things well:	1 (R)
Skate fast as winter wind across the glare;	2 (R)
Swim through the fiord, past breaker, rip and swell;	1 (R′)
Ride like the Snow-Fiend on my snow-white mare.	2 (R′)
Shall a maid do what Viking may not dare?	2
I wed no lover I can aught excel—	1
Skate, swim and ride with me, and I declare,	2
Who wins my hand must do these three things well!	1 (R)
Bind on your skates, and after me pell-mell;	1
Follow me, Carles, and catch my streaming hair!	2
(Keep the black ice—O Bolstrom, if you fell!)	1
Skate fast as winter wind across the glare!	2 (R)
Thrice have I swum from this gray cliff to where	2
On the far side, the angry surges yell;	1
(Into the surf! O Bolstrom, have a care!)	2
Swim through the fiord, past breaker, rip and swell!	1 (R′)

Bring me my Frieda, none but I can quell;	1
(Watch her eye, Bolstrom, when you mount—beware!)	2
Ride bareback now and find the master-spell;	1
Ride like the Snow-Fiend on my snow-white mare!	2 (R′)
Skohl! Viking, Skohl! Am I not bold and fair?	2
Who would not barter Heaven, and venture Hell,	1
Striving the flower of my love to wear?	2
(Mind my words, Bolstrom, hark to what I tell!)	1
Who wins my hand?	R

This, for its unartificial mood throughout, is an admirable example of formal verse.

THE GLOSE

The glose, which might be described as a more elaborate rondeau redoublé, has an independent Romance origin. For all that it is familiar in Spanish and Portuguese verse, it is comparatively rare in French poetry, and rarer in English; so rare, that Gleeson White could discover none in English. There have been several examples since his time.

The glose begins, like the rondeau redoublé, with a quatrain —here called the *texte*—usually a quotation from another poem. The glose proceeds to comment on or amplify this texte, line by line, in four stanzas of ten lines each; closing each, as in the rondeau redoublé, with one of the lines of the texte, in the original order. But there is no requirement that the rhymes be restricted to two. Each stanza has the sixth, ninth and tenth (the refrain) line rhyming on the same sound; the others are arranged in some rhyme-scheme by the writer, preferably with identical rhyme-schemes throughout the stanzas. The final refrain of the rondeau redoublé is not used in the glose.

The glose was first employed on religious and philosophical themes; but in France, like the once sacred triolet, it altered to parody or light humor. Here is *Rags and Dreams,* one of my two published examples of the form:

"If I'd as much money as I could tell,	1 (R)
I never would cry old clothes to sell,	1 (R′)
Old clothes to sell, old clothes to sell,	1 (R″)
I never would cry old clothes to sell."	1 (R‴)

The flow of my dreams is at youth's high flood,	2
A spring flood, freighted with strange and new	3
Wonders of stars, and a touch of mud;	2
For all things are sweet to youth's wild blood.	2
And fire-shod visions come to me too,	3
Of a people hungry for stars as well,—	1
Hungry for fare that the mangered few	3
Grasp and hoard; there's a world to do,—	3
Hunger and darkness I could dispel,	1
If I'd as much money as I could tell.	1 (R)

But whether or not, it matters not;	4
I am caught in the mire as well as they;	5
I am bound to squirm in a bitter spot	4
Where blindness grows, and high dreams rot;	4
I coin my visions, to make them pay;	5
I traffic in things that decay and smell,	1
Stopping my ears to the call of gay	5
Life, and the words that the visions say:	5
Ah, if I had the heart to rebel,	1
I never would cry old clothes to sell!	1 (R')

But here I stay, and here I stay,	
And life is only a bitter jest	
That a madman dreamed, and idiots play;	
Tossing each precious thing away,	
Crowning the lowest, strangling the best;	
And death will come ringing his pedlar's bell	
And gather the breath out of the breast,	
Calling our fairest and loveliest	
Visions, but rags that shrink and swell,	
Old clothes to sell, old clothes to sell.	1 (R'')

Well, I can call, as well as he—	
And these dreams he despises so	
I say will sooner or later be,	
Not dreams, but fair reality;	
In dreams and rags and mud will flow	
The dreamer's passion, the will's hard spell;	
And very death will change, and glow	
With life; we will reap the dreams we sow;	
And then, from earth or heaven or hell,	
I never would cry old clothes to sell.	1 (R''')

The stanza unit here is 2,3,2,2,3,1,3,3,1,1(R). Each stanza has only three rhyme-sounds; but, with the exception of the rhyme dictated by the texte, (1) in this instance, there is no rhyming link between each pair of stanzas. Since the texte may follow any quatrain rhyming, as 1,2,1,2; 1,2,2,1; 1,2,3,2, etc., this means that the sixth, ninth and tenth lines in each stanza contain the link to the texte and the other stanzas in rhyming; and this may not be as uniform as in the example given, if a second or even a third rhyming sound is introduced into the texte quatrain. This is the only restriction on the rhyme-scheme; but there is always a gain in symmetrical rhyming of the various stanzas.

Jean Francois Sarazin formed what he called a glose on the sonnet *de IOB* by Benserade. It consisted of fourteen quatrains following the sonnet, used as a texte; each quatrain being terminated by a line, in proper order, of the sonnet. Thus the possibilities of the underlying idea of the glose are unlimited.

THE VILLANELLE

The villanelle, in France, was primarily a round song sung by men on a farm (from the Latin *villa*). Its structure was originally loose. Later it followed the fashion of the other fixed forms, and rigidified. Even as late as 1625, French villanelles approached the ballade in structure. But one written by Jean Passerat (1534-1602) and appearing posthumously, "J'ai perdu ma tourterelle," became so popular that it set the pattern since followed.

The villanelle is written in tercets, all rhymed 1,2,1; followed by a concluding quatrain, 1,2,1,1. The first and third lines of the first stanza are used alternately as terminal refrains in the tercets; and both together comprise the refrain of the concluding quatrain. It is usual to restrict the villanelle to five tercets. More may be used, providing the concluding quatrain is as above.

Oscar Wilde's villanelle, *Theocritus,* follows the strict pattern:

O Singer of Persephone!	1 (R)	
In the dim meadows desolate,		2
Dost thou remember Sicily?	1 (R')	
Still through the ivy flits the bee	1	
Where Amaryllis lies in state;		2
O Singer of Persephone!	1 (R)	
Simaetha calls on Hecate,	1	
And hears the wild dogs at the gate;		2
Dost thou remember Sicily?	1 (R')	
Still by the light and laughing sea	1	
Poor Polypheme bemoans his fate;		2
O Singer of Persephone!	1 (R)	

And still in boyish rivalry   1
  Young Daphnis challenges his mate;   2
Dost thou remember Sicily?   1 (R')

Slim Lacon keeps a goat for thee;   1
  For thee the jocund shepherds wait;   2
O Singer of Persephone!   1 (R)
Dost thou remember Sicily?   1 (R')

Edwin Arlington Robinson, in *The House on the Hill,* pours deeper poetry into the form; indeed, this villanelle might be considered a text of much of his singing, with its bleak burden,

> There is ruin and decay
>   In the House on the Hill:
> They are all gone away,
> There is nothing more to say.

This whole villanelle is an admirable example of formal verse, with the refrain coming in naturally and logically, and the conclusion more dignified and distinguished than what had gone before: the broadened theme of the poem, summing up all the rest. In writing such formal verse successfully, it is well to save the more effective rhymes and statements for the conclusion, even though this means subordinating an earlier stanza, by the use of a less effective rhyme. The overtones may be far lighter, as in this example by William Ernest Henley:

> Yes, the overword is plain,—
>   If it's trivial, if it's trite—
> In the clatter of the train:
> "I shall see my love again!"

Or the madder slang villanelle, by the same poet, ending:

> Which, Joe, is why I ses to you—
>   Aestheticlike, and limp, and free—
> Now *ain't* they utterly too-too,
> Them flymy little bits of Blue?

THE RONDEAU-TRIOLET FAMILY

The Triolet—Eustache Deschamps (1346?-1406?), in his *Art poétique,* listed three kinds of rondeaus. The first kind, which he called a *simple rondeau,* has eight lines, commencing with a two-lined refrain; the first refrain line reappearing as the fourth line;

and the complete two-line refrain serving again as the seventh and eighth lines. The rhyme-scheme is:

1 (R) ,2 (R) ,1,1 (R) ,1,2,1 (R) ,2 (R)

From the beginning of the fifteenth century, when Charles d'Orléans gave the fourteen-line rondel the form it now has, the name of the simple rondeau was changed to *triolet*.

The first triolets known are in the *Cléomadés* of Adenèz-le-Roi (1258-1297). At first, the triolet was usually written with a ten-syllable line; it then shifted in France to eight and often six syllables, altering from grave subjects to light and frothy ones. Froissart was noted for his triolets. The oldest in England are of a devotional nature, written in 1651 by Patrick Carey, a Benedictine monk at Douai. French triolets begin on the French masculine rhyme; this rule has no meaning in English. The triolet (a little trio, or three) received its name, says Helen Louise Cohen, because it was originally a three-part song; the *Britannica* derives the name from the triple repetition of the first line. After long neglect in English, Robert Bridges in 1873 revived the form, with his:

All women born are so perverse,	1 (R)
No man need boast their love possessing,	2 (R)
If nought seems better, nothing's worse;	1
All women born are so perverse,	1 (R)
From Adam's wife that proved a curse	1
Though God had made her for a blessing.	2
All women born are so perverse,	1 (R)
No man need boast their love possessing.	2 (R)

We are more used to a far lighter touch:

Rose kissed me today,
　　Will she kiss me tomorrow?
Let it be as it may,
Rose kissed me today.
But the pleasure gives way
　　To a savour of sorrow;—
Rose kissed me today,—
　　Will she kiss me tomorrow?
　　　　　　A Kiss, AUSTIN DOBSON

A famous American triolet is:

A pitcher of mignonette
　　In a tenement's highest casement;

Queer sort of a flower-pot—yet
That pitcher of mignonette
Is a garden of heaven sent
  To the little sick child in the basement— .
The pitcher of mignonette
  In the tenement's highest casement.

                                        H. C. BUNNER

For all the emotional appeal in the first six lines, this violates the second inviolable rule of the fixed forms, by altering the precise wording of the refrain: "A pitcher," "That pitcher," "The pitcher." Moreover, the last couplet here is mere surplusage, in no way called for, except by the rules for the form. In writing fixed forms, the rules must be followed strictly until the genius comes, who overrides them, to advantage. Here is an almost-triolet by Leigh Hunt, more famous than any triolet in the language:

Jenny kissed me when we met,   1
  Jumping from the chair she sat in.   2
Time, you thief, who love to get   1
  Sweets into your list, put that in!   2
Say I'm weary, say I'm sad,   3
  Say that health and wealth have missed me,   4
Say I'm growing old, but add   3
  Jenny kissed me.   4 (R)

The first half of line one, reappearing as the refrain in line eight, prophesies or echoes the use of the refrain in certain longer rondeaus. This form is worth crystallizing into an accepted pattern, and into much wider use than it has received.

Writing the Triolet—One of Henley's delightful triolets states:

Easy is the Triolet,
  If you really learn to make it!
Once a neat refrain you get,
Easy is the Triolet.
As you see!—I pay my debt
  With another rhyme. Deuce take it,
Easy is the Triolet,
  If you really learn to make it.

Suppose you decided to write a triolet, and arrived at this opening couplet, to be used as your "neat refrain":

Drink deep—the glass
  Is full—and near!

Now this should be filled in as your fourth, seventh and eighth lines, making your pattern now appear as:

> Drink deep—the glass
> Is full—and near!

> Drink deep! The glass

> Drink deep—the glass
> Is full—and near!

Only three lines now remain to be filled in, but in such a manner that the refrain comes in naturally and aids in the development of the verses as a whole. Once this is done, you have your triolet complete:

> Drink deep—the glass
> Is full—and near!
> Come, lad and lass,
> Drink deep! The glass
> Too soon will pass
> And disappear.
> Drink deep—the glass
> Is full—and *near!*

The Rondel—The rondel—the word is merely the old form for *rondeau*—took the form we are familiar with in the fourteenth century, with Charles d'Orléans (1391-1465) as its foremost user. French versification distinguishes between rhymes feminine, which possess the *e* mute for their final letter, and rhymes masculine, which do not. In France, the rondel may use first a rhyme masculine or a rhyme feminine; but its solitary other rhyme must be of the opposite kind. This rule is not recognized in English versification.

The rondel is a poem of fourteen lines on two rhymes. The first two lines constitute a refrain, which reappears as the seventh and eighth lines, and as the concluding couplet. The pattern thus is:

1R,2R,2,1; 1,2,1R,2R; 1,2,2,1,1R,2R

Clumsy rondels appeared in fifteenth century England; and then, after an eclipse of four centuries, the form was revived. Here is an example:

Love comes back to his vacant dwelling—	1 R	
The old, old Love that we knew of yore!		2 R
We see him stand by the open door,		2
With his great eyes sad, and his bosom swelling.	1	

He makes as though in our arms repelling	1	
He fain would lie as he lay before;—		2
Love comes back to his vacant dwelling—	1 R	
The old, old Love that we knew of yore!		2 R

Ah! who shall help us from over-spelling	1	
That sweet, forgotten, forbidden lore?		2
E'en as we doubt, in our hearts once more		2
With a rush of tears to our eyelids welling,	1	
Love comes back to his ancient dwelling—	1 R	
The old, old Love that we knew of yore!		2 R

AUSTIN DOBSON

It is strange that the tendency, in this revival of the French forms, was to use what must either be called accent verse, or be described as an irregular blending of iambs and anapests, with a few other feet used at times, as the opening foot here, consisting of one accent only (Love); for it seems misdescription to call this merely an iamb lacking its first syllable. The badge of the rondel is the repetition twice of the couplet refrain. In English, such refrains are largely restricted to poems to be sung; and with no stipulation that the refrain (or chorus of the song) fit each time into the development of the theme. In the French forms, the refrain must be woven into the very fabric of the form; and this is an over-formalization of verse, especially when applied to serious poetry. Theodore de Banville says that the art of the rondel consists in the gay and natural introduction of the refrain, which should always seem inevitable, while slightly changing the point of view in each re-use. When we get a rondel with the refrain used as naturally as the pedlar's call in *The Umbrella Man,* or the brief insistent demand in *Ain't Cha Comin' Out,* we will have arrived at a perfect use of the form. At times its mood can be very light:

> Paper, inviolate, white,
>   Shall it be joy or pain?
>   Shall I of fate complain,
> Or shall I laugh tonight?
>
> Shall it be hopes that are bright,
>   Shall it be hopes that are vain?
> Paper, inviolate, white,
>   Shall it be joy or pain?

> A dear little hand so light
> A moment in mine hath lain;
> Kind was its pressure again—
> Ah, but it was so slight!
> Paper, inviolate, white,
> Shall it be joy or pain?
> *Cosmo Monkhouse*

As always, we have the recurrent tendency toward accent verse.

The Thirteen-Line Rondel—Some French rondels after Charles d'Orléans omit either the expected fourteenth or thirteenth line, de Banville most usually omitting the thirteenth. This gives an opportunity for a more sharpened climax, and makes the retained refrain line at the end more emphatic. Otherwise, this thirteen line form follows the pattern already given for the rondel. Here is an example:

> Summer has seen decay
> Of roses white and red,
> And Love with wings outspread
> Speeds after yesterday.
>
> Blue skies have changed to grey,
> And joy has sorrow wed:
> Summer has seen decay
> Of roses white and red.
>
> May's flowers outlast not May;
> And when the hour has fled,
> Around the roses dead
> The mournful echoes say—
> Summer has seen decay.
> GEORGE MOORE

In dealing with the vocabulary of poetry, we have already discussed such regrettable inversions as the two in the preceding rondel ("of fate complain," "in mine hath lain,"), the examples here ("joy has sorrow wed" and "roses dead"), and such archaic language use as "outlast not." Such blemishes are not inevitable in the use of the fixed forms. The use of the refrain here is more natural than in several of the examples quoted, especially in its final use.

The Rondelet—The rondelet is a brief old French form, which never achieved marked popularity, for all that its structure was similar to and simpler than that of the triolet. It consisted of seven lines, of which the first, third and seventh are a four-syllabled refrain, to which the fourth rhymes; and this fourth, and the second, fifth and sixth lines, which rhyme on a second rhyming sound, are eight syllables each. The pattern then is:

    1R, 2, 1R, 1, 2, 2, 1R.

An example in English by May Probyn is:

"Which way he went?"	1R
I know not—how should I go spy	2
Which way he went?	1R
I only know him gone. "Relent?"	1
He never will—unless I die!	2
And then, what will it signify	2
Which way he went?	1R

The Chaucerian Roundel—A ten-line form of the rondel, which Chaucer named a roundel, is attributed to him:

So hath your beauty fro your hertè chased	1 R
Pitee, that mee availeth not to pleyne;	2
For daunger* halt your mercy in his cheyne.	2
Giltless my deth thus have ye purchased;	1
I sey you soth, me nedeth not to fayne;	2
So hath your beauty from your hertè chased.	1 R
Alas, that Nature hath in you compassed	1
So grete beauty, that no man may atteyne	2
To mercy, though he stewe** for the peyne.	2
So hath your beauty fro your hertè chased.	1 R

The rhyming pattern here is 1R,2,2; 1,2,1R; 1,2,2,1R. As might have been expected, this came into English poetry with eleven and ten syllables to the line: the form interpreted as iambic pentameter. It was only on the revival that the tendency went to briefer lines and to accent verse. An example in English is:

> "Laugh while you may; for laughter will have ending!"
> I heard it chuckled grossly from a low
> Valley, whose foul depths I hoped not to know.
>
> I swung instead up the high hill, ascending
> To greet the sun. But still a faint echo,
> "Laugh while you may; for laughter will have ending."

* Power, dominion.
** Starve.

[378]

Then, at the crest, I saw what was past mending,
And climbed down, and lived on. And long ago
I have warned others who strained upward so:
"Laugh while you may; for laughter will have ending."
Terminal, CLEMENT WOOD

The Rondeau—In its perfect form, the rondeau, most popular of its family, consists of thirteen eight- or ten-syllabled lines, divided into three stanzas of unequal length, knit together by two rhymes and a refrain taken out of the first line. In Clément Marot's time (1495-1544) the laws of the rondeau were laid down; and, according to 17th century Vincent Voiture (1598-1648), this was the approved type:

When you are old, and I am passed away—   1
Passed, and your face, your golden face, is grey—   1
  I think, whate'er the end, this dream of mine,   2
  Comforting you, a friendly star will shine   2
Down the dim slope where still you stumble and stray.   1

So may it be; that so dead Yesterday   1
No sad-eyed ghost, but generous and gay,   1
  May serve your memories like almighty wine,   2
    When you are old.   R

Dear Heart, it shall be so. Under the sway   1
Of death the past's enormous disarray   1
  Lies hushed and dark. Yet though there come no sign,   2
  Live on well pleased! Immortal and divine,   2
Love shall still tend you, as God's angels may,   1
    When you are old.   R

W. E. HENLEY

A rondeau thus consists of fifteen lines, with this stanzaic pattern: 1,1,2,2,1; 1,1,2,R; 1,1,2,2,1,R. In England, Dr. Lawrence, a friend of Burke's, wrote rondeaus; but it was a century later before the form had any great vogue there and in the United States. It is the use of the refrain, appearing only twice, which gives structure and emphasis to the rondeau. Here the briefened refrain returns to one of its original uses: to give the improvisatore a time for rest, in which to bring his forces into focus, and recover breath for the next flight. It both rivets the structure and deepens the emotional appeal. Unlike most rondel forms, the restrained use of the refrain permits it to appear with complete naturalness. If there is an effect of artificiality in the rondeau, it comes from the limitation of the rhymes to two sounds in thirteen rhymed lines. Yet the genuine poet or adept versifier may surmount this hurdle, too.

In English, the rondeau is more common in 4-accent verse, or in strict eight syllables to the line. Here is a splendid example:

> A man must live. We justify
> Low shift and trick to treason high,
>   A little vote for a little gold
>   To a whole senate bought and sold
> By that self-evident reply.
>
> But is it so? Pray tell me why
> Life at such cost you have to buy?
>   In what religion were you taught
>   A man must live?
>
> There are times when a man must die.
> Imagine, for a battle-cry
>   For soldiers, with a sword to hold,—
>   For soldiers, with the flag unrolled,—
> This coward's whine, this liar's lie,—
>   A man must live!
>   *A Man Must Live,* CHARLOTTE PERKINS GILMAN

The dignity and climactic effect of the ending are especially notable here. A skilled light use of the same form appears in *A Song to One,* by T. A. Daly:

> If few are won to read my lays
> And offer me a word of praise,
>   If there are only one or two
>   To take my rhymes and read them through,
> I may not claim the poet's bays.
>
> I care not, when my Fancy plays
> Its one sweet note, if it should raise
>   A host of listeners or few—
>   If you are one.
>
> The homage that my full heart pays
> To Womanhood in divers ways,
>   Begins and ends, my love, in you.
>   My lines may halt, but strong and true
> My soul shall sing through all its days,
>   If you are won.

The refrain here plays upon three punning variations of the identical sounds, "If few are won," "If you are one," "If you are won." In a refrain by Michael Lewis, the refrain similarly includes "My lady's eyes," "My lady sighs," "My lady's size." So long as the sounds are identical (as they are not in the Lewis example; for the connecting consonantal sounds before the final IZ sound here are, respectively, *z*, *s*, and *z-s*), any such witty use of the refrain is a merit, especially in light verse.

Variations in the Rondeau—The stanzaic scheme of the rondeau, already given, is by no means universally followed. Here are a few of the variations, clearly permissible, especially where the alteration adds to the naturalness of the whole:

1,2,1,1,2; 1,2,1,R; 2,1,2,2,1,R. Arlo Bates.
1,1,2,2,1; 1,2,1,R; 1,2,2,1,1,R. W. E. Henley, five times.
1,2,2,1,1; 2,2,1,R; 3,4,3,4,4,R; another,
1,2,2,1,1; 2,2,1,R; 3,4,4,3,3,R; and also
1,2,2,1,1; 2,2,1,R; 3,4,3,3,4,R, all by Edmund Gosse.

There is also a twelve-line rondeau by Austin Dobson:

1,2,2,1; 1,2,R; 1,2,2,1,R.

And two sixteen-line patterns by Edmund Gosse:

1,2,2,1,1; 2,2,1,R; 3,4,4,3,4,3,R; and also
1,2,2,1,1; 2,2,1,R; 3,4,3,4,4,3,R.

The Twelve-Line Rondeau—The rondeau used by Villon contained only twelve lines, two of them being the refrain, consisting only of the opening word. Here is John Payne's translation of it:

Death, of thy rigour I complain,	1
That hast my lady torn from me,	2
And yet wilt not contented be,	2
Till from me too all strength be ta'en	1
For languishment of heart and brain.	1
What harm did she in life to thee,	2
Death?	R
One heart we had between us twain;	1
Which being dead, I too must dree	2
Death, or, like carven saints, we see	2
In choir, sans life to live be fain,	1
Death!	R

The Roundel—The roundel, probably based upon rare early French variants, is chiefly associated with the name of Swinburne, due to his volume *A Century of Roundels*, containing a hundred examples of the form, the line-lengths ranging from four to sixteen syllables. As used by Swinburne, the roundel consisted of eleven lines, two of which are the briefer refrain lines. The refrain consists either of the opening word of the first line, or of half or some portion of that line; and, if it consists of more than one word, it is usually rhymed with the second rhyming sound, that found in the second line. The simple rhyme scheme is:

1,2,1,R; 2,1,2; 1,2,1,R

Where the refrain rhymes, this would be phrased:

1,2,1,2R; 2,1,2; 1,2,1,2R.

One of Swinburne's typical examples is:

A roundel is wrought as a ring or a star-bright sphere,	1
With craft of delight and with cunning of sound unsought,	2
That the heart of the hearer may smile if to pleasure his ear	1
A roundel is wrought.	2 R
Its jewel of music is carven of all or of aught—	2
Love, laughter or mourning—remembrance of rapture or fear—	1
That fashion may fancy to hang in the ear of thought.	2
As a bird's quick song runs round, and the hearts in us hear	1
Pause answer to pause, and again the same strain caught,	2
So moves the device whence, round as a pearl or tear,	1
A roundel is wrought.	2 R

Less extended examples are:

If rest is sweet at shut of day
  For tired hands and tired feet,
How sweet at last to rest for aye,
  If rest is sweet!

We work or work not through the heat;
  Death bids us soon our labours lay
In lands where night and twilight meet.

When the last dawns are fallen on grey
  And all life's toils and ease complete,
They know who work, not they who play,
  If rest is sweet.
      A Roundel of Rest, ARTHUR SYMONS

Meet me, love, where the woodbines grow
  And where the wild rose smells most sweet;
And the breezes, as they softliest blow,
      Meet;

[382]

Passing along through the fields of wheat,
  By the hedge where in spring the violets glow,
And the bluebells blossom around one's feet;

Where latest lingers the drifted snow,
  And the fir-tree grows o'er our trysting-seat,
Come—and your love, as long ago,
    Meet.
          The Trysting-Tree, CHARLES SAYLE

THE BALLADE FAMILY

The Ballade—The princely ballade reached its most elaborate and finished form in 14th century France. The name is an earlier form of the word *ballad,* and was connected with the dance (cf. *ballet*), but both soon departed from their connection with the dance, as *lyric* from its association with the lyre. The ballade, as a fixed form, had its roots in the *canzone di ballo* of the Italian, and in lost Provençal forms; but, as we know it, it was in the France of Charles the Wise (1364-1380) that it flourished into tremendous popularity. The ballades of Jehannot de Lescurel, just before the middle of the century, lacked the envoy as we know it; and often had refrains several lines long. As early as 1339, in *Li Regret Guillaume,* lamenting the death of Count William of Hainault, there are thirty ballades, each with a one-line refrain. Of these, thirteen use an eight-syllable line; eleven, a ten-syllable line; and the balance are seven or nine. It was in the *puys d'amour* that the envoy, hitherto a feature of several types of songs, became attached to the ballade, almost always with a conventional address to the Prince in the envoy's first line. Eustache Deschamps, Chaucer's friend, left at least 1,175 ballades. Froissart the chronicler, Guillaume de Machault, and most of all François Villon, prince of all ballade-makers, crystallized the form forever. In the late 19th century, Théodore de Banville revived the form in France, which had been made illustrious in the interim by Clément Marot and 17th century Voiture and La Fontaine, thereafter suffering eclipse from the attacks of Molière and Boileau.

The ballade is used extensively in no other language except French and English. During the 15th and 16th centuries many English ballades were written, with intermittent attention to the French rules, by Chaucer, Gower, Lydgate and their contemporaries. But these lacked the envoy. In the nineteenth century, the forgotten form was reintroduced almost simultaneously by Swinburne, Austin Dobson, Andrew Lang, Edmund Gosse and W. E. Henley. G. K. Chesterton is a noted later ballade-maker.

There are two normal types of the ballade:

1. The ballade with eight-line stanzas. It has three stanzas of eight lines each, rhyming 1,2,1,2; 2,3,2,3R. The envoy of four lines rhymes 2,3,2,3R.

2. The ballade with ten-line stanza. It has three stanzas of ten lines each, rhyming 1,2,1,2,2,3,3,4,3,4R. The envoy of five lines rhymes 3,3,4,3,4R.

The former is far the more popular in English verse.

The strict rules of formal verse-rhyming must be followed throughout. These include:

1. No rhyme-sound used once may be repeated in any part of the ballade, except that the refrain must be unchanged.

2. The rhyme-scheme must be identical from stanza to stanza.

3. Each stanza and the envoy must close with the refrain.

4. The envoy always takes the rhyme-scheme of the last half of the preceding stanza.

In France, an eight-syllabled refrain dictated an eight-line stanza; one of ten syllables, a ten-line stanza. This rule is not strictly followed in English.

5. The stanza should carry an unbroken sense throughout; it may not be split into two quatrains, or otherwise.

6. The envoy was at first addressed to the patron of the poet; Prince! Princess! Sire! or some mythical or symbolic personage. The envoy is both a dedication and a climax, and should be richer in wording and more stately in imagery than the earlier stanzas.

Thus the ballade always consists of three stanzas and an envoy, with a refrain line repeated at the close of each stanza and the envoy. The entire poem contains either three or four rhyme-sounds, according to whether the stanza has eight or ten lines; and these must be repeated without identities throughout. These rules were laid down by Henri de Croi, whose *L'art et science de rhetorique* appeared first in 1493.

The Eight-Line Stanza Ballade—An example will best illustrate the pattern:

Where are the passions they essayed,	1
And where the tears they made to flow?	2
Where the wild humours they portrayed	1
For laughing worlds to see and know?	2
Othello's wrath and Juliet's woe,	2
Sir Peter's whims and Timon's gall?	3
And Millament and Romeo?	2
Into the night go one and all.	3 R

Where are the braveries, fresh and frayed?	1
The plumes, the armours—friend and foe?	2
The cloth of gold, the rare brocade,	1
The mantles glittering to and fro?	2
The pomp, the pride, the royal show?	2
The cries of war and festival?	3
The youth, the grace, the charm, the glow?	2
Into the night go one and all.	3 R

The curtain falls, the play is played:	1
The Beggar packs beside the Beau:	2
The Monarch troops, and troops the Maid;	1
The Thunder huddles with the Snow.	2
Where are the revellers high and low?	2
The clashing swords? The lover's call?	3
The dancers gleaming row on row?	2
Into the night go one and all.	3 R

Prince, in one common overthrow	2
The Hero tumbles with the Thrall;	3
As dust that drives, as straws that blow,	2
Into the night go one and all.	3 R

Ballade of Dead Actors, W. E. HENLEY

Here the rhyme scheme is identical, stanza to stanza. The
envoy repeats the rhyme scheme of the second half of the preceding stanza. The rhymes are:

1: S (essayed), TR (portrayed), FR (frayed), K (brocade),
PL (played), M (Maid).

2: FL (flow); N (know), W (woe), unconsonanted vowel
(Romeo), F (foe), FR (fro), SH (show), GL (glow), B (Beau),
SN (Snow), L (low), R (row), thR (overthrow), BL (blow). Remember, fourteen rhymes are required for this sound; make sure
that that many are available.

3: G (gall), V (festival), K (call), thR (thrall), and the refrain
rhyme, the unconsonanted vowel (all).

No identities; the rhyming is perfect. The stanzas are complete
integers, in spite of the punctuation of the third. The envoy is

properly addressed. Here we have a ballade that meets every requirement. And it is packed full of poetry, in addition:

The Thunder huddles with the Snow

being merely one of many impressive lines.

The Ten-Line Stanza Ballade—The pattern for this can be obtained from the following opening stanza of Swinburne's version of Villon's *Epitaph in Form of a Ballade:*

Men, brother men, that after us yet live,	1
Let not your hearts too hard against us be;	2
For if some pity of us poor men ye give,	1
The sooner God shall take of you pity.	2
Here are we five or six strung up, you see,	2
And here the flesh that all too well we fed	3
Bit by bit eaten and rotten, rent and shred,	3
And we the bones grow dust and ash withal;	4
Let no man laugh at us discomforted,	3
But pray to God that he forgive us all.	4 R

and its envoy:

Prince Jesus, that of all art lord and head,	3
Keep us, that hell be not our bitter bed;	3
We have naught to do in such a master's hall.	4
Be not ye therefore of our fellowhead,	3
But pray to God that he forgive us all.	4 R

This follows the required rhyme scheme, both for stanza and envoy. The rhymes required are: 6 of rhyme 1, 9 of rhyme 2, 12 of rhyme 3, and 5 of rhyme 4, including the refrain word. Since the stipulation for the eight-line stanza ballade is 6 of rhyme 1, 14 of rhyme 2, and 5 of rhyme 3, the briefer ballade is slightly more of a strain on the rhyming potentialities of the language. With such forms, and with the chant royal, it is difficult to write without rhyming faults, especially identities, unless the *Mental Rhyming Dictionary* technique is used; remembering, after the possible rhymes have been grouped under the different consonantal sounds, "One rhyme only from each group." Swinburne, in this very ballade, uses these identities instead of rhyme:

give, forgive; live, alive; righteously, wearily; well-head, head, fellowhead.

At times, the above rhyming pattern is varied. Here are especial variations:

[386]

Stanzas, 1,2,2,1,2,1,2,2,1R—nine lines only; refrain, 2,1,2,2,1R. *A Ballade of Aspiration,* W. E. Henley.

Stanzas, 1,1,2,1,2,3,4,3,4,4R; refrain, 3,4,3,4,4R. *A Ballad at Parting,* Swinburne.

Stanzas, 1,2,1,2,2,3,4,3,3,4R; refrain, 3,4,3,3,4R. *Ballad,* John Payne.

Yet in all these variations, the envoy always repeats the pattern of the last half of the stanza; and the rhyming pattern of each of the stanzas is identical.

Instead of following the French rule of ten syllables to the line, ten lines to the stanza, the liberties taken in English ballades are exemplified by these openings by Swinburne to ballades of ten lines to the stanza: and of course in these the rhythm of each line follows the opening:

> Song wakes with every wakening year.—*A Ballad of Appeal.*
> Sea to sea that clasps and fosters England, uttering evermore.
> —*Ballad at Parting.*
> The sea is awake, and the sound of the song of the joy of her waking is rolled.—*In the Water.*

Writing the Ballade—It is clear that, with a complicated form requiring as many as twelve or fourteen non-identical rhyming sounds in one poem, it is necessary to keep our rhyming pattern filled in as we write, as in the case of the Italian sonnet, already illustrated.

Let us assume that Austin Dobson, writing his *On a Fan That Belonged to the Marquise de Pompadour,* had indicated his rhyme-progression as he wrote. He would first write down his rhyme-scheme in column 2, and prepare for his three rhyming sounds as they developed, filling in as he wrote the lines. His worksheet would then resemble:

	Rhyme Scheme	(1) ĪT	(2) Ū	(3) ĂN
Chicken-skin, delicate, white,	1	HW		
Painted by Carlo Vanloo,	2		L	
Loves in a riot of light,	1	L		
Roses and vaporous blue;	2		BL	
Hark to the dainty *frou-frou!*	2		FR	
Picture above, if you can,	3			K
Eyes that could melt as the dew,—	2		DY	
This was the Pompadour's fan.	3 R			F

	Rhyme Scheme	(1) ĪT	(2) Ū	(3) ĂN
See how they rise at the sight,	1	S		
Thronging the *Oeil de Boeuf* through,	2		thR	
Courtiers as butterflies bright,	1	BR		
Beauties that Fragonard drew,	2		DR	
Talon-rouge, falbala, queue,	2		KY	
Cardinal, Duke—to a man,	3			M
Eager to sigh or to sue,—	2		S	
This was the Pompadour's fan!	3R			F
Ah! but things more than polite	1	L		
Hung on this toy, *voyez vous!*	2		V	
Matters of state and of might,	1	M		
Things that great ministers do;	2		D	
Things that, maybe, overthrew	2		thR	
Those in whose brains they began;	3			G
Here was the sign and the cue,—	2		KY	
This was the Pompadour's fan!	3R			F
Envoy				
Where are the secrets it knew?	2		NY	
Weavings of plot and of plan?	3			PL
—But where is the Pompadour, too?	2		T	
This was the Pompadour's *fan!*	3R			F

The value of this progressive check-up becomes at once apparent. We must, of course, have accurate sound-differentiation here. *Blue* is BLŪ, not BLYŪ; *dew* is DYŪ; *do,* DŪ; *queue* and *cue* both KYŪ, etc. Running down the list, in order to delete any identities that have crept in, we find:

> Rhyme 1: light, polite—both L sounds.
> Rhyme 2: through, overthrew—both thR; and queue, cue—both KY.

These three identities would have to be eliminated, to make the ballade accurately rhymed.

It is easy to say, if the masters err so, why not forgive the later followers? The rules of the ballade and similar forms admit of no excuses. A slight fault in rhyming is no more acceptable than an egg slightly bad. This is a delightful, but triply faulty, ballade.

In light verse, ballades with far shorter lines than any example given are occasionally encountered.

Ballade with Double Refrain—This form of the ballade, found first in old French, uses two refrains: one occurring at the end of the first half of the stanza (fourth or fifth line) and one at its end (eighth or tenth line); while, in the envoy of the eight-line stanza ballade, the refrains are the second and fourth lines, with couplet rhyming here; and, in the envoy of the ten-line stanza ballade, they would appear in the second or third line, and in the fifth line. It is usual to select two antithetical refrains, and develop each half-stanza upon the contrasting refrain used to close it. Austin Dobson's *The Ballade of Prose and Rhyme* is an excellent example:

When the roads are heavy with mire and rut,	1
In November fogs, in December snows,	2
When the North Wind howls, and the doors are shut,	1
There is place and enough for the pains of prose;—	2 R
But whenever a scent from the whitethorn blows,	2
And the jasmine-stars to the casement climb,	3
And a Rosalind-face at the lattice shows,	2
Then hey!—for the ripple of laughing rhyme!	3 R

When the brain gets dry as an empty nut,
  When the reason stands on its squarest toes,
When the mind (like a beard) has a "formal cut,"
  There is place and enough for the pains of prose;—
  But whenever the May-blood stirs and glows,
And the young year draws to the "golden prime,"—
  And Sir Romeo sticks in his ears a rose,
Then hey!—for the ripple of laughing rhyme!

In a theme where the thoughts have a pedant-strut,
  In a changing quarrel of "Ayes" and "Noes,"
In a starched procession of "If" and "But,"
  There is place and enough for the pains of prose;—
  But whenever a soft glance softer grows,
And the light hours dance to the trysting-time,
  And the secret is told "that no one knows,"
Then hey!—for the ripple of laughing rhyme!

Envoy

In a work-a-day world,—for its needs and woes,	2
There is place and enough for the pains of prose;	2 R
But whenever the May-bells clash and chime,	3
Then hey!—for the ripple of laughing rhyme!	3 R

The rhyming pattern here is 1,2,1,2R,2,3,2,3R for the stanzas; and 2,2R,3,3R for the envoy.

The Double Ballade—The double ballade consists of six, instead of three, stanzas of eight or ten lines each, rhymed as in the models already studied. Ordinarily the envoy is omitted. Henley, however, a distinguished user of the form, always uses an envoy. His *Double Ballade of Life and Fate* follows the regular eight-line-to-the-stanza pattern for stanza and envoy. But he took liberties with the form when he cared to. His *Double Ballade of the Nothingness of Things* has eleven lines to each of its six stanzas, rhymed 1,2,1,2,2,3,3,4,5,4,5R; and an envoy rhymed 3,3,5,4,4,5R:

> Prince, pride must have a fall
> What is the worth of all
>   Your state's supreme urbanities?
> Bad at the best's the game.
> Well might the sage exclaim:—
> "O Vanity of Vanities!"

His *Ballade of Truisms* has only three stanzas, like a simple ballade; but it has twelve trochaic lines to each stanza, with the last syllable omitted. Each stanza has this metric pattern: 4,2,4 trochaic feet, repeated four times. The rhyming pattern is: 1,1,2,1,1,2,2,2,1,2,2,1R. The envoy repeats the pattern of the last half of preceding stanza:

Time the pedagogue his cane	2
Might retain,	2
But his charges all would stray 1	
Truanting in every lane—	2
Jack with Jane!—	2
If it could be always May. 1 R	

The Chant Royal—The chant royal, a kindred form to the ballade, was first mentioned by Ruteboeuf, a trouvère of the thirteenth century. It has five stanzas, identical in pattern, of eleven lines each, and an envoy of five lines. The whole is written on the five rhyming sounds used in the first verse; hence the sixty lines have only five rhyme-sounds. While it has been conjectured that the chant royal is an extended ballade, or a ballade conceived upon a larger scale, there is uncertainty as to which form came first. Henri de Croi, writing in 1493 on the Champt Royal and its dignity, throws no light on its origin. In the Middle Ages, the form was largely used in praise of the Virgin Mary. Eustache Deschamps, writing at about the same time as de Croi, pointed out that these Marian chants royaux, which he called *serventois,* lacked the *envoi.* In old French, Clément Marot's were the most admired examples. Many early chants royal unfolded an allegory in the five stanzas, giving the key in the envoy.

Unknown to medieval England, the form was introduced into England in the late nineteenth century. It is unknown outside of France and England. Théodore de Banville holds that the form belonged essentially to an age of faith, when it could be used to develop the exploits of a hero of royal race, or the processional splendors of religion.

The rhyming pattern is usually 1,2,1,2,3,3,4,4,5,4,5R; the envoy, 4,4,5,4,5R. There is a briefer form, with only ten lines to the stanza, and using six in the envoy: the stanzaic rhyme-scheme being 1,2,1,2,2,3,3,4,3,4R, with an envoy of 3,3,4,3,3,4R. An amusing example of the full form is furnished by H. C. Bunner, in *Behold the Deeds!* (*Being the Plaint of Adolphe Culpepper Ferguson, Salesman of Fancy Notions, held in durance of his Landlady for a failure to connect on Saturday night*):

I would that all men my hard case might know;   1
  How grievously I suffer for no sin: 2
I, Adolphe Culpepper Ferguson, for lo!   1
  I, of my landlady am lockéd in,   2
    For being short on this sad Saturday,   3
    Nor having shekels of silver wherewith to pay;   3
She has turned and is departed with my key;   4
Wherefore, not even as other boarders free,   4
  I sing, (as prisoners to their dungeon stones   5
When for ten days they expiate a spree):   4
  Behold the deeds that are done of Mrs. Jones!   5 R

One night and one day have I wept my woe;
  Nor wot I, when the morrow doth begin,
If I shall have to write to Briggs & Co.,
  To pray them to advance the requisite tin
    For ransom of their salesman, that he may
    Go forth as other boarders go alway—
As those I hear now flocking from their tea,
Led by the daughter of my landlady
  Piano-ward. This day, for all my moans,
Dry bread and water have been servéd me.
  Behold the deeds that are done of Mrs. Jones!

Miss Amabel Jones is musical, and so
  The heart of the young he-boarder doth win,
Playing "The Maiden's Prayer," *adagio*—

That fetcheth him, as fetcheth the banco skin
    The innocent rustic. For my part, I pray:
    That Badarjewska maid may wait for aye
Ere she sits with a lover, as did we
Once sit together, Amabel! Can it be
    That all that arduous wooing not atones
For Saturday shortness of trade dollars three?
    Behold the deeds that are done of Mrs. Jones!

Yea! she forgets the arm was wont to go
    Around her waist. She wears a buckle whose pin
Galleth the crook of the young man's elbów;
    I forget not, for I that youth have been.
        Smith was aforetime the Lothario gay,
        Yet once, I mind me, Smith was forced to stay
Close in his room. Not calm, as I, was he:
But his noise brought no pleasaunce, verily.
    Small ease he gat of playing on the bones,
Or hammering on his stove-pipe, that I see.
    Behold the deeds that are done of Mrs. Jones!

Thou, for whose fear the figurative crow
    I eat, accursed be thou and all thy kin!
Thee will I shew up—yea, up will I shew
    Thy too thick buckwheats, and thy tea too thin.
        Ay! here I dare thee, ready for the fray!
        Thou dost *not* "keep a first-rate house," I say!
It does not with the advertisements agree.
Thou lodgest a Briton with a puggaree,
    And thou hast harboured Jacobses and Cohns,
Also a Mulligan. Thus denounce I thee!
    Behold the deeds that are done of Mrs. Jones!

Envoy

Boarders! the worse I have not told to ye: 4
She hath stolen my trousers, that I may not flee   4
    Privily by the window. Hence these groans,   5
There is no fleeing in a *robe de nuit*.   4
    Behold the deeds that are done of Mrs. Jones!   5 R

Here we require ten rhymes each on the (1), (2) and (3) sounds;
seven (including the refrain sound) on the (5) sound; and a full
eighteen on the (4) sound. In this example, the rhyming throughout is accurate, and the product qualifies as a perfect chant royal
in light verse. Since the form is so accurate, the method already
outlined of checking the rhymes as they come, (see under "Writing
the Sonnets," and ballade) should be used, to prevent identities
instead of rhymes. In order to achieve an envoy the proper culmi-

nation of the stanzas, it is often necessary to shift the strongest
and most vigorous rhyming sounds to it, and to substitute other
rhyming sounds in the various stanzas.

THE SESTINA

The sestina, the most elaborate flowering of Provençal ingenuity in versification, differs from all of the forms so far considered (except the tanka, hokku, and cinquain), in that it was
not rhymed. It was invented by the troubadour Arnaut Daniel,
who died in 1199. Rarely used in French poetry, it is well known
in Italy, Spain and Portugal, and Dante and Petrarch were among
its users. In its pure form, it consisted of six stanzas of six lines
each of blank verse—the number six giving it its name. The
difficulty arose from the stipulation that the six terminal words
of the first stanza must also be the terminal words of the other
stanzas, according to a stipulated order. The Provençal order was:

1,2,3,4,5,6; 6,1,5,2,4,3; 3,6,4,1,2,5;
5,3,2,6,1,4; 4,5,1,3,6,2; 2,4,6,5,3,1.

After these six stanzas came a tornado, tornada or envoy of three
lines, in which the six key words were repeated **two to a line**,
in this order:

2,5; 4,3; 6,1.

If there was any symbolism in this rigid order, it has long ago been
lost. Other original rules included the requirement that each
terminal word be a two-syllabled noun—a rule no longer followed. Here is a typical example, *Homes*, by Charlotte Perkins
Gilman; the numbers referring to the positions of the key terminal words:

We are the smiling comfortable homes	1
With happy families enthroned therein,	2
Where baby souls are brought to meet the world,	3
Where women end their duties and desires,	4
For which men labor as the goal of life,	5
That people worship now instead of God.	6
Do we not teach the child to worship God?—	6
Whose soul's young range is bounded by the homes	1
Of those he loves, and where he learns that life	5
Is all constrained to serve the wants therein,	2

Domestic needs and personal desires,—	4
These are the early limits of his world.	3

And are we not the woman's perfect world	3
Prescribed by nature and ordained of God,	6
Beyond which she can have no right desires,	4
No need for service other than in homes?	1
For doth she not bring up her young therein?	2
And is not rearing young the end of life?	5

And man? What other need hath he in life	5
Than to go forth and labor in the world,	3
And struggle sore with other men therein?	2
Not to serve other men, nor yet his God,	6
But to maintain these comfortable homes,—	1
The end of all a normal man's desires.	4

Shall not the soul's most measureless desires	4
Learn that the very flower and fruit of life	5
Lies all attained in comfortable homes,	1
With which life's purpose is to dot the world	3
And consummate the utmost will of God,	6
By sitting down to eat and drink therein.	2

Yea, in the processes that work therein—	2
Fulfilment of our natural desires—	4
Surely man finds the proof that mighty God	6
For to maintain and reproduce his life	5
Created him and set him in the world,	3
And this high end is best attained in homes.	1

Are we not homes? and is not all therein?	1, 2
Wring dry the world to meet our wide desires!	3, 4
We crown all life! We are the aim of God!	5, 6

Only in her tornado or envoy did Mrs. Gilman depart from the accustomed pattern; and her arrangement is more climactic, considering her terminal key words.

In writing the sestina, the first thing to do, after the terminal words of the first stanza have been arrived at, is to write down the words in their proper order to terminate the other five stanzas, and to halve and terminate the three concluding lines. Then these last six stanzas must be filled in, with as natural a development as the versifier is capable of. The exercise is similar to that parlor game in which terminal words are furnished, for the contestants to see which can create the best verse out of them. In this game, the terminals are usually rhymed; the sestina at least avoids that limitation.

The poets who preferred rhyme had to exercise their ingenuity on rhymed sestinas. It was at once clear that, if the venerable terminal word-order of the Provençal poets was followed, there would be couplet-rhyming every so often. This was ingeniously avoided. Swinburne, in his sestina "I saw my soul at rest upon a day," used only two rhyme-sounds: the order of his terminal words being—

1,2,3,4,5,6; 6,1,4,3,2,5; 6,5,1,4,3,2;
2,5,6,1,4,3; 3,2,1,6,5,4; 4,3,2,6,5,1; tornada, 1-4, 2-3, 5-6.

This was followed by James Branch Cabell in *The Conqueror Passes,* and by Clinton Scollard in *Cupid and the Shepherd.* In *Rizzio's Love-Song,* Swinburne used three rhymes, rhyming the first stanza 1,2,1,3,2,3. He applied these six terminal words (numbered here 1,2,3,4,5,6, as is the sestina custom) as follows:

1,2,3,4,5,6; 6,1,5,4,3,2; 2,6,5,1,4,3;
3,2,1,6,5,4; 4,3,2,1,6,5; 5,4,2,3,6,1; tornada, 6-2, 3-4, 5-1.

This form found no imitators. He even wrote a double sestina, *The Complaint of Lisa,* rhyming his twelve terminal words 1,2,3,1,2,4,3,5,6,5,4,6 in the first stanza, and thereafter proceeding intricately, often with the rhyming sounds far apart. There are one hundred and fifty lines altogether in this double sestina. The result hardly seems worth the effort.

MORE RECENT FORMS

The Quatern—The quatern is a variation of the kyrielle, in which the first line of stanza one, used as a refrain, appears as the second line of stanza two, the third line of stanza three, and the fourth line of stanza four. The rhyming pattern is:

1R,2,1,2; 2,1R,2,1; 1,2,1R,2; 2,1,2,1R.

It was invented by Vivian Yeiser Laramore, and she used lines of four feet, although it is possible that others will vary this. An example is:

And we have reached the end, you say:	1 R
There is a limit to all things,	2
And each can go his separate way,	1
Forgetting joint adventurings.	2

Life has grown dulling tiny stings,		2
And we have reached the end, you say,	1 R	
Each with sick soul that clings, and clings		2
As if to hamper till doomsday.	1	

Too much "love, honor and obey,"	1	
A role not fit for queens and kings. . . .		2
And we have reached the end, you say—	1 R	
(How dreadfully the cold word rings!)		2

Have you forgot that spring of springs,		2
And our high flights, that gathered gay	1	
Stardust to glitter on our wings?		2
—And we have reached the end, you say!	1 R	

Against an Ultimatum, CLEMENT WOOD

The Sonnette—The sonnette was derived by Sherman Ripley from an old Italian form, the *sonnetto*. It consists of seven 5-foot iambic lines, rhymed 1,2,2,1; 3,2,3. An example is:

Out of the silver dark incredible white	1	
Mountains, man-shaped, tower over the plain;		2
Not rough and jagged, as if the earth's pain		2
Had spewed them forth, but straight-lined, with no slight	1	
Departure from the measuring-rod. They loom	3	
More stark than earth's raw hills. We shrink, and strain		2
Away from each gross undying tomb.	3	

Pyramids by Moonlight, ALVIN WINSTON

Other Forms—Much ingenuity has been expended in varying the syllabic count of the hokku, tanka, and cinquain. For those who wish to use them, see page 397, for the chief variations.

In addition to the variations (page 398) on the syllable-count poems, including Mr. Northe's sixty-seven forms, we also have:

The Paean, a form invented by Evelyn M. Watson. It has thirteen lines, rhymed 1,2,1,2,3,3,3; 1,2,3,4,4,4. The opening quatrain is iambic pentameter, followed by a brief triply-rhymed tercet. A couplet (1,2) repeats the theme, followed by a brief echo (3), and a terminal triply-rhymed tercet in iambic pentameter. Iambic hexameter can be used instead of pentameter, if desired.

Name	Invented by	Syllable Count	Remarks
Hokku	Japanese	5,7,5	Entirely iambic.
Tanka	Japanese	5,7,5,7,7	
Cinquain	Adelaide Crapsey	2,4,6,8,2	Unless otherwise stated, no verse rhythm required in any of these.
Double Cinquain	Berta Hart Nance	4,8,12,16,4	
Lanterne	Lloyd Frank Merrell	1,2,3,4,1	Arranged in form like a Japanese lantern: a shaped whimsey.
Pensee	Alice Maude Spokes	2,4,7,8,8	A complete thought; strong end words.
Quintet	Mary Owen Lewis	3,5,7,9,3	Strong end words.
Vignette	Flozari Rockwood	2,4,4,6,7,3	Strong end words.
Septet	Mary Owen Lewis	3,5,7,9,7,5,3	
Cameo	Alice Maude Spokes	2,5,8,3,8,7,2	Strong end words.
Sept	Etta Josephean Murfey	1,2,3,4,3,2,1	
Hexaduad	Gee Kaye	2,2,6,6,8,8,4,4,6,6,4,4	Couplet rhymes.
Inverted Hexaduad	Gee Kaye	2,6,8,4,6,4,4,6,4,8,6,2	Couplet rhyme; first two lines transposed for last two.

FORMS INVENTED BY JAMES NEILL NORTHE

(Where indicated, these may be Double (D)—pairs of lines of the same number of syllables; Twin (T), whole pattern repeated; Inverted (I), syllables in second half reversed; or several of these devices may be utilized in the same verses.)

Without Lanterne typography.

Cinquo	1,2,3,4,1	
Shadorma	3,5,3,3,7,5	
Hotan	5,7,5,3,5,3,5,7,5	
Cinquaino	2,8,6,4,2	D, T, I, ID, IT
Quintine	1,3,5,7,9	D, T, I, ID, IT
Quinquina	9,7,5,3,1	D, T, I, ID, IT
Twi-Quin-Sep	3,5,7	All of these hereafter may be also
		D, T, I, ID, IT
Tri-Sep-Quin	3,7,5	
Quin-Tri-Sep	5,3,7	
Quin-Sep-Tri	5,7,3	
Sep-Tri-Quin	7,3,5	
Sep-Quin-Tri	7,5,3	
Double Hokku	5,5,7,7,5,5	
Double Tanka	5,5,7,7,5,5,7,7,7,7	Variations called T, D, DI
		Variations called D, T, I, IT, ID. To give the count for this last,
Inverted Double Tanka	5,5,7,7,5,5,7,7,7,7,7,5,5,7,7,5,5.	

The Raccontino, a form invented by Etta Josephean Murfey, is a poem in couplets. The even-numbered lines are on the same rhyming sound. The terminal words of the odd-numbered lines, taken with the title, tell a brief story (*raccontino*). The number of couplets is unlimited. An example is *Autumn Scherzo,* by the originator of the form:

> When Autumn records
> On the scroll of a leaf
>
> The cycle of life
> And a frost-gendered grief,
>
> The tale of decay
> Holds our senses in fief. . . .
>
> While we thrill to the pain
> Of a beauty too brief.

The raccontino here is: "Autumn scherzo records life, decay, pain."

The Trine, by Evelyn M. Watson, uses three rhymed couplets of any length, followed by single lines using successively their rhyme sounds. The rhyme scheme thus is 1,1,2,2,3,3,1,2,3.

The Quaternion is Miss Watson's similar invention, in units of four, not three. Its rhyme scheme is 1,1,2,2,3,3,4,4,1,2,3,4.

The Donata, also by Miss Watson, uses the main accented words in the first line of each stanza as the rhyming sounds for the formal rhyme scheme of the stanza.

Muted Rhyme, by Miss Watson, inserts occasional rhyme in a blank verse pattern, this frequently being internal rhyme. It partakes of the nature of Amy Lowell's unsuccessful polyphonic prose.

Closed Rhyme, by Margaret Scott Copeland, has initial rhyme as well as terminal rhyme. The authorship is said to be claimed also by her husband, James Neill Northe.

TYPES OF LIGHT VERSE

Vers de société is smart sophisticated verse, which glides smoothly between the Scylla of seriousness and the Charybdis of boisterous merriment. It never oversteps the bounds of etiquette, and blandly welcomes sentiment, while sternly exiling passion. Here is an example from Sir John Suckling:

> Why so pale and wan, fond lover?
>   Prythee, why so pale?
> Will, if looking well can't move her,
>   Looking ill prevail?
>   Prythee, why so pale?
>
> Why so dull and mute, young sinner?
>   Prythee, why so mute?
> Will, when speaking well can't win her,
>   Saying nothing do't?
>   Prythee, why so mute?
>
> Quit, quit, for shame! this will not move,
>   This cannot take her;
> If of herself she will not love,
>   Nothing can make her:
>   The Devil take her!

There is always present an overtone of courtliness, like the Provençal verse. Pope's *Rape of the Lock* is an extended example. Other noted users of this type of verse include Herrick, Swift, Thomas Moore, Praed, Thackeray, Calverley, the English revivers of the ballade and rondeau, Dorothy Parker, and Samuel Hoffenstein.

Occasional verse is verse written for some especial occasion, and may have any mood and treatment.

Satirical verse is verse ridiculing any customs, manners and beliefs of which the poet disapproves. It ranges from the classic onslaughts of Juvenal, Horace, Voltaire, Pope, Dryden, and Byron, to frothy modern light verse. At times it uses dialect to advantage, as in James Russell Lowell's *Bigelow Papers*.

Humorous verse and *witty verse* are merely humor and wit dressed up in the devices of verse. Humorous verse ranges from the buffooneries of *Midsummer Night's Dream* and *Tam o' Shanter* to homely favorites such as *Casey at the Bat* and Oliver Wendell Holmes's *The One-Horse Shay*. Witty verse includes the Little Willies already given, and much *vers de société*. An admirable example is Arthur Guiterman's *A Pure Mathematician*:

> Let Poets chant of Clouds and Things
>   In lonely attics!
> A Nobler Lot is his, who clings
>   To Mathematics.

Sublime he sits, no Worldly Strife
   His Bosom vexes,
Reducing all the Doubts of Life
   To Y's and X's.

And naught to him's a Primrose on
   The river's border;
A Parallelopipedon
   Is more in order.

Let Zealots vow to do and dare
   And right abuses!
He'd rather sit at home and square
   Hypothenuses.

Along his straight-ruled paths he goes
   Contented with 'em,
The only Rhythm that he knows,
   A Logarithm.

Punning verse is witty verse marked by puns. Thomas Hood was the chief user of this form in English, as in *Faithless Nelly Gray,* where every stanza presented its puns:

"Why then," said she, "you've lost the feet
   Of legs in war's alarms,
And now you cannot wear your shoes
   Upon your feats of arms!" . . . .

And there he hung till he was dead
   As any nail in town—
For though distress had cut him up,
   It could not cut him down.

A dozen men sat on his corpse,
   A verdict for to tell;
They went and told the sexton, and
   The sexton tolled the bell!

Much *newspaper chain verse,* in which successive wits add a stanza to the original pattern, is of this type:

When many fiction writers try
   Their thoughts to give us hot,
We get e-rot-ic novels, with
   The accent on the rot.
             Lippincott's Magazine

When some hair-dressers seek to give
   Us hair to fit the hat,
We get er-rat-ic coiffures, with
   The accent on the rat.
             Boston Traveler

If I were a copy-reader, forced
  To suffer such attacks,
Some poet would get an ax-sent, with
  The accent on the ax.
Lippincott's Magazine

Nonsense verse is verse which substitutes nonsense for common sense. Lewis Carroll is famous for it, as in the *Jabberwocky* from *Through the Looking-Glass:*

'Twas brillig, and the slithy toves
  Did gyre and gimble in the wabe;
All mimsy were the borogoves,
  And the mome raths outgrabe.

"Beware the Jabberwock, my son!
  The jaws that bite, the claws that catch!
Beware the Jubjub bird, and shun
  The frumious Bandersnatch!"

He took his vorpal sword in hand:
  Long time the manxsome foe he sought—
Then rested he by the Tumtum tree,
  And stood awhile in thought.

And, as in uffish thought he stood,
  The Jabberwock, with eyes of flame,
Came whiffling through the tulgey wood,
  And burbled as it came!

One, two! One, two! And through and through
  The vorpal blade went snicker-snack!
He left it dead, and with its head
  He went galumphing back.

"And hast thou slain the Jabberwock?
  Come to my arms, my beamish boy!
O frabjous day! Callooh! Callay!"
  He chortled in his joy.

'Twas brillig, and the slithy toves
  Did gyre and gimble in the wabe.
All mimsy were the borogoves,
  And the mome raths outgrabe.

The lengthier *Hunting of the Snark* is probably the masterpiece in English of nonsense verse. Much of Edward Lear, as *The Pobble That Had No Toes, The Jumblies,* and *The Dong with a Luminous Nose,* and most of W. S. Gilbert's *Bab Ballads,* come within this category. This is one of the most difficult fields in verse in which to achieve success.

Dialect verse is verse written in any dialect, such as Negro, Irish, German, French-Canadian, and so on. Its more usual moods are the sentimental, as in *Mighty Lak a Rose,* and the humorous or witty. In Negro dialect, the writings of Irwin Russell, Paul Lawrence Dunbar, Belle R. Harrison, and my own group including *The Glory Road,* are outstanding. Here is *General Work,* from this group:

> You lookin' fuh a couple fuh gin'ral wu'k?
> Lawd, boss, mah wife is de fines' cook—
> Plain, or fancy, or out of a book.
> Her beaten biscuits is slick as slick,
> An' her rolls is light, an' her batty-cakes thick!
> Her cakes is sump'n' dey don' make no mo',
> F'um angel-food to Lady Baltimo'.
> She's a swell wash-lady; an' she sho' kin clean
> Lak nobody else you ever seen.
> She's a fu's'-rate nu'ss; she can men' an' sew,
> An' you oughta see her make a gyarden grow!
> She kin wait on table, too, fu's'-class,
> An'————
>
> Me? I'm handy at mowin' grass.
> Can us do yo' gin'ral wu'k?

Good dialect verse is tricky to write. To begin with, the full dialectic pronunciation cannot as a rule be given on all words; or the product would be unintelligible to most readers. A Negro or a white Southerner might, under proper circumstances, say "Ah mo'nuh" or "Gwuh' f'm yuh"—and how would the reader know, without explanation, that these expressions mean "I'm going to" and "Go away from here"? There must, then, be a compromise in the writing: enough of the dialect must be given to plant in the reader's mind a clear impression of the character speaking, but *not* so much that it mystifies and repels. There is one important warning. Much dialect verse is written in this general technique:

> Sum niggers iz peculyer,
> I reitteratez agen;
> They mus' cum f'um Atlanta
> An' not from Bummin'ham.

Here *sum* is no dialect pronunciation of *some,* but the phonetic spelling indicating proper pronunciation. The same is true of *iz* for *is, peculyer* for *peculiar, reitteratez* for *reiterates, cum* for

come, and *agen* for *again.* This might be an example of somebody's misspelling. But written dialect is as much a matter of the
accurate *sounds* of mispronunciation as rhyme is a matter of
accurate sound. The example of bad grammar, "niggers is," could
properly come under dialect; but not the phonetic spelling of
words pronounced alike by the characters and all users of correct
English. Again, why *f'um* and *from* in the same poem? Consistency
is no vice here. This is as inept a usage as using *you* and *thou*
to refer to the same person in a poem. *Mus', f'um, an'* and *Bum-
min'ham* alone stand out as dialect properly used here.

In writing dialect verse, it is important to get the actual speech
rhythms and typical conversational phrases of the characters, as
well as the correct phonetic spelling of words mispronounced
by the character. To give the proper dialect effect, care should
be taken to include some of the words in emphatic places among
those thus in the dialect: as in a refrain, for instance. This applies
to all dialects.

Another method is to write in the idiom, without the phonetic
misspellings at all; and leave it to the reader to insert the dialect,
in his reading. This was done by Vachel Lindsay in *The Congo*
and *Simon Legree,* and more effectively by James Weldon Johnson, in his Negro sermons in *God's Trombones.* Here is a typical
passage:

> And God said: Go down, Death, go down,
> Go down to Savannah, Georgia,
> Down in Yamacraw,
> And find Sister Caroline.
> She's borne the burden and heat of the day,
> She's labored long in my vineyard,
> And she's tired,—
> She's weary—
> Go down, Death, and bring her to me.

The reader can read this straight, letting the mere idiom of the
Negro preacher give the overtone of his spoken dialect; or he can
insert the dialect. Either way would be as effective as if *Jawja,
Gawd, fin',* and *Cal'line* had been used. To one unfamiliar with
the dialect, this method would not be fully effective.

Parody, in verse, is an imitation of another example of verse,
usually with intent to burlesque it. Carolyn Wells differentiates
between its three stages:

1. Word-rendering, the substitution of such words in the original pattern as will replace the serious motives of the original with a trivial or frivolous one.

This line from a parody of Gray's celebrated *Elegy*, by Gelett Burgess and Burges Johnson, is an outstanding example.

> The short and simple flannels of the poor.

Only one word is altered here: "annals" to "flannels"; yet this makes the parody line more memorable than the original. The effectiveness of this parody depends upon how well known the poem being parodied is; and on the width of the chasm between the original serious meaning and the new frivolous one. Similar word-renderings would be the chestnut popularization of Mark Antony's famous funeral oration from *Julius Caesar,* commencing:

> Friends, Romans, countrymen, lend me your ears;
> I will return them next Saturday,

clear down to such variants as,

> To sneeze or not to sneeze, that is the question,

and other amusing embroideries of familiar poems.

2. Form-rendering, imitating the entire style of the author; preferably of an author with mannerisms.

Alvin Winston's *Recessional: 1938; after Rudyard Kipling's Recessional: 1897,* is of this type:

> God of our Incomes, known of old
> As something, before '29,
> Beneath whose nodding we behold
> Dividends fail and bonds decline,
> Lord God of Costs, please let us get
> Some income yet, some income yet!
>
> Prosperity's gay spending dies;
> Dictators come, as kings depart;
> Our budget's all self-sacrifice,
> As sales drag bottom on the chart.
> Lord God of Costs, please let us get
> Some income yet, some income yet!
>
> For jobs, we look to WPA;
> Relief grows gross, and sinks with graft;
> Lo, all our boom of yesterday

Is one with Hoover and with Taft.
Judge of our Paychecks, let us get
Some income yet, some income yet!

As Congress chants "Hail to the Chief!"
Fascists and Nazis hiss and sting;
The universe is On Relief,
And Bennie Goodman turns on swing.
Lord God of Costs, please let us get
Some income yet, some income yet!

If labor goes upon a souse
As Communist or CIO,
And leaves Mae West and Micky Mouse
For lie-down strikes fortissimo,
Lord God of Costs, please let us get
Some income yet, some income yet!

For hopeless heart that puts his trust
In more Relief and less man's work,
Until the whole damn country's bust,
With no ambition but to shirk,
From panaceas all absurd
Thy mercy on thy people, Lord.

Amen.

To be effective, a form-rendering parody should be faithful to the full form of the poem it parodies; and usually gains by repeating even the same rhyming sounds, where this is possible.

3. Sense-rendering, utilizing both the author's style and his typical themes, carried out as he would have used them, but subtly exaggerating both style and theme.

This type of parody is often used effectively by taking as its theme or text some familiar incident or verse, and developing it as various poets would have used it. Here are typical examples from my *The Jack-and-Jiliad:*

Alexander Pope Ouijahs This Improvement

A swain and nymph who tended lowing kine
Mounted at eve a hill's embosked incline,
With garlanded receptacle, to bring
The vital fluid from th' enamelled spring.
The fountain's brink no sooner did they gain,
Than down they were dejected to the plain,
Jack with contused poll, and luckless Joan
An animated avalanche of moan.
Homeward they wended them 'neath callous skies

With lengthening re-ululated cries.
'Tis thus that youth essays th' inviting goal,
And mourns too late, alas, the stumbling sole.

Carl Sandburg Slings It in Slang

I wish I had never seen you, Jill.
I wish I had never asked to take you
To the Annual Clambake of the teameos.
I wish you had never asked me to leave
That bunch of slobs of the half-baked West
To climb the hill for a bucket of water
To make pink lemonade for them bums.
    I wish we never went.
    I wish we never fell
    And bust the union bucket—
    It set me back a dollar;
    And smashed my new straw crown—
    It bled me one forty-nine.

Robert Frost Delivers it Drily

Something inspired his tired feet to stumble;
And she, who clutched his hand, without a grumble
Fell too. They picked him up and brought him in,
As pale as cellar straw. *She* didn't skin
A single finger; but the boy was stiff.
The doctor came. Jack breathed. Doctor said, "If
You're careless twice—" Jack brushed away some dirt.
" 'Twasn't the fall, but falling first, that hurt."

Elinor Wylie Skims It Thin

She tends green bruises
On Jack and herself;
The poultice oozes
All over the elf.

His freckled head is double
Its usual size;
A sharp straw of stubble
Punctures her eyes.

Her smile is blurry
Where goblins creep. . . .
She should worry!
Water is cheap.

From T. S. Eliot's "The Waste Water"

"What is left of our jug of limpid aqua?"
    Nothing again nothing.

[407]

"Do
"You mean nothing? Do you taste nothing?
    Ain't you ever learnt
"Nothing?"
                    I learnt
They made themselves water, into which they Houdinied.
O O O O that TSEliotic rag,
So intellectual,
But hardly perpetual.
HURRY UP PLEASE ITS BUST
HURRY UP PLEASE ITS BUST

Edna St. Vincent Millay Brings the Singing Children to the Spring's Edge

Up through the bushes, upon a foggy day,
Jack and Jill went climbing up the steepest way;
And Jack had a bucket, and Jill a spray of brier,
And the sun rose dripping, a bucketfull of fire.

Up to the spring-edge—when Jack had a stumble,
And Jill, a-clutching wildly on his arm, began to tumble,
And Jack broke his cranium, and worse luck was Jill's,
And they gave all their money for the doctor bills.

Edwin Arlington Robinson Muddies It

Yes, yes—the Cricket is no harbinger,
And Spring's a season gone before its start.
I shall not weed the nettles, with the art
That asks the rooted pyramid to stir.
Take Jill, now; could you really censure her
For such a vagrancy of hand and heart
That could not soothe a joy nor rasp a smart,
Nor doff a robe of scentless miniver?

Yet Jill was less than this; for when the flood
Plunged him to his indubitable doom,
And bade her shred the echo of a tomb,
She knew that stream and soil, in fine, were mud. . . .
And was she more than what she must profess
By being so? Or was she not? No . . . . Yes.

Mosaic or *composite verse* is verse in which the lines are selected from one poet or more, and rearranged into a new pattern, serious or amusing. Here is a mosaic verse, in the Rubaiyat quatrain, composed of lines from Shakespeare's sonnets:

I have no precious time at all to spend
Than that which on thy humour doth depend—
    A bliss in proof; and, proved, a very woe:
So do our minutes hasten to their end.

Gentle thou art, and therefore to be won.
My mistress' eyes are nothing like the sun;
  And yet, by heaven, I think my love as rare;
Now see what good turn eyes for eyes have done!

How careful was I, when I took my way!
The worst was this: my love was my decay.
  Such is my love, to thee I so belong,
That time will come and take my love away.

Sometime all full with feasting on thy sight,
Thy edge should blunter be than appetite,
  And would corrupt my saint to be a devil,
Who are as black as hell, as dark as night.

The curious may locate these lines in Sonnets lvii, xcii, cxxix, lx; xli, cxxx, cxxx, xxiv; xlviii, lxxx, lxxxviii, lxiv; and lxxv, lvi, cxliv, cxlvii.

Macaronic verse consists of a mingling of two or more languages. Here is a classic example:

> In tempus old a hero lived,
>   Qui loved puellae deux;
> He ne pouvait pas quite to say
>   Which one amabat mieux.

Appreciation of this is restricted to those familiar with the various languages included.

Archaic verse is verse written in or parodying the speech of some earlier period, as in this rather slug-footed limerick classic:

> When that Seinte George hadde sleyne ye draggon,
> He sate him downe furninst a flaggon;
>   And, wit ye well,
>   It soon befell
> He had a bien pleasaunt jag on.

Shaped whimsies are verses whose typographical set-up follows the theme. Here is the famous *Song of the Decanter,* by Warfield Creath Richardson, which enjoyed a wide, and at times anonymous, repute as an argument for temperance:

SONG OF THE DECANTER

There was an old decanter
and its mouth was gaping
wide; the rosy wine had
ebbed away and left
its crystal side: and
the wind went
humming —
humming up
and down: the
wind it flew,
and through
the reed-like
hollow neck
the wildest
notes it blew.
I placed it in
the window,
where the blast
was blowing free, and
fancied that its pale mouth
sang the queerest strains to me.
"They tell me — puny conquerors! the
Plague has slain his ten, and war his
hundred thousands of the very best of men;
but I"—'twas thus the Bottle spake—"but I have
conquered more than all your famous conquerors, so
feared and famed of yore. Then come, ye youths and
maidens all, come drink from out my cup, the beverage
that dulls the brain, and burns the spirits up; that
puts to shame your conquerors that slay their scores
below; for this has deluged millions with the lava
tide of woe. Tho' in the path of battle darkest
streams of blood may roll; yet while I kill
the body, I have damned the very soul.
The cholera, the plague, the sword
such ruin never wrought, as I
in mirth or malice on
the innocent have
brought. And
still I breathe
upon them, and
they shrink before my
breath, while year by year my
thousands go my dusty way of death."

Many of the shaped whimsies of Aimee Jackson Short are as
amusing as they are deftly wrought. Here is—

THE UMBRELLA MAN

One
day in May when Chamberlain
went out for exercise, he blithely strolled
down Oxford Street, beneath sun-brightened skies. But
suddenly he felt a qualm—what was it he forgot? Could he
have failed to tell the king about the Irish plot; or could he
have some conference set for this very hour; and did he warn the
royal guards to double guard the Tower? Now while he pondered many
things, a cloud shut out the sun, but Chamberlain kept wondering what
he had or hadn't done; until a downpour dashed all thoughts of state
and protocol. "By Jove! I recollect," he cried, "I left my parasol!"
"Ah!"   "Ah"   "Ah"   "Ah"   "Ah"
!   !   !   !   !

"
C
h
e
w
!
        !"
Ah
    !   ew
    Ch-

Typographical oddities in verse include, in addition, such
devices as having certain lines, as the terminals in each stanza,
represent the way a person walks when sober, and when intoxi-
cated; of when he falls down; or anything else that ingenuity
can make the type represent. Franklin P. Adams, most famous
of America's witty "colyumists," utilized in various verses all
of the variously named fonts of type. He utilized the signs on
the railroad time-table similarly, in *Signal Service:*

Time-table! Terrible and hard
  To figure! At some station lonely
We see this sign upon the card:
*

* Train 20: Stops on signal only.

We read thee wrong; the untrained eye
  Does not see always with precision.
The train we thought to travel by
†

Again, undaunted, we look at
  The hieroglyphs, and as a rule a
Small double dagger shows us that
‡

And when we take a certain line
  On Tues., Wednes., Thurs., Fri., Sat., or Monday,
We're certain to detect the sign:
§

And this is only half of what F. P. A. has to say on this fascinating form of puzzle.

Acrostic verse is verses where some specified group of letters—as, the opening letters of each line; or the closing ones; or the first letter of the first line, the second of the second, the third of the third, etc.; or letters arranged otherwise—name a person, or convey a message. Many of the verses of Edgar A. Poe and his contemporaries used this device. Here is an acrostic by the early American versifier George Washington, better known as president:

    *F*rom your bright sparkling Eyes I was undone;
    *R*ays, you have; more transparent than the Sun,
    *A*midst its glory in the rising Day
    *N*one can you equal in your bright array;
    *C*onstant in your calm and unspotted Mind;
    *E*qual to all, but will to none Prove kind,
    *S*o knowing, seldome one so Young, you'll Find,
    *A*h! woe's me, that I should Love and conceal
    *L*ong have I wished, but never dared reveal,
    *E*ven though severely Love's Pains I feel;
    *X*erxes that great, wasn't free from Cupid's Dart,
    *A*nd all the great Heroes, felt the smart.

Verse has also been employed to contain riddles, charades, anagrams, palindromes (reversible messages, reading the same both ways, such as *Madam, I'm Adam; Able was I ere I saw Elba;* and the more amazing *Paget saw an Irish tooth, sir, in a waste gap*), and other puzzles; in writing alphabets in verse; in using echo

† Runs only on North-west division.
‡ Train does not stop at Ashtabula.
§ $10 extra fare ex. Sunday.

verses, whose terminal lines echo, often with a change of meaning, the conclusion of the preceding line, as in this stanza from a sestina with echo by Barnaby Barnes (1569-1609):

Echo! What shall I do to my Nymph when I go to behold her?
ECHO: Hold her!
So dare I not! lest She should think that I make her a prey then.
ECHO: Pray then!
Yea, but at me, She will take scorn, proceeded of honour!
ECHO: On her!
Me bear will She (with her, to deal so saucily) never!
ECHO: Ever!
Yea, but I greatly fear She will have pure thoughts to refuse such.
ECHO: Few such.
Then will I venture again more bold, if you warn me to do so!
ECHO: Do so!

There are tongue-twisters in verse, such as the familiar one from *Mother Goose:*

Peter Piper picked a peck of pickled peppers;
A peck of pickled peppers Peter Piper picked.
If Peter Piper picked a peck of pickled peppers,
Where's the peck of pickled peppers Peter Piper picked?

There are also trick lines which alter their meaning, when read differently: as the second half of the first line with the first half of the next, and so on.

VII

MISCELLANEOUS

Now that we have surveyed thoroughly the problems of what verse and poetry are; the vocabulary of poetry; the types of poetry; its repetitional devices of rhythm, accent and sound; the patterns by which lines are grouped into stanzas; and, finally, the pattern of the poem as a whole, including the fixed forms, a few final matters remain to be considered.

FIGURATIVE LANGUAGE IN POETRY

Figurative language is as much at home in prose as in poetry. The essence of most figurative language is likening one thing to another. To see such a resemblance, the mind has to make a generalization, or recognition of kinship between two or more things; and the power of generalization. Lester Ward says, is the highest power that the intellect displays. Man's method toward mental comprehension of truth is the method of generalization: seeing what resemblances exist in things apparently remote and different. As when Newton observed an apple falling, and deduced from it that the same force that pulled the apple down toward the earth (and, in small, the earth upward toward the apple) functioned throughout the solar system and the universes, and explained their positions and movements. Such generalizations appeal to the esthetic or the mental emotions; but these are strong, too, and need the rousing effect of generalizations and figurative language in poetry. Poetry without them tends to be dull, flat, and two-dimensional. Only figurative language at times can afford the effect of three- or more dimensional existences.

The simpler figures, as applied to poetry, will be indicated here.

1. A *simile* is an expressed comparison.

As idle *as* a painted ship
Upon a painted ocean. . . .

I pass, *like* night, from land to land.
The Rime of the Ancient Mariner, COLERIDGE

The presence of the *as* and the *like* make these similes.

2. A *metaphor* is an unexpressed or implied comparison.

Blossomed the lovely stars, the forget-me-nots of the angels.
Evangeline, HENRY WADSWORTH LONGFELLOW

(Pelican fishing), feathered plunging thunderbolt.
Pelicans Fishing, CLEMENT WOOD

Many metaphors use the verbs to imply the comparison:

The ship *ploughs* the sea. (As if it were a plough.)
The very deep *did rot.* (As if the ocean could rot.)

At times the implicit comparison is in the adjective:

A marble brow (that is, a brow like marble.)
A copper sky.

It can appear in some use of the noun:

A volley of oaths.
The realms of gold.

The danger here is in mixing inharmonious metaphors. Yet we have the classic example from *Hamlet,*

Or to take arms against a sea of troubles.

3. An *allegory* is a presentation of a meaning implied, but not expressly stated. It is in essence a prolonged metaphor, in which actions symbolize other actions, and often the characters are types or personifications. Bunyan's *Pilgrim's Progress* and Spenser's *Faerie Queene* are famous examples. *Fables* belong to this group, since the acts and words attributed to animals or inanimate objects symbolize human beings or human relationships.

4. *Personification* is that form of metaphor in which life and human attributes are attributed to inanimate objects, plants and animals, and forces of nature.

Love took up the glass of Time, and turned it in
his glowing hands.
Locksley Hall, ALFRED TENNYSON

[415]

Apostrophe is that form of personification in which the personified object (or, a dead or absent person) is directly addressed:

Milton, thou shouldst be living at this hour!
WILLIAM WORDSWORTH

O Death, where is thy sting.

Lafayette, we are here!

5. *Metonomy* is the use of one word for another that it suggests; as, the effect for the cause, the cause for the effect, the sign for the thing signified, the container for the thing contained, and the like. A hackneyed instance can lose all force:

The kettle is boiling.

Here we accept without thought that the meaning is that the water in the kettle is boiling. Common examples of metonomy are:

The pen is mightier than the sword.

To tend the homely slighted shepherd's trade.
Lycidas, JOHN MILTON

The shepherd's trade here, of course, refers to poetry. *Synechdoche* is an instance of metonomy in which the part is named for the whole, or the whole for the part: *heads* of cattle, factory *hands,* a fleet of ten *sail,* I like to read *Keats,* a man's own *roof.*

6. *Irony* is saying one thing and meaning its opposite. Examples,

For Brutus is an honorable man.
Julius Caesar, WILLIAM SHAKESPEARE

My, what a George Washington *you* turned out to be!

7. *Euphemism* is a figure of enlargement, meaning literally "speaking well of a thing." Thus the Greeks called the Furies the "Eumenides" or well-wishers, in an effort to earn their good will. Similarly, Christians refer to the devil as "the old Nick," "the old gentleman," "old Scratch," and use other placating terms. A different motive appears in calling a spade "an agricultural implement," in an effort to elegantize the language. The use of such euphemisms as "daughters of joy," "street-walkers," "girls on the turf" and the like, for prosti-

tutes, showed the same tendency, in some cases coupled with the same Mrs. Grundyism that calls syphilis and gonorrhea "social diseases." Euphemisms for death are common, from "passed on," "departed," "went west," "in Abraham's bosom," "is with the angels," "is in his final sleep," to the more humorous "kicked the bucket" or "croaked."

8. Another figure of enlargement is *hyperbole*—exaggeration for the purpose of emphasis. Poetry is full of examples:

> Two of the fairest stars in all the heaven,
> Having some business, do entreat her eyes
> To twinkle in their spheres till they return.
> What if her eyes were there, they in her head?
> The brightness of her cheek would shame those stars,
> As daylight doth a lamp; her eyes in heaven
> Would through the airy regions stream so bright
> That birds would sing, and think it were not night.
>
> *Romeo and Juliet*, WILLIAM SHAKESPEARE

> Here's the smell of the blood still: all the perfumes
> of Arabia will not sweeten this little hand. . . .

> Will all great Neptune's ocean wash this blood
> Clean from my hand? No; this my hand will rather
> The multitudinous seas incarnadine,
> Making the green one red.
>
> *Macbeth*, WILLIAM SHAKESPEARE

Here we have frantic poetic exaggeration at its greatest. The height of the poetry achieved is often measured by the leap above reality that the hyperbole takes.

9. *Climax* is a figure of arrangement, by which words, phrases, clauses, sentences, or longer divisions of composition, are so arranged that the thought mounts continuously in intensity to its close.

> Many a time and oft
> Have you climb'd up to walls and battlements,
> To towers and windows, yea, to chimney-tops,
> Your infants in your arms, and there have sat
> The live-long day, with patient expectation,
> To see great Pompey pass the streets of Rome. . . .
> And do you now put on your best attire?
> And do you now cull out a holiday?
> And do you now strew flowers in his way
> That comes in triumph over Pompey's blood?
> Be gone!
>
> *Julius Caesar*, WILLIAM SHAKESPEARE

[417]

Anti-climax is the same figure, with the concluding statement made weak in intensity, often to the point of ridiculousness. Samuel Hoffenstein, in *Poems in Praise of Practically Nothing,* arrives at his anti-climax when desired, even if the course leading to it has digressions:

> Your life's a wreck; you're tired of living,
> Of lending, spending, borrowing, giving;
> Of doubt and fear, of hope and question,
> Of women, children, and digestion;
> There isn't a single dream you cherish—
> You simply pine and pray to perish.
> You haven't the nerve to take bichloride,
> But you stay up nights till you're gaunt and sore-eyed;
> You don't eat greens, as the doctors tell you,
> And you drink the very worst they sell you;
> You've earned, at least, let's say, cirrhosis—
> And what do you get for it? Halitosis!

A more consistent example, in prose, would be:

> This man robbed as a child, stole from his parents, became a gangster, murdered hundreds of men, and always played golf on Sunday.

10. Rhetorical questions are classed as a figure of speech, under the name of *Interrogation.* They are questions in which the speaker implies an answer, often in the negative; and in which no answer at all is really expected. Examples are found throughout Mark Anthony's funeral oration in *Julius Caesar:*

> Did this in Caesar seem ambitious?

and as the refrain line to many ballades, as Villon's most famous one:

> Where are the snows of yesteryear?

Poetry requires the illumination of apt and original figurative language, to waken its maximum emotional response. Another effective device is, in place of the direct statement, an *allusiveness,* which implies figurative language. Here is Elinor Wylie's *The Crooked Stick:*

First Traveler: It's the sort of crooked stick that shepherds know.
Second Traveler: Some one's loss.
First Traveler: Bend it, you make of it a bow. Break it, a cross.
Second Traveler: But it's all grown over with moss!

Here the implications—the shepherd's crook, the bow, the Christian cross, and the moss indicating disuse, broaden the simple wording immeasurably. She achieves the same effect at the end of *A Crowded Trolley Car:*

> One man stands as free men stand,
> As if his soul might be
> Brave, unspoken; see his hand
> Nailed to an oaken tree.

She does not mean any physical nailing: only the allusion to the Christ story, as if the man had suffered similar spiritual martyrdom, as the price of standing like a free man. Again,

> I was, being human, born alone;
> I am, being woman, hard beset;
> I live by squeezing from a stone
> The little nourishment I get.

The allusion here is to the unspoken, "And if a man ask for bread, will you give him a stone?" Or Robinson's magnificent evocation, at the end of *Eros Turannos,* of an embroidered version of the story of the Gadarenean swine:

> Meanwhile, we do no harm; for they
> That with a god have striven,
> Not hearing much of what we say,
> Take what the god has given;
> Though like waves breaking it may be,
> Or like a changed familiar tree,
> Or like a stairway to the sea
> Where down the blind are driven.

Take the allusion to *Midsummer Night's Dream* in *Ben Jonson Entertains a Man from Stratford:*

> Shakespeare, who alone of us
> Will put an ass's head in Fairyland
> As he would add a shilling to more shillings,
> All most harmonious,

or the more dreadful passage in *Cassandra,*

> And though your very flesh and blood
> Be what your Eagle eats and drinks,
> You'll praise him for the best of birds,
> Not knowing what the Eagle thinks.

Samuel A. DeWitt uses a device as strong, in the historical allusion in *To Thaddeus C. Sweet,* dealing with the ousting of Socialist assemblymen from the New York State legislature:

> For what you did and what you said
> Farmers dropped their scythes and bled;
> And for the puppets in round rows
> Bare feet tracked the olden snows—
> Feet that wrote for tyrant George
> A bloody print at Valley Forge;
> And you forget that there are men
> Glad to march that way again.

A hint, a fugitive reference, may be all that is needed to open the reader's mind and heart to a resemblance that emphasizes the spoken message of poem or verses immeasurably. It is devices like this that give wings to your words.

WORD MUSIC IN POETRY

The most intangible trait which great verse and poetry must possess has been left to the last; and no critic ever improved on Pope's wording of it:

> True ease in writing comes from art, not chance,
> As those move easiest who have learned to dance.
> 'Tis not enough no harshness gives offense;
> The sound must seem an echo to the sense.
> *An Essay on Criticism*

This last line should be calligraphed in letters of gold, and used as the poet's constant wall-motto: "The sound must seem an echo to the sense." But to explain how this must be done throughout your verse is not easy.

The practice of the masters aids us. Here Pope's very use of the word *harshness* illustrates the whole thesis; the word is as harsh as its meaning. He proceeds,

> Soft is the strain when Zephyr gently blows,
> And the smooth stream in smoother numbers flows;

and then, a sudden change—

> But when loud surges lash the sounding shore,
> The hoarse rough verse should like the torrent roar.

He proceeds with words tense and panting with muscular strain:

> When Ajax strives some rock's vast weight to throw,
> The line too labours, and the words move slow.

The shrewd use of spondees here supplements the use of such harsh knotty words as *Ajax, rock's, vast*. This alters swiftly to the gracility and speed of winged beauty:

> Not so when swift Camilla scours the plain,
> Flies o'er the unbending corn, and skims along the main.

The word *Camilla* dances as surely as *Ajax* retards and strains. The sound must seem an echo to the sense. . . .

We find the spirit of this sung more lightly in the first song of Prince Nanki-Poo, in W. S. Gilbert's *The Mikado*. To demonstrate how differing word-usage and tone-music may be used to express differing emotions, the minstrel prince—and he speaks for each one of us—calls upon the inner evocatory qualities and overtones in the words themselves, to evoke the desired mood in the hearer and reader. Here all the repetition devices in sounds are called upon, including one not hitherto considered: the repetition of familiar groups of words, to evoke emotions they have already stored up in previous usage. In delicious light verse, the Mikado's son proceeds to establish this:

> A wandering minstrel I—
> A thing of shreds and patches,
> Of ballads, songs and snatches,
> And dreamy lullaby!
> My catalogue is long,
> Through every passion ranging,
> And to your humors changing,
> I tune my simple song!

First we have a dolorous strain that Ophelia might have moaned, while dirging her way to her watery grave:

> Are you in sentimental mood?
> I'll sigh with you,
> Oh, willow, willow!
> On maiden's coldness do you brood?
> I'll do so, too—
> Oh, willow, willow!

From this he snaps into jingoistic patriotism:

> But if patriotic sentiment is wanted,
> I've patriotic ballads cut and dried;
> For where'er our country's banner may be planted,
> All other local banners are defied!

Suddenly his mood goes chantey:

> And if you call for a song of the sea,
> We'll heave the capstan round,
> With a yeo heave-ho, for the wind is free,
> Her anchor's a-trip and her helm's a-lee,
> Hurrah for the homeward bound!
> Yeo-ho—heave-ho,
> Hurrah for the homeward bound!

The sound, as an echo to the sense. . . . The onomatopoetic theory of the origin of much of our language—that the word imitates a sound in nature—is clearly illustrated by many words:

> coo, hiss, hum, drone, bump, thud, smash, buzz, tingle, chatter, bicker, squeak, murmur, scream, shriek, bubble, gargle, growl, howl, roar, slash, lash, crash.

These are mainly words denoting sound; but the list is infinitely longer, and involves many derivatives from all languages, where the original sound-echoing nature of the word has veered immensely in meaning, although still with overtones of the original sound. Classic poetry furnishes two famous lines illustrating this: Homer's line describing a heavy stone rolling down a mountainside, and Vergil's description of a horse's hoofs galloping over a hard plain. Far more informative are Pope's lines, such as the one describing the immense labor of Sisiphus,

> Up the high hill he heaves a huge round stone,

and that giving the crashing debacle:

> Thunders impetuous down, and smokes along the ground.

A far greater poet, Shakespeare, in the third line of dying Hamlet's charge to his friend Horatio, clogs the word-sounds artificially so that they must be pronounced to fit the meaning:

> If ever thou didst hold me in thy heart,
> Absent thee from felicity awhile,
> And in this harsh world draw thy breath in pain
> To tell my story.

Milton caught the spirit of this, when he had the gates of Paradise swing welcomingly:

> Heaven opened wide
> Her ever-during gates, harmonious sound
> On golden hinges turning,

contrasted with this entrance to the gates of Hell:

> On a sudden open fly,
> With impetuous recoil and jarring sound,
> The infernal doors; and on their hinges grate
> Harsh thunder.

This use of the word *harsh* in Pope, Shakespeare and now Milton is no accident; the word's tone-music sets the key for the desired emotional response. The harshest line in English verse, deliberately so written, is Browning's famous thought-demanding puzzler:

> Irks care the crop-full bird, frets doubt the maw-crammed beast?

To the extreme contrary is Swinburne's lilting line from one of the choruses to *Atalanta in Calydon:*

> With lisp of leaves and ripple of rain.

Between these two extremes lie most of the rest of English poetry and verse. It is the writer's task to choose, in each instance, in preference, the words whose precise sounds convey the mood and idea he seeks to evoke.

As Sidney Lanier points out in *The Science of English Verse,* obviously *lal lal lal* is easy to pronounce; *bag bag bag* is much more difficult and retarding; while such a line as—

> Thou, stalwart, shouldst stiffest stand

cannot be said rapidly at all. These successive *st* sounds require in each instance an entirely new adjustment of the vocal organs, and necessitate a perceptible interval of time between one *st* and the next. The poet has the whole gamut of consonantal and vowel sounds, flowing and retarding, to choose from. For ordinary purposes, he will choose sounds that melt flowingly into one another. For especial purposes, he will utilize the eruptive and retarding sounds.

A few examples of sounds which perfectly echo the sense they convey may aid. All of *Kubla Khan* illustrates Coleridge's mastery of this evocatory word-magic:

> Through caverns measureless to man
> Down to a sunless sea. . . .

> Five miles meandering with a mazy motion. . . .

> A damsel with a dulcimer
> In a vision once I saw. . . .

> Weave a circle round him thrice,
> And close your eyes with holy dread;
> For he on honey-dew hath fed,
> And drunk the milk of Paradise.

Keats became an enduring master of the same magnificent evocation of the music in words:

> Season of mists and mellow fruitfulness!
> Close bosom-friend of the maturing sun.
>   *To Autumn*

> O what can ail thee, knight-at-arms,
> Alone and palely loitering?
> The sedge has wither'd from the lake,
> And no birds sing.
>   *Ballad: La Belle Dame Sans Merci*

> St. Agnes Eve—ah, bitter chill it was!
> The owl, for all his feathers, was a-cold;
> The hare limp'd trembling through the frozen grass. . . .

> With jellies soother than the creamy curd,
> And lucent syrops, tinct with cinnamon;
> Manna and dates, in argosy transferr'd
> From Fez; and spicéd dainties, every one,
> From silken Samarcand to cedared Lebanon.
>   *The Eve of St. Agnes*

Swinburne, for all of his soporific quality from its overuse, is one of the masters of the language in evoking from words all of the music innate in them:

> Where beyond the extreme sea-wall, and between the remote
>   sea-gates,
> Waste water washes, and tall ships founder, and deep death waits;
> Where, mighty with deepening tides, clad about with the sea as
>   with wings,
> And impelled of invisible tides, and fulfilled of unspeakable things,

White-eyed and poisonous-finned, sharp-toothed and serpentine-
curled,
Rolls, under the whitening wind of the future, the wave of the
world.

Hymn to Proserpine

By the ravenous teeth that have smitten
    Through the kisses that blossom and bud,
By the lips intertwisted and bitten
    Till the foam has a savor of blood,
By the pulse as it rises and falters,
    By the hands as they slacken and strain,
I adjure thee, respond from thine altars,
    Our Lady of Pain.

Dolores

Tennyson is repeatedly as magical—often throughout the pastel
tapestry of *The Idylls of the King,* the tense ballad *The Revenge,*
and most of all in *The Princess* and its songs:

Sweet and low, sweet and low,
    Wind of the western sea,
Low, low, breathe and blow,
    Wind of the western sea!
Over the rolling waters go,
Come from the dying moon, and blow,
    Blow him again to me;
While my little one, while my pretty one, sleeps. . . .

Ah, sad and strange as in dark summer dawns
The earliest pipe of half-awaken'd birds
To dying ears, when unto dying eyes
The casement slowly grows a glimmering square;
So sad, so strange, the days that are no more. . . .

Myriads of rivulets hurrying thro' the lawn,
The moan of doves in immemorial elms,
The murmuring of innumerable bees.

G. K. Chesterton is full of the same appropriate wedding of sound
to sense:

And men brake out of the northern lands,
    Enormous lands alone,
Where a spell is laid upon life and lust
And the rain is changed to a silver dust
    And the sea to a great green stone.

The Ballad of the White Horse

For every tiny town or place
    God made the stars especially;

[425]

> Babies look up with owlish face
> And see them tangled in a tree. . . .
>
>   Likelier across these flats afar,
>   These sulky levels smooth and free,
>   The drums shall crash a waltz of war
>   And Death shall dance with Liberty.
>   Likelier the barricades shall blare
>   Slaughter below and smoke above,
>   And death and hate and hell declare
>   That men have found a thing to love.
>   *Dedication to The Napoleon of Notting Hill*

Dim drums throbbing, in the hills half heard,
Where only on a nameless throne a crownless prince has stirred,

and all the magical rest of *Lepanto*. There was never a more distinguished user of the evocation of the latent tone music in words, to set the key of the mood, than Edgar A. Poe:

> And the Raven, never flitting, still is sitting, still is sitting,
> On the pallid bust of Pallas just above my chamber door;
> And his eyes have all the seeming of a demon's that is dreaming,
> And the lamplight o'er him streaming casts his shadow on the
>   floor;
> And my soul from out that shadow that lies floating on the floor
>   Shall be lifted—nevermore.
>
>   *The Raven*

What these masters did, every versifier must strive to do, to evoke from his words the full magic of which they are the sealed containers. This calls for careful critical analysis, once the verses have been written, of the mood sought to be conveyed throughout; and a careful excision of offending and jarring elements, and a substitution of those words whose tone and overtones evoke the mood desired. For moods come from the emotions; and, where the object is to awaken emotions in a certain direction, are of far more importance than mere mental accuracy. Sooner or later, the mind's best accuracy is discovered to be inaccurate. The emotion's accuracy does not alter.

The extremest instances of letting the sound echo the sense are found in the direction of light verse. Of this kinship is Poe's *The Bells:*

> Hear the sledges with their bells—
>   Silver bells!
> What a world of merriment their melody foretells!

[426]

How they tinkle, tinkle, tinkle
    In the icy air of night,
While the stars, that oversprinkle
All the heavens, seem to twinkle
    With a crystalline delight!

Or Southey's tour-de-force, *How the Water Comes Down at Lodore,*

And thumping and plumping, and bumping and jumping,
And dashing and flashing, and splashing and clashing,
    And so never ending,
    And always descending,
Sounds and motions for ever and ever are blending,
    All at once and all o'er,
    With a mighty uproar,
And this way the water comes down at Lodore.

Much of the appeal of Vachel Lindsay was based upon a use of this device that became exaggerated at times, as in this effort to catch the sound of automobile horns, somewhat as Gershwin did in *An American in Paris:*

Hark to the calm-horn, balm-horn, psalm-horn,
Hark to the faint-horn, quaint-horn, saint-horn. . . .

Hark to the pace-horn, chase-horn, race-horn. . . .
They tour from Memphis, Atlanta, Savanna,
Tallahassee and Texarkana. . . .
Cars from Concord, Niagara, Boston,
Cars from Topeka, Emporia, and Austin. . . .
            The Santa Fé Trail

Oh, the longhorns from Texas,
The jay hawks from Kansas,
The plop-eyed bungaroo and giant giassicus,
The varmint, chipmunk, bugaboo,
The horned toad, prairie-dog and ballyhoo,
From all the newborn states arow,
Bidding the eagles of the west fly on,
Bidding the eagles of the west fly on.
            Bryan, Bryan, Bryan, Bryan

He would trade engender for the red bartender,
He would homage render to the red bartender,
And in ultimate surrender to the red bartender,
He died of the tremens, as crazy as a loon. . . .
The moral, the conclusion, the verdict now you know,
    The saloon must go!
    The saloon must go!
The saloon, the saloon, the saloon must go!

Here at last art is replaced with ineffective artlessness.

But the lesson does not escape us. All verse, all poetry, gain by an actual welding of sound and overtone to the emotions intended to be evoked by the message sought to be conveyed. Poetry requires it, used with shrewd reticence; light verse can gain by a direct and aggressive use of mimetic sounds, or noises imitating the actual noises of things. So it is that the sound echoes truly the sense.

CRAFTSMANSHIP IN THE MASTERS

Three hundred and thirty-three years ago, English ears first heard these words uttered upon a stage:

> Tomorrow, and tomorrow, and tomorrow,
> Creeps in this petty pace from day to day
> To the last syllable of recorded time,
> And all our yesterdays have lighted fools
> The way to dusty death. Out, out, brief candle!
> Life's but a walking shadow, a poor player
> That struts and frets his hour upon the stage
> And then is heard no more; it is a tale
> Told by an idiot, full of sound and fury,
> Signifying nothing.

This quotation from *Macbeth* contains not a single word or phrase which is out of our living speech today. To the extreme contrary, the last volume of a contemporary, George Sterling, *Sonnets to Craig*, contains these word usages:

Opening sonnet: thy, thy, for a space, lest, thing, ere, of all my worship leave no trace, this my heart, thee, against thy snows be set, seraph.

Thereafter: guerdon, elysian hair, dross before thy magic gold, wandereth, lureth, saith, art crueller, nectar of thy bliss, love's gage, ministrant to doom, be found the rose, thy mystic beam, thou dost take, for when 'tis night, 'mid desert sands, a sweet amaze, aught in Paradise, Aye, thou, thy beatific grace, amain, elysian dew, And found them autumn's tawny seeds a few, thou settest, Lo! the abyss, thy like, thy beauty, thine image, thy soul, thy lure, mine art's.

There is the case for the living vocabulary, summed up: with the advocate for the living usage more than three centuries dead; and the spokesman for the dead vocabulary one we have greeted and hobnobbed with. George Sterling was an authentic poet. At least one of his sonnets, the one to the black vulture, earns its way into the anthologies. But this omitted the stock poeticisms that he had been taught were the essence of poetry; and, where these appear, the verse becomes so doughy that man is glad to forget it.

It is not the words that make the poetry, remember; it is their use. When Shakespeare wrote,

> It is a tale
> Told by an idiot, full of sound and fury,
> Signifying nothing,

he lifted *idiot* by his magnificent usage into poetry. When Wordsworth wrote,

> Why bustle thus about your door?
> What means this bustle, Betty Foy?
> Why are you in this mighty fret?
> And why on horseback have you set
> Him whom you love, your Idiot Boy?
> *The Idiot Boy*

the word *idiot* is as unpoetic as the rest of the passage. The living speech, the colloquial, can be magical, poetic, as in this sonnet sestet by John V. A. Weaver:

> It is some lie that under a windswept tree,
> Touching your lips, I touched my vanished youth,
> And found again a young, new ecstasy.
> It is a lie, I say. This—this is Truth!
> Now—I shall rest. For youth and you are gone.
> Tomorrow I shall put my flannels on.

If you are so Victorian that a reference to under-attire awakens your half-ashamed risibilities, you are in the minority today. The majority sees the poignant poetry here.

Edwin Arlington Robinson will be remembered for lines as colloquially magical as:

> The man who had made other men
> As ordinary as arithmetic. . . .

> I'll bet the king had warts or carbuncles,
> Or something wrong in his divine insides,
> To make him wish that Adam had died young. . . .

> I'll have to tell you, brother Bedivere,
> That crowns and orders, and high palaces, . . .
> Will not go rolling down to hell just yet
> Because a pretty woman is a fool. . . .

> Where summer now lay buried, and the first
> Red leaves of autumn, flying silently,
> Became a scattered silence on the grass.

The same poet can sag into lines as incredible bookish as:

> Born with a face
> That on a bullfrog would ensure for life
> The lucubrations of a celibate. . . .
>
> Less to remembering an obscure monition
> Than to confessing an assured renascence.

Robert Frost is the modern master of the use of colloquial idioms and words, which emotion transmutes into pure gold:

> The trial by market everything must come to. . . .

> What to make of a diminished thing. . . .

> The having anything to sell is what
> Is the disgrace in man or state or nation. . . .

> The melancholy of having to count souls
> Where they grow fewer and fewer every year
> Is extreme where they shrink to none at all. . . .

> Good fences make good neighbors. . . .

> The slow smokeless burning of decay. . . .

> We love the things we love for what they are.

For the use of slang, we may go back to Shakespeare:

> So do I still, by these pickets and stealers.

If Hamlet could say this, there is every justification, in its proper usage, for Carl Sandburg's use of it in *Cahoots* and elsewhere:

> Play it across the table.
> What if we steal this city blind?
> If they want anything let 'em nail it down.

We gain, sometimes, by watching the masters at work, and see how their first essays were later altered, to the betterment of the product. For what they did is what we must do. John Livingston Lowes's *Convention and Revolt in Poetry* includes a classic treatment of this. Thus Coleridge, in the full fire and fury of the creation of *The Rime of the Ancient Mariner*, wrote first a stanza,

> The fair breeze blew, the white foam flew,
> The furrow *followed free;*
> We were the first that ever burst
> Into that silent sea.

And then Coleridge's ponderous intellect set to work, and emitted the second line with more scientific accuracy:

> The furrow *stream'd off free.*

A footnote explained that only to those on shore or some other point of vantage did the furrow seem to follow; that, from on shipboard, it clearly seemed to flow away from the ship. Eleven years afterwards, Coleridge restored the line to its first reading, realizing that the line, as first written, was inevitable in music, alliterative, assonantal, and perfect.

Similarly, in Tennyson's early *The Miller's Daughter* these lines appeared:

> I came and lay
> Beneath those gummy chestnutbuds. . . .

> A water-rat from off the bank
> Plunged in the stream. With idle care
> Downlooking through the sedges rank,
> I saw your troubled image there.
> Upon the dark and dimpled beck
> It wandered like a floating light,
> A full fair form, a warm white neck,
> And two white arms—how rosy white!

This, published at the age of twenty-three, met with a barrage of hostile criticism. Ten years later, the poem reappeared. The gummy chestnutbuds had gone: how could their gumminess add to the poetic feeling?

> I came and sat
> Below the chestnuts, when their buds
> Were glistening to the breezy blue. . . .

> Then leapt a trout. In lazy mood
> I watch'd the little circles die;
> They past into the level flood,
> And there a vision caught my eye;
> The reflex of a beauteous form,
> A glowing arm, a gleaming neck,
> As when a sunbeam wavers warm
> Within the dark and dimpled beck.

Notice how thorough-going the revision is. This is not great poetry; but, as verse, it is infinitely improved in the second version. The admirable fifth line of the second stanza in the original version is shifted to the terminal position; otherwise, only *form, neck* and *arm* remain. The obtruding water-rat has gone forever. Tennyson even interposed an additional stanza, to prelude the entrance of the girl. So the masters labor over their lines.

The opening of Keats's *Hyperion,* the masterpiece of his genius, at first contained:

> Not so much life as a young vulture's wing
> Would spread upon a field of green-eared corn.

On second thought, he substituted an eagle for a vulture. Holding that this broke the illusion of stillness, Keats pencilled on the margin of the manuscript,

> Not so much life as on a summer's day
> Robs not at all the dandelion's fleece.

But again he held that the dandelion's volatile fluff danced away with the illusion of stillness; and finally we had the perfect lines,

> Not so much life as on a summer's day
> Robs not one light seed from the feathered grass,
> But where the dead leaf fell, there did it rest.

Perhaps you think that free verse is written freely, and left to remain as it first appeared. The successive editions of *Leaves of Grass* dissipate this misconception forever. Whitman's first title for one of the most effective poems was *Out of the Rocked Cradle.* This was retitled *Out of the Cradle Endlessly Rocking,* which set the mood from the start. As a third line, this unneeded excrescence appeared:

> Out of the boy's mother's womb, and from the nipples
> of her breasts.

This went out. A line at first appearing as—

> From those beginning notes of sickness and love there
> in the transparent mist

had *sickness* altered to *yearning,* and omitted *transparent.* The line—

When the snows had melted, and the Fifth Month grass
was growing

reappeared as:

When the lilac-scent was in the air and Fifth-month
grass was growing.

The ninth line of the first carol ended, originally,

If we two but keep together.

Notice the tremendous improvement in the present version,

While we two keep together.

And similar amendments marked this poem throughout, and most
of the others.

A study of the plays of Shakespeare, in the order in which
they were written, indicates the incredible growth of his genius,
in the direction of naturalness, and accent rhythm in place of the
artificial meters. The youthful *Comedy of Errors* started with
a rhymed couplet, followed by end-stopped lines:

Aegeon. Proceed, Solinus, to procure my fall,
And by the doom of death end woes and all.

Duke. Merchant of Syracusa, plead no more.
I am not partial to infringe our laws;
The enmity and discord which of late
Sprung from the rancorous outrage of your duke
To merchants, our well-dealing countrymen,

and this bumpety seven-accent rhythm, dear to the vulgar,

Dromio of Ephesus. Say what you will, sir, but I know what I know;
That you did beat me at the mart, I have your hand to show;
If the skin were parchment, and the blows you gave were ink,
Your own handwriting would tell you what I think.

The development proceeds, through the major chronicle plays
and the mature comedies, to the great tragedies, where there is an
almost complete balance of end-stopped and run-on lines:

Maecenas. Now Anthony must leave her utterly.

Enobarbus.   Never; he will not.
Age cannot wither her, nor custom stale
Her infinite variety; other women cloy
The appetites they feed, but she makes hungry
Where most she satisfies; for vilest things

[433]

> Become themselves in her, that the holy priests
> Bless her when she is riggish.

Even here, all the lines are run-on after the first two. And so on to *The Tempest* and the last few plays, where something freer even than accent verse dominates: a free verse unheard since the prehistory of English versification.

We might start on a far lower flight, to show a similar growth. A certain young versifier commenced in the mood of his sonnet *On Woman:*

> Ah! who can e'er forget so fair a being?
> Who can forget her half-retiring sweets?
> God! She is like a milk-white lamb that bleats
> For man's protection.

In another sonnet with the same title he wrote:

> But when I mark
> Such charms with mild intelligences shine
> My ear is open like a greedy shark,
> To catch the tunings of voice divine.

What with this picture of woman bleating like a lamb, and man's ear likened to a shark's mouth, would you predict much of a future for this versifier? And yet, lifting always his verse to match that music only his inner ear heard, soon enough he offered to the world *The Eve of St. Agnes,* the *To a Grecian Urn,* the magnificent torso of *Hyperion,* with lines like:

> Be thou therefore in the van
> Of circumstance; yea, seize the arrow's barb
> Before the tense string murmur.

During his brief poetic lifetime, John Keats progressed from a crude and uninspired use of rhyme, to a deft use of it, and out of the use of this ornament to the magnificent naturalness of a blank verse that peers Shakespeare's. Milton, a deft young rhymester under the Stuarts, with his *L'Allegro, Il Penseroso,* and the rest, matured into the sonorous blank verse flight of *Paradise Lost.* Always the growth, against the complaints of the admirers of the young style, has been in the direction of a discarding of all that is alien to native English verse: rhyme, that monkish child of the decadent Roman empire and nascent Christianity; meter, that altered warping of naturalness that held down with iron heel the natural poetry of Greece, of Rome, of the Romance world, and of islanded England . . . a growth toward the accent verse that was the first recorded dawn-song in England, and may have been so in all these lands; first born of that free verse in which man naturally sang first, when poetry first formed on his lips.

What importance has this to you: that the growth of the individual poets hailed as great, and parallel to it through the ages the growth of English and American poetry as a whole, has been this Hegelian return—the original thing itself, on a higher level? Let us be content with the minimum benefit: that it reassures you not to beware of such tendencies as your verse shows toward breaking the old patterns; but, to the contrary, to encourage them, as in line with the development of the best in English verse and poetry. You may end as a deft user of all the possible artifices and ornaments: meter and its formal embroideries, rhyme, consonance, assonance. But even so you will know that, even to you, the moment may come when the thing you have to say is of such surpassing importance that you do not wish to cloud and dilute its effectiveness by any alien extraneous device—the moment when your own living idiom, unornamented, will be your highest poetry.

The craftsmanship of the masters speaks for itself. They were not content with what came first, and easiest. They weighed this product line by line, stanza by stanza, and from the standpoint of the poem as a whole. Some of them, like Whitman, never regarded a poem as a thing ended until death had ended them. The greater among them did not remain content with the technique mastered first; but they moved into sector after sector, conquering each, until in the end they had returned to the less ornamented and more natural speech that the race used first as its convention for poetry.

Somewhere, somehow, your own course as versifier will parallel this startide, in small or in large. For this is the road toward mastery; and a part of you, at least, will be content with nothing less.

THE POET AS SELF-CRITIC

The role of self-criticism in the poet and versifier is second only in importance to that of original creator. Among some few poets, this role is carried out before the first line of the poem is written down. In the vast majority of cases, it is a separate and distinct process. Each poet must work out his ritual of self-criticism for himself, by experiment ascertaining what methods give him the best results. A few general suggestions may be of assistance.

The first concerns timing. There are certain improvements which may occur at once, after the poem has been first written down; and these should, of course, be made at once. But it constantly happens that the actual process of writing has distracted the poet's attention from some integral part of the poetic concept; and only an interval that permits the poet to return to his product from a new slant permits, as a rule, this omitted material to recur to the emotional self, which after all cannot be contented until the full original poetic concept has been written down. This distraction often comes from the difficulties involved in the particular stanza- or poem-pattern being used; and the first product must be allowed to cool and become sufficiently weaned from its creator, before an unbiased and critical view of it is possible. Once flaws have been detected, the poet should seek to recreate the poem to any extent necessary, in order to correct them. This may be a matter of hours, of days, of weeks, or longer. But, until the poem best expresses the creator's ability, it should never be regarded as a finished thing, even if it has been permitted an interim publication.

It is strongly recommended that all intermediate drafts of the poem, and memorandum of all changes, be preserved. The poet may later recur to some discarded reading as preferable; as Coleridge in the example quoted from *The Ancient Mariner*. The preserved first and later drafts are of value to the poet in self-understanding, and for posthumous study.

It is possible here only in generalizations. But a definite differentiation must be made between the poet as original creator, and the poet as subsequent critic. Where pure natural poetry is being produced, there are many poets who ignore mental control of the process entirely, and let the unconscious dictate what is to be written down:

> The will beneath, as rank as swampland fennel,
> Lashes dog reason back into his kennel.

In proportion as the poetry or verse is written to a definite pattern, stanzaic or poem (as, sonnet, ballade, etc.), the critical mind must function during creation, to remind the creator of the pattern to which he is writing. Obviously, in writing formal stanzas or a sonnet, it would be ridiculous if the form were ignored, while writing. For, even if the poetic concept were written down first in prose or free verse, there would come a creative moment where it would have to be poured into the poetic mold; and here the poet is predominantly creator, yet with the intellect guiding the fitting of the concept into the mold. Since the creative part is the more important, every flash of so-called inspiration should be jotted down, as for example, on the margins, for later study, with a view to whether or not it can be fitted into the mosaic of the preconceived form. When we come to formal light verse, the intellect may even assume the rôle of joint dictator. But the creative part must never be given less than full leeway, in the first draft at least.

Thereafter, the rôles differ. There must be co-operation between creator and critic, alternating if not simultaneous. The critic must mark all words and lines that fall below the standard, or fail to fit the pattern. Then the creator must be called upon to replace these with words and lines that come up to the standard. This process may have to alternate many times, before the final result is right. The creator speaks the inner poetic urge, which cannot be taught. The critic has stored within him, fully absorbed, all that this and similar books can teach him; and is an expert at ways of saying what the creator must say. There is one nebulous yet indisputable advantage that the process of criticism, including self-criticism, carries with it. An outsider, or the poet himself, may not at first see what is wrong with a word or line, and may merely register a general dissatisfaction, or even suggest a wrong diagnosis and remedy. But the attention, once focussed upon a faulty part of the verses, sets the creative side to work upon it; and in the end some improvement is almost sure to eventuate, even if it be far from what is first suggested by outsider or the poet as self-critic.

ON TRANSLATING POETRY

Translating poetry is as impossible as altering a Chinese tune into Occidental music, or recapturing *Loch Lomond* in Chinese orchestration. In these two cases, the very scales of music differ; the intervals are all different, and differently originated—one from a fixed-string instrument like the harp, the other from an unfixed one, like a violin or certain wind-instruments. The tune of one land cannot reappear in the musical idiom of a land with music differently based, and still be the same tune.

Poetry, at its height (and this includes light verse at its height) calls for a technical utilization of the poetic devices of the land of its origin. Each word used has its own overtones, its own invisible cargo of associations, which do not exist in the second language, and cannot be carried over into it. The poet uses, at his best, a word-usage where every word evokes emotions far beyond its meaning or sound; an emotional tug that can be felt, but cannot be measured or rendered in any equivalent form. Take these two magical lines from Keats:

> Magic casements, opening on the foam
> Of perilous seas, in faery lands forlorn.

If this were translated, word for word, into a language with words of identical meaning, it would still not be translated poetry. For the word-music would differ completely; the associations would differ; and the resultant would not be the poetry of Keats in another language: it would be merely what the poetry of Keats meant, a vastly different thing. This cannot be translated even into English. Accurately glossed or paraphrased, it would give:

> Supernatural windows, unclosing on the bubbles
> Of dangerous oceans, in enchanted countries dejected.

The poetry is gone forever. The same is true of all poetry: it is untranslatable. To that extent Coleridge is right, in describing poetry as the best words in the best order. It is rather the inevitable words in the inevitable order; and there is no more a duplication of these words or this order possible, than there is possible a duplication of yourself, or this moment at which I first write down these words.

We may be able to sense, by studying out Villon's old French, the magic in the line:

> Mais ou sont les neiges d'antan?

No translation of this into English or any other language can recapture the music, or, indeed, the meaning with its overtones, of the original. Here are some of the versions in English—for it has been tried repeatedly:

> But what is become of last year's snow?. . . .

> But where, oh where, be last year's snows?

(But this has overtones of "Where, oh where has my little dog gone?")

> But where are the snows of yester-year?

"Is become" is a poeticism; "where be" a worse one; "yester-year" another: we say, in the living language, *yesterday*, but never *yester-year*. Yet this last has already built up its own associations, and commends itself to many readers: though *not* as a translation of Villon's music or meaning. Do your best with it:

> But where are yesterday's snows?

However, more than "yesterday" is meant.

> But where are the snows of years gone by?. . . .

> But where are the snows of the years that are dead?. . . .

> But where are the snows that are past?

Each of these lines may be poetic, or may fail; but each is a different utterance from Villon's. Even "But where are the—" is not quite a right rendering; for Villon wrote in a language with accent missing or minor, while we write in a language where accent is central. And he has only eight syllables to his line pattern, without accentual differentiation; and in each of these the vowel music differs, the consonantal music is altered, the overtones are not the same.

Turn for a moment to the evocative effect of single words. Alfred Noyes climaxes his resounding chant *Marchaunt Adventurers,*

> Englande!—Englande!—Englande!—Englande!

Even the spelling (unheard by the reader, of course) gives an overtone of the more heroic and less "umbrellaed" past. Those who feel with him the glory that included Prince Hal and Hotspur, Agincourt and Crecy, Sidney, Drake, Sir Henry Morgan, the shattered Armada, the sun never setting on a spreading empire, feel in this a magnificent emotional climax. Differently used (as if Shelley had used it in his justly bitter *Masque of Anarchy*), the same line might have aroused detestation. A translation of this, the fourfold repetition of a country's name, by a poet, and to hearers, who cannot possibly throb to the remembered glories, is meaningless, or prosy, or even an evocation of hatred. Put it in Lissauer's *Hymn of Hate,* if you doubt this. To France, remembering red centuries with no love spanning the channel,

Angleterre! Angleterre! Angleterre! Angleterre!

would never translate any of the quality of Noyes's line. Nor could we thrill to

Greenland! Greenland! Greenland! Greenland!

as poetry (unless by an extreme stretch of our receptive imagination).

Translation of poetry is impossible.

Yet, until man mounts to the wisdom of one speech, universally used and comprehensible, international understanding calls for a sharing in each land of the poetic achievements of the others. Architecture, sculpture, painting, dancing, can be seen with eyes that use an international language; music, to all races with similar musical idioms, can be heard by ears which use an international language. But what are we to do with words too specialized to be universal? The only answer is the poetic recreation of a poem in the new language.

When Edward Fitzgerald made the quatrains of Omar Khayyam a part of the heart heritage of the English race, he had no more to go on, to English comprehension, than the following literal translations indicate: for all that the originals were part of the prized poetic heritage of Persia:

I desire a flash of ruby wine and a book of verses,
Just enough to keep me alive—and half a loaf is needful;

[440]

And then, that thou and I should sit in the wilderness
Is better than the Kingdom of a Sultan.

Everywhere that there has been a rose or tulip bed,
It has come from the redness of the blood of a king;
Every violet shoot that grows from the earth
Is a mole that was once on the cheek of a beauty.

I have travelled far in wandering by valley and desert,
It came to pass that I wandered in all quarters of the world;
I have not heard from anyone who came from that road,
The road he travelled, no traveller travels again.

Hell is a spark from my useless worries,
Paradise is a moment of time when I am tranquil.

There is clearly no summons here to waken the English soul—no musical word-usage, none of our idiom, none even of our visualizing. Yet, out of this material Fitzgerald wrought poetry as enduring as:

A Book of Verses underneath the Bough,
A Jug of Wine, a Loaf of Bread—and Thou
    Beside me singing in the Wilderness—
Ah, Wilderness were Paradise enow.

I sometimes think that never blows so red
The Rose, as where some buried Caesar bled;
    That every hyacinth the garden wears
Dropt in her Lap from some once lovely head.

Strange, is it not? that of the myriads who
Before us pass'd the door of Darkness through,
    Not one returns to tell us of the Road,
Which to discover, we must travel, too.

Heav'n but the Vision of fulfilled Desire,
And Hell the Shadow from a Soul on Fire,
    Cast on the Darkness into which Ourselves,
So late emerged from, shall so soon expire.

To achieve this, Fitzgerald had to treat the literal translation merely as the nebulous material out of which poetry was to be created. The creation involved all the poetic resources of the English language, and the result is authentic English poetry. It is so that all recreation (not translation) of foreign poetry is to be done.

Dr. Charles Prosper Fagnani, of Union Theological Seminary, gave this accurate translation of the first five verses of Genesis i:

At the beginning of Elohim's forming the heavens and the earth, when darkness was upon the face of the abyss, Elohim said, "Let there be light," and there was light.

Elohim saw that the light was excellent.

And Elohim separated the light from the darkness and he called the light Day and the darkness he called Night.

Evening came, and Morning came,
One day.

If this had been planned as a translation of poetry, it would have been a complete failure. For the original was authentic poetry, no doubt of that; at the time it was written, such early science as a description of the formation of the universe, the solar system and the earth was always written in verse. From a religious point of view, it is a statement of fact; and accuracy in translation is far more important than recreation in English poetry. From the standpoint of English poetry, those masters of word-music who gave us the King James Bible, that co-former of the style of so much of our prose and poetry, recreated it thus:

In the beginning God created the heaven and the earth.

And the earth was without form, and void; and darkness was upon the face of the deep. And the Spirit of God moved upon the face of the waters.

And God said, Let there be light; and there was light.

And God saw the light, that it was good; and God divided the light from the darkness.

And God called the light Day, and the darkness he called Night. And the evening and the morning were the first day.

The accuracy is all with Fagnani; the poetry is all with the earlier version, which is a recreation, not a translation. Which of these we prefer depends upon the use to which we intend to put it.

In translating the poems of Sappho, it did not take me long to understand that the artificial Sapphic stanza, so alien to natural English verse, even when based on accent rather than quantity, only blurred and turned into prose her authentic poetry. The stanza, after all, had been adopted to fit a musical setting, long lost, and to accompany a formal dance, long forgotten. In the end, so important was it to communicate the direct poetry of the

[442]

great singer, I used a simple free verse, as the most translucent medium in which to let her speak. The result, from scrupulously eliminating any ornamenting devices that Sappho could not have used, at least rendered her poetry faithfully:

Of Atthis

My dear one said
she would rather lay aside her robes for me
than for anyone,
even though Zeus himself
came storming after her.

So she spoke.
But when a girl talks to a ravenous lover,
her words should be written upon the wind
and on soft tumbling water.

To Her Brother, Returning from Naukratis

Golden Nereids,
grant me my brother's safe return,
I entreat you,
that his heart's will may be won,
and that, sponging clean his former errors,
he may become a joy to his friends
and a withering to his enemies,
so that we may flush with shame
before no man.

And his sister
may he desire to hold in due honor;
and the keen pain and the barbed words
with which, when he left, in his pain
he sought to slit my heart,
being cut to the bone by my scoldings,—
in the gay greeting of his homeland kin
may he choose to fling them lightly away,
when he returns on some near day
and plucks a wife, if he desires one,
from among decent young women.

But for you, with whom in vagabond love he mated,
thinking that to be beautiful
which is a public marketplace,
you with your nose sniffing the ground,
go off and hunt elsewhere,
you obscene and evil bitch!

[443]

To the Evening Star

O evening star,
fairest of all stars that shine,
you bring back all
that heart-uplifting dawn
has scattered wide.

You bring home the sheep,
you bring back the goats and the whimpering kids,
you bring home the child to its mother.

Into the West

All things end.
The skyblue and the purple,
the saffron and the vermilion,
wed with the tombing darkness.

The day grays, and falters
toward its nightly sepulture in the west.

The doves fly lower.
Their seeking grows small,
they cease the labor of their wings.

I walk quietly
into the west.

A Last Word

So you women have boasted
that you are more fortunate than I.
Youth is much, and the love of men and girls,
and one's own to suckle.

I do not complain.
I have received abiding joy
from the golden Muses,
and when I die
I shall not be forgotten.

Some one, I tell you,
will remember me hereafter.

It is well to return thus to poetry speaking without excessive ornamentation. For it was so that poetry commenced; and the unadorned magic can have more potency than a spilth of baubles and tinsel. It would be untrue to the original to translate Pope or Swinburne without the excessive ornamentation that badged them. It would be as untrue to Sappho to mar her magnificent naturalness with obtruding bangles.

VOLUMES OF POETRY

In arranging any poem in its final form, and increasingly as the poem is long and inclusive, the same principles apply that hold good for a plea, a speech, an argument. The opening should establish a point of contact with the audience, as far as possible; the ensuing portions should build up consistently, with increasing emotional appeal, to the climax; and this should be the strongest, most enduring and most effective part of all.

The same principle applies to the preparation of a collection of poems for a volume. If possible, without unnatural straining, the poems increase in effectiveness as they are grouped naturally by subject matter, type of appeal, or the like. The opening section should have both contact and enough emotional appeal to give the reader momentum enough to carry him through the beginning of the build-up toward the climax. The last section should be the most effective of all, especially to the more thoughtful readers.

MARKETING POETRY

The poetic product cannot reach its audience, except by means of publication. The poet and versifier, since he must eat and drink and sleep and clothe himself, like all the rest of mankind, at times looks to the product of his versifying to furnish an income, or at least to contribute toward it. Robert Frost's line,

The trial by market everything must come to,

is applicable here. It is incumbent on the poet to find out what the various markets are, and their financial returns, and thereafter to cultivate such of them as he cares to. This applies as surely to the poet who does not need an addition to his income; for he can always donate his returns to the advancement of poetry in some way, if he has no closer hobby to which to apply it.

Poetry and verse form the main source of income of some writers. Miss Millay is said to be in this class, and probably Phyllis McGinley. So are or were Walt Mason, Edgar A. Guest, Berton Braley, and quite a few more. The same thing is certainly true of many lyricists for musical comedies, musical shows and popular songs. The direct income from the sale of verse is supplemented by some returns that far exceed the checks from periodicals in size: including the right of reprint in anthologies, which often pay well; royalties on musical settings, from sale of sheet music, mechanical recordings, royalties for the use of songs in moving pictures, radio, television, and other public performances; royalties from volume publication; and other minor rights. In the first publication of a poem which is copyrighted, the poet should be careful to see that all rights, except those directly needed by the periodical, book, or song—these are called first American serial rights, in the case of a periodical—are at once re-assigned to the author. Usually a publisher makes no objection to this. If it is not specifically granted, it is usually implicit. And yet, the poet makes no mistake who has "First American serial rights only" typed or stamped on each poem submitted for acceptance.

The number of poets, however, who make an appreciable amount from their poetry is not too large; even when we add to this related incomes from lectures on poetry, book reviews of poetry, and services as teacher or critic of poetry and verse. Barring certain specialized fields, such as song-lyrics, greeting-card verse, advertising verse and light verse, the paying markets for poetry are limited to a small number of newspapers and far less than half of the general magazines. When aimed for any of these specialized fields, of course the verse must be slanted directly toward their editorial requirements. In the case of the general magazines, the usual stipulation is that the poem be comparatively brief—it is usually inserted as a filler after prose, to permit the next article or story to start at the top of a page—and, in addition, that it be on a subject of wide appeal to the magazine's readers. The exceptional long poem may be accepted by magazines of many types, including ones as divergent as *The Atlantic Monthly, The Nation* and *The New Republic, The Commonweal,* the Sunday magazines of certain daily newspapers and even their daily editions for timely poems, adventure magazines for certain adventure poems, many of the leading women's magazines, even general magazines like *Collier's, Esquire, The New Yorker.* But the poem must have unusual appeal, to be considered on a parity with prose by such markets. The poet should familiarize himself with such markets and the type of verse they prefer, and govern himself to some extent by these, in his submissions.

But this is looking at it from the standpoint of income; and that is not the major objective of the poet, which is primarily to let his verses, his word, his say, have as wide a hearing as possible. This at once adds to the market enormously. There are many magazines devoted exclusively to poetry; and a few of these pay, and pay well. Many poets make a practice of trying the paying markets first, and, rather than see the poem go unpublished, then start it on the rounds of the non-paying magazines, and the large number of newspapers which throw their columns over to poems. There is an inner satisfaction and social recognition in being hailed as the author of poems that appeal. They may always be located so for musical setting or anthology use, and they have had their first day in court through these publications, even though they have brought in no additions to the income.

Anthologies are of four classes. There are, first of all, those which pay the poet for the privilege of inclusion; and these naturally have the highest standing. There are those where inclusion means an especial recognition of merit. Of such were Braithewaite's *Anthologies of Magazine Verse,* annual events for many years, and Thomas Moult's later volumes. Among these may be included anthologies commemorating especial events, as a world's fair or some historical anniversary; and state and other grouped anthologies, not of the pay-as-you-enter class. A third group are really joint publications of poems by a limited group of poets, such as the *Others* anthologies and similar ones. To these the individual poets may be asked to contribute a pro rata of the cost, in return receiving a pro rata of the returns. The last group are anthologies in which the poet pays for insertion, either directly or by the required order of one or many more copies of the book, often at an excessive price. These sag downward until some of them are definitely in the racketeering class; and the poet would do well to avoid them.

Volume publication must be the intermediate objective of the poet, on his way to ultimate recognition. Some few volumes of poetry, such as Robinson's *Tristram* and Stephen Vincent Benet's *John Brown's Body,* both book-of-the-month club choices, as well as all of Miss Millay's and Dorothy Parker's volumes, bring in ample financial returns. This is unusual. A small number of additional volumes are published to balance the lists of certain publishers—perhaps to balance the profits made from best selling prose; or in order for a publisher to monopolize all of the publications of a remunerative author. In general, the poet is asked to underwrite, in whole or in part, the cost of publishing most volumes of poetry. If he can secure an outlet for his volume, he may break even or make some profits; if not, as a rule the volume ends up definitely "in the red." But this is only from a standpoint of immediate income. The poet's return in reputation, depending on the critical reception of the volume, in the esteem of his friends, in self-esteem, in opening the contents to possible use in song-settings, is more than often definitely "in the black." If the volume must come within this latter class, great care should be exercised in selecting a publisher who will give the volume a fair chance, in sending out the proper list of review copies to the right places, and in giving the book every opportunity for book-store sales.

To avoid the embarrassment of having a poem, whether sold or donated, appear more than once in periodicals, it is well to keep an accurate list of its submissions, and the result of each submission.

The writer of prose is accustomed to the receipt of rejection slips, and thrills when the variety of an acceptance and a check replaces the expected declination. The writer of poetry and verse may as well accustom himself in advance to the same lot, increasingly. It is consoling to blame it on the obtuseness of the editors. The fault quite as often lies with the poet, in not knowing his markets well enough, or failing to master his technique sufficiently. Both these faults can be easily remedied. This at least is due to the poem, and alike to the poet himself. For the inner glow of achieving, both in writing and publication, a bid for man's most enduring immortality, that of being hailed as one of the poets or spokesmen for the race, is no light goal to aim for.

BIBLIOGRAPHY

Alden, Raymond MacDonald: *English Verse,* 1903.

Brewer, R. F.: *Manual of English Prosody,* 1869.

Campion, Thomas: *Observations in the Art of English Poets,* 1602.

Cohen, Helen Louise: *Lyric Forms from France,* 1922.

Daniel, Samuel: *Defense of Rhyme,* 1603.

Dowden, Edward: *Shakespeare Primer,* 1877.

Eastman, Max: *Enjoyment of Poetry,* 1913.

Gascoigne, George: *Certain Notes of Instruction Concerning the Making of Verse or Rhyme in English,* 1575.

Hood, Tom: *Rules of Rhyme, a Guide to Versification, with a Compendious Dictionary of Rhymes,* 1877.

Lanier, Sidney: *The Science of English Verse,* 1880; *Shakespeare and His Forerunners,* 1908.

Lowes, John Livingston: *Convention and Revolt in Poetry,* 1919.

Mott, Lewis F.: *The Provençal Lyre,* 1901.

Percy, Thomas: *Reliques of Ancient English Poetry,* 1876.

Pound, Louise: *Poetic Origins and the Ballad,* 1921.

Poole, Joshua: *English Parnassus, or a Help to English Poesie,* 1679.

Puttenham: *Art of English Poesy,* 1589.

Stedman, Edmund Clarence: *The Nature and Elements of Poetry,* 1892.

Sterner, Lewis G: *The Sonnet in American Literature,* 1930.

Untermeyer, Louis: *The Forms of Poetry,* 1929.

Webbe, William: *Discourse of English Poetry,* 1586.

White, Gleeson: *Ballades and Rondeaus,* 1887.

Wood, Clement: *The Complete Rhyming Dictionary and Poet's Craft Book,* 1936.

Wood, Clement: *Hunters of Heaven: The American Soul as Revealed by Its Poetry,* 1929.

INDEX

Index